New Complete Geography
Fourth edition

Charles Hayes

Gill & Macmillan

Gill & Macmillan
Hume Avenue
Park West
Dublin 12
with associated companies throughout the world
www.gillmacmillan.ie

© Charles Hayes 2009

Illustrations by Kate Shannon

978 07171 4093 0

Colour reproduction by Typeform Repro Ltd
Design, diagrams and print origination in Ireland by Design Image

Contents

Syllabus Section: The Human Habitat

Unit 1: The Earth's Surface: Shaping the Crust

1.	The Restless Earth	1
2.	Rocks	10
3.	Weathering and Erosion: An Introduction	16
4.	Mechanical Weathering: The Effects of Frost	17
5.	Chemical Weathering by Rainwater: The Burren Area	18
6.	Mass Movement	25
7.	The Work of Rivers	29
8.	The Work of Moving Ice	42
9.	The Work of the Sea	52

Unit 2: The Restless Atmosphere

10.	Our Planet's Heating System: Sun, Wind and Ocean Currents	61
11.	Different Weathers: The Effects of Ascending and Descending Air	71
12.	Water in the Atmosphere	78
13.	Measuring and Forecasting Weather	82
14.	Factors that Affect Climate	90
15.	An Introduction to Climate Types	94
16.	Hot Climates: Focus on Hot Deserts	95
17.	Losing to the Desert: Drought and Desertification	98
18.	Gaining from the Deserts: A Major Irrigation Scheme	100
19.	Temperate Climates: Focus on Mediterranean Lands	103
20.	Cold Climates: Focus on Boreal Lands	109

Unit 3: How Our Life Support System Works

21.	Natural Vegetation and Climate	111
22.	Our Living Soil	113
23.	Soil and Natural Vegetation	120

Maps and Photographs

Map and Photograph Interpretation

24. Ordnance Survey Maps: An Introduction   122
25. More on Maps of 1:50,000 Scale   126
26. City Street Maps and Town Plans   149
27. Aerial Photographs   156
28. Activities with Maps and Photographs   172

Syllabus Section: Population, Settlement and Urbanisation

Unit 4: Population and Human Migration

29. Population: A Growing Concern   180
30. Population Make-Up   188
31. People on the Move   193
32. Where are the People?   198
33. Some Effects of High and Low Population Densities   206
34. Life and Death in an Unequal World   216

Unit 5: Settlement Patterns

35. Norman Settlements in Ireland   220
36. Patterns in the Distribution of Towns   222
37. New Settlement Patterns in the Dutch Polders   226
38. The Functions of Nucleated Settlements   229
39. Change in Urban Functions over Time   238
40. Movement, Communication Links and the Growth of Settlements   243

Unit 6: Urban Geography

41. Urban Growth: The Story of Dublin   248
42. Functional Zones within Cities   253
43. How Land Values Affect Land Use in Cities   256
44. Variations in City Housing   258
45. On the Move: City Traffic Patterns   260
46. Urban Problems   264
47. Urban Solutions   268
48. Urban Problems in Kolkata   272

Syllabus Section: Economic Activities

Unit 7: Primary Economic Activities

49.	Economic Activities: An Introduction	275
50.	Water: A Vital Natural Resource	277
51.	Energy Sources: Focus on Oil and Gas	282
52.	Using Our Peat Bogs	289
53.	Over-Fishing	295
54.	Farming: An Example of a System	299

Unit 8: Secondary Economic Activities

55.	Secondary Activities as Systems	303
56.	Industry in Ireland	306
57.	Change over Time in the Location of Industry	314
58.	Women in Industry	318
59.	Classifying Global Regions According to Industry	322
60.	Acid Rain	324
61.	Disagreements about Industry	328

Unit 9: Tertiary Economic Activities

62.	Tertiary Activities	331
63.	Tourism and Tourist Attractions	333
64.	Fun in the Sun – Mediterranean Tourism	340
65.	Rich World – Poor World	345
66.	Exploitation: Past and Present	348
67.	Aid to the South	355
68.	Sudan – Things that Hinder Development	361
69.	Rich and Poor Regions within European States	366
70.	Reducing Economic Inequality – Different Viewpoints	372

Acknowledgements	376

eTest.ie – what is it?

A revolutionary new website-based testing platform that facilitates a social learning environment for Irish schools. Both students and teachers can use it, either independently or together, to make the whole area of testing easier, more engaging and more productive for all.

Students – do you want to know how well you are doing? Then take an eTest!

At eTest.ie, you can access tests put together by the author of this textbook. You get instant results, so they're a brilliant way to quickly check just how your study or revision is going.

Since each eTest is based on your textbook, if you don't know an answer, you'll find it in your book.

Register now and you can save all of your eTest results to use as a handy revision aid or to simply compare with your friends' results!

Teachers – eTest.ie will engage your students and help them with their revision, while making the jobs of reviewing their progress and homework easier and more convenient for all of you.

Register now to avail of these exciting features:

- Create tests easily using our pre-set questions OR you can create your own questions

- Develop your own online learning centre for each class that you teach

- Keep track of your students' performances

eTest.ie has a wide choice of question types for you to choose from, most of which can be graded automatically, like multiple-choice, jumbled-sentence, matching, ordering and gap-fill exercises. This free resource allows you to create class groups, delivering all the functionality of a VLE (Virtual Learning Environment) with the ease of communication that is brought by social networking.

Inside the Earth

The earth's layers

Figure 1 shows that the inside of the earth consists of several **different layers**.

Crust (This thin outer shell of the earth is made up of solid rock)

Mantle (The mantle is so hot that some rocks there are semi-molten and flow about in slow-moving currents)

Core (The centre part of the earth is very hot)

Plate (big slab of the Earth's crust)

Plate boundary (where plates meet)

The earth is a bit like a huge apple. It has a 'skin' which we call the **crust**, a softer inside which we call the **mantle** and a centre called the **core**.

Did you know ... that the American and European continents are moving away from each other ... at about the same speed as your fingernails grow!

More about the earth's crust

1. The crust is rather like a huge jigsaw puzzle. It is broken into pieces called plates. The places where plates meet are called **plate boundaries**.
2. These huge plates do the following:
   - They **float** on the heavier, semi-molten rock of the mantle.
   - They move around slowly, carrying our continents with them as 'passengers'. This movement is called **continental drift**.
   - They **collide** with and **separate** from each other. These movements cause *activities* such as **folding**, **earthquakes** and **volcanic activity** to happen at plate boundaries. The activities then give rise to *landscape features* or *landforms* such as fold mountains and volcanic mountains.

Our Moving Plates

Figure 2 shows the world's principal *plates*. It also shows *plate boundaries* where plates **separate** from each other, where plates **collide** and where plates **slide past** each other.

The principal crustal plates
(a) *Learn the names and locations of these plates.*
(b) *With the help of your atlas, decide whether plates separate, collide or slide past each other at each of the following places: California (Western USA); Iceland; the Andes mountains.*

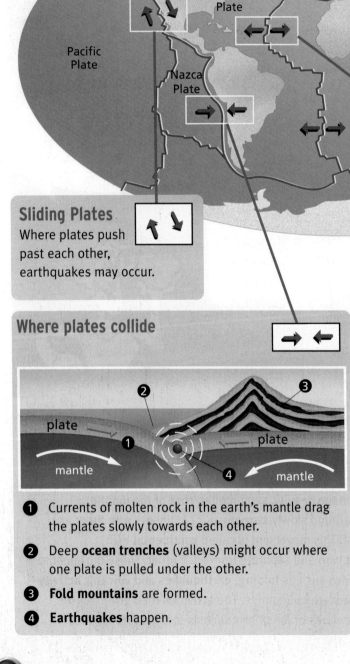

Key
— plate boundary
← direction of plate movement

Eurasian Plate

American Plate

Pacific Plate

Pacific Plate

African Plate

Nazca Plate

Australian Plate

Sliding Plates
Where plates push past each other, earthquakes may occur.

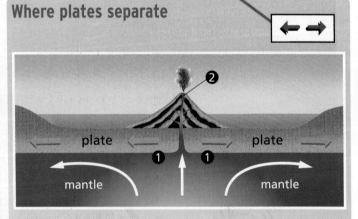

Where plates collide

plate

plate

mantle

mantle

❶ Currents of molten rock in the earth's mantle drag the plates slowly towards each other.

❷ Deep **ocean trenches** (valleys) might occur where one plate is pulled under the other.

❸ **Fold mountains** are formed.

❹ **Earthquakes** happen.

Where plates separate

plate

plate

mantle

mantle

❶ Currents of molten rock in the earth's mantle slowly drag plates apart from each other.

❷ Where the plates separate, volcanic material rises up from the mantle to form **volcanic islands**, **volcanic mountains** and long **mid-ocean ridges**.

Folding

When moving **plates collide** with each other, tremendous **compression** (pushing together) occurs where the plates meet. This compression may cause the earth's crust to become **very slowly buckled and arched upwards**, forming fold mountains (Figure 3).

Fold mountains form where plates collide

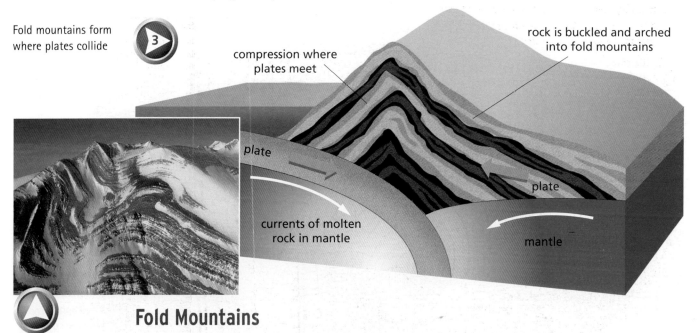

Fold Mountains

How do you know that this rock has been folded?

The world's youngest fold mountains include the *Alps* in Europe, the *Rocky Mountains* in North America and the *Andes* in South America. These mountain ranges were formed during the **Alpine foldings** only about 35 million years ago. They are very high because they have not yet been worn down as much as other fold mountains.

Ireland's fold mountains were formed very long ago and so have been worn down to quite low heights. Mountains in Munster, for example, were formed 250 million years ago during the **Armorican foldings**.

These pictures show MacGillycuddy's Reeks in Co. Kerry (left) and the Andes in South America (right).
(a) Which mountains are higher? Why?
(b) With the help of your atlas, locate the Andes in Figure 2. Which two plates collided to form these mountains?

Earthquakes

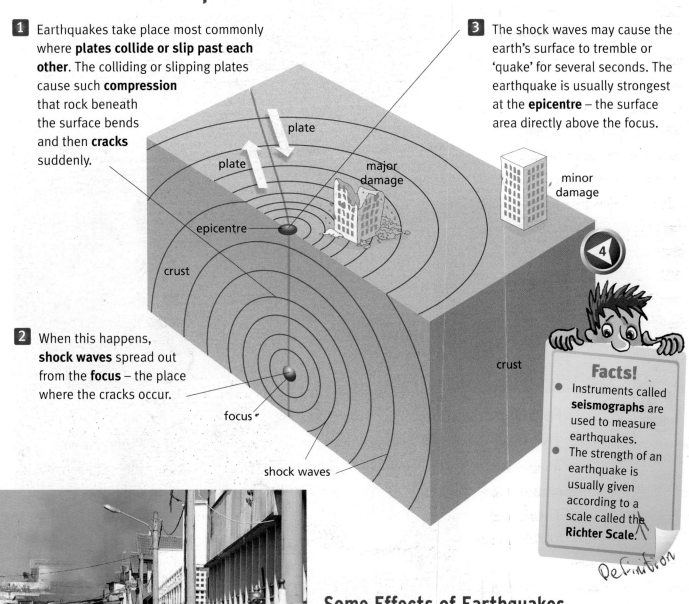

1 Earthquakes take place most commonly where **plates collide or slip past each other**. The colliding or slipping plates cause such **compression** that rock beneath the surface bends and then **cracks** suddenly.

2 When this happens, **shock waves** spread out from the **focus** – the place where the cracks occur.

3 The shock waves may cause the earth's surface to tremble or 'quake' for several seconds. The earthquake is usually strongest at the **epicentre** – the surface area directly above the focus.

plate

plate

major damage

minor damage

epicentre

crust

focus

crust

shock waves

Facts!
- Instruments called **seismographs** are used to measure earthquakes.
- The strength of an earthquake is usually given according to a scale called the **Richter Scale.**

Definition

Some Effects of Earthquakes

Strong earthquakes can result in terrible loss of life and property:

- **Buildings** close to the epicentre sway and collapse.
- **Roads** crack and railway lines bend.
- Gas pipes break, causing terrible **fires**.
- Huge tidal waves called **tsunamis** can result from earthquakes beneath the seabed. In December 2005 a giant tsunami destroyed coastal towns and killed up to 300,000 people in Indonesia and other countries in Asia (see photograph).

Devastation following the terrible tsunami of 2005

Earthquakes in California

California, in the United States of America, has suffered severe earthquakes because it is situated where the Pacific and North American plates push past each other (Figure 5). In 1906 a strong earthquake rocked the city of **San Francisco**. Buildings collapsed. Gas pipes were broken, causing fires which destroyed much of the city. In 1989 another strong earthquake hit the city. It measured 7.1 on the *Richter Scale*.

At the present time, compression is known to be building up in the earth's crust beneath San Francisco. Some Californians speak of their fear of 'the Big One' which may one day destroy their city. But wide streets and specially reinforced 'earthquake-proof' buildings are expected to lessen the effects of any further Californian earthquakes.

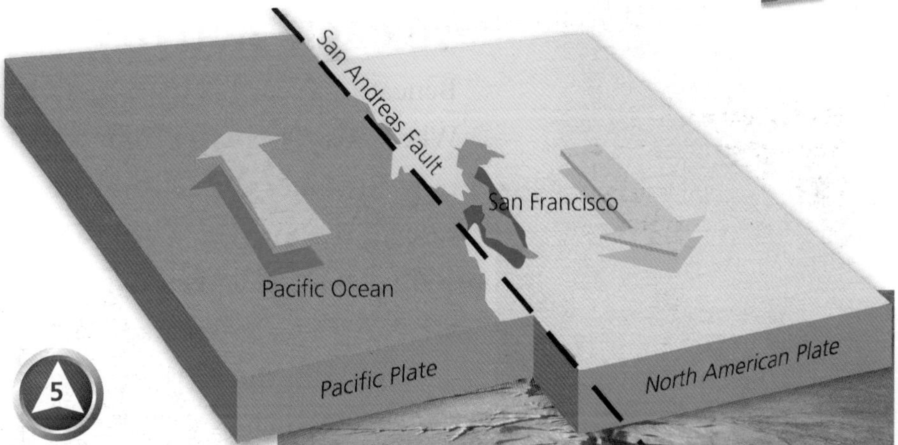

5 Plate movements in California

The *San Andreas Fault* in California is a large crack in the earth's crust which marks part of the boundary (meeting place) between the Pacific and North American plates

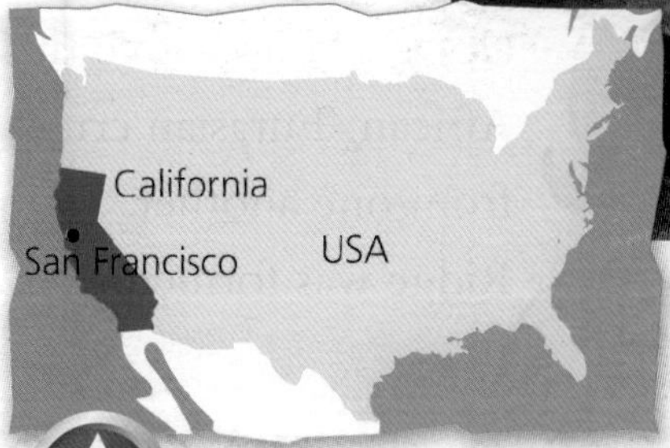

6

Earthquake damage in San Francisco

Volcanic Activity

Beneath the earth's crust there is hot, liquid rock called **magma**. Where plates separate from or collide with each other, the magma can sometimes force its way up through cracks in the crust until it reaches the surface. When the magma reaches the surface, it cools and hardens. It is then called **lava**.

● Where plates separate, lava may pour quietly through long cracks in the earth's surface. This lava may build up **mid-ocean ridges** such as the Mid Atlantic Ridge.

● Lava may also force its way violently through a small hole called a **vent**. When this happens, a **volcanic mountain** is formed.

The Mid Atlantic Ridge

Deep beneath the middle of the Atlantic Ocean there lies a long, narrow chain of mountains called the Mid Atlantic Ridge (Figure 7). This ridge runs roughly in a north-south direction, with some of its peaks rising above the surface of the sea to form volcanic islands.

The Mid Atlantic Ridge is volcanic in origin. It lies along a zone where the American and the African/Eurasian crustal plates are slowly moving away from one another. Figure 7 shows how the Mid Atlantic Ridge was formed.

A volcanic eruption in Iceland
Volcanic ash produces fertile soil for farms on the lower slopes of the mountain. The volcano is also an important tourist attraction. But violent eruptions can still endanger the lives and property of those living nearby.

Study a wall map or atlas for signs of the Mid Atlantic Ridge. Try to find some of the islands that form part of the ridge.

Volcanic Island (Iceland)

America

Mid Atlantic Ridge

Atlantic

Ocean

Europe

3

American Plate

1

2

Eurasian Plate

1

Mantle

7

How the Mid Atlantic Ridge was formed

1 The American and Eurasian plates float on heavy, semi-molten rock. Moving currents of the semi-molten rock drag the plates apart.

2 As the American and Eurasian **plates move apart**, a long **crack** occurs in the earth's crust.

3 **Molten magma** from beneath the crust wells up through this crack. The magma then cools and hardens to form a long ridge beneath the Atlantic Ocean.

Iceland – the Land of Ice and Fire

Iceland is not only a place of winter snow and ice. It is also a volcanic island of the Mid Atlantic Ridge and contains several volcanic mountains. Volcanic activity causes hot springs to rise from the ground and this provides hot water for the houses in Reykjavik, Iceland's capital city. Many tourists visit Iceland to see its unique volcanic scenery.

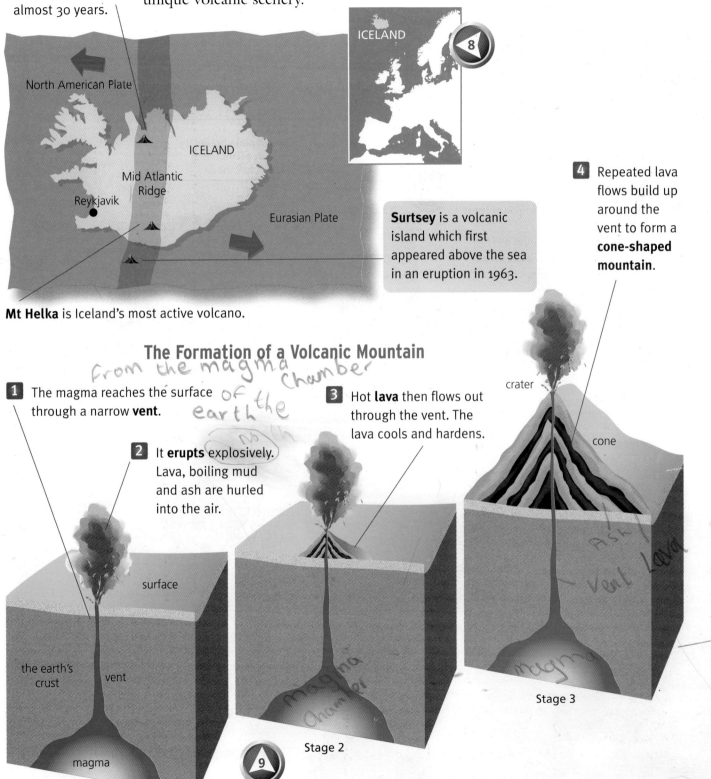

Mt Krafla has been erupting continuously for almost 30 years.

North American Plate

ICELAND

Mid Atlantic Ridge

Reykjavik

Eurasian Plate

Surtsey is a volcanic island which first appeared above the sea in an eruption in 1963.

Mt Helka is Iceland's most active volcano.

ICELAND

8

4 Repeated lava flows build up around the vent to form a **cone-shaped mountain**.

The Formation of a Volcanic Mountain

from the magma chamber

1 The magma reaches the surface *of the* through a narrow **vent**. *earth* ~~no th~~

2 It **erupts** explosively. Lava, boiling mud and ash are hurled into the air.

3 Hot **lava** then flows out through the vent. The lava cools and hardens.

crater

cone

surface

the earth's crust

vent

magma Chamber

Ash

Vent Lava

magma

magma

Stage 1

Stage 2

Stage 3

9

How a volcanic mountain is formed

7

Types of volcano

Active	still erupt regularly	Etna and Vesuvius (Italy)
Dormant	have not erupted for a long time, but may erupt again	Cotopaxi (Ecuador)
Extinct	have not erupted in historic times	Slemish, Co. Antrim

The Pacific Ring of Fire

Figure 10 shows that earthquakes and active volcanoes occur near the meeting places of the earth's great crustal plates. The largest earthquake and volcanic zone lies along the edges of the Pacific Ocean. This zone is known as the **Pacific Ring of Fire**.

The locations of active volcanoes and earthquake zones

(a) Why do you think the Pacific Ring of Fire is so called?

(b) Why do volcanoes, earthquakes and fold mountains occur near the Pacific Ring of Fire? Answer precisely. Consult Figure 2 if necessary.

(c) Explain why Ireland does not experience major earthquakes or volcanic activity.

Volcanic mountains in Japan

(a) Identify a volcanic cone and crater in the photograph.

(b) Identify Japan in Figure 10.

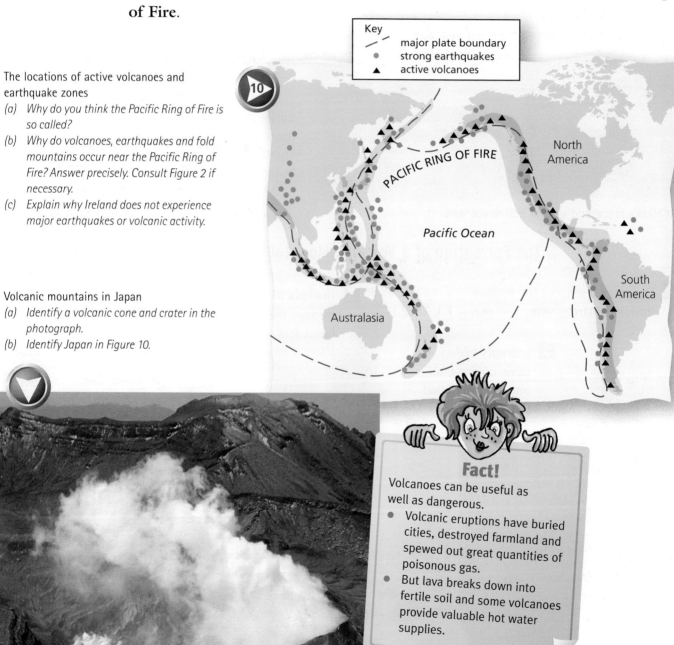

Key
- ⌐⌐⌐ major plate boundary
- ● strong earthquakes
- ▲ active volcanoes

PACIFIC RING OF FIRE

North America

Pacific Ocean

South America

Australasia

Fact!

Volcanoes can be useful as well as dangerous.

- Volcanic eruptions have buried cities, destroyed farmland and spewed out great quantities of poisonous gas.
- But lava breaks down into fertile soil and some volcanoes provide valuable hot water supplies.

Rapid Revision

- The crust of the earth is divided into **plates**. Convection currents in the mantle below cause the plates to move slowly, carrying our continents with them. This process is called **continental drift**. It causes the boundaries of plates to **collide** with and **separate** from each other.

- **Folding** can occur where plate boundaries collide. Compression causes parts of the crust to become raised and buckled into mountains. The Rocky Mountains, the Andes and the mountains of Munster are all examples of fold mountains.

- **Earthquakes** can occur where plates collide or slip past each other. The compression and cracking of rock causes shock waves to spread from the focus of an earthquake. When these waves reach the surface, the ground trembles, causing great damage to life and property. San Francisco has suffered severe earthquake damage.

- **Mid ocean ridges** may be formed where plate boundaries separate beneath the oceans. Magma makes its way to the surface along long cracks to form long ridges, such as the Mid Atlantic Ridge. Some higher parts of this ridge stick up above the surface of the ocean in the form of volcanic islands. Iceland is such an island.

- **Volcanic mountains** are also formed where plates collide. Magma reaches the surface violently through a vent. Layers of ash and lava gradually form a volcanic cone, which will have a crater at its top. Mount Vesuvius in Italy is an example of an active volcano. Slemish in Ireland is an extinct volcano. Some other volcanoes are dormant. They have not erupted for a long time, but they may erupt again.

- The world's largest earthquake and volcanic zone lies around the rim of the Pacific Ocean. It is called the **Pacific Ring of Fire**.

 Activities

1. Describe briefly but clearly the meaning of each of the following terms: *continental drift*; *fold mountains*; *epicentre*; *San Andreas Fault*; *magma*; *volcanic cone*; *crater*; *Pacific Ring of Fire*.

2. Explain each of the following statements very briefly (write one sentence for each).
   (a) Why the continents of Europe and America are moving very slowly away from each other.
   (b) Why the mountains of Munster were once higher than they are now.
   (J.C. Ordinary Level)

3. (a) Describe THREE types of damage caused when a volcano erupts.
   (b) Explain TWO ways volcanoes can be useful to people.
   (J.C. Ordinary Level)

4. Describe how plate movements lead to the formation of earthquakes and volcanoes. (J.C. Higher Level)

See Chapter 1 of your Workbook

Rocks

The earth's crust is made up of many different types of rocks. Most of these rocks have different **physical characteristics**. They may differ in colour, hardness, density (their weight) or texture (how they feel). *But rocks are usually divided into three groups depending on their* **origins** *or how they were formed*. These groups are described below.

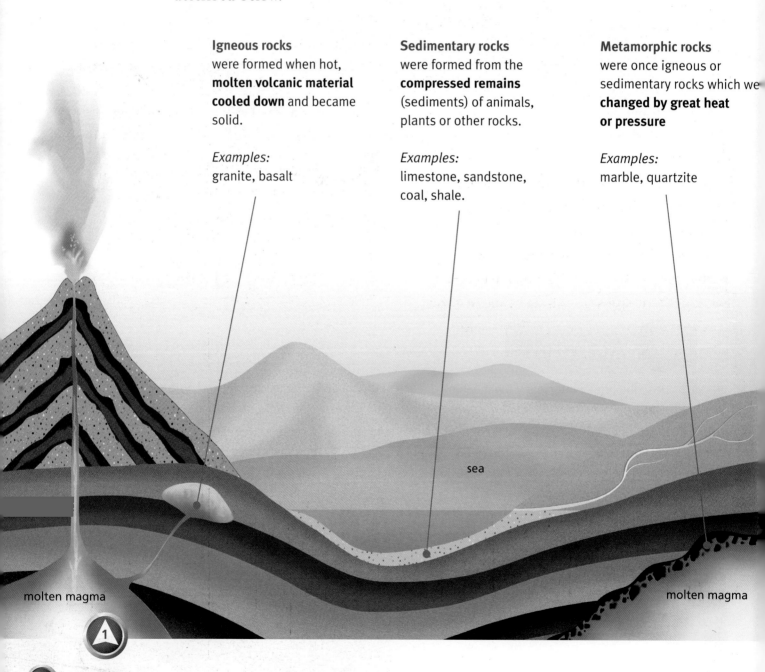

Igneous rocks
were formed when hot, **molten volcanic material cooled down** and became solid.

Examples:
granite, basalt

Sedimentary rocks
were formed from the **compressed remains** (sediments) of animals, plants or other rocks.

Examples:
limestone, sandstone, coal, shale.

Metamorphic rocks
were once igneous or sedimentary rocks which we **changed by great heat or pressure**

Examples:
marble, quartzite

sea

molten magma

molten magma

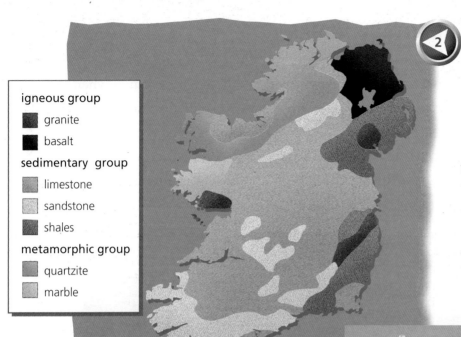

igneous group
- granite
- basalt

sedimentary group
- limestone
- sandstone
- shales

metamorphic group
- quartzite
- marble

2 This is a geological map of Ireland. It shows the general distribution of the most common rock types.
Which rock is most common:
(a) in Ireland;
(b) in your own county;
(c) in the Antrim Mountains;
(d) in the Wicklow Mountains;
(e) in the Burren (north Clare);
(f) in the Central Plain?

Some Igneous Rocks
Granite

Granite is a **hard, coarse, multi-coloured** rock. It contains pink or grey feldspar and crystals of mica or quartz.

It was formed when **magma cooled** deep within the earth's crust. The magma cooled so slowly that large crystals had time to form.

Granite is found in the **Wicklow and Mourne Mountains** (see Figure 2).

Granite

Basalt

Basalt is a **heavy, black** rock. It was formed when **lava cooled on the earth's surface**. The lava cooled too rapidly for any crystals to form.

Basalt is found in the **Antrim Plateau** and at the **Giant's Causeway** (see Figure 2).

Basalt formations at the Giant's Causeway, Co. Antrim
As lava cooled quickly at the surface, it dried and cracked into these regular-shaped columns.

Some Sedimentary Rocks
Sandstone

Sandstone is usually **coarse and brown/red** in colour. It is formed when large amounts of sand are worn from the earth's crust, carried away by rivers or wind and deposited on the beds of seas or lakes. The **sand grains** are then very gradually **compressed and cemented together** to form rock.

The **Macgillicuddy's Reeks, Comeragh** and other mountains of Munster are made up mostly of sandstone (see Figure 2).

Sandstone

Sedimentary rocks are usually laid down in layers called **strata**, with lines between the layers called **bedding planes**.
Can you identify strata and bedding planes in this photograph?

Sandstone is a beautiful building material

Limestone – Ireland's Most Common Rock
Origin

Limestone is made from the **remains of fish and other sea creatures**. As generations of these creatures died, their **skeletons** were piled up on the beds of shallow seas. The skeletons were crushed by the weight of later deposits and **cemented** together by the seawater until they formed slowly into solid rock.

Characteristics

1 Limestone is laid down in horizontal layers or **strata**. The divisions between the layers are called **bedding planes**.

3 Limestone is **permeable**, which means that water can pass through it. It is easy for rainwater to pass down through the many joints and bedding planes.

2 Vertical cracks or **joints** also occur in limestone.

The characteristics of limestone

5 Limestone may contain **fossils**. A fossil is the preserved remains of a plant or animal.

4 Limestone is **easily weathered** or worn away. The rainwater that passes through it is a weak carbonic acid which dissolves the calcium carbonate that makes up the limestone.

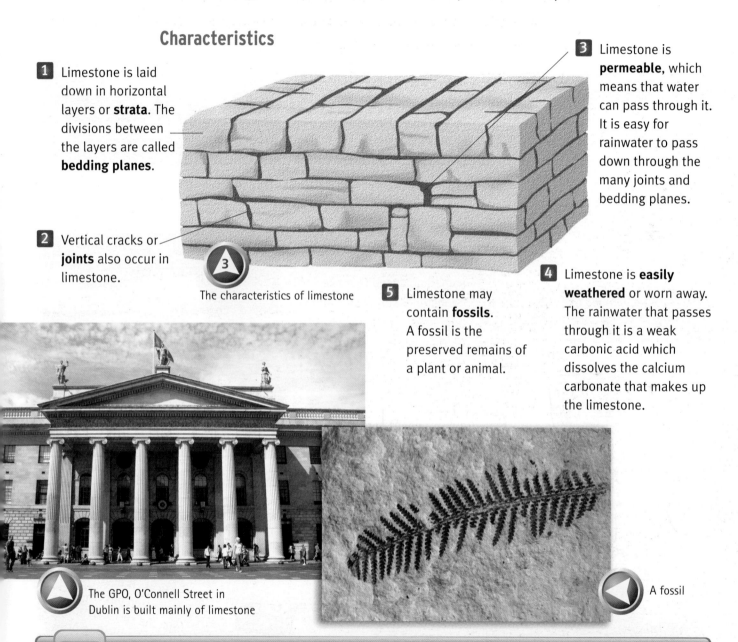

The GPO, O'Connell Street in Dublin is built mainly of limestone

A fossil

Uses of Limestone

Limestone is used in many trades.

- **Manufacturers** use limestone to make cement for the building industry. Limestone is also used to make headstones and in the manufacture of iron and steel.
- **Builders** use blocks of limestone to make public buildings. Limestone chippings are used to surface roads.
- **Farmers** use ground-up limestone as a soil conditioner.

Some Metamorphic Rocks

Igneous or sedimentary rocks can sometimes be changed completely when they come into contact with great **heat** (from magma) or with great **pressure** (due to folding). These rocks can be changed into hard, metamorphic rocks such as marble or quartzite.

Sandstone *changes to* **quartzite**

Quartzite is a **light-coloured, hard rock** which is sometimes used to surface roads. It occurs at the tops of many hills and mountains, such as at Errigal (Co. Donegal) and the Hill of Howth (Co. Dublin).

Light-coloured streaks of quartzite can sometimes be found in sandstone

Limestone *changes to* **marble**

Marble is a beautiful, **hard, crystalline rock,** which is sometimes used to make headstones, fireplaces and ornaments. It can be white (Rathlin Island), green (Connemara), red (Cork) or black (Kilkenny).

This headstone is made of marble

Rocks provide us with many **natural resources** (things from nature which are useful to people). Such resources include *energy resources* and *building materials*. These materials can be **extracted** or removed from the earth's crust in the following ways:

Liquid rock such as **natural gas and oil*** are drilled and pumped to the surface using platforms or 'rigs'. Gas is drilled from under the Celtic Sea off Co. Cork.

Shaft mines with vertical entry tunnels can be used to remove **coal** from deep beneath the earth's surface.

Rock used for **building** is usually removed directly from the surface by *quarrying*.

Peat* is also harvested directly from the surface, for example at the Bog of Allen, Co. Offaly.

* You can learn more about oil and gas in Chapter 51 and more about peat in Chapter 52.

Quarries

Rocks used as **building materials** are usually **quarried** directly from the earth's surface. So are sand and gravel, which are used for making concrete blocks and wall plaster.

Quarrying is the most common way of extracting rocks in Ireland. It is cheap and less dangerous than shaft mining. But quarrying sometimes creates dust that pollutes the air. Quarries also create visual pollution by leaving ugly scars on the earth's surface. Big trucks driving to and from quarries can create heavy traffic on local roads.

A limestone quarry near Swords, Co. Dublin

(a) What uses might be made of the stone quarried here?
(b) How might quarrying harm the environment?
(c) Name some quarries in your locality.

Carrols Quarry in Ardfert

Rapid Revision

- **Igneous rocks** are formed when molten volcanic material cools down.
  - **Granite**, which contains crystals, is formed slowly beneath the surface of the earth.
  - **Basalt** contains no crystals and is formed rapidly on the earth's surface.
- **Sedimentary rocks** are formed from the compressed remains of animals, plants or other rocks.
  - **Sandstone** is formed from compressed grains of sand.
  - **Limestone** – Ireland's most common rock – is formed from the compressed remains of sea creatures. This permeable, stratified rock is weathered by rain and may contain fossils.
- **Metamorphic rocks** are formed when other rocks change as a result of great heat or pressure.
  - Limestone changes to **marble**.
  - Sandstone changes to **quartzite**.
- Rocks provide us with **natural resources**. Fossil fuels may be extracted by mining (for coal) or drilling (for oil and gas). Rocks used for building materials are usually quarried.

Activities

1. Rocks are divided into three groups, depending on how they are formed. Choose three rocks, one from each group, and for each rock name it and explain clearly how it was formed. (J.C. Higher Level)
2. *'Rocks are useful for economic activities.'*
    Name and explain **two** ways rocks may be used in economic activities. (J.C. Ordinary Level)

See Chapter 2 of your Workbook

Weathering and Erosion: An Introduction

Rocks at the earth's surface are constantly being worn away or denuded by the forces of **weathering and erosion**.

Types of Weathering

Weathering
This is the simple **breaking down of rocks** that lie exposed to the weather. There are two types of weathering: **mechanical** and **chemical**.

Mechanical weathering breaks up rocks into smaller pieces. Its main agents (causes) are:
● **frost**
● **sudden temperature changes**
● **plants and animals**.

Chemical weathering causes rock to dissolve or otherwise decompose. Its main agent is:
● **rain**.

Denudation is carried out by ...

and ...

Erosion
This involves the breaking down of rock *and* the carrying away of rock particles. Erosion is caused by **moving water** (seas and rivers), **moving ice** and **moving air** (wind).

Transport

Deposition
Materials that are carried away by the forces of erosion are eventually **dropped** (deposited) in other areas.

This river is **eroding** rock from a mountain ...

... and depositing the eroded rock particles on low-lying ground

Mechanical Weathering: The Effects of Frost

In Chapter 3, we learned that frost is one of the chief agents of mechanical weathering.

Pieces of rock which are broken off by this **freeze–thaw** action tumble downslope and collect in heaps. These piles of rock fragments are called **scree**.

How Frost Can Weather Rocks

1 By day ...

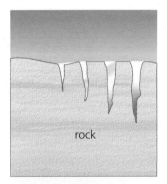

rock

... **water collects** in cracks in rocks.

2 By night ...

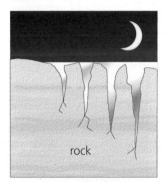

rock

... when temperatures drop to 0°C, **the water freezes** and turns to ice. As it does so, it expands by about 10 per cent. This widens the cracks and puts a strain on the rock.

3 After a long time ...

rock

... **freezing and thawing** occur so frequently that the rock is gradually split and broken up.

Where Frost Weathering Occurs

Frost action occurs in areas where:

* **temperatures** frequently rise above and fall below freezing point; and
* **precipitation** (rain, snow, etc.) is sufficient to provide plenty of water.

Such areas include the mountains of Ireland, where frost action is common in winter. Frost weathering is particularly severe in the great snowy mountain regions of the world. These regions include the Andes, the Alps and the Rocky Mountains.

The jagged top of this mountain is a result of weathering by frost. *Identify the scree.*

Chemical Weathering by Rainwater: The Burren Area

In the northern part of Co. Clare there is a limestone area known as the Burren (Figure 1). It is a rare and famous **karst** area – a place where the soluble limestone is exposed at the surface.

The **Burren** contains some very unusual scenery because the limestone is severely weathered by rainwater (see box below, 'How limestone is weathered by rainwater'). In this chapter we shall examine the effects of weathering by rainwater both on and beneath the limestone surface.

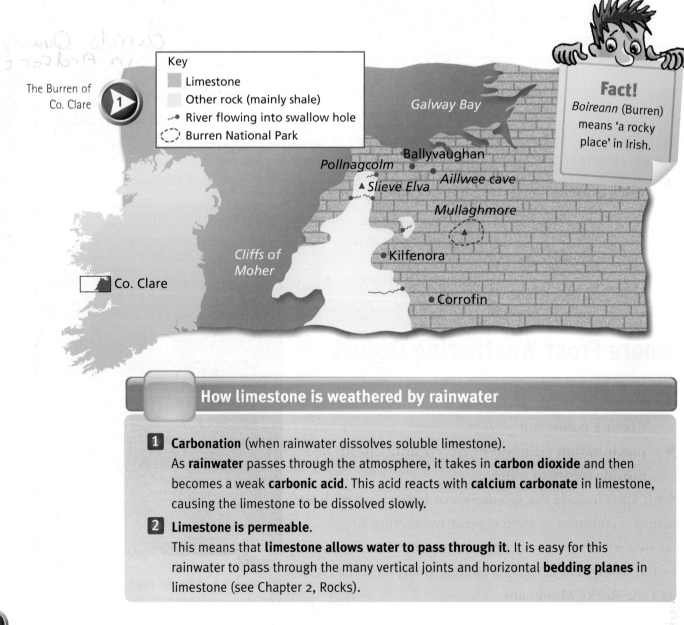

The Burren of Co. Clare **1**

Key
- Limestone
- Other rock (mainly shale)
- River flowing into swallow hole
- Burren National Park

Galway Bay

Ballyvaughan
Pollnagcolm
Aillwee cave
▲ Slieve Elva
Mullaghmore
Cliffs of Moher
● Kilfenora
☐ Co. Clare
● Corrofin

Fact!
Boireann (Burren) means 'a rocky place' in Irish.

How limestone is weathered by rainwater

1 **Carbonation** (when rainwater dissolves soluble limestone).
As **rainwater** passes through the atmosphere, it takes in **carbon dioxide** and then becomes a weak **carbonic acid**. This acid reacts with **calcium carbonate** in limestone, causing the limestone to be dissolved slowly.

2 **Limestone is permeable.**
This means that **limestone allows water to pass through it**. It is easy for this rainwater to pass through the many vertical joints and horizontal **bedding planes** in limestone (see Chapter 2, Rocks).

The Karst Surface

The photograph below shows that the surface of the Burren consists largely of bare rock.

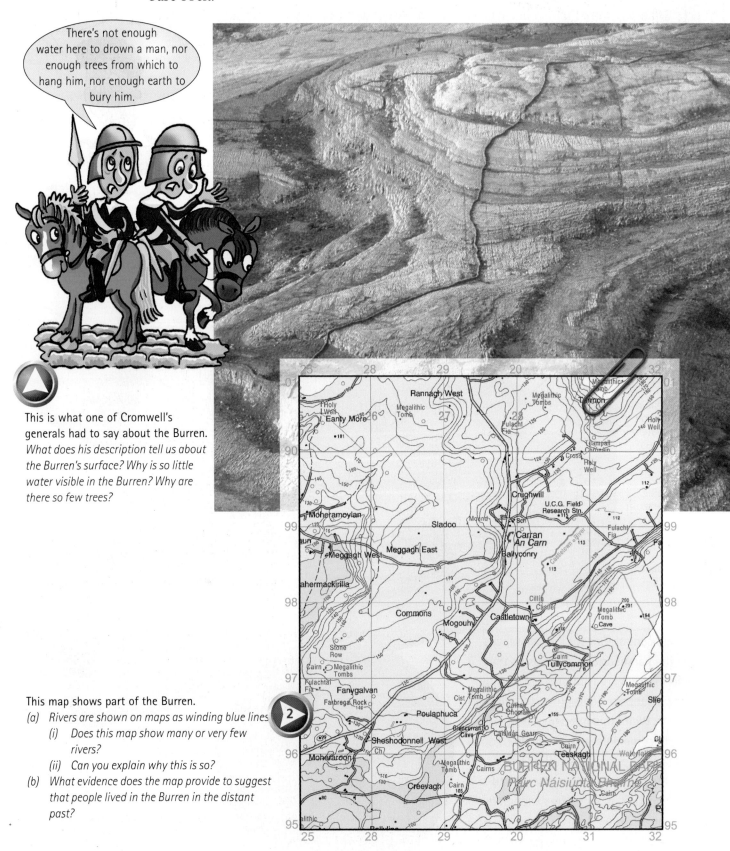

> There's not enough water here to drown a man, nor enough trees from which to hang him, nor enough earth to bury him.

This is what one of Cromwell's generals had to say about the Burren. *What does his description tell us about the Burren's surface? Why is so little water visible in the Burren? Why are there so few trees?*

This map shows part of the Burren.

(a) *Rivers are shown on maps as winding blue lines*
    (i) *Does this map show many or very few rivers?*
    (ii) *Can you explain why this is so?*

(b) *What evidence does the map provide to suggest that people lived in the Burren in the distant past?*

Surface Features

The rocky surface is called **limestone pavement**. The limestone pavement is criss-crossed by *clints* and *grikes*.

- **Grikes** are deep grooves in the pavement. They were once narrow, vertical joints, which were widened by rainwater weathering.
- **Clints** are the blocks of limestone that separate the grikes.

'Landforms' is another word for 'features'.

The gaps are the grikes.

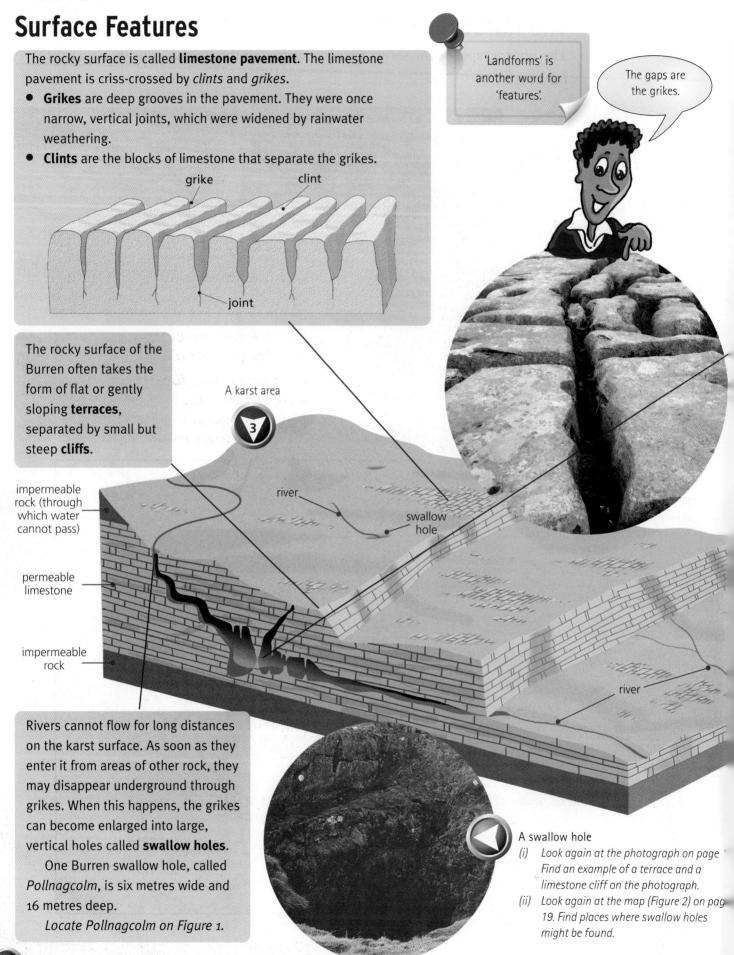

grike

clint

joint

A karst area

3

The rocky surface of the Burren often takes the form of flat or gently sloping **terraces**, separated by small but steep **cliffs**.

impermeable rock (through which water cannot pass)

river

swallow hole

permeable limestone

impermeable rock

river

Rivers cannot flow for long distances on the karst surface. As soon as they enter it from areas of other rock, they may disappear underground through grikes. When this happens, the grikes can become enlarged into large, vertical holes called **swallow holes**.

One Burren swallow hole, called *Pollnagcolm*, is six metres wide and 16 metres deep.

Locate Pollnagcolm on Figure 1.

A swallow hole
(i) Look again at the photograph on page Find an example of a terrace and a limestone cliff on the photograph.
(ii) Look again at the map (Figure 2) on pag 19. Find places where swallow holes might be found.

Underground Features

Underground rivers and seeping rainwater continue to dissolve the limestone beneath the surface of the Burren, gradually forming **passages** and **caves**. These caves contain features such as **stalactites**, **stalagmites** and **pillars**.

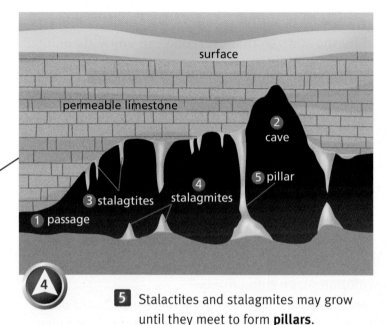

surface

permeable limestone

2 cave

5 pillar

4

3 stalagtites   stalagmites

1 passage

4

1 **Passages** are long tunnels formed by underground water dissolving the limestone.

2 Passages may become enlarged to form large **caves** or **caverns**.

3 Drops of water containing dissolved limestone may form slowly and evaporate on the roof of a cave. Each drop leaves a tiny speck of calcite (from calcium carbonate) attached to the roof. Over thousands of years, these specks develop into **stalactites** – slender columns of calcite which **hang from the cave roof**.

4 When drops of water fall onto the cave floor and evaporate, they cause calcite to build up in the form of **stalagmites**. These are thicker columns of calcite which **form on the floor**, directly under stalactites.

5 Stalactites and stalagmites may grow until they meet to form **pillars**.

How many cave features can you find in this picture?

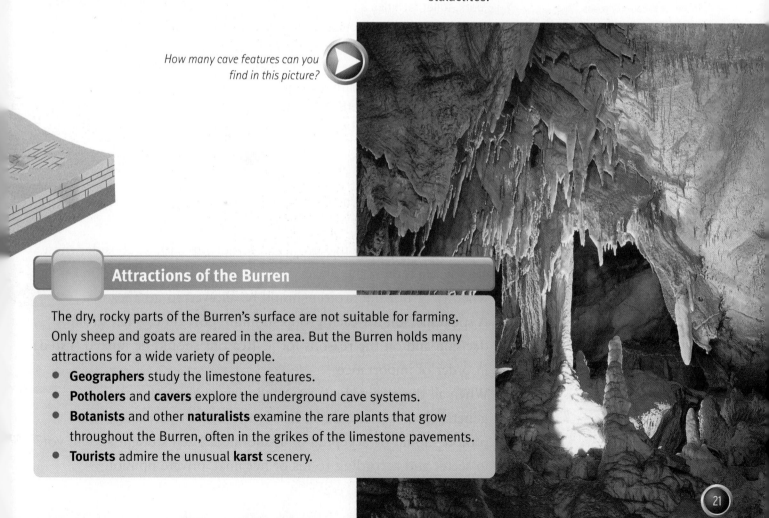

Attractions of the Burren

The dry, rocky parts of the Burren's surface are not suitable for farming. Only sheep and goats are reared in the area. But the Burren holds many attractions for a wide variety of people.

- **Geographers** study the limestone features.
- **Potholers** and **cavers** explore the underground cave systems.
- **Botanists** and other **naturalists** examine the rare plants that grow throughout the Burren, often in the grikes of the limestone pavements.
- **Tourists** admire the unusual **karst** scenery.

The visitor centre would provide some permanent jobs, as well as summer work for local students. The building of the centre would also provide work for local builders and building workers.

If the local country roads were widened, more and more cars and buses would visit this peaceful area. The area would soon become overcrowded, polluted and noisy.

The Burren area holds numerous ancient historical sites. An influx of visitors could mean that these priceless monuments could be damaged.

National Parks

National parks are big areas of beautiful countryside. Their wildlife and scenery are protected by the state so that everyone can enjoy them.

There are six national parks in Ireland. One is the Burren National Park, which occupies 1,100 hectares of karst countryside around Mullaghmore (see Figure 1 on page 18).

People sometimes disagree as to how our national parks, forests and other natural areas should be used. Such a **disagreement took place when a large visitor centre was proposed for the Mullaghmore area.**

The proposed development at Mullaghmore

- The development would include a visitor centre, in which tourists and other visitors could learn about the area. It would include a restaurant, a large car park, toilet facilities and a small sewage treatment system. There would also be a small ranger station to house the park rangers whose duty it is to protect and conserve Burren National Park.
- The centre would receive an estimated 60,000 visitors per year.
- Access roads to the centre would be widened.
- The project would cost the equivalent of €3.5 million, 75 per cent of which would come from EU grants.

Some arguments for and against the Mullaghmore project are outlined in the speech bubbles.

- Divide the class into five groups. Each group should consider these arguments carefully and then make a group recommendation on whether or not the project should be allowed to go ahead. A spokesperson for each group should report on his/her group's decision and on the reasons for it. Reasons should be ranked (listed) in order of importance.
- When all the groups have reported their recommendations, a general class vote should be held on whether the Mullaghmore project should be accepted or abandoned. Each student should vote in secret and according to his or her final, private opinion.

The centre would attract more visitors to the Burren. These visitors would spend money in restaurants, bars, shops and guesthouses. This 'spin-off' effect would bring increased prosperity to the wider Burren area.

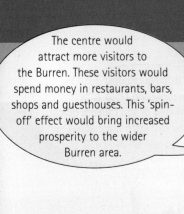

This development would give more people better access to the Burren. Many of those who oppose the Mullaghmore project are 'Burren enthusiasts' who already enjoy the area and who just want to keep it to themselves.

This area is of great botanical importance. Rare plants of Alpine and Mediterranean origins grow side by side with native varieties. The thousands of visitors would pick and trample these unique plants. They would also erode the existing small paths that run through the area.

This centre might be suitably situated in Corrofin or some other 'gateway' village of the Burren. Such villages would have the local population, car parks and other services that the centre would require. But Mullaghmore is at the very heart of the Burren National Park. It is an unspoilt place that needs conservation – not large-scale development!

The best place to learn about the Burren is surely at the heart of the Burren itself. That's why Mullaghmore is the best place to build a visitors' centre.

Tourists will come to the Burren area anyway and at present they just trample all over the place. The visitor centre would help to control visitors, by channelling them along set walking paths. The rangers at the new rangers' station would help to make sure that people do not abuse the area.

Expert bodies such as An Taisce and the Heritage Council expressed concern at the impact which this development might have. We should listen to these neutral organisations. They know what they are talking about and have the good of the country at heart.

The site of the proposed interpretative centre at Mullaghmore
What evidence is there that this photograph was taken in the karst area?

What actually happened in the end?
For ten years, a passionate dispute raged between those who favoured and those who opposed the Mullaghmore development. In the end, the project was abandoned.

Beyond the Burren ...

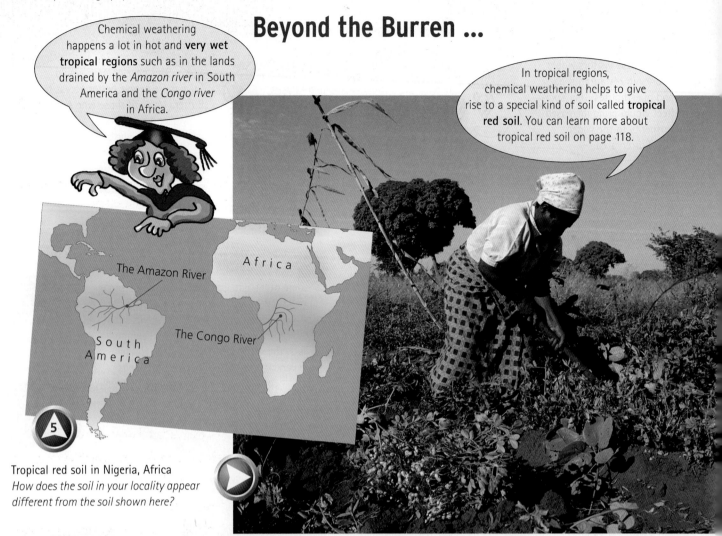

Chemical weathering happens a lot in hot and **very wet tropical regions** such as in the lands drained by the *Amazon river* in South America and the *Congo river* in Africa.

In tropical regions, chemical weathering helps to give rise to a special kind of soil called **tropical red soil**. You can learn more about tropical red soil on page 118.

Tropical red soil in Nigeria, Africa
How does the soil in your locality appear different from the soil shown here?

Rapid Revision

- The Burren in Co. Clare is a **karst** area of exposed limestone.
- Carbonic acid in rainwater passes through and reacts with the calcium carbonate in the permeable limestone. This results in the **chemical weathering** of limestone.
- The **karst surface** contains some swallow holes and bare limestone pavements with clints and grikes.
- **Beneath the surface** are passages and caverns, with stalactites on their ceilings and stalagmites on their floors. Where stalactites and stalagmites meet, pillars exist.
- A **controversy** occurred when it was proposed to build an interpretative centre at Mullaghmore within the Burren National Park. Some people favoured the project. They said that the centre would bring employment and profitable tourism to the area and that it would open up the Burren to more people. Others feared that noisy crowds might damage the unique plant life and historic monuments in this quiet area. The project was eventually abandoned.

See Chapters 3–5 of your Workbook

Mass Movement

In Chapters 3 and 4, we learned that weathering loosens and breaks up the rocks of the earth's surface. This loose, weathered material is called **regolith**. *(soil/mud/ rocks)* Regolith moves down slopes under the influence of gravity. This action is known as **mass movement**.

mass movement

> Why did mass movement occur on this Irish hillside? See below.

- **Slopes** allow mass movement to happen.
- **Water** (after heavy, prolonged rainfall) makes regolith wet and heavy and more likely to move downhill.
- A **shortage of vegetation** makes mass movement more likely. (Vegetation helps to prevent mass movement because the roots of trees and plants bind the soil together.)

Types of Mass Movement

Some of the main types of mass movement are outlined in the box. They move at different speeds, which depend largely on the steepness of the slopes on which the movements occur. Listed below are some of the main types of mass movement.

Types of mass movement	Slope	Speed
Soil creep	gentle	slow
Bogbursts, mudflows	gentle to steep	slow to rapid
Landslide	very steep	very rapid

Soil Creep

Soil creep is the **slowest** type of mass movement. Grain by grain, soil can creep down even the gentlest of slopes. Soil creep is so slow (sometimes only 1 millimetre a year) that it might not be noticed at all, except for the effect that it has on surface objects such as walls and fences (Figure 1). Anything that loosens the soil, including freeze-thaw action or the burrowing of animals, assists the movement of soil downslope.

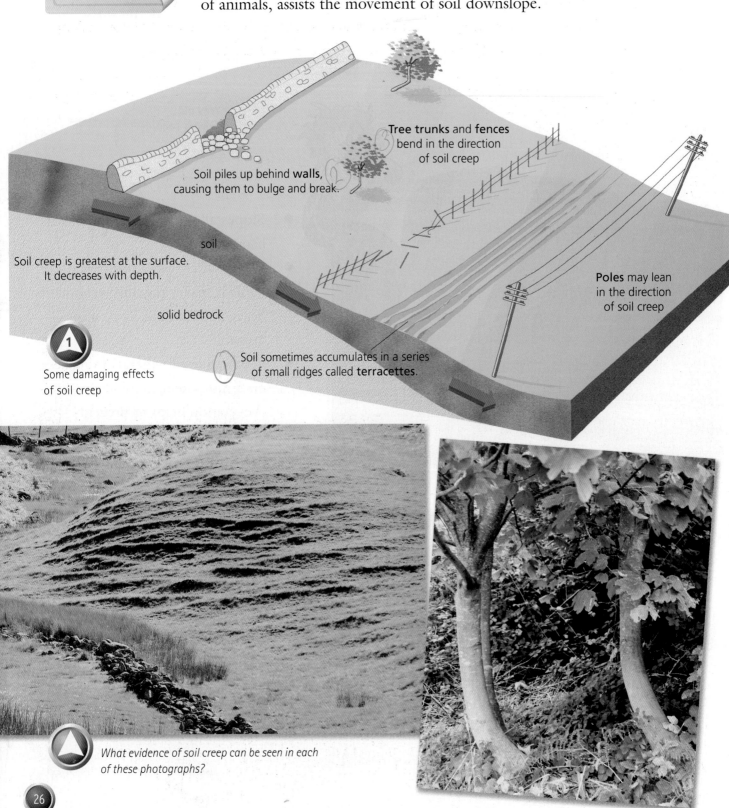

Tree trunks and fences bend in the direction of soil creep

Soil piles up behind **walls**, causing them to bulge and break.

soil

Soil creep is greatest at the surface. It decreases with depth.

solid bedrock

Poles may lean in the direction of soil creep

1 Some damaging effects of soil creep

Soil sometimes accumulates in a series of small ridges called **terracettes**.

What evidence of soil creep can be seen in each of these photographs?

Bogbursts and Mudflows

Some Irish hill slopes are covered by thick layers of **peat** or turf. **Bogbursts** may take place on such slopes after long periods of heavy rain. If the rainwater cannot drain or soak away, the peat can become heavy and saturated with water. Peat can then flow downslope like runny porridge and cause great damage over a large area.

Mudflows are rather like bogbursts. They occur when saturated regolith flows rapidly down hillsides. Small mudflows are common in Irish hill areas such as the Wicklow Glens. But not all mudflows are small. In 2005, one terrible flow killed 1,400 people in Guatemala, Central America (see Case Study below).

Case study: The village that became a graveyard

On 8 October 2005 a mountain mudflow ripped into the timber-and-tin shacks of the village of Panabaj in Guatemala. Fourteen hundred villagers were buried alive beneath a 12-metre-deep sea of mud.

Heavy rains following a tropical storm triggered the mudflow that destroyed Panabaj. But poverty was also responsible. Poor villagers had removed the trees that had once covered much of the mountain. They did so in order to grow enough food and gather enough firewood to survive. Tree roots soak up water and bind soil together. Without trees, mountain soils can turn quickly into heavy, liquid mud.

Few were rescued from the mud that engulfed Panabaj. In American Indian tradition, the lost village was declared to be a sacred place – a mass graveyard.

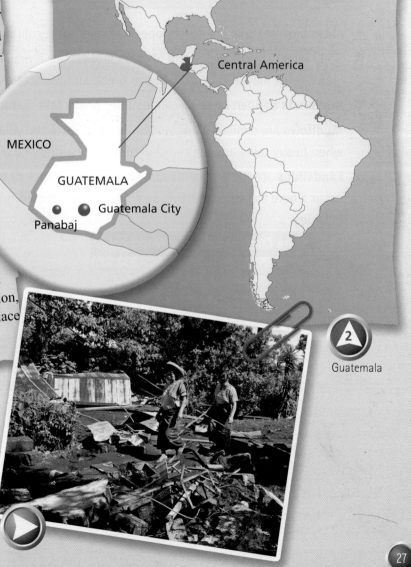

Central America

MEXICO

GUATEMALA

Panabaj · · Guatemala City

2

Guatemala

(a) *Name the village and country in which the mudflow occurred.*

(b) *Explain how nature and poverty were each responsible for the mudflow.*

(c) *Find out the meaning of the term 'deforestation'. Then explain how deforestation can lead to mudflows.*

Describe this scene following the mudflow at Panabaj

Landslides

A landslide is a **very rapid** slipping of earth or rock down a cliff or **very steep slope**. Landslides are common in mountainous areas and along coastal cliffs. Anything that undercuts the base of a slope – such as sea erosion, road building or quarrying – can trigger off a landslide (see Figure 3).

How sea erosion can cause landslides on a cliff

1 The waves erode a notch at the base of the cliff.

2 The material above the notch breaks off and collapses downwards as a landslide.

Rapid Revision

- **Mass movement** is the downslope movement of regolith under the influence of gravity.
- **Soil creep** is the slowest form of mass movement. It may cause tree trunks, poles and fences to lean over. It may also cause walls to break and terracettes to form.
- **Bogbursts** happen on peaty slopes after heavy rain. Saturated peat runs rapidly downslope.
- **Mudflows** are similar to bogbursts. Inhabitants in the village of Panabaj in Guatemala were killed when heavy rains and the removal of trees resulted in a disastrous mudflow.
- **Landslides** are the extremely rapid movement of rock or earth down very steep slopes. They may occur where the sea undercuts sea cliffs or where road-builders make steep-sided cuttings in hillsides.

See Chapter 6 of your Workbook

Test Yourself eTest.ie

A landslide on the sea cliff between Bray and Greystones, Co. Wicklow

(a) *What, in your opinion, caused this landslide to happen?*

(b) *What problems or dangers might result from a landslide such as this?*

Rivers: Some Common Features

The diagram in Figure 1 shows some common river features. Figure 2 gives a definition of each of these features. In the space provided in Figure 2 write the name of each feature next to the appropriate definition. Then learn these definitions.

Common river features

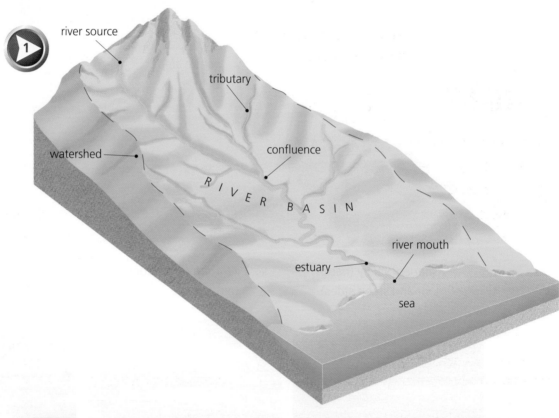

Common river features and definitions

Feature	Definition
	the place where a river begins
	a stream or river which joins a larger river
	the place where a river enters the sea, a lake or other river
	that part of a river mouth which is tidal
	the total area drained by a river and its tributaries
	the high ground which separates one river basin from another
	the place where two or more rivers meet
River course	the route taken by a river between its source and its mouth

The Three Stages of a River

A river rises in high ground (its **source**). It then flows down a slope (its **course**) until it reaches the sea (its **mouth**).

Three stages may occur in the course of a river. These are the upper or **youthful stage**, the middle or **mature stage**, and the lower or **old age stage**. The main characteristics of these stages are shown in Figure 3.

The three stages of a river

Stage	Youth (Upper course)	Maturity (Middle course)	Old age (Lower course)
Gradient (or slope) of river flow (long profile)	 steep slope	gentle slope	almost flat
Valley Shape	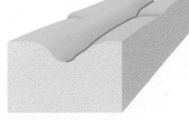 'V-shaped' valley (narrow floor and steep sides)	 Valley trough (wide floor and fairly gentle sides)	 Plain (flat, low land)
Main river processes or activities	 Small rivers flow down steep slopes and **erode** river beds **vertically** (downwards).	 Larger rivers flow rapidly down gentle slopes and **erode** river banks **laterally** (sideways).	 Large rivers flow on flat plains and **deposit** material that they had eroded further upstream

The Youthful Stage

Youthful rivers are usually small in volume (size). They usually flow down steep slopes. Such rivers generally **erode** the land over which they flow.

How rivers erode

- **Hydraulic action** is the force of moving water, which breaks fragments from the bed and the banks (sides) of the river. The material carried along by the river is called its **load**.
- **Abrasion** is when the load hits against the bed and banks of the river and erodes them rapidly. Abrasion is the most powerful way in which rivers erode.
- **Attrition** is when the stones carried in the load of the river are themselves worn down. Stones are smoothened, rounded and made smaller by the process of attrition.
- **Solution** is when chemicals in the water help to break down some rocks. Carbonic acid, for example, slowly dissolves limestone.

Features of Erosion by Young Rivers
V-shaped Valleys (Figure 4)

These valleys have **steep sides** and very **narrow floors**.

Their cross-sections are shaped like the letter V.

Examples:
In the upper courses of the Rivers **Liffey** and **Barrow**.

(a) How is this young river eroding the landscape?
(b) How is the speed of the river affected by the nature of the river bed?

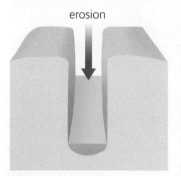

erosion

1 The river erodes **vertically** or downwards.

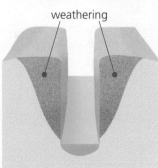

weathering

2 As the river cuts downwards its steep sides are attacked by **weathering**. This loosens and breaks up the rock and soil.

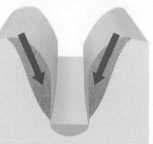

mass movement

3 **Gravity** causes the loose material to slide or creep downslope into the river.

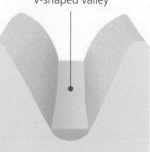

V-shaped valley

4 The river **transports** (carries) the material away. All these activities combine to form a **V-shaped valley**.

How V-shaped valleys are formed

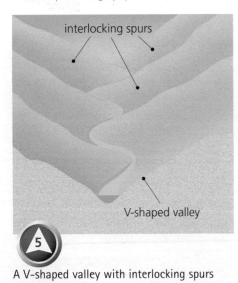

interlocking spurs

V-shaped valley

5

A V-shaped valley with interlocking spurs

Interlocking Spurs

These are areas of high ground which seem to 'lock' into each other as they stick out across a V-shaped valley (Figure 5).

Formation

A small, young river cannot remove bits of high ground (spurs) that lie across its path. So the river flows around them and continues to erode downwards. As it develops its valley, the river leaves interlocking spurs of high ground sticking out on both sides of the valley.

> *Examples*:
> In the upper courses of the **Liffey** and the **Barrow**.

(a) *Identify the interlocking spurs in this picture.*
(b) *Is the river eroding mainly down or laterally (to the sides)?*
(c) *What use is being made of the land in this upland area? How might land use be different in a lowland area?*

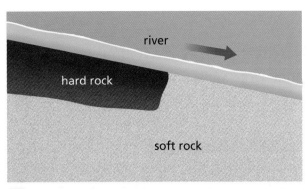

1 A **band of hard rock** lies on an area of soft rock

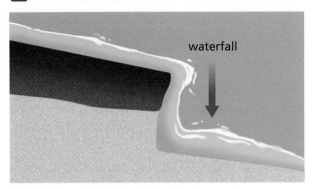

2 The river **erodes the soft rock** more quickly than the hard rock, so that a **vertical drop** develops where the hard and soft rock meet. The river falls over this drop as a **waterfall**.

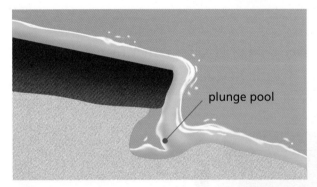

3 Falling water and stones wear away a hole called a **plunge pool** in the soft rock.

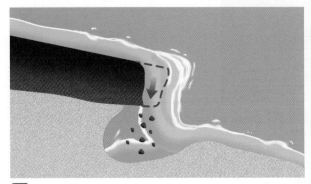

4 The hard rock above the plunge pool is **undercut** and collapses into the plunge pool. As this continues, the waterfall slowly erodes its way upstream.

Waterfalls (Figure 6)

In a waterfall, a **river falls over a vertical slope**. This happens where a sudden drop occurs in the course of a river.

Example:
Powerscourt waterfall on the River Dargle in Co. Wicklow.

 How a waterfall forms

Fact!
The world's highest waterfall is Angel Falls in Venezuela (South America). It is almost one kilometre high!

Assarnacally waterfall in Co. Donegal
Can you identify the plunge pool? How was it formed?

The Mature Stage

How rivers transport (carry) material

By the time they reach their mature stage, rivers will have received many tributaries. Mature rivers are therefore quite large and so can **carry large loads of material** along with them.

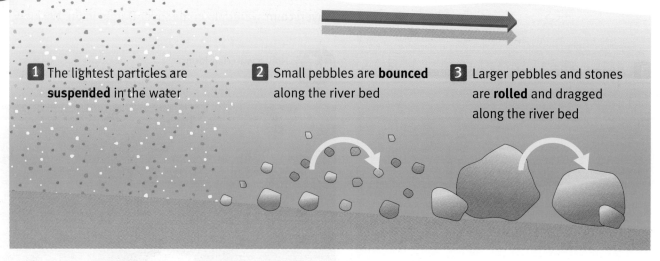

1 The lightest particles are **suspended** in the water

2 Small pebbles are **bounced** along the river bed

3 Larger pebbles and stones are **rolled** and dragged along the river bed

Features of Mature River Valleys
Valley Troughs (Figure 8)

Examples:

In the middle courses of the Rivers **Lee** and **Nore**.

These are **wide-floored** valleys with **gently sloping sides**.

Formation

As it moves down towards sea level, a river erodes **its sides** rather than downwards. So its valley becomes wider. Weathering also continues to wear away the valley sides, which become more gently sloping.

8 Mature river at Ballyduff, Co. Waterford
Can you suggest a reason why the village is sited some distance away from the river?

A Wide valley floor
B Gentle slopes at sides of valley
C River bend (meander)
D River erosion on outside bank of meander
E River deposition on inside of meander

Meanders (Figure 9)

These are **large curves** in the course of a river.

Examples:
In the middle and lower courses of the **Shannon** and the **Boyle**.

Formation

Once a river has developed a winding course, the curves in the river become wider and wider until they form meanders. Meanders are developed both by **erosion and deposition** (see Figure 9).

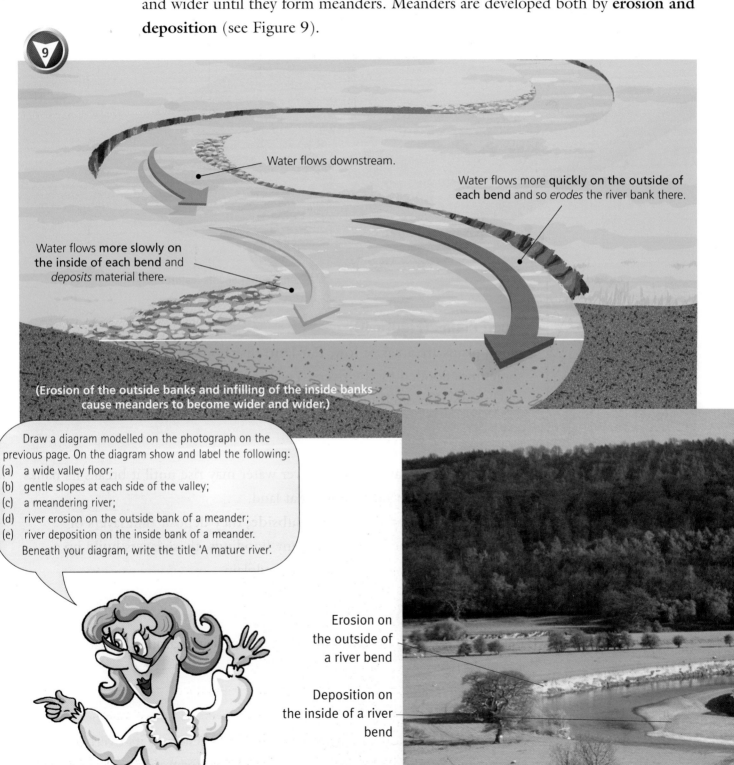

Water flows downstream.

Water flows more **quickly on the outside of each bend** and so *erodes* the river bank there.

Water flows **more slowly on the inside of each bend** and *deposits* material there.

(Erosion of the outside banks and infilling of the inside banks cause meanders to become wider and wider.)

Draw a diagram modelled on the photograph on the previous page. On the diagram show and label the following:
(a) a wide valley floor;
(b) gentle slopes at each side of the valley;
(c) a meandering river;
(d) river erosion on the outside bank of a meander;
(e) river deposition on the inside bank of a meander.
Beneath your diagram, write the title 'A mature river'.

Erosion on the outside of a river bend

Deposition on the inside of a river bend

The Old Age Stage

Old rivers **meander slowly** over almost flat plains before they enter the sea. Slowly moving rivers have little energy. So they **deposit** their loads of fine soils and mud. Soils and mud deposited by rivers is called **alluvium.**

Features of Deposition by Old Rivers

Some features of deposition
- Flood plains
- Levees
- Ox-bow lakes
- Deltas

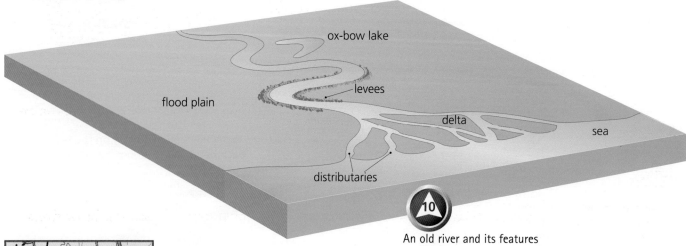

An old river and its features

Flood Plains (Figure 10)

Flood plains are areas of **low, flat land** that border old rivers and which are sometimes flooded by the rivers. They are covered in fertile **alluvial soils**, which were deposited by the river during many centuries of flooding.

Formation

- In times of **heavy rain**, the river water may rise until it breaks its banks and **floods** the surrounding flat land.
- As the floodwaters gradually **subside**, they deposit thin layers of alluvium on the land. After many floodings, these layers build up a thick, fertile covering over the floodplain.

Levees (Figure 10)

Levees are **narrow, raised banks** of alluvium found along the banks of some old rivers.

Formation

When a river overflows, it drops most of its load close to its riverbank. After many floodings, these deposits build up to form ridges of alluvium called levees.

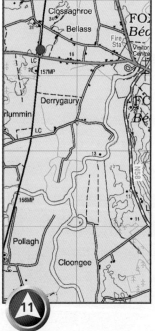

The floodplain of the River Moy, near Foxford, Co. Mayo
What 'old age' river features can you see?

Example:
The 'Lee Fields' near Cork City.

Ox-Bow Lakes (Figures 10 and 12)

Ox-bow lakes are **horseshoe-shaped lakes** found near old rivers.

Example:
On the River **Moy**, near Foxford, Co. Mayo.

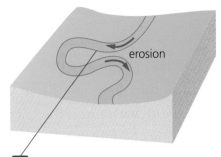 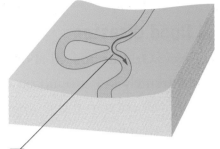 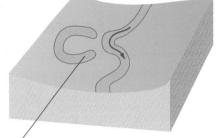

1 Erosion takes place on the outer banks of meanders, so that the neck of land between meanders becomes very narrow.

2 The narrow neck of land is eventually worn away. The river now flows straight through instead of following the meander.

3 Levee deposits later seal off both ends of the abandoned meander, which becomes an ox-bow lake.

The formation of ox-bow lakes

Deltas (Figure 10)

Deltas are **triangular-shaped areas of land** which form at the mouths of rivers. They are made up of alluvium.

Formation

Examples:
At the mouths of the **Nile** in Egypt and the **Rhone** in France.

When a river enters the sea, it loses its energy and it deposits what remains of its load.

If the sea cannot wash away these deposits, they will build up to form a **delta** at the river's mouth. Soon, the river channel becomes choked and the river is forced to break up into a number of smaller channels called **distributaries**.

(a) Is the river shown here in its upper, middle or lower course?
(b) Identify the features of river deposition which are shown.

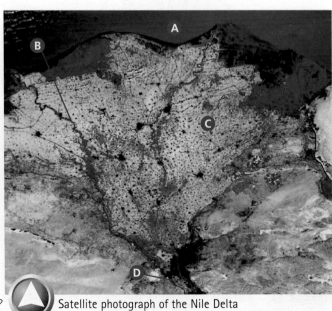

Satellite photograph of the Nile Delta
Identify each of the following by its letter: the delta, the River Nile, a distributary, the Mediterranean Sea.

> People interact with natural processes

An international flood disaster

The American city of New Orleans housed about half a million people in 2005. The city is located on extremely low ground on the **delta** of the Mississippi River. It lies between the Gulf of Mexico to the south and Lake Pontchartrain to the north (Figure 13). New Orleans was protected from sea storms and from lake and river flooding by large **levees**, topped with flood walls. There were electric pumps to pump water out of the city when needed. Wetlands or swamps outside New Orleans also helped to protect the city by soaking up any periodic flood water.

> By 2005, some people feared that New Orleans might one day suffer a disastrous flood.
> - Hurricanes (extremely strong tropical storms) are common in the Gulf of Mexico.
> - The American government under President George Bush reduced the amount of money being spent on maintaining levees and other flood defences.
> - President Bush allowed rich property developers to drain and build on the wetlands.

13 The location of New Orleans

New Orleans before the flood – a city famous for music and culture

38

Disaster struck on 29 August 2005. An exceptionally violent **hurricane** codenamed 'Katrina' crashed into the Gulf of Mexico coast. A great surge of seawater swept up the Mississippi and into Lake Pontchartrain. Some of the levees which protected New Orleans gave way. The city was invaded by a wall of water. Many people fled New Orleans as the hurricane approached. But as many as 100,000 poor people had neither the transport nor the money needed to leave. They became trapped in what was soon to become a stinking wasteland of polluted floodwater. Almost two thousand people drowned.

Government emergency assistance was inadequate and slow to arrive and many people died of thirst and baking heat. The city's population was halved following the hurricane, as hundreds of thousands of people lost their property and became **refugees** in other parts of the United States.

After Hurricane Katrina. New Orleans is reduced to a nightmare wasteland of stinking floodwater.

Activities

1. Make three statements about New Orleans and its location.
2. Explain the meanings of the terms *levee, delta, hurricane* and *refugee*.
3. *'Interaction between nature and humans can sometimes be harmful.'* How did nature and people contribute to the New Orleans disaster?

Case study: Dam Building in Ireland

Study the photograph of Ardnacrusha on the River Shannon where the ESB built a hydroelectric power station, which uses rushing water to generate electricity. As part of this **hydroelectric scheme**, a **dam** was built across the river valley. Behind the dam, trapped water has risen to form an **artificial lake**.

The damming of our rivers provides us with many benefits. It also has some disadvantages.

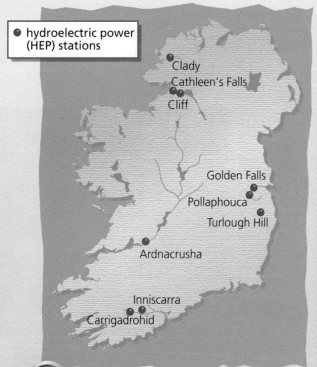

● hydroelectric power (HEP) stations

Clady
Cathleen's Falls
Cliff

Golden Falls
Pollaphouca
Turlough Hill

Ardnacrusha

Inniscarra
Carrigadrohid

14 Ireland's hydroelectric power stations
(a) Which Irish rivers have been used to make HEP?
(b) Name the power stations on each river.

The HEP station at Ardnacrusha
(a) Identify the features labelled **A**, **B** and **C** on the picture.
(b) Do you think that this valley is a suitable site for a dam. Why or why not?
(c) How can the damming of a river help to prevent flooding?

Benefits of hydroelectric dams	Disadvantages of hydroelectric dams
● They enable hydroelectric **power** to be generated for our homes, schools, etc.	● Artificial lakes **flood** settlements and valuable farmland.
● Artificial lakes can be used as **reservoirs** (storage areas) for urban water supplies.	● The survival of **salmon** and other river creatures may be threatened if their natural habitat is interfered with.
● Artificial lakes can be used for fishing and other **water sports**.	● It is difficult and **expensive** to dam a river.

Rapid Revision

- At their **youthful stages**, rivers usually erode downwards. The main **processes of erosion** are as follows:
  - **Hydraulic action** – the force of moving water
  - **Abrasion** – erosion *by* the river load
  - **Attrition** – erosion *of* the river load
  - **Solution** – chemical erosion

- **Landscape features** formed by **young rivers** include:
  - **V-shaped valleys**
  - **interlocking spurs**
  - **waterfalls**

- Rivers **transport** their loads in three ways. Very light particles are **suspended**, heavier particles are **bounced** and still heavier pebbles are **dragged** along by the river.

- **Landscape features** formed by **mature rivers** include:
  - **Valley troughs** with wide floors and gentle sides
  - Broad **meanders**.

- At their **old** stages, slow-flowing rivers **deposit** much of their loads. Landscape features of old rivers include:
  - Flat, low-lying **flood plains**
  - Horseshoe-shaped **ox-bow lakes**
  - **Levees** at the side of rivers
  - **Deltas** at the mouths of some rivers.

- Human activities can help prevent or cause **flooding**. The poor maintenance of levees and the drainage of wetlands contributed to disastrous floods in New Orleans, USA, following Hurricane Katrina in 2005.

- People sometimes change river processes by building **dams**. Dams provide hydroelectric power. They also create artificial lakes which can be used for water storage and for water sports. But the dammed lakes flood farmland. The building of dams is costly and may disrupt wildlife.

Activities

1. *V-shaped valleys, waterfalls, ox-bow lakes*
   In the case of each of the features listed above:
   (a) Say whether it has been formed by river erosion or by river deposition.
   (b) Describe with the aid of a diagram how it has been formed.
   (c) Name one example.

2. Describe three ways in which people use rivers.
   (Use Figure 15 to help you.) (J.C. Ordinary Level)

3. Describe two benefits and two possible objections to the development of a hydroelectric scheme. (J.C. Higher Level)

4. (a) Apart from hydroelectric schemes, describe one way in which people have influenced rivers. (J.C. Higher Level)
   (b) Explain how this influence has been beneficial (good) or harmful.

See Chapter 7 of your Workbook

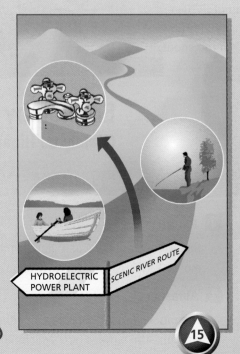

HYDROELECTRIC POWER PLANT SCENIC RIVER ROUTE

15

The Work of Moving Ice

Almost two million years ago, the climates of countries such as Ireland became colder and colder. Mountain snow piled up and gradually turned to ice. The ice moved slowly on to the lowlands as great rivers of ice called **glaciers**. Ireland had become a cold wasteland, like much of the Arctic region is today. A great **ice age** had arrived.

The picture shows a **glacier** in the Alps today.

Snowfields or areas of permanent snow and ice. They provide a constant supply of ice for the glacier.

Moraine (material deposited by the glacier.)

The front of the glacier is called its **snout**. A river of meltwater flows from the snout.

A steep-sided, **glaciated valley** lies beneath the glacier. This valley was formed at the height of the ice age by a glacier that was much larger than the one shown in the picture.

Erosion by Moving Ice
(Mainly on Highlands)

How ice erodes

1 Plucking

Sometimes the base of a glacier may melt into the ground. It may then freeze again and, as the glacier moves forward, it may 'pluck' chunks of rock away with it.

2 Abrasion

The plucked rocks become embedded in the base of the glacier. As the glacier moves, these rocks scrape and smoothe the surface over which they pass.

Features of Glacial Erosion

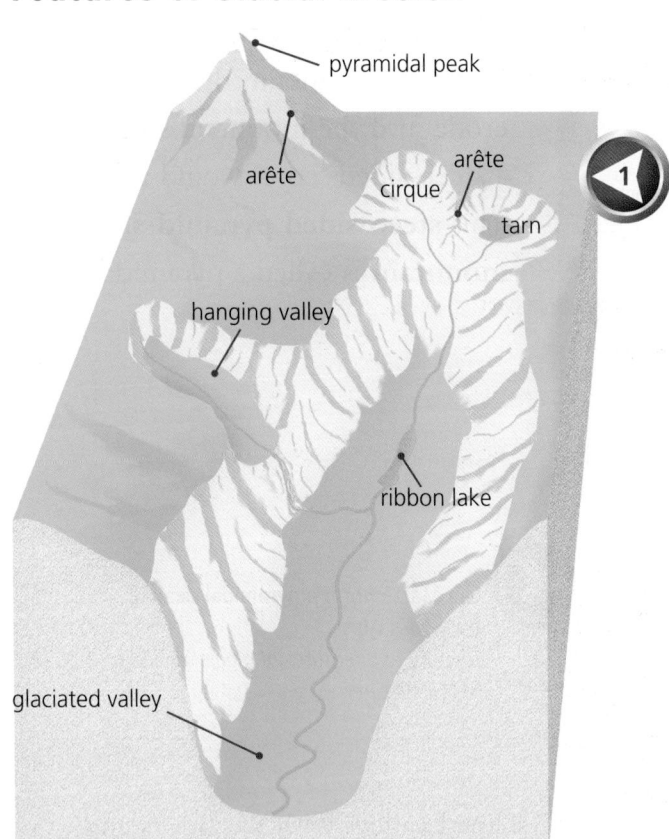

Features of glacial erosion

Figures 2 and 3 show three-dimensional images of a photograph and a map of the Coumshingaun area in the Comeragh Mountains *Identify two cirques, a tarn and an arête in this picture.*

Cirques

These are large, basin-shaped hollows in mountains. They are steep-sided on three sides. Cirques sometimes contain round lakes called **tarns**.

Each cirque was once the birthplace of a glacier. Snow piled up in these areas and became compressed into ice. The ice **eroded** (plucked and abraded) deep hollows as it began to move slowly downhill in the form of a glacier.

Example:
Coumshingaun in the Comeragh Mountains, Co. Waterford.

Arêtes

When two cirques develop side by side, the land between them becomes eroded until only a narrow ridge separates them. This narrow ridge is called an arête.

Example:
At the side of Coumshingaun cirque.

These lines on maps are called **contours**. *They show heights above sea level.*

Contours are *close together* where the land is **steep**.

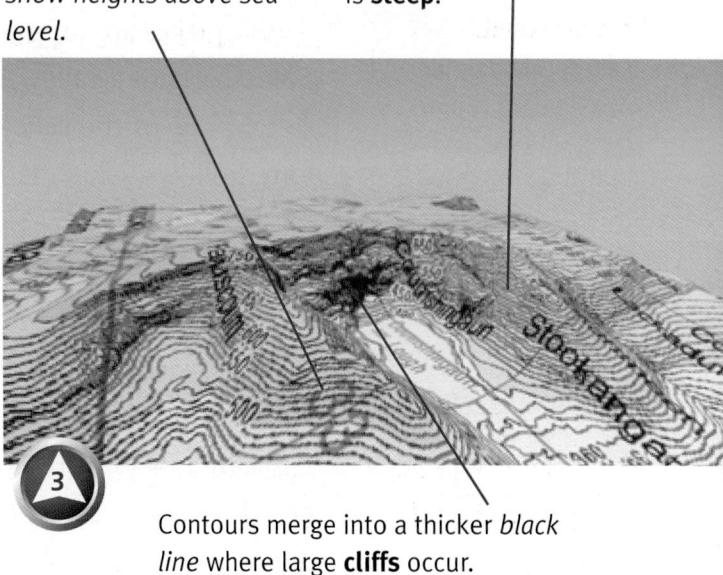

Contours merge into a thicker *black line* where large **cliffs** occur.

Pyramidal Peak

If three or more cirques formed around a mountain, they would erode into the mountain so that only a steep-sided 'core' would remain. This **steep-sided pyramid-shaped mountain** is called a pyramidal peak.

The Matterhorn, a pyramidal peak in the Swiss Alps
Identify two features of glacial erosion in this picture

Glaciated Valleys

> Example:
> At Glendalough,
> Co. Wicklow.

Glaciated valleys are deep, straight, U-shaped valleys with flat floors and steep sides.

Glaciated valleys were originally V-shaped river valleys. During the Ice Age, powerful **glaciers** deepened and straightened the valleys. The glaciers also **steepened the valley sides and flattened their floors** so that the valleys became U-shaped.

Ribbon Lakes

> Examples:
> At Upper and Lower Lakes, Glendalough.
> At Kylemore Lough, Co. Galway.

Ribbon lakes are long, narrow lakes in glaciated valleys.
Some parts of a valley floor may have **softer rocks** than other parts. The softer parts of the valley may be **eroded more deeply** by the glaciers, leaving long hollows, which later become filled with water to form lakes.

Hanging Valleys

> Examples:
> At Glendalough.
> At the side of Kylemore Lough.

Hanging valleys are tributary valleys which 'hang' above the levels of the main glaciated valleys. Rivers often flow from hanging valleys into the main glaciated valleys by means of waterfalls.

Many valleys were greatly deepened by the powerful glaciers that once occupied them. But their **tributary valleys were not deepened to the same degree**. When the glaciers melted, the floors of the tributaries remained high above the floors of the main valleys.

Figures 4 and 5 show a 3D photograph and map of Kylemore Lough in Co. Galway

(a) Identify by its label each of the following features in Figure 4:
  - a glaciated valley
  - a ribbon lake
  - a hanging valley.

(b) Identify by its label each of the following in Figure 5:
  - contours close together where slopes are steep
  - contours further apart where slopes are gentle
  - an absence of contours where the land is flat
  - the symbol for a road
  - the symbol for a house.

(c) Why do you think no houses have been built on the flat land close to the river?

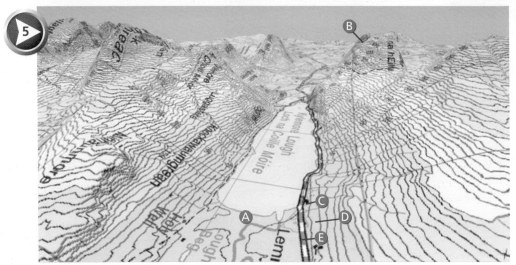

Fiords

Fiords are **drowned U-shaped valleys** which take the form of deep, steep-sided sea inlets.

Fiords were once glaciated valleys, which were drowned by rising sea levels at the end of the Ice Age. The level of the sea rose because of the vast amounts of meltwater that entered it.

Example:
Killary Harbour in Co. Mayo.

This photograph was taken in Norway, which is known as 'The Land of Fiords'
How do you know that the feature shown is a fiord?

Glendalough, Co. Wicklow

Ordnance Survey map of the Glendalough area

How many of these photograph and map questions can you do?

Examine the **photograph** of Glendalough in Figure 6.
(a) How do you know that the valley shown has been eroded by ice?
(b) Identify the feature labelled **A** on the photograph and describe how it has been formed.
(c) At what time of year do you think the photograph was taken? Explain your answer.

Now examine the **Ordnance Survey map** (Figure 7) and the **photograph** together.
(d) Name the lake labelled **A** on the photograph.
(e) A river flows at the place labelled **B** on the photograph. Can you name the general direction of its flow? (Hint: use the map.)
(f) Use the map to state the height above sea level of the place labelled **C** on the photograph.
(g) What evidence can you find (i) on the photograph and (ii) on the map to suggest that the Glendalough area is used for tourism or recreation?

Transport by Moving Ice

In general, moving ice **erodes** large quantities of rock in highland areas. It then **transports** the eroded material downslope to lowland areas and **deposits** it there. Figure 8 shows **how a glacier transports material**.

1 Some of the material is carried along on the **surface** of the glacier. This material includes lateral and medial moraines.

- **Lateral or 'side' moraines** are ridges of regolith (loose rock and soil) which falls from nearby hills on to the sides of the glacier.

- **Medial or 'middle' moraines** are ridges of regolith which run down the middle of the glacier's surface. They were formed when two glaciers met and two lateral moraines joined together to form a single medial moraine.

- **Terminal moraines** lie across the valley. They were pushed along in front of the moving glacier.

2 Some transported material is embedded **within the glacier**. Most of this fell through deep cracks or **crevasses** on the glacier's surface.

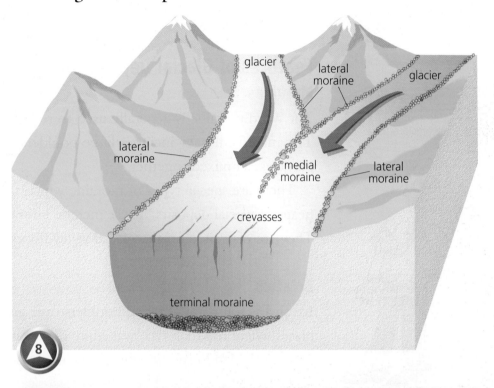

glacier · lateral moraine · glacier · lateral moraine · medial moraine · lateral moraine · crevasses · terminal moraine

8

Glaciers in the Alps

(a) *Identify crevasses in the picture.*

(b) *What types of moraines are shown at X and Y?*

(c) *What kind of moraine is shown in the picture on page 42?*

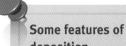

Some features of deposition
- moraines
- erratics
- drumlins
- outwash plains
- eskers

Moraines are described in Figure 8 on the previous page.

Example:
Boulders from Scotland have been deposited in Co. Dublin by moving ice.

Glacial Deposition
(Mainly on Lowlands)

As glaciers moved slowly from mountains to lowlands, they carried with them the materials that they had eroded. These materials were deposited on the lowlands by the melting ice.

Features of Glacial Deposition
Moraines

The word moraine is generally used to refer to any material laid down by ice. This material usually includes large boulders, small stones and fine soil particles, all mixed together.

There are special types of moraine which take the shape of long, narrow heaps of glacial deposits. These include **lateral**, **medial** and **frontal** moraines. They are deposited on the glacial valley floors when the glaciers melt.

Erratics

Ice sheets sometimes carried boulders over great distances, dumping them in places where the rock type was quite different. Such boulders look out of place in the landscape on which they now stand. They are called erratics.

A granite erratic found in an area of limestone in Inishmore, the Aran Islands

Examples:
In Clew Bay,
Co. Mayo.
In Lower Lough Erne,
Co. Fermanagh.

Drumlins

Drumlins are rounded, oval-shaped hills. They are made of boulder clay, which is a mixture of stones and clay. These small hills often occur in large numbers known as **swarms**. Because boulder clay is impermeable, the land between drumlins may contain marshes or small lakes.

Drumlins were formed when boulder clay was laid down by moving ice and was later smoothed and shaped by later ice movements.

A drumlin 9

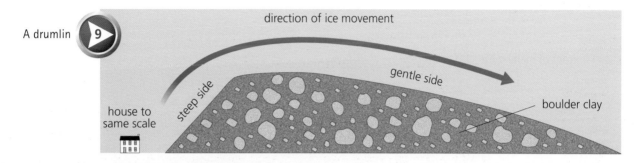

A drumlin swarm in Clew Bay. These drumlins were partially submerged (drowned) when the sea rose at the end of the Ice Age.

(a) How do you know by the shape of these islands that they are drumlins?
(b) The place labelled **A** on the photograph is shown as Rosnakilly on the map in Figure 10. Using the map to help you, name the points labelled **X** and **Y** and the island labelled **Z** on the photograph.
(c) Is there any evidence on the photograph or map that the drumlins shown were inhabited in ancient times?

49

Example:
The Curragh, Co. Kildare

Outwash Plains

Outwash plains are **low-lying areas of sand and gravel** usually found near frontal moraines.

Towards the end of the Ice Age, vast amounts of water flowed from the melting ice fronts. This **meltwater** moved through the frontal moraines on to the plains beyond. As it did so, the water flushed large amounts of sand and gravel through the moraines and deposited them on the outwash plains (see Figure 11).

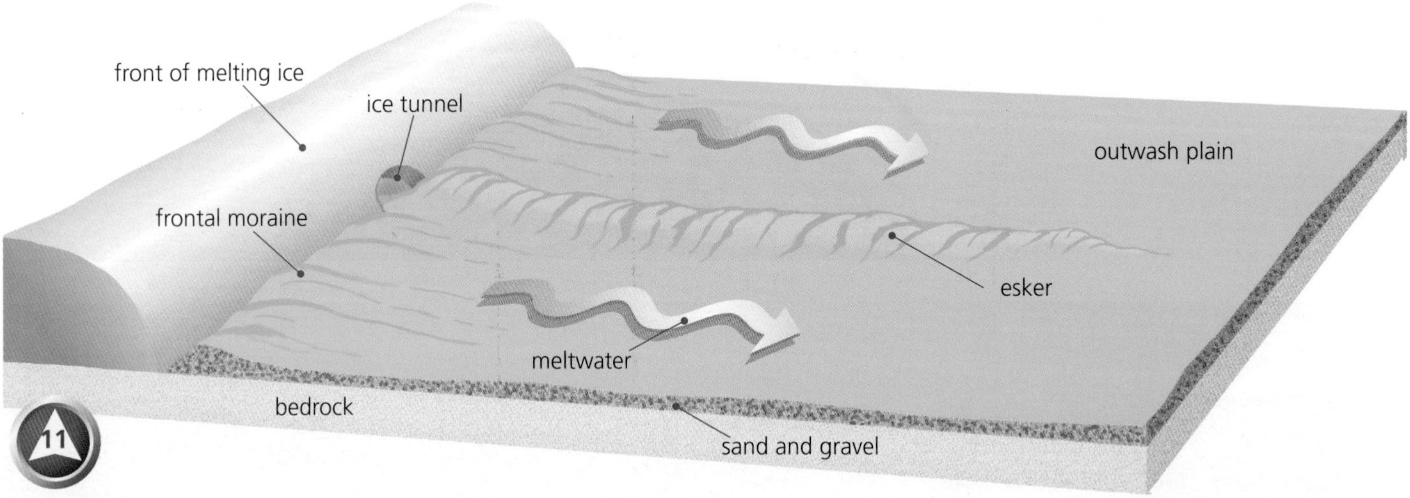

11

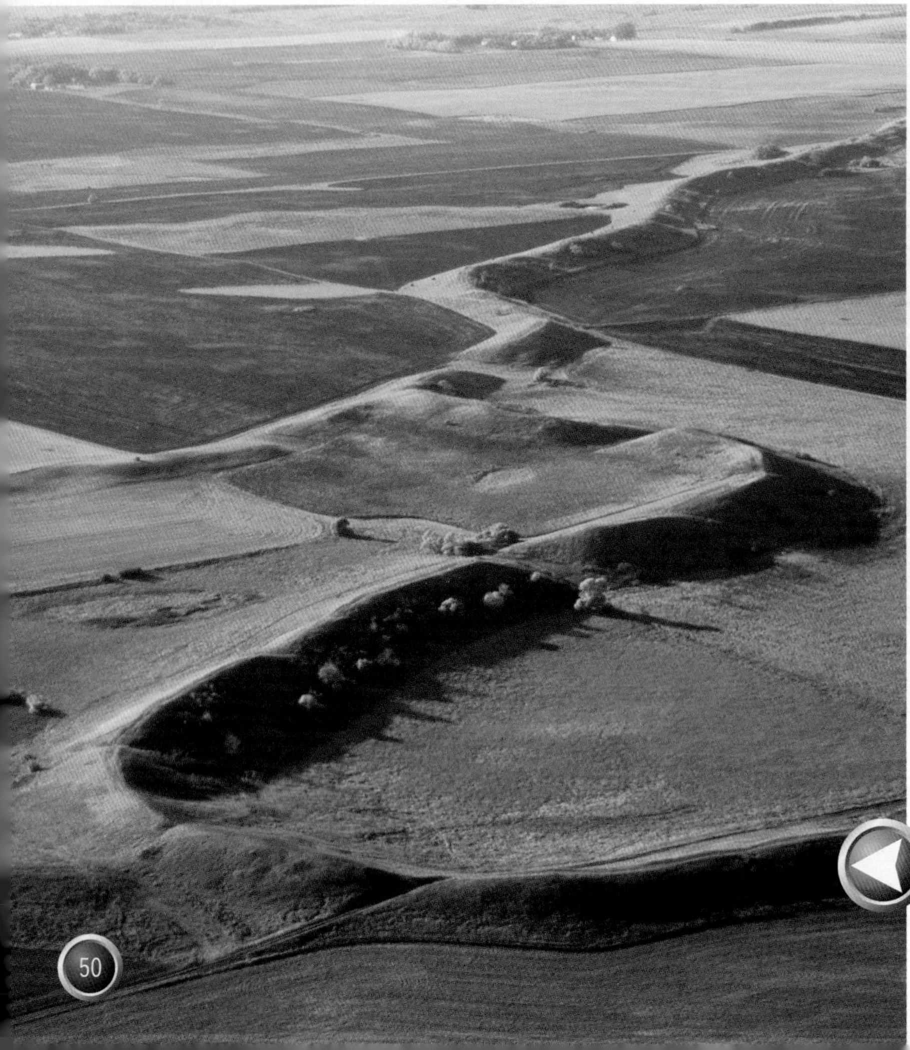

Eskers

Eskers are **long, narrow ridges** which wind across lowland areas (see Figure 11).

When the ice was melting towards the end of the Ice Age, rivers of meltwater flowed rapidly through tunnels beneath the ice. When a river left a tunnel at the front of the ice, it lost its energy and deposited material. As the ice front melted back gradually, the material was deposited in the form of a long, narrow ridge.

Example:
Between Athlone and Athenry in the Central Plain.

Can you see an esker in this photograph? Describe how the esker was formed.

Rapid Revision

Glaciers are slow-moving rivers of ice. They erode highland areas by **plucking** (pulling rocks from the ground) and by **abrading** (scraping the surface over which they pass).

Features of erosion include the following:

- *Cirques*, which are basin-shaped hollows where glaciers began.
- *Arêtes*, which are knife-edged ridges between cirques.
- *Glaciated valleys*, which have steep sides and flat floors.
- *Ribbon lakes* on the floors of glaciated valleys.
- *Hanging valleys* up on the sides of glaciated valleys.
- *Fiords*, which are drowned glaciated valleys.

Moving ice **transports** material from highlands to lowlands. Some materials are transported on the surfaces of glaciers in the form of moraines.

Features of deposition are found mainly on lowlands and include the following:

- *Lateral, medial and frontal moraines* on the floors of glaciated valleys.
- *Drumlins*, which are oval-shaped hills of boulder clay.
- *Erratics*, which are boulders carried from distant places.
- *Outwash plains* of sand and gravel laid down by meltwater from the ice.
- *Eskers*, which are long, winding ridges laid down by rivers coming out of ice fronts.

Activities

1. Describe **two** processes (two ways) by which moving ice has eroded the landscape. (J.C. Higher Level)
2. From the list of landscape features given below, identify those that are formed by glacial erosion and those that are formed by glacial deposition.
   Tarn, levee, frontal moraine, outwash plain, sea cliff, arête, drumlin, V-shaped valley, hanging valley, cirque, erratic, stalactite, fiord, meander, delta, hanging valley.
3. Describe how one feature of glacial erosion and one feature of glacial deposition have been formed over the years. Use at least one diagram in your answer. (J.C. Ordinary Level)

See Chapter 8 of your Workbook

The Work of the Sea

The work of the sea along our coasts includes **erosion**, **transport** and **deposition**.

Sea Erosion

Sea erosion is the removal by the sea of rocks and soil from the coast. It is carried out most effectively:

- by **strong waves** (usually carried by strong winds across large sea areas)
- on exposed **shorelines** made of soft rock.

How Waves Erode

1. **Hydraulic action** is the power of water as it crashes against the coast.
2. **Compressed air** becomes trapped in rock cracks by incoming waves. The pressure of the air can shatter the rock.
3. **Abrasion** is erosion of the coastline by the stones that are hurled against it by the waves.
4. The stones carried by waves are themselves smoothed and worn down. This is called **attrition**.

Features of erosion
- bays and headlands
- sea cliffs
- sea caves
- sea arches
- sea stacks
- blow holes

Features of Sea Erosion
Bays and Headlands

A **bay** is a large, curved opening into the coast. A **headland** is a piece of land sticking out into the sea.

Examples:
Dublin Bay and Howth Head, Co. Dublin.

Formation

hard rock
soft rock
hard rock
erosion
Waves
sea

Areas of hard and soft rock lie exposed to the sea

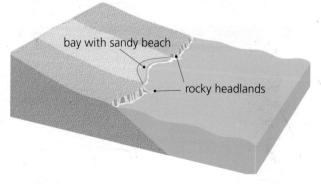

bay with sandy beach
rocky headlands

The soft rock is eroded back quickly to form bays. The hard rock resists erosion and juts out to form headlands.

Sea Cliffs

A **sea cliff** is a high rock face that slopes very steeply up from the shore.

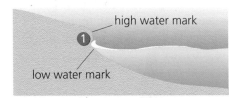

high water mark

low water mark

1 Waves erode a **notch** in the coast. *By hydraulic action and abrasion*

2 The notch gradually becomes deeper.

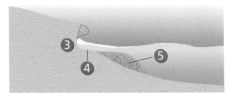

3 The area above the notch becomes so undercut that it collapses, forming a **cliff**.

4 The former base of the cliff remains as a **wave-cut platform**.

5 Material eroded from the cliff builds up to form **a wavebuilt terrace**.

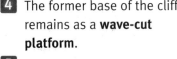

How sea cliffs are formed

Examples:
The Cliffs of Moher, Co. Clare.
At Benwee Head, Co. Mayo.

Cliffs are shown where contour lines are extremely close together

contour lines

Identify examples of headlands and bays on this Ordnance Survey map fragment

island

possible sea stacks (see page 54)

sandy beach (see page 56)

An Binn Bhui
Benwee Head

Stonefield

Sea erosion
Identify a cliff, an undercut part of the cliff and a wave-cut platform.

Sea Caves, Arches and Stacks

4 The formation of sea caves, arches and stacks

A sea stump is the remains of a sea stack which has been eroded by the sea

cave

arch

stack

stump

Sea cave

A **sea cave** is a large hole or tunnel at the foot of a cliff. **Waves find a weak spot** at the base of a cliff and gradually erode it until a cave is formed. ↳ by abrasion and hydraulic action

Example:
Cliffs of Moher.

Sea arch

A **sea arch** is a natural archway in a rocky headland.
If a **cave erodes right through a headland** (or if two caves erode through from either side), an arch may form.

Example:
Old Head of Kinsale, Co. Cork.

Sea stack

A **sea stack** is a pillar of rock sticking out of the sea near the coast.
If the roof of an **arch collapses**, its outer wall may stand out as a pillar of rock.

Example:
Ballybunion, Co. Kerry.

Example:
'McSweeney's Gun' in Co. Donegal.

Blow Holes

A **blow hole** is a hole which joins the roof of a cave with the surface above. It is called a blow hole because sea spray may be blown up through it in stormy weather.

Formation

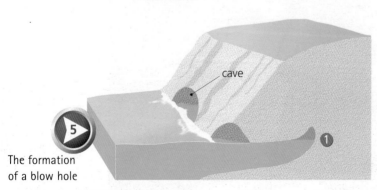

cave

5

The formation of a blow hole

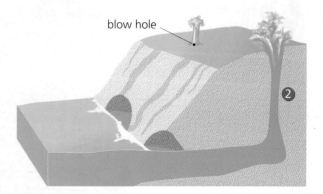

blow hole

1 When powerful waves crash into a cave, air **becomes trapped** inside the cave.

2 The **air pressure breaks a hole** in the roof of the cave.

Malinbeg, Co. Donegal
(a) Identify each of the features of **erosion** labelled on the photograph.
(b) Can you identify one feature of coastal **deposition**?

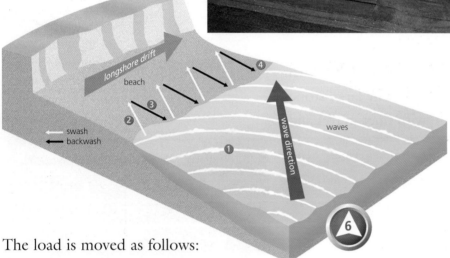

Transport by the Sea

The mud, sand and shingle (pebbles and stones) carried along by the sea are called its **load**.

The load is moved as follows:

- **Up the shore** by the force of incoming waves (the **swash**) and back **down the shore** by the pull of retreating waves (the **backwash**).
- **Along the shore** by a process known as **longshore drift** (see Figure 6).

Groynes are low walls built out into the sea to stop the movement of longshore drift
How do groynes prevent longshore drift? Why might port authorities or resort owners wish to prevent longshore drift?

How longshore drift works

1 Waves approach the shore from the side.

2 The **swash** of each wave pushes material up the beach at an angle.

3 Each **backwash** drags the material straight down following the slant of the beach.

4 As these processes repeat themselves, the material is gradually **transported along the shore in a zig-zag manner**.

Sea Deposition
How Deposition Takes Place

The sea drops its load where the **power of waves** is **reduced**.
This may occur, for example, in **sheltered bays** or in **gently sloping** coastal areas.

Features of Sea Deposition
Beaches

A **beach** is a gently sloping area of sand or shingle that occurs between high and low tide levels.

Features of sea deposition
- beaches
- spits
- bars
- tombolos

Examples:
Bray, Co. Wicklow.
Salthill, Co. Galway.

Formation

When **waves break** they **lose their power** and begin to **deposit** the material they are carrying.

The **swash** pushes materials up the beach. Some of the swash seeps into the beach. The weaker **backwash** can then pull only finer material back down. That is why large stones are often found at the top of a beach, with finer gravel and sand on the lower beach.

Sand dunes are large mounds of sand at the back of a beach. They have been deposited there by **wind**, which blows the sand up from the beach.

People sometimes plant **marram grass** on sand dunes to prevent the sand from invading nearby farmlands. The marram grass and its deep roots help to bind the sand and so prevent it from being blown inland.

A **storm beach** consists of very large stones deposited at the top of a beach by storm waves.

Beaches in Co. Clare
Identify each of the following:
- *A beach*
- *A storm beach*
- *Stones at the top of a beach*
- *Sand on the lower beach*
- *Sand dunes*
- *Marram grass*

Spits

A spit is a narrow ridge of sand or shingle. One end juts out into the sea, while the other is connected to the land.

Longshore drift stops when it reaches a bay or other sheltered place. The material carried by the longshore drift is deposited at these places and may build up gradually to form a spit (Figure 7).

Examples:
Portmarnock, Co. Dublin.
Bannow Bay, Co. Wexford.

Bars

A bar is a narrow ridge of sand or shingle which seals off the mouth of a bay.

A **spit** may grow in length until is completely **seals off a bay**. The former spit is then referred to as a bar. A *lagoon* is a small lake formed behind the bar. It was originally part of the bay, which was sealed off by the bar.

Examples:
Lady's Island Lake, Co. Wexford.
Loch Muiri, Co. Clare.

Tombolos

A tombolo is a narrow ridge of sand or shingle, which joins an offshore island to the mainland.

A **spit** may grow in length until its seaward end **reaches a nearby island**. The former spit is then referred to as a tombolo.

Examples:
Howth, Co. Dublin, was once an island until the Sutton tombolo joined it to the mainland.

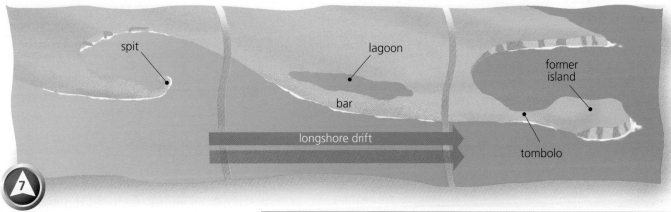

7

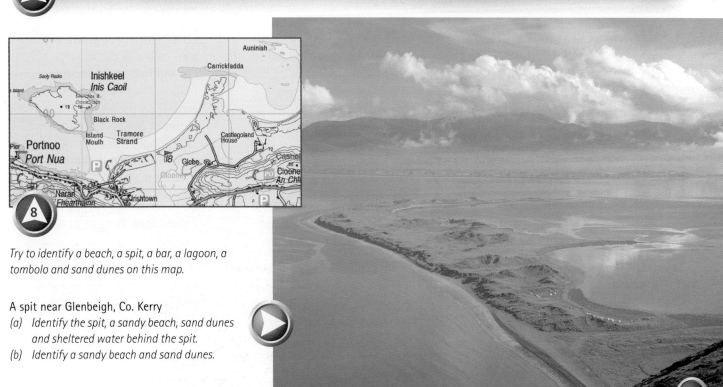

8

Try to identify a beach, a spit, a bar, a lagoon, a tombolo and sand dunes on this map.

A spit near Glenbeigh, Co. Kerry
(a) Identify the spit, a sandy beach, sand dunes and sheltered water behind the spit.
(b) Identify a sandy beach and sand dunes.

For centuries the sea had provided livelihoods for fishermen in the East Cork village of Ballycotton. But the sea has sometimes been an enemy as well. Its powers of erosion and deposition have inflicted great damage on Ballycotton and the surrounding area (Figure 9).

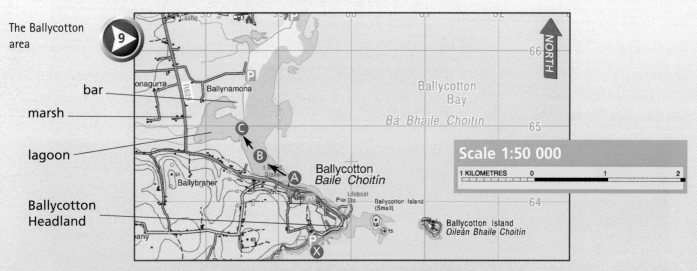

The Ballycotton area

- bar
- marsh
- lagoon
- Ballycotton Headland

Marine Processes and Problems at Ballycotton

Process	Problems	Possible coastal defence work
Ⓐ **Sea erosion** occurs on the soft boulder clay cliffs near Ballycotton headland.	Valuable **farmland**, several **houses** and some **roads** have been **eroded** away.	• Build a strong concrete **sea wall** to break the waves. • Lay out huge **boulders** (to reduce the power of the waves) on the shore. • A **pier or breakwater** (long wall jutting out to sea) would reduce erosion in the area sheltered by it.
Ⓑ **Longshore drift** removes the eroded material towards Ballycotton Bay.	Longshore drift **assists** both **erosion** near the headland and **deposition** in the bay.	Build concrete **groynes** to reduce longshore drift.
Ⓒ **Deposition** has resulted in a bar blocking the head of the bay.	The bar **blocked river drainage** into the bay. Marshes and a lagoon formed and **flooded** farmlands and roads. The marsh, however, provided an important wildlife sanctuary.	Occasionally **cut through the bar** to improve river drainage. (But this would damage the wildlife sanctuary.)

Aerial view of Ballycotton

1. Examine the **aerial photograph** of Ballycotton.
   (a) Identify each of the following features according to its numbered label and say whether each feature is formed by erosion or deposition: rocky cliff; headland; sandy beach; bar; lagoon.
   (b) Identify each of the following features in the photograph: a pier; boats in the harbour; a ploughed field; holiday cottages.

2. Examine the **aerial photograph** of Ballycotton **above and the map extract (Figure 9) together.** The photograph was taken above the spot marked with an X on the map. When the photograph was taken, the camera was pointing towards a caravan park at the top of the map.
   (a) Try to estimate the direction in which the camera was pointing when the photograph was taken.
   (b) Try to estimate the distance between the places labelled 2 and 4 on the photograph. (To do this you will have to calculate the distance between those places on the map.)

More about Coastal Defence

The following are methods used to defend our coasts against the sea.

Strong sea walls

These are made of reinforced concrete. The fronts of the walls may be curved, so as to deflect waves back out to sea.

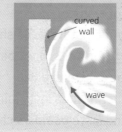

curved wall

wave

Groynes

(revise page 55)

Marram grass

(revise page 56)

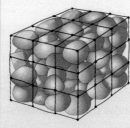
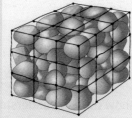

Gabions

These are steel wire cages filled with stones. When stacked on top of each other, they act like a sea wall.

Large boulders

They are placed in front of cliffs or sand dunes. They break the waves and so reduce their power.

Rapid Revision

The sea erodes by means of:

- *Hydraulic action* (erosion by water).
- *Compressed air* in the rocks.
- *Abrasion* (erosion *by* the sea's load).
- *Attrition* (erosion *of* the sea's load).

Features of sea erosion include the following:

- *Headlands* (usually of harder rock) and bays (usually of softer rock).
- *Sea cliffs*, which slope steeply up from the shore.
- *Sea caves*, which form where waves enlarge weak spots in cliffs.
- *Sea arches*, where sea caves erode through headlands.
- *Sea stacks*, which are the outer walls of collapsed arches.
- *Blow holes*, which join the roofs of caves with the surfaces above.

The sea transports its load:

- *up and down* the shore by the swash and backwash of waves.
- *along* the shore by longshore drift.

The sea deposits its load when its force is reduced.

Features of deposition include the following:

See Chapter 9 of your Workbook

- *Beaches* of sand or shingle.
- *Spits*, which protrude out from the shore.
- *Bars*, which form when spits block bays.
- *Lagoons*, which form behind bars.
- *Tombolos*, which form when spits join islands to the mainland.

Sea walls, *gabions* and *large boulders* can be used to reduce sea erosion. *Groynes* are used to reduce longshore drift.

Activities

1. For each of the following terms, write a sentence to show that you understand its meaning: *hydraulic action*; *notch*; *lagoon*; *blowhole*; *marram grass*; *groynes*.

2. Describe the ways in which the sea erodes a coast. (J.C. Higher Level)

3. Make separate lists of features of sea erosion and features of sea deposition. Name one Irish example of each feature on your list.

4. Describe how the sea helps to form one coastal feature of erosion and one coastal feature of deposition. Use at least one diagram in your answer. (J.C. Higher Level)

5. With the aid of diagrams, explain how (a) a sea cave and (b) a coastal bar is formed.

6. Say whether each of the following statements is **true** or **false**:
   (a) A cave must normally be present for a blow hole to form.
   (b) Bars are formed behind lagoons.
   (c) Cliffs, sea arches, tombolos and wave-cut platforms are all features of sea erosion.

10

Our Planet's Heating System: Sun, Wind and Ocean Currents

Key Ideas

- The sun heats the earth's surface, which in turn heats the atmosphere. This creates the Greenhouse Effect.
- Places in low latitudes are warmer than places in high latitudes.
- Winds and ocean currents help to transfer heat from low to high latitudes.

Our world is surrounded by a blanket of gases called the **atmosphere**. These gases include nitrogen (78%), oxygen (21%) and small amounts of other gases, such as carbon dioxide and ozone. The sun heats the atmosphere in the way described below under the heading 'The Greenhouse Effect'.

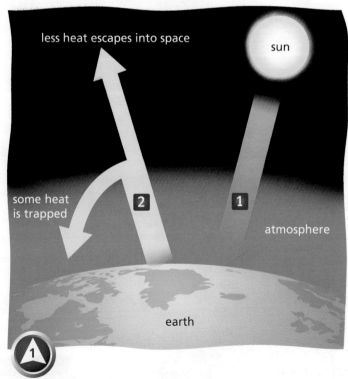

less heat escapes into space

sun

some heat is trapped

2

1

atmosphere

earth

1

The greenhouse effect

The Greenhouse Effect

1 The *sun* produces **short-wave energy**, which passes through the atmosphere and heats up the surface of the earth.

2 The *earth's surface* then returns **long-wave energy** into the atmosphere. But long-wave energy finds it more difficult to pass through gases such as carbon dioxide. So some heat remains in the atmosphere.

This is called the **greenhouse effect** because the glass of a greenhouse, like the atmosphere, allows solar energy to pass through it and traps some of the energy inside. The greenhouse effect provides us with the heat that plants and animals need to survive.

Global warming has been described as the greatest threat that humanity has ever faced. It may cause climate changes that would bring death and destruction on a massive scale. Human activities are largely to blame for global warming.

What is Global Warming?

You read on page 61 that the greenhouse effect traps heat within our atmosphere and that this enables plants and animals to survive. But human activities now produce huge amounts of '**greenhouse gases**' such as *carbon dioxide*, *methane* and *CFCs*. These gases trap more heat in our atmosphere and cause the earth and the atmosphere to become warmer.

Which Human Activities Cause Global Warming?

1
People burn more and more **fossil fuels**, such as coal, oil and gas. We burn these fuels to run cars, aircraft and heating systems and to make electricity. Burning fossil fuels releases *carbon dioxide* into the atmosphere.

2
Trees absorb carbon dioxide and so control the greenhouse effect. But the world's **forests**, especially the tropical rain forests, are being **cut down** at an alarming rate. This increases the amount of *carbon dioxide* in the atmosphere.

3
More and more **household waste** is being produced in rich Western countries. Refuse dumps containing this waste emit *methane*.

4
Very powerful greenhouse gases called CFCs have been produced in making **plastics** and using **fridges**.

Another problem
The production of CFCs and the burning of fossil fuels also damages the atmosphere's **ozone layer**, which protects us from harmful ultraviolet rays. Damage to the ozone layer increases skin cancers, wrinkling and eye disease among people.

Traffic jam in Dublin
How does this situation contribute to global warming? How else do Irish people contribute to global warming?

Some Likely Effects of Global Warming Worldwide

- Rising temperatures could melt the polar ice caps. **Sea levels** would then rise and could drown the homes of one hundred million people this century.

- Global warming would cause serious **climate change**. Some parts of the world would have more storms, rainfall and flooding. Other regions would suffer from *drought* (unusually long periods of dry weather).

- It is feared that drier conditions will result in crop failures and famines in many parts of Africa. There will also be an increase in **desertification** or the spread of deserts such as the Sahara.

How might global warming affect Ireland?

- More **extreme weather** could be expected. Summers might be drier, but winters much wetter and stormier than at present.
- Rising sea levels could **flood** low-lying parts of the country, including the centres of Dublin, Cork and Galway.
- Some scientists fear that global warming could stop the **North Atlantic Drift** flowing. Ireland's harbours might then freeze in winter.

Global warming in action
These pictures were taken of a glacier in Alaska, USA. The top picture was taken in 1952 and the lower picture in 2006. Describe and explain how the glacier has changed over time.

Think of precise ways of conserving energy

Name some types of renewable energy

What can WE do about global warming?

- **Conserve energy** so that less carbon dioxide is created.
- Use **renewable energy** instead of fossil fuels.
- **Plant more trees**. They use up carbon dioxide and so help to reduce greenhouse gases.

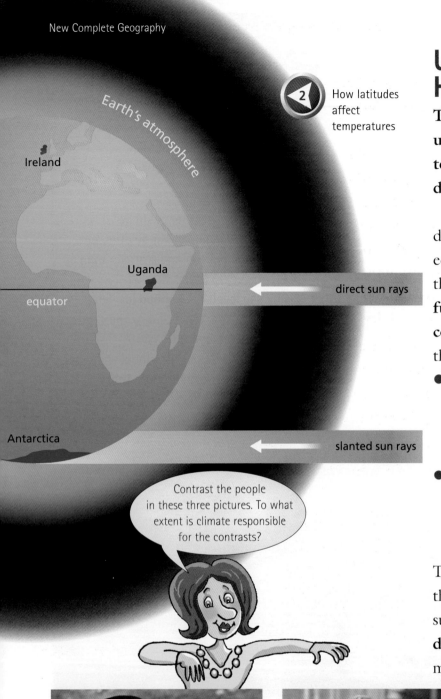

Earth's atmosphere

Ireland

Uganda

equator

direct sun rays

Antarctica

slanted sun rays

2 How latitudes affect temperatures

Contrast the people in these three pictures. To what extent is climate responsible for the contrasts?

Uneven Distribution of Heat

The heat of the sun is distributed unevenly over the earth's surface. The temperature (or heat) of any place depends largely on that place's latitude.

The latitude of a place is its angular distance from the equator. Places near the equator are in low latitudes. Places far from the equator are in high latitudes. The **further a place is from the equator, the cooler it is likely to be**. The reasons for this are explained below.

- **Near the equator** the sun shines from almost directly overhead. This means that its **rays are concentrated** on small areas, which become very hot.

- **Far from the equator** the sunrays are slanted. This causes their **heat** to be **spread** over larger areas, so temperatures are lower.

The atmosphere absorbs some heat from the sun's rays. Far from the equator, slanted sunrays have to travel through a **greater depth of atmosphere**. They therefore lose more heat before they reach the earth.

Uganda is near the equator, so it is **very hot** there

Ireland is in middle latitudes. Its temperatures are **moderate** (neither very hot nor very cold).

Antarctica is very far from the equator, so it is **very cold** there

Moving Air (Wind)

The atmosphere is not a calm place, because air moves almost constantly within it. Another word for moving air is **wind**.

Why does chimney smoke rise rather than fall to the ground?

How do Winds Happen?

We have already seen that some parts of the earth are warmer than other parts. The earth heats the atmosphere or air above it. Therefore some parts of the *atmosphere* are warmer than other parts. It is **the unequal heating of the atmosphere** that **causes winds to happen**. To understand how, study the four points below.

1. Air has weight. The weight of air is referred to as **atmospheric pressure**.
2. **Cold air** is dense and is therefore heavy. Because it is heavy it presses down on the earth. This causes **high pressure**.
3. **Warm air** is not dense and is therefore is light. Because it is light it rises up from the earth. This causes **low pressure**.
4. **Winds blow from areas of high pressure to areas of low pressure** (see Figure 3).

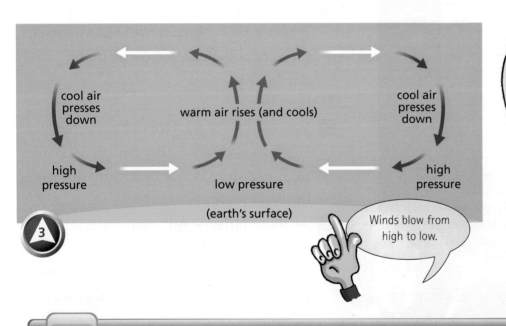

cool air presses down

warm air rises (and cools)

cool air presses down

high pressure

low pressure

high pressure

(earth's surface)

3

Winds blow from high to low.

Fill a balloon with air and let it go. Why does air (wind) blow out of the balloon?

More about winds

- **Winds are named after the direction from which they blow.** For instance, if a wind blows from the south-west towards the north-east it is said to be a south-westerly wind.
- Winds that blow *from* the direction of *the equator* are said to be **warm winds.**
- Winds that blow from the higher latitudes *towards* the equator are said to be **cool winds.**
- The winds that are most common in an area are called **prevailing winds.**

Global Air Movements

Throughout the world as a whole, general patterns of winds prevail. These are the **global air movements** (or **global winds**) of our planet.

How Our Global Wind Patterns Develop

1 **Unequal heating of our atmosphere at different latitudes** results in the creation of our global winds. Study Figure 4 to understand how this happens in the northern hemisphere (half) of the world.

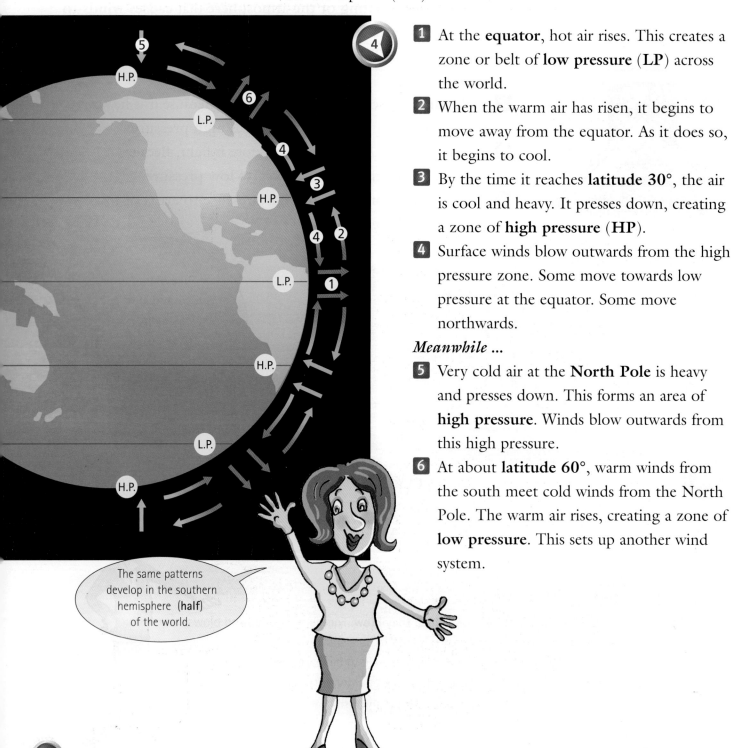

The same patterns develop in the southern hemisphere (**half**) of the world.

1 At the **equator**, hot air rises. This creates a zone or belt of **low pressure** (**LP**) across the world.

2 When the warm air has risen, it begins to move away from the equator. As it does so, it begins to cool.

3 By the time it reaches **latitude 30°**, the air is cool and heavy. It presses down, creating a zone of **high pressure** (**HP**).

4 Surface winds blow outwards from the high pressure zone. Some move towards low pressure at the equator. Some move northwards.

Meanwhile ...

5 Very cold air at the **North Pole** is heavy and presses down. This forms an area of **high pressure**. Winds blow outwards from this high pressure.

6 At about **latitude 60°**, warm winds from the south meet cold winds from the North Pole. The warm air rises, creating a zone of **low pressure**. This sets up another wind system.

2 Coriolis Force

You will notice in Figure 5 that our global winds move in 'slanted' patterns from belts of high pressure to belts of low pressure.

This happens because the **earth rotates on its axis from west to east**. The west-east rotation causes winds in the northern hemisphere to move to the right and winds in the southern hemisphere to move to the left. This is known as **Coriolis Force**.

The **unequal heating of our atmosphere** and Coriolis Force combine together to give the global wind patterns which are shown in Figure 5.

(a) Which global winds are likely to distribute heat to cooler areas? Which winds are likely to lower temperatures over the areas in which they blow?

(b) Trade winds blow between 30° and the equator. Their temperatures are usually high. Why, then, are trade winds referred to as cool winds?

(c) Which global winds prevail over Ireland? Are these winds likely to bring warm or cold conditions? Why?

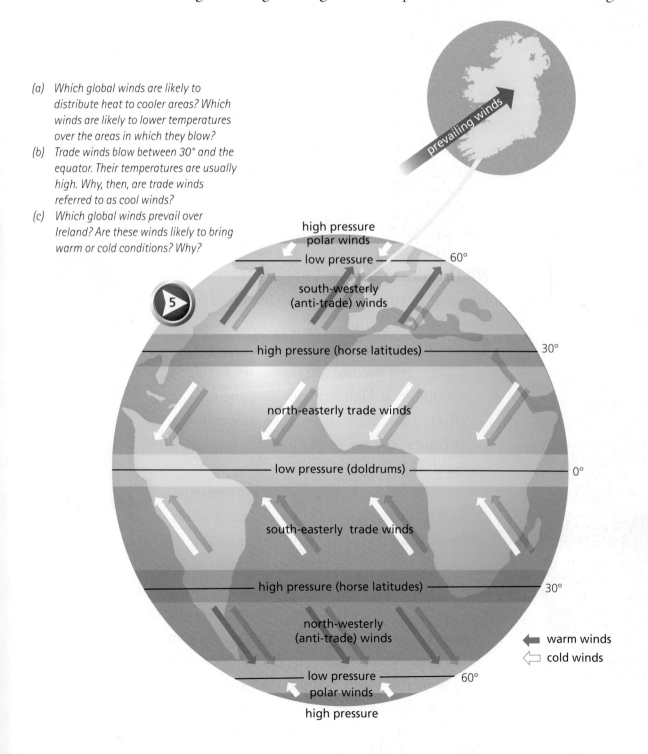

Ocean Currents

Ocean currents are like great rivers that flow slowly across the surface of our oceans.

The patterns of the main ocean currents of the Atlantic are shown in Figure 6. Those currents that flow from (cooler) higher latitudes towards (warmer) lower latitudes are called **cold currents**. Those that flow from the direction of the equator towards either of the poles are called **warm currents**.

Ocean currents of the Atlantic
(a) *Water temperature in the Canaries Current off Africa is higher than the water temperature in the North Atlantic Drift off Norway. Why, then, is the North Atlantic Drift referred to as a warm current, while the Canaries Current is referred to as a cold current?*
(b) *Why do you think ocean currents move in a general clockwise pattern in the northern hemisphere? (See below for the answer.)*

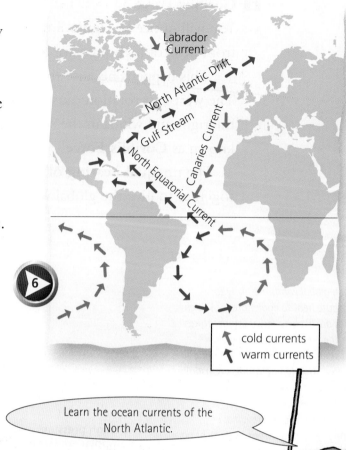

cold currents
warm currents

Learn the ocean currents of the North Atlantic.

The **rotation of the earth on its axis** helps to determine the direction of ocean currents. **Coriolis Force** causes currents in the northern hemisphere to be deflected to the right so that they flow in a clockwise direction. In the southern hemisphere, currents are deflected to the left, so that they flow in an anticlockwise direction.

What Causes Ocean Currents?

Unequal heating at different latitudes causes ocean currents. It does so in two ways:

1 Great heat at low latitudes causes water to expand and become less dense; while cold conditions at high latitudes have the opposite effect. These differences cause **convection currents** of water to move slowly between high and low latitudes.

This helps to explain why cold currents such as the Labrador Current move towards lower latitudes, while warm currents such as the Gulf Stream move towards higher latitudes (Figure 6).

2 You have seen that unequal heating sets up **global winds** (Figure 5). Friction between these winds and the sea surfaces causes ocean currents to be dragged along in the general direction of the winds. For example, south-westerly winds help to blow the North Atlantic Drift from the south-west towards the coast of Ireland.

The Effects of Ocean Currents

Ocean currents influence climate because they **transfer heat** from one area to another.

Some climatic effects of ocean currents

WARM CURRENTS

1. They **raise the temperatures of the waters** to which they flow.

2. They help to keep harbours in higher latitudes **free from ice**.

3. They warm onshore winds and so **raise air temperatures** in nearby lands.

COOL CURRENTS

1. They **lower the temperatures of the waters** to which they flow.

2. They increase the possibility of **ice** in higher latitude harbours.

3. They cool onshore winds and so **lower air temperatures** in nearby lands.

Ireland and the North Atlantic Drift

The North Atlantic Drift has a huge effect on Ireland's climate.

- It originates as the Gulf Stream in the warm Gulf of Mexico. It is therefore a warm current, which **heats the waters** off our coast. If the North Atlantic Drift did not exist, Ireland's harbours would freeze in winter!

- The North Atlantic Drift also transfers winter warmth to the **southwesterly winds** which prevail (usually blow) over Ireland. These winds keep our winters much milder than they would otherwise be.

Ireland (picture on the left) lies at similar latitudes to Labrador in Canada (right)
How and why do their winter conditions differ?

Rapid Revision

- The atmosphere or air that surrounds our planet is heated by energy from the sun. Solar energy heats the earth's surface. Then long-wave energy passes from the earth back into the atmosphere, where some of it is trapped. This process is called the **greenhouse effect** and it provides enough heat for plants and animals to thrive on our planet.

- Human activities increase greenhouse gases. This results in **global warming** and **climate change** which could cause disastrous flooding, drought and desertification. People need to conserve energy and use renewable energy sources to combat climate change.

- Places near the equator receive sunrays from almost directly overhead. These rays are more concentrated and travel through a lesser depth of atmosphere than sunrays at places near the poles. This is why **places in low latitudes are warmer** than places in high latitudes.

- Air has weight and exerts pressure. Light, warm air tends to rise and exerts **low pressure**. Heavy, cold air presses down and exerts **high pressure**. Air moves from areas of high pressure to areas of low pressure. That is how winds occur.

- Throughout the world, there are general, prevailing patterns of moving air. These are called **global winds** and they are set up by the **unequal heating** of the earth at different latitudes. The directions in which global winds blow are also determined by **Coriolis Force**, which is the effect of the rotation of the earth on its axis.

- **Ocean currents** are also caused by unequal heating at different latitudes. Unequal heating sets up convection currents between warm and cool parts of the oceans. The global winds (which are themselves caused by unequal heating) help to drag the ocean currents along in their direction. **Warm ocean currents**, such as the North Atlantic Drift, raise sea and air temperatures and keep harbours in high latitudes free of ice. **Cool currents**, such as the Labrador Current, have the opposite effect.

Activities

1. Explain what the term Greenhouse Effect means. (J.C. Ordinary Level)
2. Why are places near the equator usually warmer than places far from the equator?
3. Describe the causes of the increase in global temperatures. (J.C. Higher Level)
4. Explain how **two** of the following might help to ease the problem of global warming:
   - energy conservation
   - using renewable energy
   - planting more trees.
5. With the aid of a diagram, explain how winds happen.
6. What are ocean currents and what impacts (effects) do they have on places to which they flow? (J.C. Higher Level)

See Chapter 10 of your Workbook

11

Different Weathers: The Effects of Ascending and Descending Air

- You learned in Chapter 10 that warm air rises and creates areas of low pressure. Cool air presses down and creates areas of high pressure.
- In this chapter you will learn that ascending (rising) air and descending (pressing down) air produce different kinds of weather.

Weather is the condition of the atmosphere (temperature, pressure, etc.) over a very **short period** of time.

Don't confuse weather with climate!

Climate is the **average** condition of the atmosphere across a large area of the earth's surface and over a very **long period** of time.

Depressions and Anticyclones

Depressions

Over mid-latitude countries such as Ireland, areas of **low pressure** often take the form of **depressions** (which are also called **cyclones** or **lows**).

Depressions are typically oval in shape. They may be over 1000km long from end to end. Pressure is lowest at the centre of each depression.

Anticyclones

In mid-latitudes, areas of **high pressure** often take the form of **anticyclones** (also called **highs**).

Anticyclones also tend to be roughly oval in shape. They are often even larger in size than depressions. Pressure is highest at the centre of each anticyclone.

Atmospheric pressure is measured in units called **millibars (mb)**, which are also called **hecto pascals (hPa)**

1000

988

L

Lines on weather maps which show places of equal pressure are known as **isobars**

1004

• Dublin

1016

1020

1024

• London

H

1 (a) Identify a cyclone and an anticyclone on this weather map.
(b) What is the atmospheric pressure:
  (i) over Dublin; and
  (ii) over London?
(c) Where is the centre of the 'high'?

Weather During a Depression (Ascending Air)

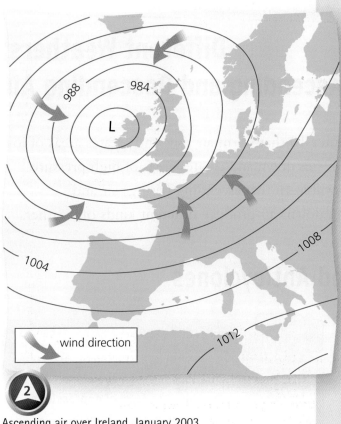

Ascending air over Ireland, January 2003

(a) What are the lines on the map known as?
(b) Give the values of each of the unnumbered lines on the map.
(c) Describe the weather conditions in Dublin.

Strong Winds

Notice that the isobars in the depression in Figure 2 are spaced closely together. Closely packed isobars indicate **strong winds**.

Strong winds blow in **towards** the low pressure areas at the **centres** of depressions. Because of Coriolis Force, the winds blow in an anti-clockwise motion in the northern hemisphere.

Much Cloud

Air rises from the low-pressure centres of depressions. But temperature decreases with height. **So as the air rises it becomes cooler**.

Cool air cannot hold as much water as warm air can. So as the air rises some of its water vapour is **condensed** or changed into tiny droplets. These droplets make up cloud.

> The main types of cloud are discussed in Chapter 12.

Much Precipitation

As the air continues to rise, **condensation continues**. The tiny **droplets** that make up cloud **join together** and become heavier until they fall as rain or as other forms of precipitation. The rain associated with depressions is called **cyclonic rain**.

> **Precipitation** refers to all forms of moisture which reach the earth from the atmosphere. Rain is the most common type of precipitation. Other kinds include hail, snow, sleet, frost and dew.

Weather During an Anticyclone (Descending Air)

Light or No Winds

Notice that the isobars in the anticyclone in Figure 3 are spaced widely apart from each other. Widely spaced isobars indicate **light winds or calm conditions**.

Any winds that do exist blow **away from the centre** of the anticyclone. Because of Coriolis Force, the winds blow in a clockwise direction in the northern hemisphere.

No Cloud

Air descends towards the centre of high pressure. As **the air descends, it becomes warmer**.

As the air becomes warmer it can hold more moisture, so it **absorbs rather than condenses** water vapour. Without condensation **no cloud** can form. So skies are clear.

Dry Weather

Since descending air results in little or **no condensation**, anticyclones bring **dry** weather conditions.

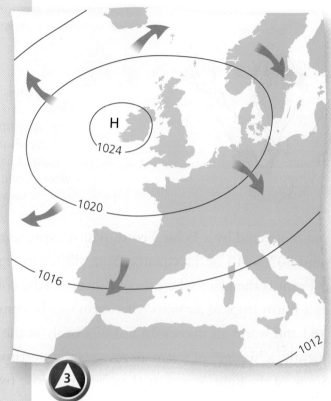

3

Descending air over Ireland, August 2002

(a) Name the principal weather feature shown on the map.
(b) From which direction is the wind shown to blow on the map:
  (i) over Germany;
  (ii) off the south coast of Iceland?
(c) Contrast the weather conditions over Dublin with the conditions over Dublin shown in Figure 2.

> **Temperatures during anticyclones:**
> Summer anticyclones bring hot weather to Ireland, but in winter anticyclones bring cold conditions. Night temperatures are especially low during winter anticyclones, because there are no clouds to blanket in the heat of the day's sunrays.

> Dry conditions are also common in the sheltered **rain shadows** of mountains where air descends from mountain slopes. (Rain shadows are discussed in Chapter 12.)

More about Depressions

Some important definitions.

An **air mass** is a large body of air in which temperatures, pressure and humidity are uniform.

A **front** is a boundary line between two air masses. A *warm front* develops where a warm air mass advances on a cold air mass. A *cold front* develops where a cold air mass advances on a warm one.

Ireland is affected by a **Polar Front**, which exists usually between 50° and 60° north of the equator. You will see in Figure 4 that the Polar Front is the place where a cold air mass (the cold polar winds) meets a warm tropical air mass (the warm south-westerly winds).

Cold and warm air masses do not mix easily at the Polar Front. Frequently, a 'wedge' of warm air invades the 'territory' of the cold air. Some of the light, warm air then begins to rise over the cold air, setting up an area of low pressure called a **depression** (Figure 5).

Depressions develop frequently over the North Atlantic. They typically move eastwards towards Ireland, where each depression brings with it a **spell of low pressure with wet, windy and unsettled weather**.

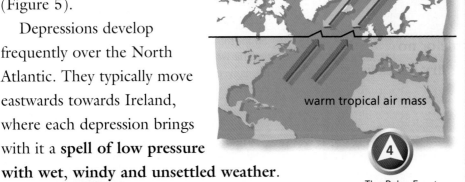

cold polar air mass

warm tropical air mass

4 The Polar Front

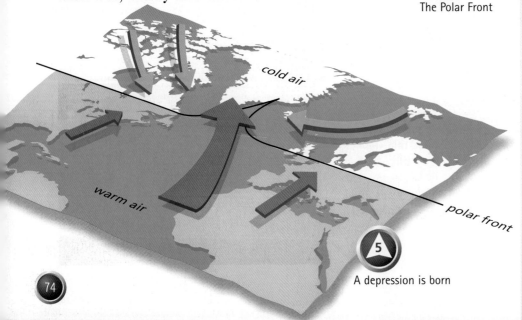

cold air

warm air

polar front

5 A depression is born

The Composition of a Depression

Figures 6a and 6b show the following factors that make up a depression.

- There is a **warm sector** (containing a wedge of warm, light air) and a **cold sector** (containing dense, polar air).
- There is a **warm front**, where air from the warm sector rises slowly over the denser cold air. As the warm air rises, it cools and condenses. Precipitation is continuous along the warm front.
- There is a **cold front** where cold air nudges under warm air and forces it to rise rapidly. Precipitation also takes place here.
- The entire depression is an area of **low pressure**. Pressure is lowest at the centre.
- **Winds blow towards the centre** of the depression. In accordance with *Coriolis Force*, winds in the northern hemisphere blow towards the centre in an anti-clockwise manner.

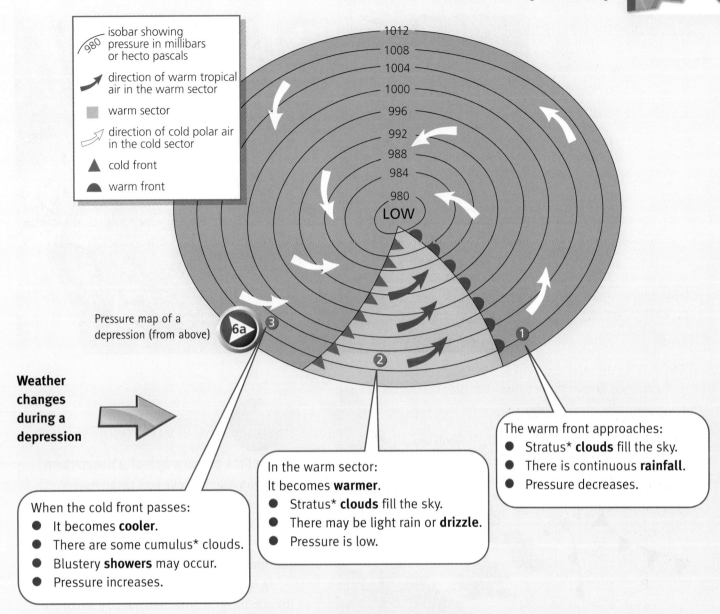

Legend:
- 980 isobar showing pressure in millibars or hecto pascals
- direction of warm tropical air in the warm sector
- warm sector
- direction of cold polar air in the cold sector
- ▲ cold front
- warm front

Pressure map of a depression (from above)

Weather changes during a depression

1012
1008
1004
1000
996
992
988
984
980
LOW

The warm front approaches:
- Stratus* **clouds** fill the sky.
- There is continuous **rainfall**.
- Pressure decreases.

In the warm sector:
It becomes **warmer**.
- Stratus* **clouds** fill the sky.
- There may be light rain or **drizzle**.
- Pressure is low.

When the cold front passes:
- It becomes **cooler**.
- There are some cumulus* clouds.
- Blustery **showers** may occur.
- Pressure increases.

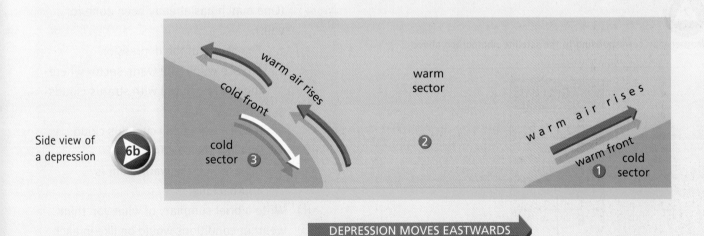

Side view of a depression

6b

warm air rises
cold front
warm sector
warm air rises
cold sector
warm front
cold sector

DEPRESSION MOVES EASTWARDS

*types of cloud are explained on page 79

75

The warm front

The warm sector

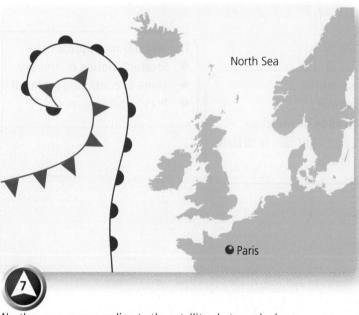

North Sea

Paris

Weather map corresponding to the satellite photograph above

Grid	
A	5
B	
C	
D	
E	

Activities

A satellite photograph of a depression

The photograph above was taken from a weather satellite and *shows a depression centred over the Atlantic Ocean north-west of Ireland*. Areas of cloud are shown in white.

(a) Identify each of the countries labelled 1 to 4 on the satellite photograph.

(b) On the grid provided, match each of the labels A to E on the photograph with each of the following features of a depression. (One match has already been done for you.)
1. The centre of the depression
2. A place within the warm sector where the sky is covered with stratus clouds
3. The cold front
4. A place with small cumulus cloud 'behind' the cold front
5. A place that the warm front is approaching.

(c) Write a brief summary of what you think weather conditions would be like in each of the places labelled A, B and C on the satellite photograph.

Rapid Revision

Ascending air (in depressions) and descending air (in anticyclones) give very different weather conditions.

Ascending air gives:
- low pressure
- strong winds
- much cloud
- precipitation
- unsettled weather

Descending air gives:
- high pressure
- calm
- clear skies
- dry weather
- settled weather

Depressions are born at the Polar Front where warm tropical air meets cold polar air. They move eastwards over the Atlantic and affect Ireland's climate, especially in winter.

- **As a depression approaches**, pressure falls, stratus clouds fill the sky and rain becomes continuous.
- **When the warm front passes over**, temperatures rise, the sky remains overcast and drizzle may fall.
- **When the cold front passes over**, temperatures drop and blustery showers may occur.

Activities

1 The satellite photograph shown here was taken in the summer of 2007. It shows a depression and an anticyclone over different parts of Europe.

(a) Is Ireland under a depression or an anticyclone? How do you know?

(b) Describe three probable contrasts between weather conditions in Ireland and in Spain when this photograph was taken.

(c) Explain *why* there was cloud over Ireland when the photograph was taken.

2 Explain the difference between each of the following:

(a) between weather and climate;

(b) between isobars and millibars;

(c) between rain and precipitation.

See Chapter 11 of your Workbook

12

Water in the Atmosphere

Most of the earth's water supply exists in the form of salt water in the oceans or as ice in the polar ice caps. A small proportion of this water, however, is constantly being refined and renewed by what is called the **water cycle**.

The water cycle (Figure 1) involves water constantly entering and leaving the atmosphere. It provides plants, animals and people with the moisture they need to survive.

Water is described as a **renewable resource**. Can you guess why?

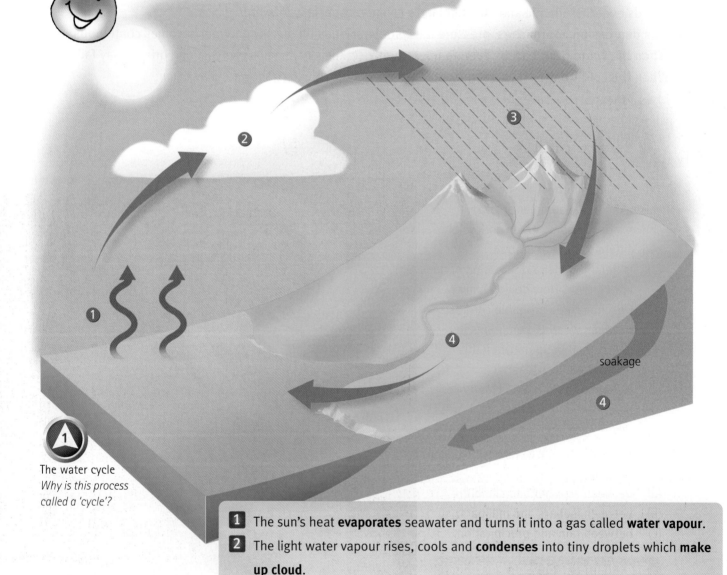

1

The water cycle
Why is this process called a 'cycle'?

soakage

1 The sun's heat **evaporates** seawater and turns it into a gas called **water vapour**.

2 The light water vapour rises, cools and **condenses** into tiny droplets which **make up cloud**.

3 Further cooling and condensation results in **precipitation** (rain, hail, snow, etc.).

4 Surface **run-off** (rivers) and **soakage** return most of the water to the sea. (Some water is evaporated immediately back into the atmosphere.)

The water cycle shows us that water is present in the air in three different forms:

- water vapour
- cloud
- precipitation

Water Vapour

Air can hold moisture in the form of water vapour. Water vapour in the air is expressed as **relative humidity (RH)**. Warm air can hold more water vapour than cool air can.

When the air can hold no more water vapour (when the RH is 100%), it is said to be **saturated**. Any extra water vapour will then undergo **condensation**. This means it will change into the **tiny droplets** that make up cloud.

Cloud

The main types of cloud are shown in the photographs.

Cirrus clouds
- are very high in the sky
- look like delicate brush-strokes

Cumulus clouds
- are at medium altitudes
- look like fluffy 'castles in the sky'
- some dark cumulus clouds bring showers

Stratus clouds
- are low in the sky
- occur in thick layers
- can bring long spells of precipitation

Precipitation

Rain is the most common form of precipitation. It occurs when **moisture-laden air is forced to rise**. This happens for three reasons, so there are three types of rainfall.

1 Relief rain

Relief rain occurs when air is forced to rise over mountains, resulting in rain on the windward side (Figure 2).

> Relief rain is common in the western mountains of Ireland, such as those in Kerry and Donegal.

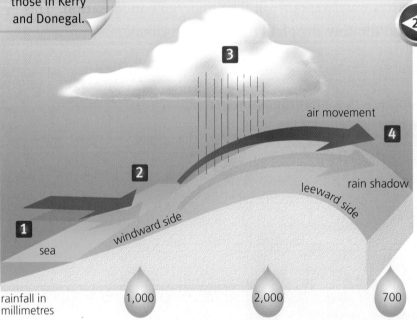

Relief rain and rain shadow

1. **Moisture-laden** winds blow in from the sea.
2. **Air rises over mountains** and is cooled.
3. Water vapour **condenses** to form cloud and rain on the windward side of the mountains.
4. When the air moves down the leeward (sheltered) slope, it has already lost most of its moisture. So the leeward side gets little rain. It is called a **rain shadow** area.

2 Convectional rain

Convectional rain occurs **when air rises from a warm land surface** (Figure 3).

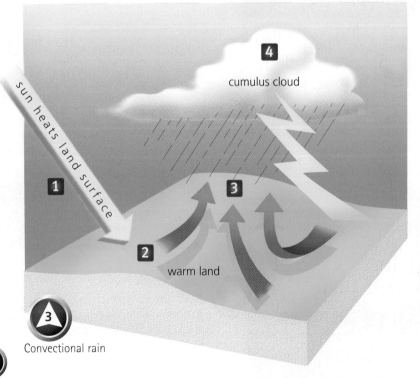

Convectional rain

> Convectional rain is common in Ireland only on hot, summer days, but it occurs frequently in some regions near the equator.

1. The sun heats the earth's **surface**.
2. **Air** over the hot land is **warmed**. It expands and rises rapidly.
3. As the **air rises**, it is cooled.
4. Water vapour **condenses** to form cumulus cloud and **heavy, thundery showers**.

3 Cyclonic (frontal) rain

This is associated with low pressure systems such as **depressions**. They contain warm and cold *air masses.* Cyclonic rain forms where these air masses meet (Figure 4).

Revise **air mass** on page 74

Cyclonic rain is very common in Ireland

light warm air mass

a 'front', where air masses meet

heavy cold air mass

1 **Warm air** is light, so it tends to **rise** over heavier, cool air.

2 Warm air **cools**.

3 Water vapour **condenses** to form stratus cloud and rain.

4 Cyclonic rain at the warm front of a cyclone

Rapid Revision

- Water constantly enters and leaves the atmosphere through the **water cycle**. Water evaporates into water vapour. Water vapour condenses into cloud and precipitation. Rivers and soakage return water to the sea.
- The amount of water vapour in the atmosphere is expressed in terms of **relative humidity**.
- **Types of cloud** include brush-like cirrus cloud, 'fluffy' cumulus cloud and layered stratus cloud.
- When air is forced to rise, its water vapour condenses and **rain** may result.
    - **Relief rain** occurs when air is forced to rise up the sides of mountain.
    - **Convectional rain** occurs when air rises from a warm land surface.
    - **Frontal (cyclonic) rain** occurs when air rises on the warm or cold fronts within depressions.

Activities

1 With the aid of a labelled diagram, explain how the water cycle works.
2 Describe the differences between each of the following:
   - evaporation and condensation;
   - cirrus cloud and cumulus cloud;
   - relief rain and cyclonic rain.
3 Name and describe the type of rainfall that you might expect to occur on a hot July afternoon in Ireland. Use a labelled diagram to illustrate your answer.

See Chapter 12 of your Workbook

Test Yourself
eTest.ie

Measuring and Forecasting Weather

How We Get Our Weather Forecasts

Watch this evening's weather forecast on television or read it in today's newspaper.

Information is gathered by **weather satellites**, weather stations and other sources.

The data is collected and sorted at the **Irish Weather Centre** (Met Éireann) and is used to make weather maps and weather forecasts.

The **weather forecasts** are published in newspapers and broadcast on television and radio.

The Importance of Weather

Weather forecasts are important to people in many professions. Here are a few examples.

Farmers need to know that the weather will be dry before they begin to harvest their crops.

Fisherfolk might not put to sea if dangerous gales are forecast.

Can you think of any other professionals for whom weather forecasts are important?

Pilots and air traffic controllers might postpone flights if bad weather threatens to endanger take-off or landing.

At the Meteorological (Weather) Station

Irish weather stations such as those at **Dublin, Cork and Shannon airports** use complicated technology to constantly measure weather conditions. But schools, too, can make their own weather stations. They can use the simpler methods described in this chapter to measure the following:

- temperature
- wind direction and speed
- humidity.
- sunshine
- precipitation

Temperature

Temperature is measured in **degrees Celsius/Centigrade** (°C) by a **maximum and minimum thermometer** (Figure 1).

The **maximum and minimum thermometer** is a glass tube containing mercury and alcohol. As temperatures rise, mercury moves up the maximum side of the tube until the highest point is reached. A piece of metal in the tube marks this point. When temperatures fall, the lowest temperatures reached are recorded on the minimum side of the tube.

A Stevenson Screen

Temperature is measured in the shade, rather than in the direct heat of the sun. To do this, *maximum and minimum thermometers* are shaded in special wooden boxes called **Stevenson screens** (Figure 2).

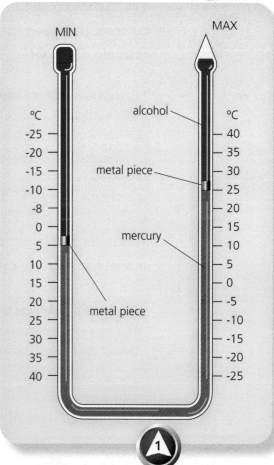

A maximum and minimum thermometer
What maximum and minimum readings is this thermometer showing? (Take the readings at the base of each metal piece.)

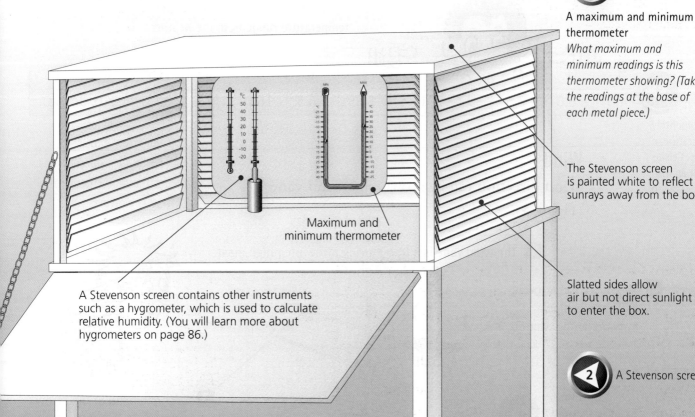

Maximum and minimum thermometer

The Stevenson screen is painted white to reflect sunrays away from the box.

Slatted sides allow air but not direct sunlight to enter the box.

A Stevenson screen contains other instruments such as a hygrometer, which is used to calculate relative humidity. (You will learn more about hygrometers on page 86.)

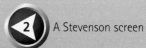
A Stevenson screen

The maximum and minimum temperature readings taken each day allow us to calculate the *mean* or *average* temperature for each day, month or year. See, for example, *Calculation 1*.

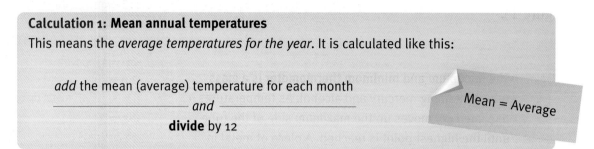

Calculation 1: Mean annual temperatures
This means the *average temperatures for the year.* It is calculated like this:

add the mean (average) temperature for each month
———————————— *and* ————————————
divide by 12

Mean = Average

Maximum and minimum temperatures also allow us to calculate daily, monthly or annual temperature **ranges**. See, for example, *Calculation 2*.

Calculation 2: Annual temperature range
This means the *difference* between the average temperature of the hottest month and that of the coldest month. It is calculated like this:

Range = Difference

the mean temperature of the hottest month   *minus*   the mean temperature of the coldest month

Calculate the **mean annual temperature** and the **annual temperature range** from the weather station data given in Figure 3.

	J.	F.	M.	A.	M.	J.	J.	A.	S.	O.	N.	D.
3	4.5	6.0	7.5	9.5	11.5	14.5	16.5	16.0	13.0	11.0	7.0	5.0

Mean monthly temperature in degrees Celsius at an Irish weather station

Wind

Wind direction can be shown on a **wind vane** (Figure 4).

If the arrow end points north, for example, it means that a northerly wind is blowing.

1 The wind vane is a free-moving arrow on a high mast.

2 The tail of the arrow is wide and is blown forward by the wind ...

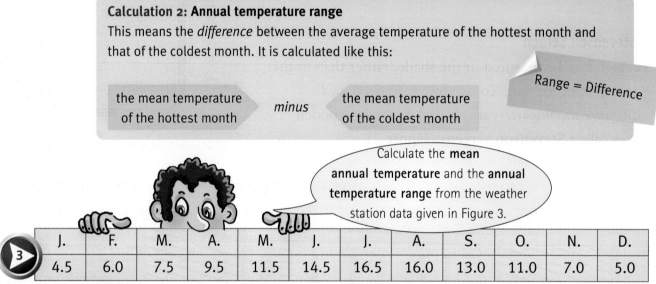

A wind vane
From which direction is the wind blowing in this diagram?

4

3 ... so the head of the arrow points in the direction from which the wind blows.

(a) Name the weather instrument shown in this picture.
(b) Can you tell the wind direction from it?

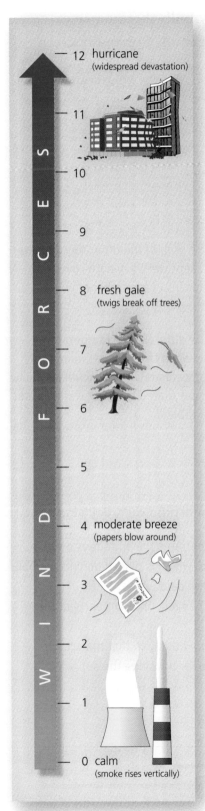

12	hurricane (widespread devastation)
11	
10	
9	
8	fresh gale (twigs break off trees)
7	
6	
5	
4	moderate breeze (papers blow around)
3	
2	
1	
0	calm (smoke rises vertically)

WIND FORCES

6

Some forces of the Beaufort Scale

The **speed** or **strength** of wind can be determined in two ways.

1 Wind speed (in **kilometres per hour**) can be measured using an **anemometer**.

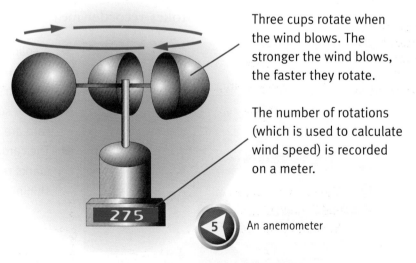

Three cups rotate when the wind blows. The stronger the wind blows, the faster they rotate.

The number of rotations (which is used to calculate wind speed) is recorded on a meter.

275

5 An anemometer

2 The **Beaufort Scale** (Figure 6) describes the strength of wind by observing its effect on the landscape. This scale (which is called after the Irishman who invented it) measures wind in twelve **forces**.

Humidity

A **hygrometer** is used to measure **relative humidity**, which expresses the amount of water vapour in the air as a **percentage**.

One common type of hygrometer uses **wet** and **dry bulb thermometers** (Figure 7). These two thermometers stand side by side in the Stevenson screen.

Wet and dry bulb thermometers

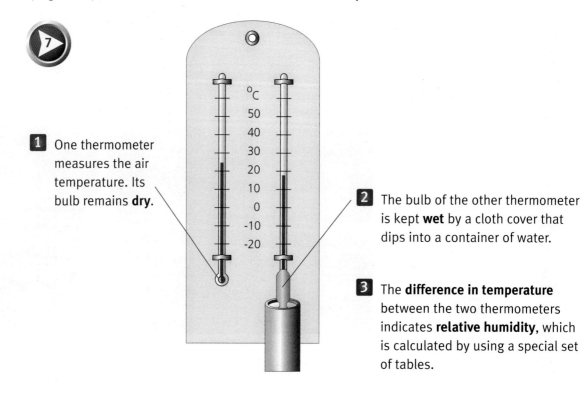

1 One thermometer measures the air temperature. Its bulb remains **dry**.

2 The bulb of the other thermometer is kept **wet** by a cloth cover that dips into a container of water.

3 The **difference in temperature** between the two thermometers indicates **relative humidity**, which is calculated by using a special set of tables.

Sunshine

A **Campbell Stokes recorder** measures the **hours** of sunshine each day (Figure 8).

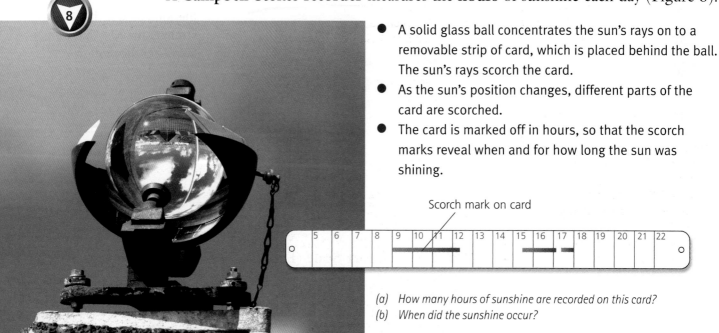

- A solid glass ball concentrates the sun's rays on to a removable strip of card, which is placed behind the ball. The sun's rays scorch the card.
- As the sun's position changes, different parts of the card are scorched.
- The card is marked off in hours, so that the scorch marks reveal when and for how long the sun was shining.

Scorch mark on card

(a)   How many hours of sunshine are recorded on this card?
(b)   When did the sunshine occur?

Precipitation

A **rain gauge** is used to measure precipitation in **millimetres (mm)**; see Figure 9.

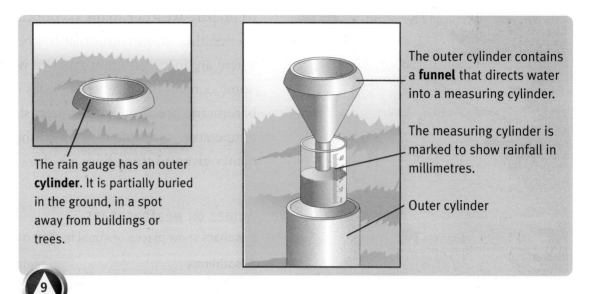

The rain gauge has an outer **cylinder**. It is partially buried in the ground, in a spot away from buildings or trees.

The outer cylinder contains a **funnel** that directs water into a measuring cylinder.

The measuring cylinder is marked to show rainfall in millimetres.

Outer cylinder

9

A rain gauge

Why is the rain gauge situated away from buildings or trees?

Month	J.	F.	M.	A.	M.	J.	J.	A.	S.	O.	N.	D.
Precipitation	153	103	100	70	87	81	98	95	122	142	145	159

10

The table in Figure 10 gives precipitation for each month of a year in an Irish weather station.

(a) *What was the wettest month and how much precipitation fell in that month?*
(b) *Name the driest month and give its precipitation.*
(c) *Calculate the total annual precipitation (add up the precipitation for each month of the year).*
(d) *Calculate the total winter precipitation. (Assume winter months to be November, December and January.)*

Figure 11 uses bar graphs to show precipitation at a weather station over a year.

11

(a) *List in rank order the three wettest months. (Begin your list with the wettest month.)*
(b) *How much precipitation fell in July?*
(c) *Name the wettest month and state its precipitation.*

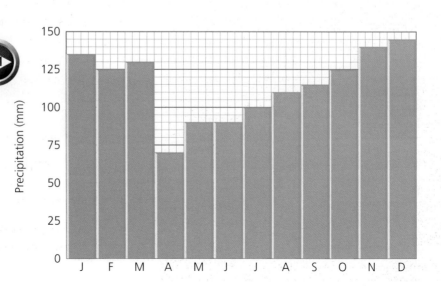

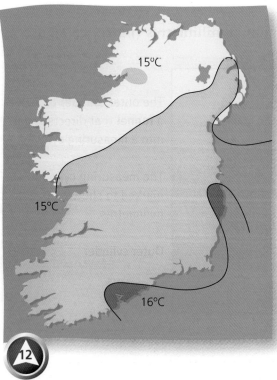

Mean July temperatures in °C throughout Ireland
(a) Where are the warmest parts of Ireland in July and how warm are they?
(b) What part of the country is coolest and what is its temperature?

Weather Maps

One of the chief tasks of the Irish Weather Centre is to prepare **weather maps (synoptic charts)** based on the weather information that has been gathered. There are many different types of weather maps. Some contain lines showing places of equal barometric pressure, while others show places of equal temperature, precipitation or sunshine levels. The names given to these lines are shown in the box.

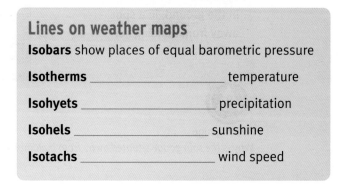

Lines on weather maps
Isobars show places of equal barometric pressure
Isotherms _____ temperature
Isohyets _____ precipitation
Isohels _____ sunshine
Isotachs _____ wind speed

Mean January temperatures
Are the following statements true or false?
(a) 'Temperatures in January decrease generally from South to North.'
(b) 'The lines on this map are called isohyets.'

Mean annual rainfall (mm) throughout Ireland
(a) What is the annual rainfall in the wettest part of Ireland?
(b) 'Rainfall generally decreases from west to east.' True or false?
(c) What is the annual rainfall in Dublin City?

Rapid Revision

- Weather **forecasts are important** to farmers, pilots and other professionals.
- Information is recorded by satellites, at weather stations, etc. The Irish Weather Centre uses the information to make weather reports.

Measuring weather

Elements of weather	Instrument used	Unit of measurement	Lines on weather maps
Temperature	Thermometer	Degrees Celsius (C°)	Isotherms
Wind direction	Wind vane	Compass directions	—
Wind speed	• Anemometer • Beaufort Scale	Kilometres (km) per hour Forces	Isotachs
Relative humidity	Hygrometer	Percentages	—
Sunshine	Campbell Stokes recorder	Hours per day	Isohels
Precipitation	Rain gauge	Millimetres (mm)	Isohyets

Activities

1 In the case of each of the items labelled A–E in the diagram:
   (a) Name the item.
   (b) Say what it is used for and how it works.

For more activities see Chapter 13 of your Workbook.

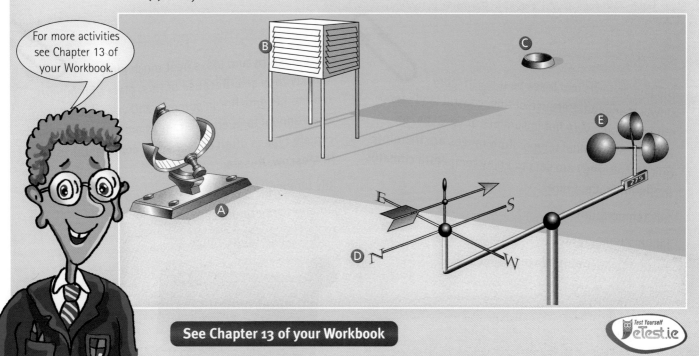

See Chapter 13 of your Workbook

Test Yourself eTest.ie

Factors that Affect Climate

> Climate is the average weather across a large area of the earth's surface and over a very long period of time (35 years or more).

There are many different types of climate in the world, each with its own special characteristics. **A number of factors work together to influence climate**.

These factors include:

- **latitude**
- **distance from seas and oceans**
- **prevailing winds**.

Revise page 64.

Factors Affecting Climate
Latitude

The latitude of a place is its **distance from the equator. The further a place is from the equator, the cooler it is likely to be**. The reasons for this are explained on page 64.

Distance from Seas and Oceans

Study Figure 1 on page 91 and then fill in the blanks in the statements below.

The sea absorbs and loses heat much more slowly than land. Because of this, coastal lands tend not to become very hot in summer or very cold in winter. Their annual temperature ranges are therefore quite small. They are said to enjoy **temperate climates**.
In Shannon, Co. Clare:

July temperatures are _____

January temperatures are _____

Annual temperature range is _____

Land absorbs and loses heat much more quickly than sea. Because of this, places far inland tend to become hot in summer and very cold in winter. Their annual temperature ranges are large and their climate type is often described as **continental**.
In Moscow, Russia:

July temperatures are _____

January temperatures are _____

Annual temperature range is _____

> **Ocean currents** also affect climates. Revise on page 69.

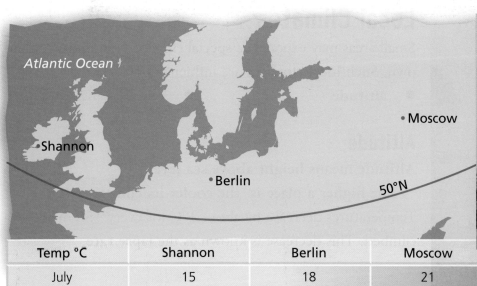

Temp °C	Shannon	Berlin	Moscow
July	15	18	21
January	8	-1	-15

In what part of Europe might this picture have been taken? Explain.

1 Temperature conditions at three places in Europe

Prevailing Air Masses or Winds

The wind that blows most frequently over an area is called the **prevailing wind**.

The direction of prevailing winds can have important effects on the climates of the places to which they blow. The effects of various winds on Ireland's climate are outlined in Figure 2.

The effects of different air masses (winds) on Ireland's climate **2**

Prevailing winds are especially important.

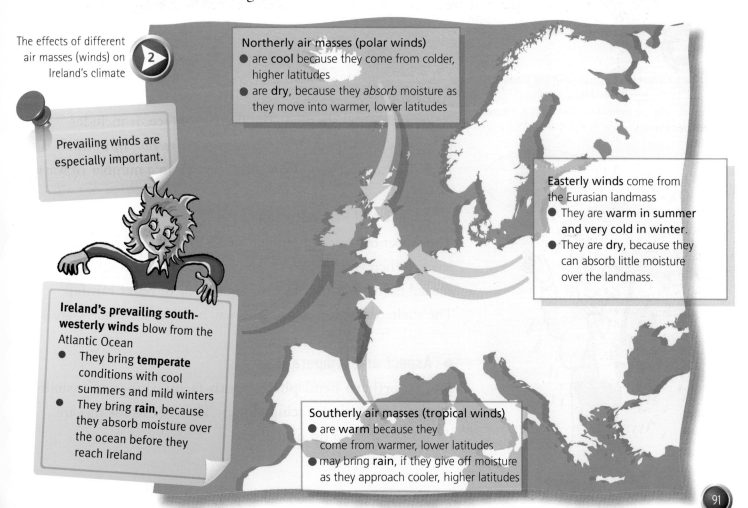

Northerly air masses (polar winds)
- are **cool** because they come from colder, higher latitudes
- are **dry**, because they *absorb* moisture as they move into warmer, lower latitudes

Easterly winds come from the Eurasian landmass
- They are **warm in summer and very cold in winter**.
- They are **dry**, because they can absorb little moisture over the landmass.

Ireland's prevailing south-westerly winds blow from the Atlantic Ocean
- They bring **temperate** conditions with cool summers and mild winters
- They bring **rain**, because they absorb moisture over the ocean before they reach Ireland

Southerly air masses (tropical winds)
- are **warm** because they come from warmer, lower latitudes
- may bring **rain**, if they give off moisture as they approach cooler, higher latitudes

Mount Kilimanjaro is situated in hot lands very close to the equator in Africa
Explain why the summit of Kilimanjaro is always covered in snow.

This was explained on page 80. Revise!

Local Climates

Small areas may experience special climatic conditions of their own. Such **local climates** are influenced by:

- **altitude**
- **relief**

Altitude

Altitude means height above sea level.

   The higher a place is, the cooler its climate will be. Temperatures decrease by about 1°C for every 150 metres climbed. This decrease is known as the **lapse rate**.

Why temperatures decrease with height

- The **atmosphere** forms a kind of blanket above us which absorbs and holds in the heat radiated from the earth's surface. The higher we climb, the thinner this 'air blanket' above us becomes and the less heat it can hold. So temperatures fall as altitudes increase.
- High mountains are likely to be windier than lowlands. This **exposure to wind** can further reduce temperatures. This is called the **chill factor**.

Relief

Relief means the **shape of the land's surface**. It includes things such as **aspect**, which means *the direction in which a slope faces*. Aspect can affect local climates in a number of ways.

• Aspect and Precipitation

The aspect of coastal mountain slopes affects local precipitation levels. When wind blows in from the sea, the seaward slopes of coastal mountains may receive high levels of **relief rainfall**. The sheltered or leeward slopes may be dry, rain shadow areas.

• Aspect and Temperatures

In the **northern hemisphere, south-facing slopes are usually warmer than north-facing slopes.** The reasons for this are shown in Figure 3 on page 93.

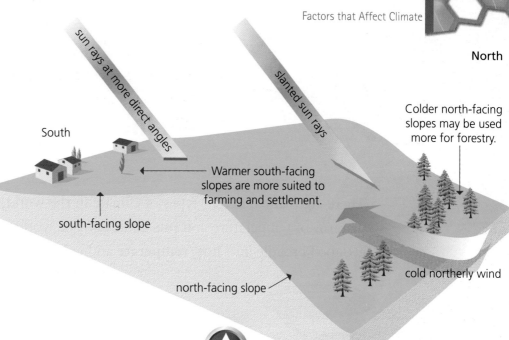

North

1 Sunrays arrive at more **direct angles** on south-facing slopes. So they are more concentrated and give more heat.

2 South-facing slopes get **longer periods of daily sunshine,** while north-facing slopes are sometimes in the shade.

3 South-facing slopes are **sheltered from cold northerly winds.**

South

sun rays at more direct angles

slanted sun rays

Colder north-facing slopes may be used more for forestry.

Warmer south-facing slopes are more suited to farming and settlement.

south-facing slope

north-facing slope

cold northerly wind

Aspect and local temperatures (in the northern hemisphere)
How would this situation differ in the southern hemisphere?

Rapid Revision

The **factors that influence the climates of large regions** include the following:

- **Latitude:** The further a place is from the equator, the cooler it is likely to be.
- **Distance from the sea:** Coastal lands tend to have temperate climates with small annual temperature ranges. Places far from the sea tend to have warmer summers and much colder winters.
- **Prevailing winds:** Ireland's prevailing south-westerly winds bring moderate temperatures and much rain.

The **factors that influence local climates** include:

- **Altitude:** Temperatures decrease with height above sea level.
- **Relief:** (a) The windward slopes of coastal mountains get relief rain.
  (b) Places with southerly aspects tend to be warmer than places with northerly aspects.

Activities

1 *Distance from the equator; height above sea level; distance from the sea; ocean currents.*
Choose two of these factors and explain how each of them influences the climate of a place.
(J.C. Ordinary Level)

2 *Ireland has a mild climate with rain all year round.* Explain briefly why the climate of Ireland is like this.
In your answer write about temperature and rainfall. (J.C. Ordinary Level)

3 Describe the effects over Ireland of polar and tropical air masses. Refer to temperature and rainfall in your answer. (J.C. Higher Level)

See Chapter 14 of your Workbook

An Introduction to Climate Types

There are many different types of climate in the world, each with its own particular patterns of temperature and precipitation. The world's main climates can be grouped broadly into **hot**, **temperate** and **cold**. They are listed below.

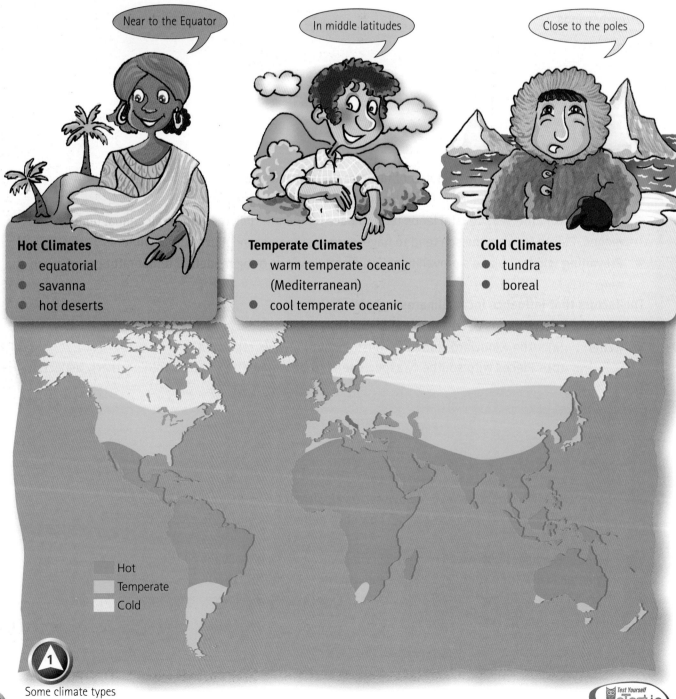

Near to the Equator

In middle latitudes

Close to the poles

Hot Climates
- equatorial
- savanna
- hot deserts

Temperate Climates
- warm temperate oceanic (Mediterranean)
- cool temperate oceanic

Cold Climates
- tundra
- boreal

Hot
Temperate
Cold

1 Some climate types

Test Yourself eTest.ie

Hot Climates: Focus on Hot Deserts

Figure 1 shows the locations and the main features of some of the world's hot climate types.

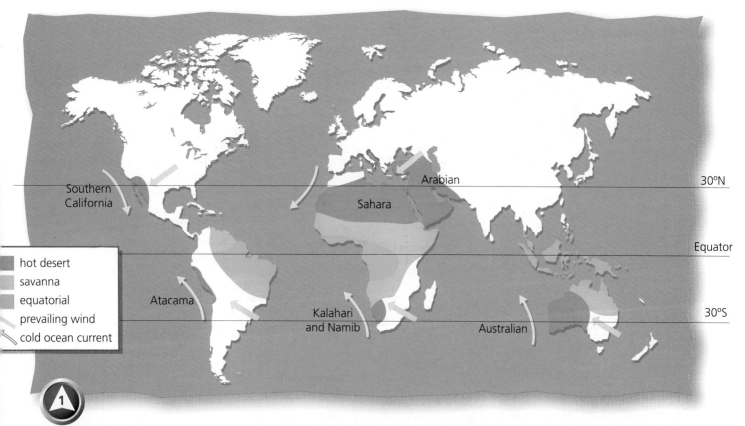

Legend:
- hot desert
- savanna
- equatorial
- prevailing wind
- cold ocean current

Map labels: Southern California, Atacama, Sahara, Arabian, Kalahari and Namib, Australian, 30°N, Equator, 30°S

1

Some hot climates
(a) Name six large hot deserts.
(b) With the help of your atlas, name one country in each of the desert regions you have named in (a) above.
(c) What kind of ocean currents flow off the coasts of hot deserts?
(d) Which climate type is found only very near to the Equator?

Focus on Hot Desert Climate

Where are the Hot Deserts?

The hot deserts of the world are shown in Figure 1. They are situated:

- **between 15° and 30°** north and south of the equator – areas which are in the paths of the trade winds.

- usually on the **western sides of land masses** near cold ocean currents.

Hot Desert Climate

Main features		Reasons why
Very dry – usually less than 100mm of rain per year	⇨	Most desert regions are in the paths of the **trade winds**. As these winds blow towards the equator, they become warmer and so absorb moisture. They are therefore dry winds. Now and then, winds blow in from the western seas. But these winds must pass over **cold ocean currents**. As they do so, they are cooled and lose all their moisture before they can reach the land.
Hot – usually over 30°C in summer	⇨	Deserts are in the tropics, where the **sun** shines from almost **vertically overhead** in the summertime.
Big range in day and night temperatures	⇨	**Cloudless skies** allow daytime temperatures to rise rapidly. But with no clouds to blanket it, the heat escapes quickly after nightfall. Temperatures can drop by an amazing 40°C during the hour following sunset. Night is sometimes called 'the winter of the desert'.

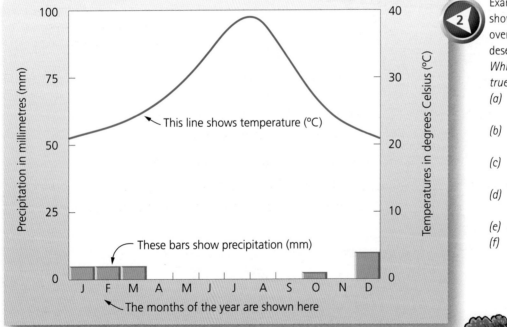

This line shows temperature (°C)

These bars show precipitation (mm)

The months of the year are shown here

Precipitation in millimetres (mm)

Temperatures in degrees Celsius (°C)

J F M A M J J A S O N D

2 Examine this climate chart, which shows temperature and precipitation over the year at a place in the Sahara desert.
Which of the following statements are true?
(a) *The mean temperature of the hottest month is over 35°C*
(b) *No month has a mean temperature of less than 30°C*
(c) *There is no precipitation in this place*
(d) *Most months have no precipitation*
(e) *Precipitation is highest in summer*
(f) *Total annual precipitation is less than 40 mm*

Natural vegetation is plant life that has not been planted or altered by people. It is always related to climate.

Read more about natural vegetation in Chapter 21.

Natural Vegetation

Desert vegetation is very **scarce**, owing to the severe shortage of water. Plants which survive in hot deserts must adapt to hot, dry conditions. They must be able to:

- **find water** underground
- **store water**
- **survive the heat** of the desert sun.

The **giant cactus**:

- has a *spongy interior* which can store water
- has *waxy skin* which holds in moisture
- has *grooves* like an accordion which allow the plant to swell and hold more water in times of rain

Plants are widely spaced, so there is less competition for water.

The **mesquite** bush has *tap roots* which are long enough to find water up to 30 metres below ground.

The **desert dandelion** *blooms only at night.* Its flowers stay closed during the day to escape the drying effects of the hot sun.

Rapid Revision

- Hot deserts are **situated** on the western sides of landmasses between 15° and 30° north and south of the equator. They include the Sahara, Kalahari and Australian deserts.

- Hot desert **climates** are very dry, hot and have large day-night temperature ranges.

- **Vegetation** is scarce in hot deserts. Plants adapt to hot, dry conditions by being widely spaced and having deep roots. The giant cactus has a spongy interior to absorb water and a waxy skin to help keep the water inside the plant.

 ## Activities

1 **True or false?**
  (a) Hot climates include equatorial, hot desert and Mediterranean types.
  (b) Hot desert climates exist only between 15° and 30° north of the equator.
  (c) Hot deserts are permanently hot places.

2 In the case of hot desert climate:
  (a) Describe what the climate is like – refer to rainfall and temperature.
  (b) Explain why the climate occurs.
  (c) Describe how the climate affects vegetation. (J.C. Higher Level)

See chapter 16 of your Workbook

Losing to the Desert: Drought and Desertification

In many parts of the world land is slowly turning to desert – a process that is known as **desertification**. The most severe desertification is taking places at the edges of existing deserts.

The **Sahel** region lies like a belt across Africa on the southern fringes of the Sahara desert (Figure 1). The Sahel has suffered particularly badly from desertification.

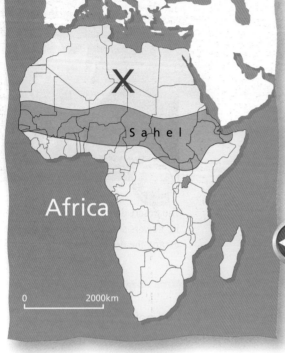

1 The Sahel region in Africa
(a) With the help of your atlas, identify six countries of the Sahel.
(b) Name the desert labelled X on this map.

Fact!
The population of the Sahel has doubled in the past 20 years!

2 Causes of desertification
(a) Which of the causes below are natural and which are human?
(b) What is global warming? (Refer back to page 62 if you need to.)

Causes of Desertification in the Sahel

Desertification is the result of a combination of natural and human causes. These are outlined in Figure 2.

 Severe Drought

Scientists believe that **global warming** is causing increased drought in parts of Africa.

▼

Severe **droughts** have occurred since the 1970s. Droughts are unusually long rainless periods during which crops fail and soils become dry and dusty.

Rapid population growth

High birth rates and improved health care have resulted in **rapid population growth**. More people need more *food*, *fuel* and *housing*. So:
- More **trees** have been cut for fuel and housing.
- More sheep, goats and cattle have **overgrazed** the land and stripped away its natural grass cover.
- Land has been **over-cultivated**, so that its fertility has declined.

The **soil becomes bare and exposed** and therefore can be blown away by the wind. The eroded land then becomes barren.

Desertification has taken place.

Effects of desertification

1 Desertification has affected millions of hectares of **land** and threatens the livelihoods of nearly 100 million people in countries such as Mali and Ethiopia.

2 It has contributed to the outbreak of terrible **famines**.

3 It has forced millions of people to leave their desertified homelands and **migrate** to other areas. These areas then become overpopulated and overgrazed and this causes more desertification.

The effects of desertification in Mali
Describe the scene

Fact!
Nigeria alone loses 40 acres of land to desertification each second!

What Can be Done?

Desertification in the Sahel is being fought using the following methods:

- **Irrigation schemes** are being used to increase the amount of grazing land available.

- Efforts are being make to **restrict the numbers of cattle**, sheep and goats which graze semi-desert regions.

- **Drought-resistant grasses and trees** are being planted. Their roots help to bind the soil together and prevent it from being blown away in the wind.

Rapid Revision

- **Desertification** is the process by which land turns to desert. It especially affects the Sahel region on the southern fringe of the Sahara.
- **Unreliable rain** supplies and drought have helped to cause desertification. Overpopulation (which has led to deforestation, overgrazing and over-cultivation) is also a cause. Once soil is bare and exposed it becomes eroded by wind and desertified.
- Desertification has caused **farmland losses, famine** and **mass migration** in the Sahel. People try to **prevent desertification** by planting trees, restricting cattle numbers and irrigating land.

See Chapter 17 of your Workbook

Gaining from the Deserts: A Major Irrigation Scheme

The good things provided by nature are called **natural resources**. Water is a basic natural resource, which allows people and animals to live and crops to grow.

Irrigation is the **artificial watering of the land** to encourage plant growth and to increase soil fertility.

Small-scale irrigation is practised by millions of farmers in dry areas throughout the world. Major irrigation projects also exist. One major project is connected with the *Aswan Dam Scheme* in the Nile Valley, Egypt.

Case study: The Aswan Dam Project

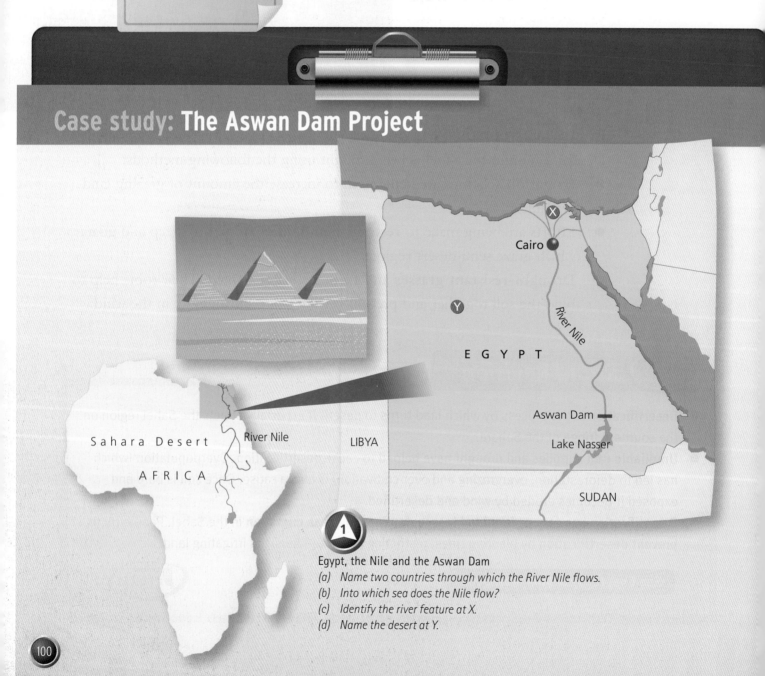

Sahara Desert
River Nile
AFRICA
LIBYA

Cairo
River Nile
Y
E G Y P T
Aswan Dam
Lake Nasser
SUDAN

1

Egypt, the Nile and the Aswan Dam
(a) Name two countries through which the River Nile flows.
(b) Into which sea does the Nile flow?
(c) Identify the river feature at X.
(d) Name the desert at Y.

The **River Nile** provides Egypt with almost all of its fresh water. In times past the river flooded during parts of the year, but did not provide enough water for farming during the rest of the year. To ensure an even and reliable supply of water the Egyptian government built a great dam at Aswan during the 1960s.

The **Aswan Dam** is half a kilometre wide and is the highest dam in the world. It holds back the waters of the Nile to form *Lake Nasser*, which is one of the world's largest artificial lakes. Much of the lake water is pumped to farmlands to irrigate crops.

But the Aswan Dam project has brought problems as well as benefits to the Egyptian people. These are outlined below.

Problems

1. When the Nile flooded each year it deposited rich **alluvial mud** which kept its floodplain fertile. Now that the river no longer floods, farmers need expensive fertilisers to enrich their soils.

2. Much land was **flooded** when Lake Nasser was created. Up to 90,000 local people had to move to new homes.

3. The sites of ancient Egyptian **tombs** were flooded when Lake Nasser was created.

4. High temperatures cause some of the surface water in Lake Nasser to evaporate. This causes a build-up of **salts** in the remaining irrigation water. Salty water can poison the land.

Benefits

1. A regular supply of water irrigates land in Egypt and in neighbouring Sudan. **Irrigation** has caused Egypt's agricultural income to increase by 200 per cent.

2. The Aswan project provided **clean water** for millions of Egyptians. This helps to prevent the spread of diseases such as dysentery.

3. The dam is used to provide half of all Egypt's **electric power.**

4. Boats can now sail up and down the Nile all through the year. This helps **transport, fishing** and **tourism**. Lake Nasser is also used for fish farming and to provide water sports for tourists.

Irrigation in Egypt
Explain how this system of irrigation works

A satellite photograph of Aswan

Match the labels A–D on the photograph with each of the following features.

- *The River Nile*
- *Lake Nasser*
- *The Aswan Dam*
- *A desert area*

Rapid Revision

- **Irrigation** is the artificial watering of land. The **Aswan Dam Project** is a big irrigation scheme in Egypt. The River Nile is dammed and Lake Nasser has formed behind the dam.

- A regular supply of water **irrigates** farmlands and so helps to provide food for Egypt's growing population. Lake Nasser provides **drinking water**. It also provides water for **hydroelectricity, fishing** and **tourist** water sports.

- But the Nile floodplain is now deprived of the **alluvial mud** which the river once provided. Lake Nasser **flooded** peoples' homes and ancient tomb sites. The build-up of **salts** in Lake Nasser damages water quality.

 ## Activities

1. With reference to an irrigation scheme you have studied:
   (a) Name the scheme
   (b) Outline its operation
   (c) Discuss two benefits of the scheme to the local population.
       (J.C. Higher Level)

2. '*Major irrigation schemes can create as well as solve problems.*'
   Describe three problems created by a major irrigation scheme of your choice.

See Chapter 18 of your Workbook

Temperate Climates: Focus on Mediterranean Lands

Figure 1 shows the locations of some of the world's **temperate climate types**.

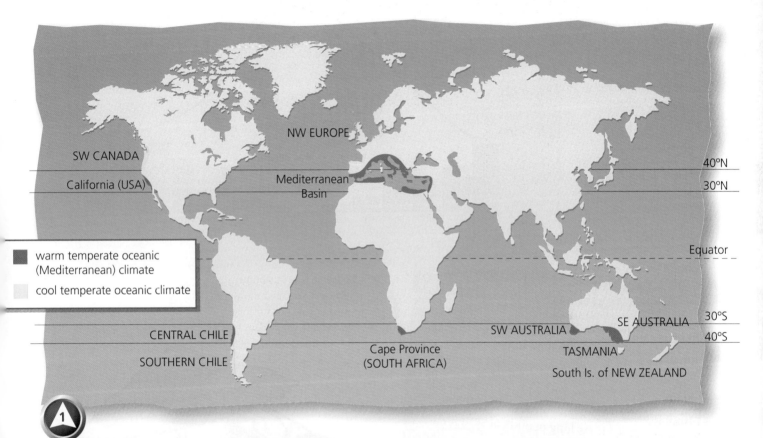

warm temperate oceanic (Mediterranean) climate

cool temperate oceanic climate

SW CANADA

California (USA)

NW EUROPE

Mediterranean Basin

40°N

30°N

Equator

CENTRAL CHILE

SOUTHERN CHILE

Cape Province (SOUTH AFRICA)

SW AUSTRALIA

SE AUSTRALIA

TASMANIA

South Is. of NEW ZEALAND

30°S

40°S

1

The world's temperate climate types
Which climate type does Ireland experience? Describe the general location throughout the world of this type of climate.

Focus on Mediterranean Climate (Warm Temperate)

The greatest area of this type of climate is around the Mediterranean Sea. That is why it is called 'Mediterranean' climate.

Name six areas of the world which enjoy a Mediterranean type climate.

Location

The Mediterranean lands of the world are shown in Figure 1. They are situated:

- **between 30° and 40°** north and south of the Equator
- on the **western sides of landmasses**.

Climate of the Mediterranean

The graph in Figure 2 shows a **Mediterranean-type climate**. This climate has **hot, dry summers**, with average temperatures of nearly 30°C and almost no rain in July and August. **Winters are wet and mild** (about 8°C in January).

(a) Which is the hottest month and what is its mean temperature?

(b) What is the total annual rainfall?

(c) Name the three driest months and give the approximate rainfall figures for each.

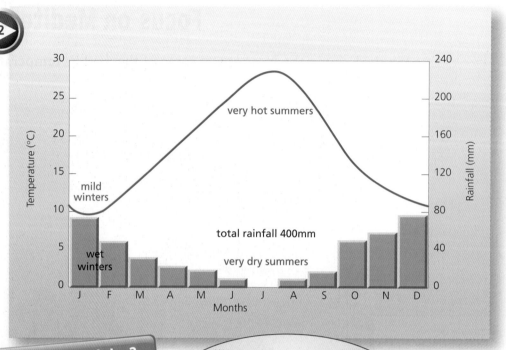

Why are summers hot and dry?

- Because this area is less than 40° from the equator, the **sun is quite high in the sky**. The sun's rays are therefore concentrated and give great heat.
- **High pressure** usually dominates the area in summer. This brings long periods of settled, dry weather.

Why are winters mild and wet?

- Although the **sun** is lower in the sky in winter, it is **still high enough** to give quite warm conditions.
- During winter, the prevailing **winds blow in from the Atlantic Ocean** in the west. These winds are mild and damp. When they rise over mountainous areas, relief rainfall occurs. Westerly winds also bring depressions and these result in wet, unsettled conditions.

We come here in summer for lovely clear skies and the almost guaranteed hot sunshine. No wet and windy days here! Such a change from Ireland!

Natural Vegetation

The natural vegetation of Mediterranean lands has to survive long, hot periods of **summer drought** (see box below). Mediterranean vegetation includes the following:

- Evergreen **trees** such as pine, cypress and cork oak.
- **Shrubs**, such as myrtle and laurel.
- Following the removal of trees, **'garigue'**-type vegetation developed. This consists of tough grasses and sweet-smelling herbs such as rosemary, lavender and thyme.

pine

cork oak

laurel

cypress

lavender

rosemary

How Mediterranean plants adapt to summer drought

- They usually have **small waxy leaves or sharp thorns** that do not lose much moisture through transpiration. (Transpiration is the loss of moisture through the leaves or bark of a plant.)
- Trees such as the cork oak and olive have **thick, protective bark**. These help to stop heat getting in or moisture getting out through transpiration.
- **Long tap roots** reach far underground for water.

Most natural vegetation has been removed from Mediterranean areas for farming and other activities. Some Mediterranean farmers use irrigation to improve crop yields.

(a) What is irrigation?

(b) What evidence of irrigation can be seen in this Mediterranean farm?

Some Links between the Mediterranean Climate and Human Activities

Human activities interact with climate. On the one hand, climate influences agriculture, industry, tourism and other human activities. On the other hand, human activities themselves contribute to the climate changes that are now threatening our planet.

Study Figure 3. Describe as fully as you can the links shown (or any other links) between the Mediterranean climate and human activities.

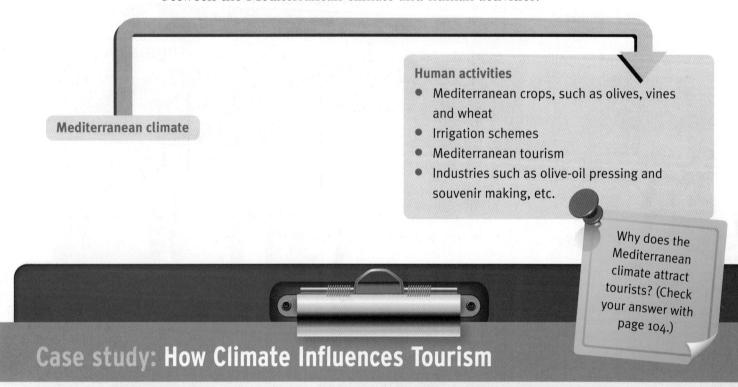

Mediterranean climate

Human activities
- Mediterranean crops, such as olives, vines and wheat
- Irrigation schemes
- Mediterranean tourism
- Industries such as olive-oil pressing and souvenir making, etc.

Why does the Mediterranean climate attract tourists? (Check your answer with page 104.)

Case study: How Climate Influences Tourism

4 Tourist areas along the Mediterranean coast
Name four European countries with Mediterranean tourism.

The **economies** of many Mediterranean coastal areas (see Figure 4) are now dominated by beach tourism. Hundreds of thousands of people **work directly** in the tourist industry. They find employment in hotels, restaurants, bars and travel companies. Many more are **employed indirectly** by tourism. They work in the building of tourist hotels and apartments, in the manufacture of souvenirs or in shops or other services supported by holidaymakers.

Beach tourism in Spain
Contrast this tourist resort with the mountain resort in the picture below.

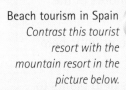

Learn more about Mediterranean tourism in Chapter 64.

Mountain tourism in the Alps in winter
Why is snow 'especially slow to melt' on north-facing slopes?

Climate and Mountain Tourism

Climate can also help attract tourists to great European mountain ranges, such as the Alps. The photograph below explains how this is so.

High altitudes reduce temperatures greatly. This means that precipitation often comes as powdery snow. The snow lies deeply on the ground throughout winter. It is especially slow to melt on north-facing slopes.

High pressure gives long winter periods of calm, dry weather with blue skies. These conditions are ideal for skiing.

Summer tourism in these mountains usually takes the form of mountain walking, climbing and sightseeing. High altitudes and mountain breezes keep temperatures pleasantly warm and fresh, rather than very hot. The highest mountains are snow-covered throughout the year and attract climbers in summer.

Rapid Revision

- The Mediterranean lands are **situated** on the western sides of landmasses between 30° and 40° north and south of the equator. The largest single Mediterranean region lies on the shores of the Mediterranean Sea.
- **Summers** are hot and dry because of low latitudes and high pressure. Winds from the Atlantic help to make **winters** mild and moist.
- **Natural vegetation** adapts well to the climate. Waxy leaves, thick bark and long roots help plants to survive the hot, dry summer conditions. Most natural vegetation is now cleared for agriculture. Irrigation is commonly used. Overgrazing has resulted in soil erosion.
- Climate affects **human activities**. For example, hot, dry and sunny summers are the basis of a huge tourist industry in Mediterranean lands. Deep snow and calm, dry conditions attract winter tourists to Alpine resorts.

Activities

Month	J	F	M	A	M	J	J	A	S	O	N	D
Temperature in °C	9	11	12	16	20	25	28	29	19	17	15	12
Precipitation in mm	72	55	29	20	14	4	0	4	15	52	61	79

1   The table above shows temperature and rainfall figures for a Mediterranean town.
   (a)   Name the hottest month and the coolest month and state the temperature for each.
   (b)   Calculate the annual temperature range.
   (c)   Calculate the total annual rainfall.
   (d)   Calculate the average monthly precipitation for the first three months of the year.
   (e)   Calculate the mean monthly temperature for the hottest three months of the year.
2   Explain why weather conditions are so different in summer and winter in Mediterranean areas.
   (J.C. Higher Level)
3   Name four species of natural vegetation of Mediterranean lands and explain how such vegetation adapts to the Mediterranean climate.
4   Name any four Mediterranean tourist resorts in Europe and explain why the Mediterranean climate attracts tourists from countries such as Ireland.
5   Explain how climate affects mountain tourism in one named European country.

See Chapter 19 of your Workbook

Cold Climates: Focus on Boreal Lands

Figure 1 shows the locations of the world's main cold climate types.

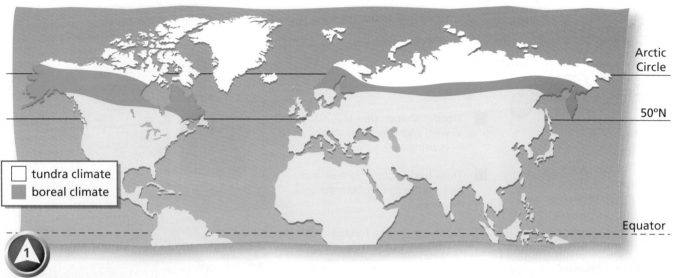

The world's cold climates

(a) Describe the general location of tundra climate.

(b) Examine the location of the boreal lands. Unscramble the 'words' below to name six countries in which boreal lands exist.
SUA, DACANA, RAWONY, WESEND, DAFNNIL, SUSAIR

Focus on Boreal Lands

Location

The word boreal means 'northern'. The **boreal lands** of the world stretch across the northern hemisphere **between 50°N and the Arctic Circle (66½°N).**

Climate

The climate of this region is of the **cool continental type**.

Main features	Reasons why
Very cold winters, with mean January temperatures of -29°C in places.	• These lands are in **high latitudes.** The sun's rays reach them at oblique angles and give little heat.
Short but surprisingly **warm summers,** with mean July temperatures of 16°C.	• In **summer,** when the northern hemisphere is **tilted towards the sun,** these lands get long hours of daylight. This causes the heat of the land to increase gradually.
Light precipitation – less than 400 mm per year.	• The **polar winds** are too cold to hold much moisture.

Natural Vegetation

The natural vegetation of boreal regions is dominated by vast forests of **coniferous trees**, such as pine, spruce and fir. These forests are called **taiga** and they contain one-third of the world's trees.

Most conifers are **evergreen** – they do not shed their needle-like foliage in autumn. This permanent foliage allows the conifers to start developing as soon as their short growing season begins.

Figure 2 shows other ways in which conifers are equipped to survive the long, cold winters and limited precipitation levels of boreal climate.

> **Logging** is one of the most important activities in the taiga. The government in Sweden insists that, for every tree cut, at least two saplings (young trees) must be planted. This is called **sustainable logging**.

■ **Slender shape** offers little resistance to wind and so reduces the risk of trees being blown over during storms.

■ **Thick bark** retains moisture and protects the conifer from the cold, dry wind.

■ **Thin, needle-like foliage** is not withered by cold, biting winds.

■ **Downward-sloping** and springy branches allow snow to slide off.

■ **Shallow roots** can develop in the thin layers of soil above the **permafrost** (permanently frozen ground).

Describe this view of taiga in Russia.

See rapid revision on page 112

Natural Vegetation and Climate

(a) What is a river basin? (Check page 29 if necessary.)

(h) Find the Amazon and Congo rivers on a map of the world.

What is natural vegetation?

Natural vegetation is plant life that has not been planted or altered by people. Few areas of the world still possess their natural vegetation. The natural vegetation of Ireland, for example, was deciduous forest. These ancient forests have been almost completely destroyed to make way for agriculture.

Regions where natural vegetation is still widespread include the equatorial forests of the Amazon River Basin in South America and of the Congo River Basin in Africa.

How Natural Vegetation Is Related to Climate

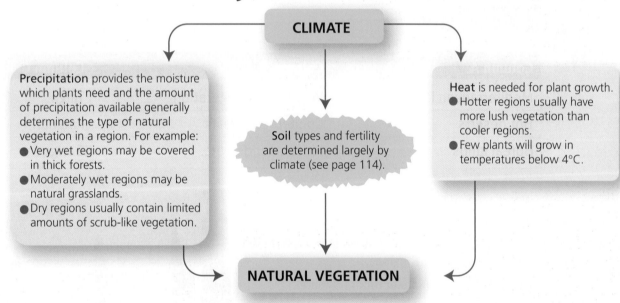

CLIMATE

Precipitation provides the moisture which plants need and the amount of precipitation available generally determines the type of natural vegetation in a region. For example:
- Very wet regions may be covered in thick forests.
- Moderately wet regions may be natural grasslands.
- Dry regions usually contain limited amounts of scrub-like vegetation.

Soil types and fertility are determined largely by climate (see page 114).

Heat is needed for plant growth.
- Hotter regions usually have more lush vegetation than cooler regions.
- Few plants will grow in temperatures below 4°C.

NATURAL VEGETATION

How Natural Vegetation is Adapted to Climatic Conditions

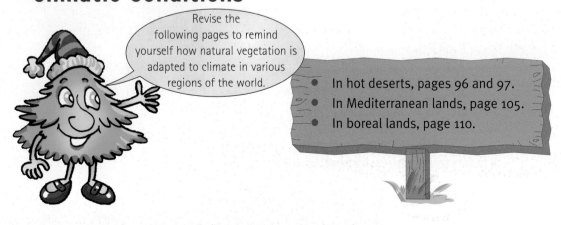

Revise the following pages to remind yourself how natural vegetation is adapted to climate in various regions of the world.

- In hot deserts, pages 96 and 97.
- In Mediterranean lands, page 105.
- In boreal lands, page 110.

Rapid Revision

Chapter 20

● **Cold** climates include boreal and tundra types.

● The **boreal lands** lie between 50°N and the Arctic Circle. Because of their high latitudes, they have long, **cold winters** and **short summers**. Cold, northerly winds provide very **little precipitation**.

● Boreal regions are covered in vast coniferous forests called **taiga**. Conifers have thick bark, needle-like foliage, downward-sloping branches and shallow roots. These features help trees to survive in cold, dry conditions. Logging is an important activity in the taiga.

Chapter 21

● **Natural vegetation** is vegetation that has not been planted or adapted by people.

● **Climate helps to determine natural vegetation**. It provides the moisture and heat needed for vegetation to thrive. Climate also influences soil fertility and this in turn influences vegetation.

Activities

1

Column A	Column B	Column C
Mediterranean lands	Very limited vegetation	Taiga
Hot deserts	Coniferous forests	Kalahari
Boreal lands	Pine, lavender, etc.	Garigue

(a) Match each of the words in column A with the correct words and phrases in columns B and C.

(b) Explain fully how natural vegetation is adapted to climate in hot desert regions.

2 In the case of boreal climate **or** tundra climate:

(a) Briefly describe its temperature and precipitation.

(b) Describe one way in which climate has influenced how people earn a living.

3 (a) State whether the climate of the area shown in the photograph is Mediterranean, Equatorial or Boreal.

(b) Briefly describe the temperature and precipitation of the climate you identify.

(c) Describe one way in which climate has influenced how people earn a living.

See Chapters 20 and 21 of your Workbook

Our Living Soil

Soil is a *thin layer of loose material on the surface of the land*. Without it, plants could not grow and there would be no food for land animals – including people. Soil, therefore, is an essential **natural resource**.

A **natural resource** is something that is created by nature (natural) and is useful to people (a resource).

The Composition of Soil

Soil is a **living thing**. It contains several vital ingredients. All these ingredients work together to make the soil fertile.

Mineral particles

Mineral particles are the biggest ingredient of soil. Most are tiny particles. They come from the underlying rock, called the **parent rock**, which is broken down by weathering and erosion.

Some minerals are **soluble**. They can dissolve in water and become liquid.

Living organisms

Numerous creatures live in the soil. Some of these are visible to the naked eye – insects and earthworms, for example. But the vast majority of creatures are too small to be seen without the aid of a microscope. These are called **micro-organisms**.

Micro-organisms help to break down plant litter to form humus. So they play a vital role in making the soil fertile.

Plant remains

When dead plants, leaves and other forms of **plant litter** enter the soil, they decay to form a dark, jelly-like substance called **humus**. Humus nourishes plants. It also helps to hold soil particles together.

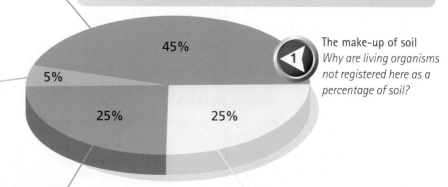

45%

5%

25%

25%

The make-up of soil
Why are living organisms not registered here as a percentage of soil?

Water

As water moves through the soil it dissolves soluble minerals. It then distributes these minerals to plants that can absorb them in liquid form through their roots. The dissolved minerals are called **nutrients** because they nourish the plants.

Air

Air is found in the spaces between soil particles. Air supplies the oxygen and nitrogen that plants and living organisms need to survive.

Soil micro-organisms such as these are so tiny that millions of them could fit on a teaspoon.

The earthworm helps to make the soil fertile. As it moves beneath the surface, it helps to mix the soil and to circulate air through it.

How Soil is Formed

A number of factors work together over a long period to produce soil. These factors include **climate**, **parent rock**, **vegetation** and **people**. Figure 2 below shows how this happens.

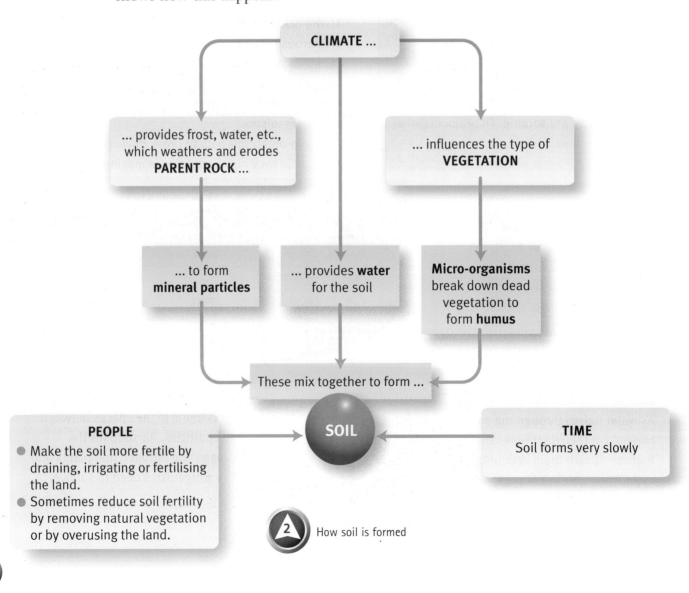

CLIMATE ...

... provides frost, water, etc., which weathers and erodes **PARENT ROCK** ...

... influences the type of **VEGETATION**

... to form **mineral particles**

... provides **water** for the soil

Micro-organisms break down dead vegetation to form **humus**

These mix together to form ...

SOIL

PEOPLE
- Make the soil more fertile by draining, irrigating or fertilising the land.
- Sometimes reduce soil fertility by removing natural vegetation or by overusing the land.

TIME
Soil forms very slowly

2   How soil is formed

Some Processes in Soil Formation: a Closer Look
The Breakdown of Vegetation into Humus

Dead leaves, twigs and other forms of **plant litter** build up on the surface of the soil. **Micro-organisms**, such as bacteria and fungi, cause the plant litter to decay into a black jelly-like substance called **humus**.

Oxygen is needed to assist the breakdown of plant litter into humus. So **air** in the soil plays an important role in the process of **humification**. Humus helps to make soil fertile.

Micro-organism

Oxygen

Humification of plant litter

Fertile soil

The Movement of Water through Soil

In rainy areas such as Ireland, rainwater percolates (soaks) downwards through the soil.

Water often dissolves minerals, humus and other plant nutrients on the upper parts of the soil. Then, as the water seeps downwards, it washes these plant nutrients down beyond the reach of many plant roots. This process is known as **leaching**. Too much leaching is bad for the growth of vegetation because it deprives plants of many of the nutrients they need.

Where leaching is severe, the dissolved minerals may be washed downwards until they reach a depth at which the soil has become saturated. Here, minerals may build up to form a crusty layer called a **hard pan**. The hard pan is usually *impermeable* – it does not allow water to pass through it.

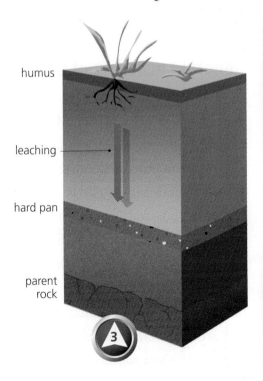

humus

leaching

hard pan

parent rock

3

Fact!
In hot regions water can move *upward* through the soil towards the surface. This movement is called **capillary action**.

Identify plant litter and a hard pan in this soil cutting

Soil Profiles

A **vertical section of the soil from the surface downwards** is called a **soil profile.**

Different soil types have different soil profiles. Figure 4 shows a typical profile. You will notice that it contains a number of layers. These layers are called **horizons**, because they occur more or less horizontally.

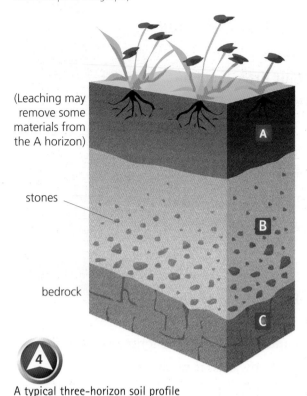

(Leaching may remove some materials from the A horizon)

stones

bedrock

4

A typical three-horizon soil profile

A The **A horizon** – sometimes called the **humus horizon** – is nearest the surface. It is usually dark in colour because it contains dark-coloured humus. It also contains plant litter.

B The **B horizon** lies just below the A horizon. It may contain less humus and so may be lighter in colour. Because it is near the underlying bedrock, it usually has a more stony texture than the A horizon.

C The **C horizon** consists of the underlying bedrock or parent rock of the soil.

Different Soil Types

The **formation of humus** and the **movement of water through the soil** combine to create several **different soil types**. Examples of these soil types are:

- brown soils
- podzols
- tropical red soils

General Locations of Main Soil Types in Ireland

- **Brown soils** are Ireland's most common soil type. They occur mainly in the drier parts of the country, such as in the Midlands and in eastern counties. *Name six counties where brown soils predominate.*
- **Podzols** are found in many of Ireland's damp highland areas. *Name three highland areas where podzols are prominent.*

Legend:
- brown soils
- podzols
- damp gley soils
- poor peaty soils

5

Ireland's main soil types

Brown soils

- Brown soils usually developed in places where the natural vegetation was once **deciduous forest**. The plant litter from broad-leaved deciduous trees provided plenty of rich, dark humus.
- Brown soils occur in areas of **moderate rainfall**. Because of this, they are not heavily leached and do not contain hard pans.
- **Plenty of humus** and the **absence of severe leaching** combine to:
  1. give these soils a dark **brown** colour;
  2. make them **fertile**, well drained and suited to **arable** (tillage) as well as to **cattle** farming

Podzols

- Podzols often occur beneath areas of **coniferous forest** or **heathland**. These vegetation types seldom provide enough rich humus to make the soil fertile.
- Podzols occur in areas of **high rainfall**. Because of this, they are usually leached heavily. Hard pans often form beneath their surfaces.
- **Shortages of humus** and the occurrence of **severe leaching** combine to:
  1. give podzols a **grey** (rather than a dark) appearance near the surface;
  2. make the soil rather **infertile** and suited only to **rough grazing** or to the growth of **coniferous forests.**

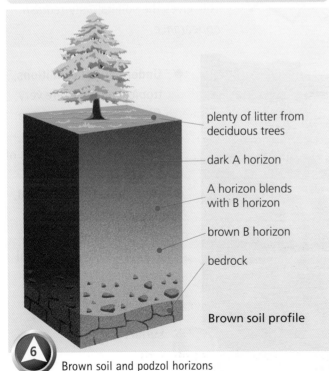

plenty of litter from deciduous trees

dark A horizon

A horizon blends with B horizon

brown B horizon

bedrock

Brown soil profile

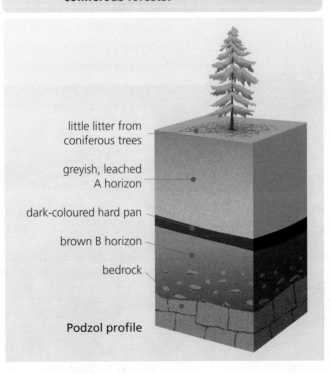

little litter from coniferous trees

greyish, leached A horizon

dark-coloured hard pan

brown B horizon

bedrock

Podzol profile

6 Brown soil and podzol horizons
Contrast the two profiles shown

Tropical Red Soils

Areas of tropical red soils

(a) *With the help of your atlas and the information in this figure, name five **countries** in Latin America, five countries in Asia and five in Africa which have large areas of tropical red soils.*

(b) *Which **continents** possess tropical red soils?*

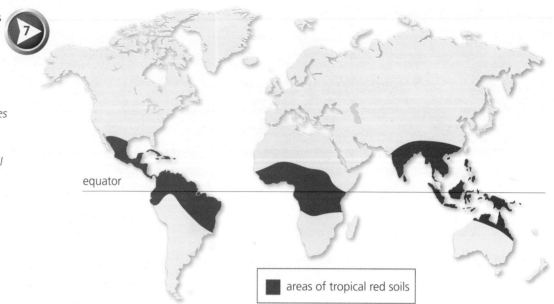

equator

■ areas of tropical red soils

These soils are **deep** and **rusty-red** in colour. They are found in **tropical regions** close to the Equator for the following reasons:

1 The equatorial or tropical **climates** of these regions are very hot and very wet. These conditions give rise to a great deal of *chemical weathering*.

2 Dense **tropical forests** deposit large amounts of plant litter on the soils. Decaying plant litter creates acids that assist *chemical weathering*.

3 Severe **chemical weathering** helps to break down rocks to great depths and so gives rise to *deep soils*. It also breaks down iron in rocks into a substance called iron oxide or rust. This gives the soil its *rusty-reddish appearance*.

- **Under natural conditions**, tropical red soils are very *fertile*. This is so because tropical forests provide them with large amounts of humus.
- **When forests are cleared**, the soils are deprived of their humus and lie exposed to heavy tropical rain. They then become heavily *leached*, *infertile* and severely *eroded* by surface water.

Rapid Revision

- Soil is a natural resource that has several **ingredients**. Its main ingredient is mineral particles, which are the remains of denuded rock. Micro-organisms help to break down plant remains into humus. Other ingredients are water and air.

- **Climate** is important in the formation of soil. It provides the agents of weathering and erosion that breaks down rock into mineral particles. It provides water for the soil. It also provides the vegetation that decays to humus. **Human activities** may help to make the soil more fertile or less fertile.

- **Humification** is the process by which plant litter decays into humus. **Leaching** is the process by which water carries plant nutrients down through the soil. **Capillary action** is a process by which water emerges through the soil.

- A **soil profile** is a vertical section through the soil. The A horizon is nearest to the surface and may contain much humus. Below that is the B horizon, which has less humus and is more stony. The C horizon is mainly bedrock.

- **Brown soils** are found in lowland areas of limited rainfall that were once covered with deciduous forests. They are fertile soils and are suited to arable farming as well as to cattle farming. **Podzols** are found in rainy uplands that were under coniferous forests. Podzols are grey and infertile and suited mainly to rough grazing. **Tropical red soils** are rusty-red in colour and are found in hot, wet tropical regions. When cleared of natural vegetation, they may become heavily leached and eroded.

Activities

1. (a) Name five ingredients that make up soil.
   (b) Explain how each of *two* of the ingredients you name affects soil formation. (Based on J.C. Question)

2. Name and describe two processes that assist in the formation of soils in Ireland.

3. (a) Name and describe fully one Irish soil type that you have studied.
   (b) Draw a diagram to show the horizons (layers) in this soil type. Label your diagram carefully. (J.C. Ordinary Level)

4. The picture shows part of an equatorial rainforest in Indonesia.
   (a) Name the type of soil you would expect to find in this region.
   (b) Describe the characteristics of the soil type you name.
   (c) Explain how human activities effect soil in the region shown.

See Chapter 22 of your Workbook

Soil and Natural Vegetation

Soil Influences

- **The soil nourishes vegetation by providing it with essential nutrients** such as nitrogen and calcium.

   When all the essential nutrients are present, the soil is fertile. Rich vegetation, with a wide variety of plant species, can grow in such soil.

   When some essential nutrients are absent, the soil will be infertile. Fewer and usually smaller plants will grow in it.

- **The depth of soil influences vegetation growth.**

   Some deep-rooted plants such as oak and beech trees need deep soil in order to thrive. Deep soils are found most usually in river valleys and in lowland areas.

   Only shallow-rooted plants, such as grasses and coniferous trees, can thrive in shallow soils. Such soils are most common on mountain slopes that have been eroded.

... and Vegetation

(a) Contrast (describe the differences between) the vegetation shown in these two pictures.

(b) How would the soil differ between the two places shown in the pictures?

How trees reduce the effects of leaching

1. Deep **roots** soak up leached nutrients and transfer them to the leaves.
2. When **leaves** fall and decay, the nutrients are returned to the soil's surface.

Vegetation...

- **Vegetation provides humus which nourishes the soil**.

    Some types of vegetation, such as **deciduous trees**, provide large amounts of plant litter. This type of litter decays quickly to form humus. The humus fertilises the soil and also helps to give the soil's A horizon a dark brown appearance.

    Other vegetation types, such as **coniferous trees**, provide small amounts of plant litter which does not break down easily into humus. The soil beneath these vegetation types tends not to be fertile. Its A horizon is sometimes rather grey in colour.

- Vegetation can reduce the effects of **leaching** by returning leached nutrients to the surface of the soil (see Figure 1).

- Vegetation can prevent **soil erosion** by forming a protective cover over the soil. This cover protects the soil from both water and wind erosion. Disastrous soil erosion has happened in areas where natural vegetation has been removed.

...Influences Soil

Rapid Revision

- **Soil influences vegetation.** It provides *nutrients* that are needed by plants. The *depth* of soil also influences the type of vegetation that grows.

- **Vegetation influences soil.** It provides *humus* to fertilise the soil. It reduces the effects of *leaching*.
    It also helps to prevent soil *erosion*.

See the local study in Chapter 23 of your **Workbook**.

24

Ordnance Survey Maps: An Introduction

Map A (scale 1:20,000,000)

Map B (scale 1:50,000

Map C (scale 1:8,500)

Map D (scale 1:1000)

A **map** is a **scaled-down drawing or plan of all or part of the earth's surface**. Maps are drawn to different scales, depending on the type of information that they need to show.

- **Small-scale maps** show **large areas** in little detail.
- **Large-scale maps** show **small areas** in greater detail.

Four map fragments of different scales
Examine these fragments of four maps of different scales.
(a) Which map has the largest scale?
(b) Which map shows the greatest detail?
(c) Which map shows the least detail?
(d) Which map would be most useful for each of the following:
  (i) people wishing to find their way around a city;
  (ii) people studying house sizes within a street;
  (iii) tourists on a car holiday around Ireland;
  (iv) people studying the location of a town in relation to the countryside around it?

Scale

Scale is the relationship between a distance on a map and its corresponding distance on the ground.

For example, if the scale of a map is one centimetre to one kilometre (1cm:1km), a length of 6 centimetres on the map would represent 6 kilometres on the ground.

REPRESENTATIVE FRACTION
(RF) is given as a ratio. The RF 1:50,000 tells us that any one unit of measurement on the map corresponds to 50,000 similar units on the ground.

LINEAR SCALE is a line divided into kilometres and parts of a kilometre (or into miles and parts of a mile).

SCÁLA 1:50 000   SCALE 1:50 000

1 KILOMETRES   0   1   2   3   4   5   6   7   1 KILOMETRES 8
1 STATUTE MILES   0   1   2   3   4   1 STATUTE MILES 5
2 ceintimeadar ša chilimeadaí (taobh chearnog eangal) 2 centimetres to 1 kilometre (grid square side)

Three ways of showing scale

STATEMENT OF SCALE
The scale is stated. (In this case it is 2cm to 1km.)

Measuring Distances on Maps

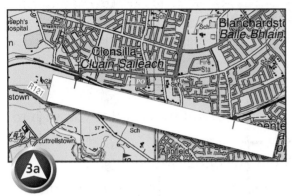

To measure the distance between two railway stations

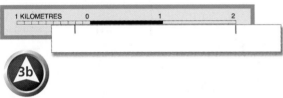

The answer is 2.2 kilometres

Straight Line Distances

The straight line or shortest distance between two points is sometimes called the distance 'as the crow flies'. This distance can be calculated as follows.

1 Place a straight edge of paper on the map so that it passes through the two points (see Figure 3a).

2 Carefully mark the edge of paper where each point touches it (see Figure 3a).

3 Place the edge of paper on the map's linear scale and measure precisely the distance between the two marks (see Figure 3b).

Curved Line Distances

Curved line distances, such as those along roads or railways, can be measured as follows.

1 Lay the straight edge of a strip of paper on the starting point and put a pencil mark on both the paper and the map ('A' on Figure 4a).

2 Keeping these two marks together, place the paper edge along the centre of the road. Mark the map and the paper at the spot where the road begins to bend away from the paper ('B' on Figure 4b).

3 Keeping these last marks together, place the paper edge along the next straight piece of road and again mark the map and the paper where the road leaves the paper edge ('C' on Figure 4c).

4 Repeat these steps until you reach the end of the measurement. Mark the end point on the paper.

5 Use the map's linear scale to measure the distance between the starting and finishing marks on the paper.

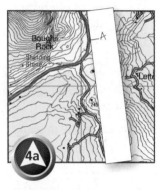

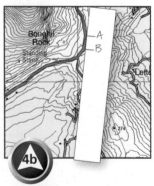

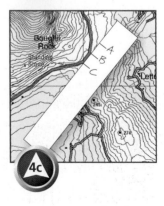

Activities

1 Measure in kilometres the shortest distance between the peak of Torc Mountain (.535) and the peak of Shehy Mountain (.571) on the **Killarney Area** map on page 133.

2 Measure the N15 road on the **Sligo Area** map on page 148. (This road runs from the top of the map to where it meets the N16 road.)

Calculating Areas on Maps

To Calculate Regular (Rectangular) Areas

You will notice that your 1:50,000 Ordnance Survey map contains 'boxes' called grid squares. The side of a full grid square measures one kilometre (km). This makes it very easy to calculate area from a map. Do the following:

1. Count the number of grid squares across the base of the area that you wish to calculate.
2. Count the number of grid squares up the side of the area.
3. Multiply the number across by the number up the side. This gives you the area in square kilometres (sq km).

Example:

To calculate the area of the map in Figure 5:

1. Number of grid squares across the base = 6
2. Number of grid squares up the side = 3.5
3. Area = 6 x 3.5 = 21 sq km.

 Activities

1. Calculate in square kilometres the area of the **Central Dublin** map on page 134.
2. Calculate the area of that part of the **Sligo Area** map that lies south of the line marked 41 (page 148).

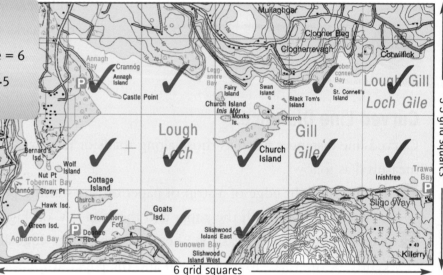

6 grid squares

3.5 grid squares

To Calculate an Irregularly Shaped Area

The total area of each grid square on a 1:50,000 map is one square kilometre. This allows us to calculate easily the approximate area of any irregularly shaped feature (a lake, for example). Do the following:

- Count all the squares which are at least half-filled by the feature which you wish to measure. This number will represent the approximate area of the feature in sq km.

Example:

To calculate the approximate area of Lough Gill shown in Figure 5:

1. Number of squares at least half filled by the lake (these squares have been ticked) = 13.
2. Approximate area of the lake = 13 sq km.

Activities

1. Calculate in square kilometres the approximate size of Lough Leane (exclude Muckross Lake) on the **Killarney Area** map on page 133.
2. Calculate approximately the area of seawater shown on the **Central Dublin** map on page 134.

Directions

Directions are usually given in the form of compass points. Figure 6 shows the main points of the compass. Learn these directions very carefully. Then do the exercise attached to Figure 7.

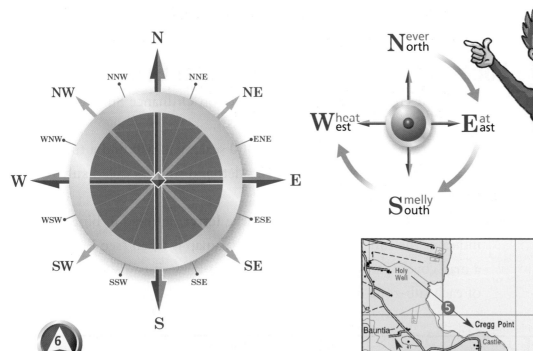

To help you remember the four main compass points

Never
North

Wheat
West

Eat
East

Smelly
South

6

1 Identify the following directions from the **Central Dublin** map on page 134:
   (a) from Ballsbridge to Dollymount;
   (b) from Ringsend to Rathgar;
   (c) from Ringsend to Trinity College;
   (d) from Killester to Trinity College.

2 In which direction would you travel if you walked along the Bull Wall from Clontarf? (see the **Central Dublin** map on page 134.)

3 In which general direction does the Drumcliff River flow? (**Sligo Area** map, page 148.)

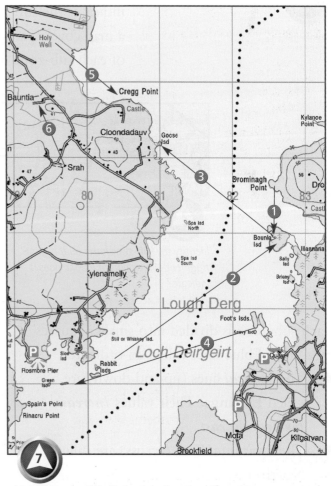

7

Identify each of the following directions from this map.
1. *from Drominagh Point to Bounla Island;*
2. *from Rabbit Islands to Bounla Island;*
3. *from Bounla Island to Goose Island;*
4. *from Foot's Islands to Green Island;*
5. *from the Holy Well to Clegg Point;*
6. *from Srah to Bauntia.*

25

More on Maps of 1:50,000 Scale

1 Sub-zones

Locating Places – the National Grid

The **National Grid** is used to locate places on Ordnance Survey (OS) maps.

In the margin of each map of 1:50,000 scale, you will find a tiny map of Ireland. This tiny map is divided into lettered squares called **sub-zones** (Figure 1).

● Each OS map has printed on it a large **letter** outlined in blue. This indicates the sub-zone from which that map is taken (see Figure 2). If a map covers parts of more than one sub-zone, it will show the letters of each sub-zone it occupies.

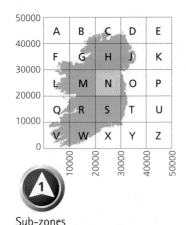

2

Identify the sub-zone letter on this map fragment. Which part of Ireland does it indicate?

Each sub-zone is divided into smaller squares by a grid of blue lines called co-ordinates.

● The *vertical* lines (up and down) are called **Eastings.** Their values *increase towards the east*.

● The *horizontal* lines (across) are called **Northings**. Their values *increase towards the north*.

Both Eastings and Northings are numbered from 00 to 99 (see Figure 3).

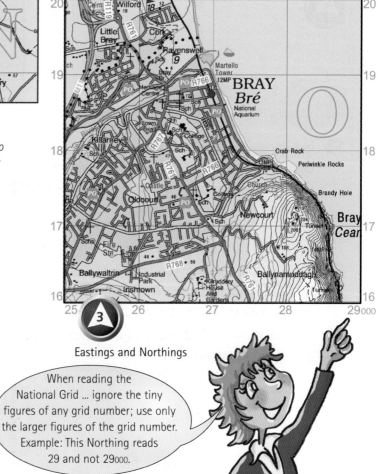

3 Eastings and Northings

When reading the National Grid ... ignore the tiny figures of any grid number; use only the larger figures of the grid number. Example: This Northing reads 29 and not 29000.

Grid References

The locations of places on OS maps are expressed in the form of grid references.

Four-Figure Grid References

Four-figure grid references are used to give the location of any single square on a map, so they give us the general location of features within that square.

How to get a four-figure grid reference

Step 1:   Give the sub-zone **letter**.

Step 2:   Give the two-digit number of the **Easting** on the *left* side of the square.

Step 3:   Give the two-digit number of the **Northing** on the *bottom* side of the square.

Think of 'LEN'
Letter – Easting – Northing

For example:

- The four-figure grid reference for the National Aquarium in Figure 3 is O 27 18.
- What is the grid reference for the golf course (⚑) in Figure 3?
- Which square is indicated by the reference O 28 17?

Activities

1. Give four-figure grid references for each of the following places on the Central Dublin map on page 134: Rathgar; Ringsend; Killester.
2. Identify the main feature at O 21 34 and at O 20 31 on that map.

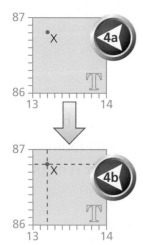

Six-Figure Grid References

Six-figure grid references are needed to give the exact locations of small features.

To calculate a six-figure grid reference

To get a six-figure grid reference we must imagine that the distance between each pair of Eastings and between each pair of Northings is divided by ten, as in decimal measurement (see Figure 4a). This will enable us to give a third figure for both the Easting and Northing readings.

For example:

- The place marked X in figure 4b is within sub-zone 'T'.
- It is at Easting 13.2.
- It is at Northing 86.8.
- Decimal points are not included in grid references.
- So the six-figure reading for the place marked X is **T 132 868**.

Activities

1. Find six-figure grid references for the following features in Figure 3: the most northerly church; boating activities.
2. Examine the **Killarney Area** map on page 133. Give a six-figure grid reference for Crow Island and Lamb Island in Lough Leane.

To Locate a Feature from a Six-Figure Grid Reference

Example: To locate the position of N 996 173 in Figure 5.

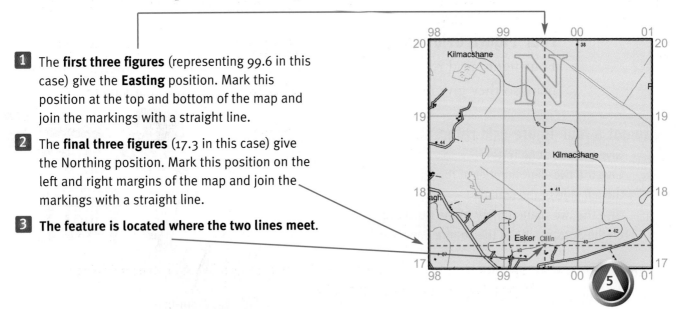

1 The **first three figures** (representing 99.6 in this case) give the **Easting** position. Mark this position at the top and bottom of the map and join the markings with a straight line.

2 The **final three figures** (17.3 in this case) give the Northing position. Mark this position on the left and right margins of the map and join the markings with a straight line.

3 **The feature is located where the two lines meet.**

Activities

1 What features are located at O 261 175 and at O 265 192 in Figure 3?

2 What features are located at each of the following places on the **Sligo Area** map on page 148?
(a) G 686 360; (b) G 681 421; (c) G 703 442.

Symbols

Many features are shown on OS maps by means of symbols. Symbols may be given in the key or legend found at the base of each map. A selection of symbols found on 1:50,000 maps is given in figures 6 and 7. You will learn about other symbols later in this chapter.

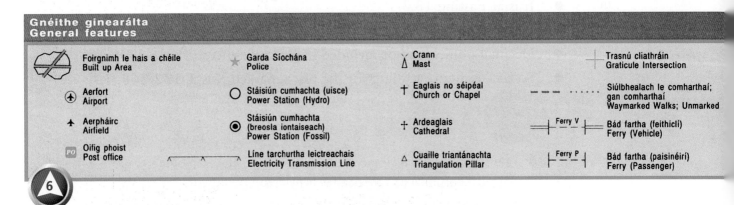

Some map symbols

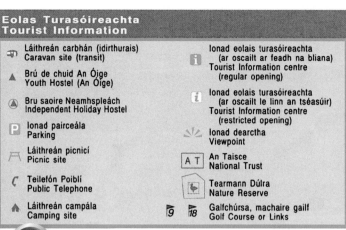

Láithreán carbhán (idirthurais) Caravan site (transit)	Ionad eolais turasóireachta (ar oscailt ar feadh na bliana) Tourist Information centre (regular opening)
Brú de chuid An Óige Youth Hostel (An Óige)	Ionad eolais turasóireachta (ar oscailt le linn an tséasúir) Tourist Information centre (restricted opening)
Bru saoire Neamhspleách Independent Holiday Hostel	Ionad dearctha Viewpoint
Ionad pairceála Parking	An Taisce National Trust
Láithreán picnicí Picnic site	Tearmann Dúlra Nature Reserve
Teilefón Poiblí Public Telephone	Galfchúrsa, machaire gailf Golf Course or Links
Láithreán campála Camping site	

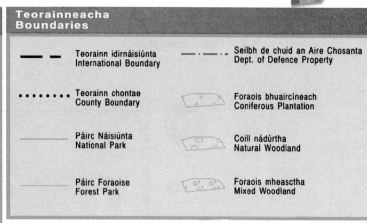

Teorainn idirnáisiúnta International Boundary	Seilbh de chuid an Aire Chosanta Dept. of Defence Property
Teorainn chontae County Boundary	Foraois bhuaircíneach Coniferous Plantation
Páirc Náisiúnta National Park	Coill nádúrtha Natural Woodland
Páirc Foraoise Forest Park	Foraois mheasctha Mixed Woodland

7

Some map symbols

Activities

1 On the **Killarney Area** map (page 133), identify the symbol at each of the following places:
(a) V 968 842 (b) V 965 905 (c) V 978 873

2 On the **Central Dublin** map (page 134), identify the symbol at each of the following places:
(a) O 206 337 (b) O 187 371 (c) O 206 316

How Height is Shown on Maps

Height above sea level is given in metres on modern maps. The following methods are used to show height.

Method	Explanation	Symbol
Triangulation pillars	They are sometimes used to show the exact heights of hill or mountain peaks.	
Spot heights	They show the exact height of points on a map.	
Contour lines	A contour is a line joining places of equal height. Contours usually occur at intervals of 10 metres.	
Colour layers	Areas of different heights are shown by bands of different colours. Shading varies gradually from green (low ground) to brown (high ground).	

8

Examine Figures 9 and 10. Figure 10 shows a slightly 3-D version of the Ordnance Survey map in Figure 9.

- *Match the locations A–E (shown on Figures 9 and 10) with the appropriate height selected from those listed in the box in Figure 11.*
- *Estimate the height of each of the places marked 1–3.*
- *Using a pencil, shade lightly the area shown which is between 150 and 160 metres in height.*

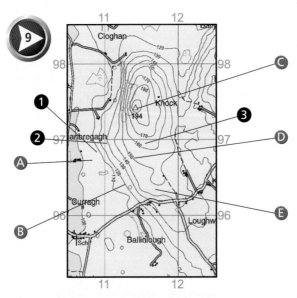

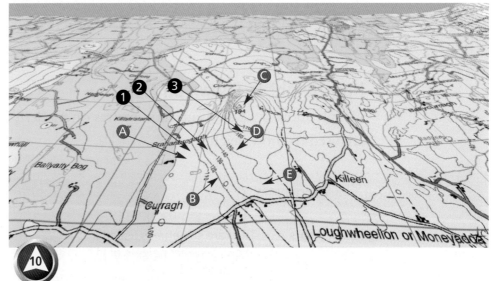

Height in metres	
152	145
105	85
175	120
194	305

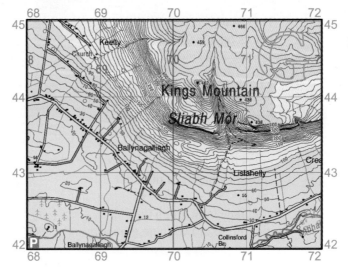

Examine Figure 12

Calculate the height of each of the following places:

(i)   *G 710 430*
(ii) *G 680 445*
(iii) *G 700 430*
(iv) *The highest point on the map*

Showing Slope

Steepness

Steepness of slope is shown on maps by the closeness of contours.

The steeper the slope, the closer the contours.

1. **No** or very few contours show **flat** land
2. **Widely spaced** contours show **gentle** slopes
3. **Close** contours show **steep** slopes
4. Contours **merge** together to show **cliffs**.

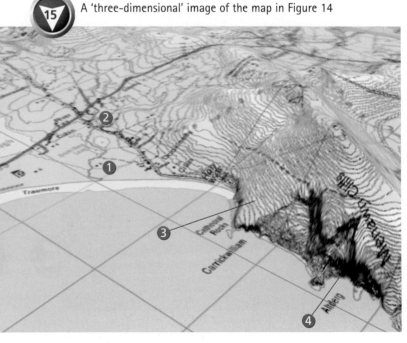

An OS map showing part of Achill Island

A 'three-dimensional' image of the map in Figure 14

(a) Identify the steepness of the slope shown at each of the places labelled **1–4** in **Figure 15**.

(b) How are contours used to show those four slopes in **Figure 14**?

Types of Slope

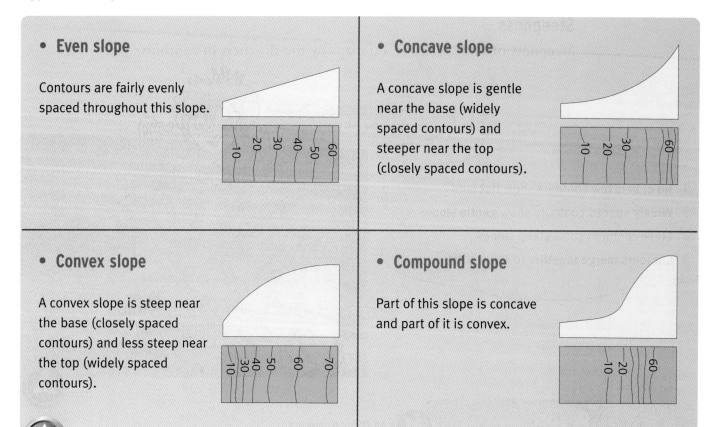

- **Even slope**

Contours are fairly evenly spaced throughout this slope.

- **Concave slope**

A concave slope is gentle near the base (widely spaced contours) and steeper near the top (closely spaced contours).

- **Convex slope**

A convex slope is steep near the base (closely spaced contours) and less steep near the top (widely spaced contours).

- **Compound slope**

Part of this slope is concave and part of it is convex.

Identify the type of slope from A to B in each of Figures 16–19.

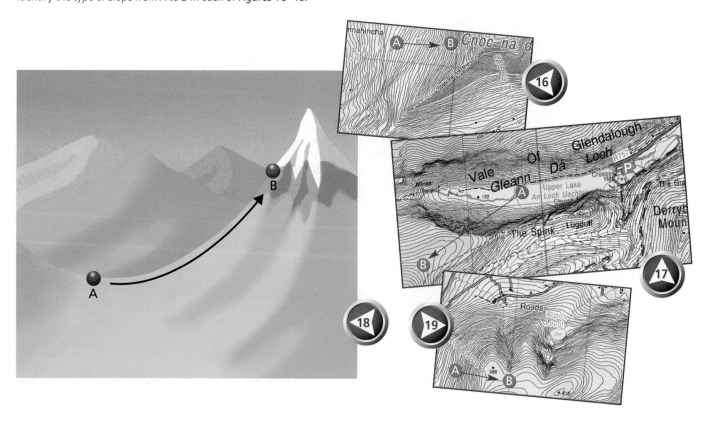

Killarney Area

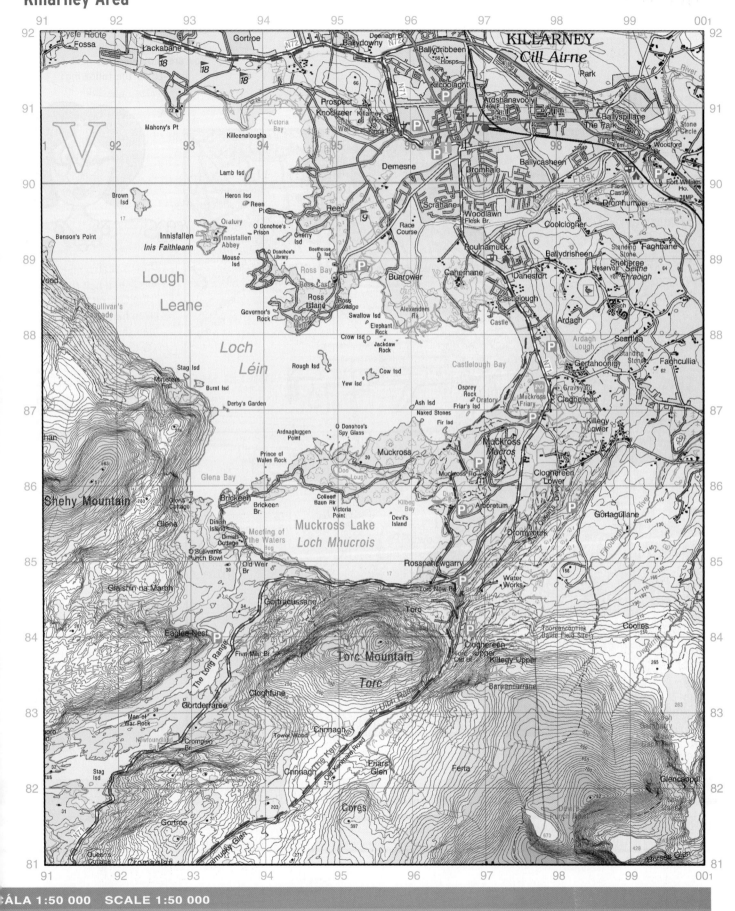

SCÁLA 1:50 000 SCALE 1:50 000

1 KILOMETRES 0 1 2 3 4 5 6 7 1 KILOMETRES 8

STATUTE MILES 0 1 2 3 4 1 STATUTE MILES 5

2 ceintiméadar sa chiliméadaf (taobh chearnog eangal) 2 centimetres to 1 kilometre (grid square side)

Drawing Sketch Maps

You may be asked to draw a sketch map of an Ordnance Survey map.
You are shown on the next page how to do the following:

Central Dublin

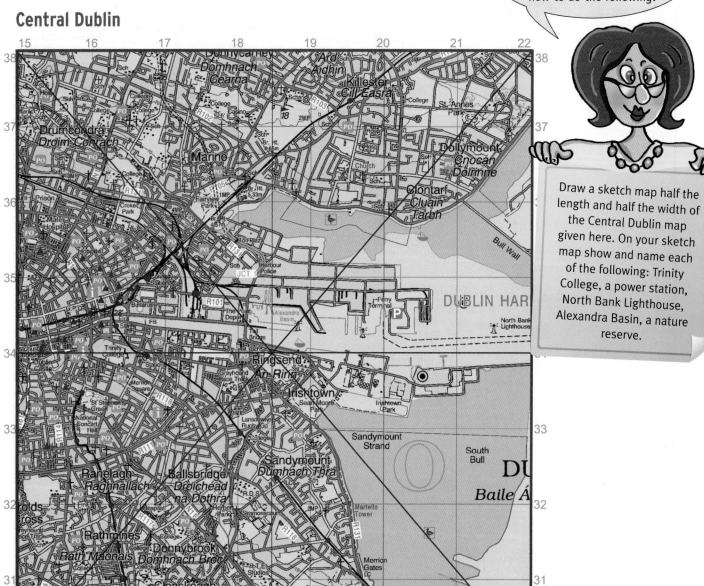

Draw a sketch map half the length and half the width of the Central Dublin map given here. On your sketch map show and name each of the following: Trinity College, a power station, North Bank Lighthouse, Alexandra Basin, a nature reserve.

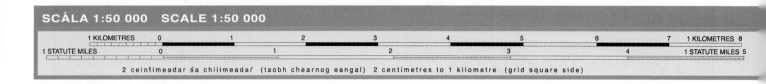

SCÁLA 1:50 000   SCALE 1:50 000

1 KILOMETRES   0   1   2   3   4   5   6   7   1 KILOMETRES 8

1 STATUTE MILES   0   1   2   3   4   1 STATUTE MILES 5

2 ceintiméadar sa chilíméadaí (taobh chearnóg eangal) 2 centimetres to 1 kilometre (grid square side)

How to Draw a Sketch Map

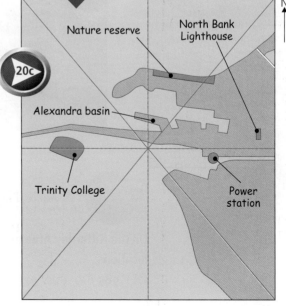

1 Draw a rectangular **frame** of the sketch, as shown in Figure 20a. Your frame must always be the same *shape* as the frame of the map. (In this case make the frame half the length and half the width of the map.)

2 Using a pencil, lightly divide both the OS map and the sketch into **segments** as shown in Figures 20b and 20c. You will use these segments to guide you when positioning features on the sketch.

3 Insert the **coastline** (if any) on the sketch. Insert and name the other **required features**, omitting any unnecessary details (Figure 20c).

4 Give the sketch a **title**. Indicate **north** with a direction arrow near the sketch (Figure 20c).

Sketch map of Central Dublin area

Activities

1 Draw a sketch map of the **Killarney Area** map on page 133. On your sketch map show and name each of the following: Lough Leane; Innisfallen Island on Lough Leane; the River Flesk; a delta at the mouth of the River Flesk; a tarn (glacial lake) called the Devil's Punch Bowl.

2 Draw a sketch map of the **Sligo Area** map on page 148. Show and name each of the following: Sligo Harbour; the highest point on the map; Sligo town; the N4 and N15 roads; a nature reserve; a golf course.

Relief

Relief refers to the **shape of the land surface**. Study the definitions of the relief features labelled A to I in the table below.

Some of the features labelled in the box appear on the photograph and map in Figures 21a and 21b. Using a pencil, write in the appropriate blank spaces the label for each feature shown.

Relief Features

A.	**Mountain**	A steep-sided landform, usually over 400 metres in height
B.	**Hill**	A steep-sided landform, usually less than 400 metres in height
C.	**Ridge**	A long, narrow area of high land
D.	**Col**	A dip or gap between two areas of high land
E.	**Spur**	A protruding (sticking out) piece of high ground
F.	**Valley**	A long, narrow depression, usually occupied by a river
G.	**Estuary**	The part of a river mouth which is tidal
H.	**Bay**	A large coastal inlet
I.	**Headland**	A cliff-like area jutting into the sea

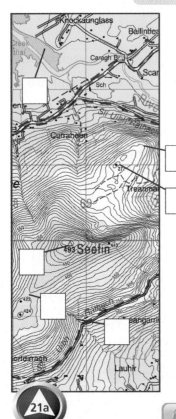

21b
A mountainous, coastal area in Co. Mayo

21a

A mountainous, coastal area in Co. Kerry

Activities

On the **Killarney Area** map on page 133 identify the relief features at each of the following locations:

(a) V 985 819 (b) V 973 877 (c) V 912 893 (d) V 942 835 (e) V 956 820.

Water Features and Drainage

Here are the **symbols** for water features used in 1:50,000 OS maps.

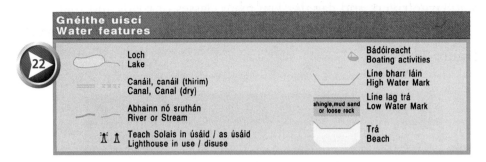

Drainage

Drainage refers to the way and the extent to which water flows off the land surface. It refers especially to **rivers**, **lakes** and **marshes**. Study the drainage features labelled in the box.

The features labelled in the box appear on the map in Figure 23. Using a pencil, write in the appropriate blank spaces the label of each feature shown.

Drainage features

A.	**Well-drained area**	An area containing a rather straight river or rivers
B.	**Poorly drained area**	An area with a lot of surface water, containing marshes, bogs or many lakes
C.	**Tributary**	A smaller river that joins a larger one
D.	**V-shaped valley**	A valley with steep sides and a narrow floor which was eroded by a young river
E.	**Flood plain**	Flat, low-lying land at the sides of an old river. River flooding may result in an absence of houses
F.	**Meander**	A large curve in the course of a river

 Activities

Using the **Sligo Area** map on page 148, give a four-figure grid reference for each of five different drainage features shown on the map.

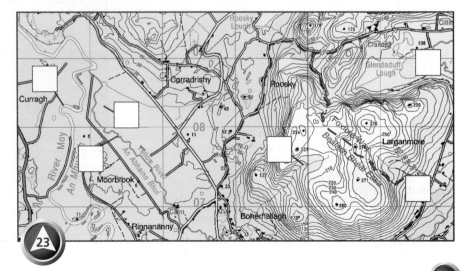

Communications

Most transport is carried out on **roads**. Other types of transport include **rail, air, sea, large rivers** and **canals**. The main classes of roads and their functions (what they do) are outlined in Figure 24. Symbols relating to railways are given in Figure 25.

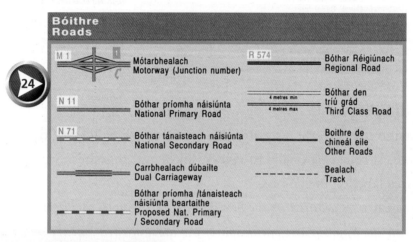

Landscape and Routeways

Relief and drainage influence routeways in a number of ways. Figure 26 gives some examples of this.

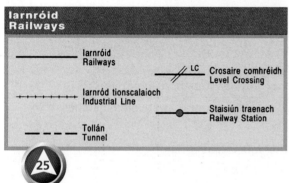

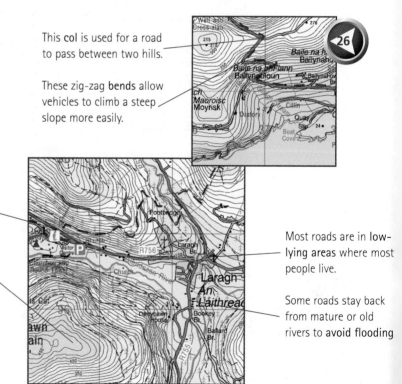

This **col** is used for a road to pass between two hills.

These zig-zag **bends** allow vehicles to climb a steep slope more easily.

This road follows a **river valley** so as to maintain a gentle gradient.

Few roads are built on **hills** because few people live there. Many hills have steep slopes and this would make road-building difficult and expensive.

Most roads are in **low-lying areas** where most people live.

Some roads stay back from mature or old rivers to **avoid flooding**

Describe how relief influences roads on the **Killarney Area** map on page 133.

Antiquities

Defence/Homes

Pre-Norman times
- Crannog (ancient lake dwelling)
- Clochan (a cluster of dwellings)
- Ring Fort
- Dun
- Lios
- Rath
- Hill Fort
- Promontory Fort (on a headland)
- Round Tower

Norman times
- Motte and Bailey (type of castle)
- Castle

Burial Places

Pre-Norman times
- Megalithic Tomb
- Dolmen
- Cromlech
- Standing Stone
- Cairn
- Mound
- Riolig
- Graveyard
- Ogham Stone
- Standing Stone/Gallaun

Religious

Pre-Norman
- Stone Circle
- Holy Well
- Cillin

Norman and later
- Friary
- Abbey
- Mass Rock
- Church

- Battlefield

Settlement

A settlement is a place where people live. In this section we will study settlement under the following headings:

- **Former settlement** – refers to ancient or historic sites of human settlement.
- **Rural settlement** – includes isolated houses and small villages.
- **Urban settlement** – refers to cities and towns.
- **Placenames** – we shall examine the meanings of common names of places.

Former Settlement

Former or ancient settlement is shown on maps by the presence of **antiquities**. These are shown and named in red print. Some common antiquities are listed in the box on the left.

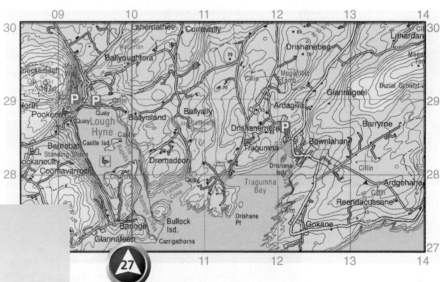

27 What evidence of former settlement do you find on this map? What does the evidence suggest about the way of life or the beliefs of the people who once lived here?

Describe the former settlement shown here.

Identify evidence of ancient settlement at each of the following locations on the **Killarney Area** map (page 133):
(a) V 934 893 (b) V 971 882
(c) V 997 906 (d) V 988 868.

Rural (Country) Settlement

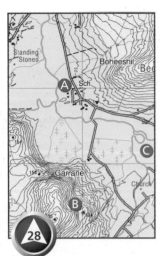

28

Explain why people live in the area labelled A, but not in the areas labelled B or C.

Density of settlement refers to the number of houses per square kilometre in any area.

Factors that affect the density or the location of rural settlement:

- **Altitude** – Altitude is height above sea level. Most people live on land below 200 metres (coloured green on OS maps). Land above that is often too cold or too windy to attract much settlement.

- **Slope** – Most people live on flat or fairly gently sloping land, where it is easier to farm and to build roads and houses.

- **Aspect** – Aspect is the direction in which a slope faces. South-facing slopes get most heat from the sun and so may favour settlement.

- **Drainage** – Well-drained land is more suitable to settlement than poorly drained land, which may be marshy or liable to flood.

Give two reasons why the area labelled A has no human settlement and two reasons why the area labelled B has settlement.

Rural Settlement Patterns

Settlement pattern refers to the general shape or pattern in which houses are distributed. Rural settlements may form the three general patterns shown below.

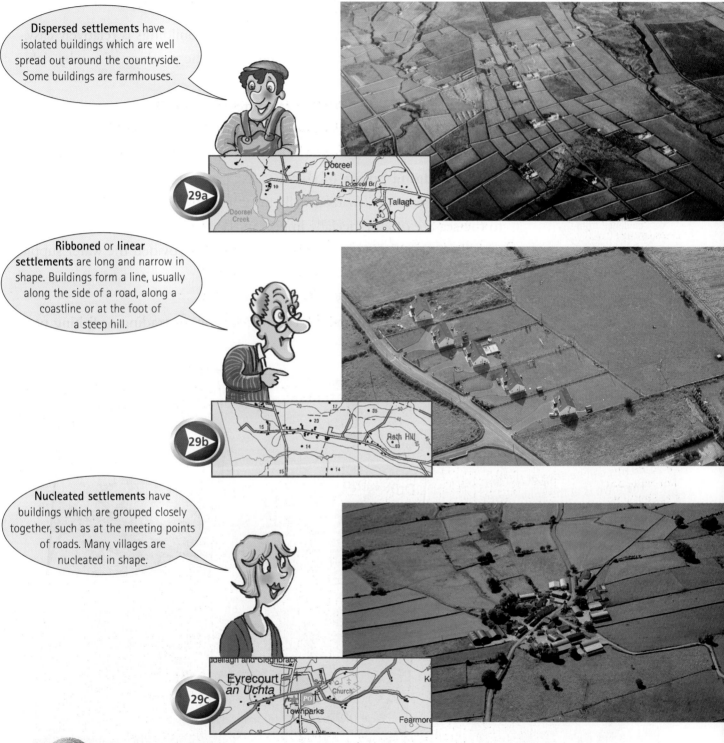

Dispersed settlements have isolated buildings which are well spread out around the countryside. Some buildings are farmhouses.

29a

Ribboned or **linear settlements** are long and narrow in shape. Buildings form a line, usually along the side of a road, along a coastline or at the foot of a steep hill.

29b

Nucleated settlements have buildings which are grouped closely together, such as at the meeting points of roads. Many villages are nucleated in shape.

29c

Activities

Identify the general settlement pattern at the following places in the **Sligo Area** map on page 148:
(a) G 65 35; (b) 64 44; (c) G 63 41.

Urban Settlement

The Location of Towns

Most towns develop at the following locations:

- **On flat or gently sloping lowlands**

  At such places, the construction of roads and buildings is relatively easy. Towns may have become market centres for the produce of nearby rich agricultural land.

- **Where roads or other transport routes meet**

  At such places people meet together, trade may develop and settlements may grow.

- **At the bridging points of rivers**

  Where bridges exist, roads usually meet and towns develop. Bridges near to the sea are often especially important because busy coastal roads pass over them. Local rivers might in the past have provided the water supplies needed by towns.

- **At coastal locations**

  Many towns developed at coastal locations as trading or fishing ports.

When using a map to describe the location of a town always refer to actual evidence from the map.

Sample answer

The location of Drogheda (Figure 30)

Drogheda is built on gently sloping low land. For example, a spot height of 27 metres can be seen at O 079 770.

The town is at the convergence of several roads, such as the R152 and R166. There is a railway station at O 100 748.

Drogheda is at two bridging points (St Mary's Br. and Boyle Br.) of a river.

The river at Drogheda is wide and the existence of a quay at O 109 757 suggests that the river itself may once have contributed to trade in the town. The river might also have supplied water to the town in the past.

Activities

Describe the location of **Killarney** (on page 133) and of **Sligo** (on page 148). Refer to the maps in each description.

Urban Functions

The functions of towns are the **services and activities that they provide for people**. Most towns have several functions that attract people and help the towns to grow. Some, though not all, urban functions can be identified on 1:50,000 OS maps.

Function	Explanation	Clues on 1:50,000 maps
Defence (a former function)	Some towns originated near castles or towers, which were easily defended	Castles or towers in or near the town
Church (a former function)	Some towns originated near old abbeys or monasteries which once provided alms, education and health services	Monasteries, abbeys, priories or old churches in or very near the town
Market (usually a former function)	Many towns once provided markets for the produce of the surrounding countryside. Some still have co-operative marts	Well-drained lowlands nearby
Port	Commercial (cargo) ports tend to be large. Fishing ports tend to be smaller	Deep, sheltered bays or estuaries, piers, docks, lighthouses or beacons
Tourist resort	Some towns have developed largely because of the tourist opportunities they provide	**Scenic:** mountains, lakes, woodlands **Coastal:** beaches, dunes, cliffs **Cultural:** antiquities **Facilities:** caravan parks youth hostels golf courses tourist information centres
Manufacturing	Most towns contain some factories, though these are usually not shown on 1:50,000 maps. The presence of an industrial estate, which would contain several factories, is sometimes indicated.	Industrial estate (Ind Est)
Other services	Almost all towns provide a wide range of commercial services (shops, offices, etc.) and recreational services (bars, cinemas, etc.). Such services are not normally shown on 1:50,000 maps. But some services are indicated, as shown on the column to the right.	school — sch. college — coll. church — † convent — conv garda station — ★ hospital — hosp parking — P fire station — Fire Stn

 Activities

Describe four different functions or services in the town of **Bray** (Figure 3, page 126). Refer to the map in your answer.

Placenames

The origins of some places are easily discovered from their names. The name Newbridge, for example, would suggest a settlement that was founded near what was then a new bridging point of a river.

To understand the origins of many placenames, we must first know the meanings of the Irish words that make up the original meanings of the names. A list of Irish words commonly used in placenames is given below.

	Meaning
Sliabh (Slieve/Sleve)	Mountain
Cnoc (Knock)	Hill
Drom (Drum)	
Gleann (Glen)	Valley/Glen
Abhainn (Owen)	River
Áth	Crossing point of a river
Inis (Inish/Inch)	Island
Carraig (Carrick)	Rock
Baile (Bally)	Small settlement
Teampaill (Temple)	Church
Cill (Kil)	Church
Mainistir (Monaster)	Monastery
Ros (ross)	Wood
Lios (Lis)	
Dún (Doon)	Ancient fort
Rath	
Caher	

	Meaning
...**mór** (more)	Large
...**beag** (beg)	Small
...**ín** (een)	Little
...**ard**	High
...**dubh** (duff)	Black
...**buí** (boy)	Yellow
...**rua** (roe)	Red/brown
...**gorm**	Blue
...**sean** (shan/shane)	Old

> The placename Shankill, for example, appears to come from the words 'sean' (old) and 'cil' (church). Shankill may have developed on or near the site of an old church.

Activities

1. Suggest origins for each of the following placenames: Ardmore; Carrick on Shannon; Ballyduff; Killybegs; Owenboy; Caher; Kilkenny; Templemore; Knockgorm; Dunmore.

2. Attempt to explain the origins of each of the following placenames given in the map of the **Sligo Area** (page 148): Drumcliff (G 67 41); Rathcormack (G 68 41); Castletown (G 67 43).

Recreation, Tourism and Maps

Many tourist or recreational features and facilities can be found on Ordnance Survey maps.

Remember:
When describing tourist attractions:

1. *Name* a feature that would attract tourists.
2. Use a grid reference to *locate* this feature.
3. Explain *why* the feature named would attract tourists.

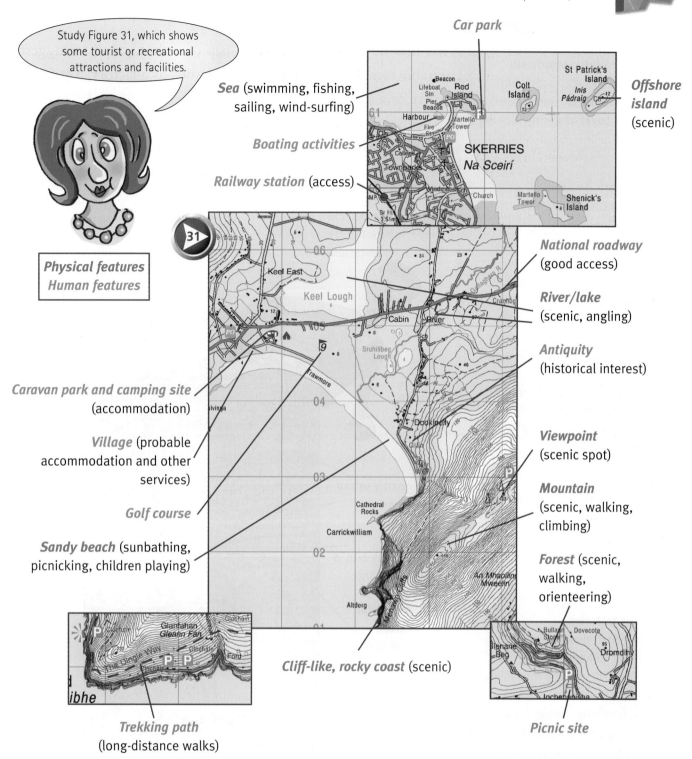

Study Figure 31, which shows some tourist or recreational attractions and facilities.

Physical features
Human features

Car park

Sea (swimming, fishing, sailing, wind-surfing)

Boating activities

Railway station (access)

Offshore island (scenic)

SKERRIES
Na Sceirí

National roadway (good access)

River/lake (scenic, angling)

Antiquity (historical interest)

Viewpoint (scenic spot)

Mountain (scenic, walking, climbing)

Forest (scenic, walking, orienteering)

Caravan park and camping site (accommodation)

Village (probable accommodation and other services)

Golf course

Sandy beach (sunbathing, picnicking, children playing)

Cliff-like, rocky coast (scenic)

Picnic site

Trekking path (long-distance walks)

Activities

1. Examine the **Killarney Area** map on page 133. Describe some human and physical features that might attract tourists to the area represented by the map.

2. Examine the **Sligo Area** map on page 148. Describe four reasons why Rosses Point might make a good holiday base for a family of people with different recreational interests.

Locating a factory

1 Site

Choose a **large empty site** for buildings, car parks and any future expansion of the factory. **Level or gently sloping ground** is best, because it is easier (and cheaper) to develop.

2 Transport

Good **roads** (or a **railway station**) nearby could bring raw materials to and finished products from the factory. Workers will also use road and possibly rail transport.

A large **port** nearby might make it easier to import raw materials or to export finished products.

A nearby **airport** might be useful for the movement of management staff or of light, valuable products.

3 Town

A nearby town would provide **workers** (but a factory *within* a town might look ugly. It would also add to traffic congestion, noise pollution and air pollution).

4 Other factories

Other factories nearby might provide **linkages** with a new factory. This means they might provide it with raw material or with a nearby market for its products. Many modern factories are now located in **industrial estates** on the outskirts of urban areas.

Locating Large Buildings

You may be asked to use an OS map or a photograph to suggest a suitable location for a large building, such as a factory, a leisure centre or a school.

Consider the factors listed in the box to help you choose a suitable location.

Example: With the help of the map in Figure 32, explain fully why the place labelled 'X' might be a good location for a modern factory.

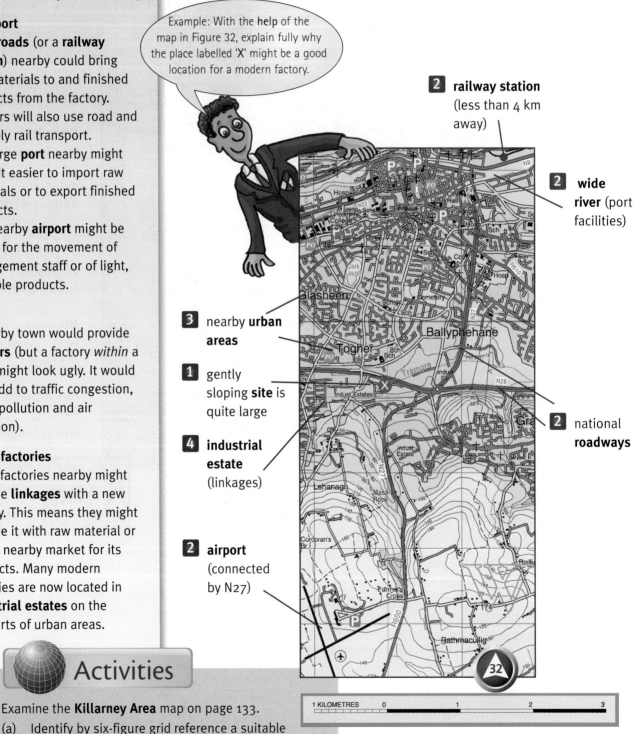

2 railway station (less than 4 km away)

2 wide river (port facilities)

3 nearby **urban areas**

1 gently sloping **site** is quite large

4 industrial estate (linkages)

2 airport (connected by N27)

2 national **roadways**

Figure 32

Activities

Examine the **Killarney Area** map on page 133.

(a) Identify by six-figure grid reference a suitable location for a large shopping centre.

(b) Referring to the map, give three reasons why you think the location you have chosen is a good one.

1 KILOMETRES   0   1   2   3

Selecting an Industry

You may be asked to select an industry that could be built on a map (or photograph) location of your choice.

- You can usually opt for a '**computer**' factory. Computer industries are *footloose*. They can succeed in a wide variety of locations.

- You can select an industry which would **process local raw materials**. This could be a cheese or meat-processing plant in a lowland rural area or a fish-processing plant close to a busy fishing port.

Other Buildings

The factors listed on the previous page on the location of a factory can also be adapted for the location of a school, hotel, leisure centre, shopping centre or other large building. (See sample question and answer below.)

Sample question

Suggest and account for (explain) a suitable location for a large post-primary school within the map area shown in Figure 33.

Sample answer

The school could be built at S 514 566 (at Pennefatherslot).

1. There seems to be quite a large empty site. A scarcity of contours shows that the land is almost flat. This would make it easier (and cheaper) to build here.

2. An adjoining third-class road leads to larger roads such as the nearby N77. Such roads (and perhaps the nearby railway station) would allow students and teachers to travel easily to and from school.

3. Nearby suburbs, such as at S 513 569, would probably provide students for the school.

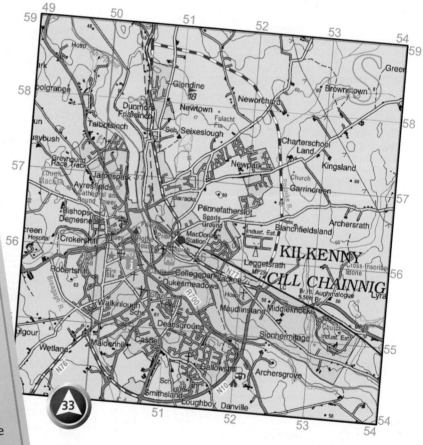

Activities

Examine the **Sligo Area** map on page 148. Describe some advantages and possible objections to building a large pharmaceutical plant factory at G 707 373.

Sligo Area

46 45

62 63 64 65 66 67 68 69 70 71

45
Ballyglilgan
Cooldrumman
27
Barrow
Keelty
466
Lissadell House
Church
Barrow
Urlar Ho.
Castle
Castletown
459
Kings Mountain
Sliabh Mor

44
Cullagh
Milltown
Cartronmore
Ballynagalliagh

43
Carney
Fearann Uí Chearnaigh
Carney River
Finned
Finned Point
Fulacht Fia
Coolbeg
Megalithic Tomb
Drumcliff
Lisl

42
Drumcliff Bay
Beacon
Curraghatee
Castle
Round Tower
High Cross
Yeats Grave
Ballynagalliagh
Br
Collinsford Br
Moated Site
G
Drumcliff
Droim Chliabh
Drumcliff River
Clooneen
Cloonderry

41
Rosses Lower
Ballinphunta
Curraghmore
Curraghnagap
Kintogher
Rathcormack
Drum

40
Bomore Point
Rosses Point
An Ros
Doonweelin
Doonierin
Tully
Springfield
Rahaberna
Kiltycooly

Deadman's Point
Sch
Pier
Hosp
Sch
Teesan
Carncash

39
Metal Man
Midden
Mound
Star-shaped Fort
Oyster Island
Beacon
Ballyweelin
Cregg
Castle
Ballincar
Ballinvoher
Lisnalurg
Shannon Oughter

38
Sligo Harbour
Shannon Eighter
Rathbraghan
Standalone Point
Horse Island
Cartron

37
Dorrins Strand
Cummeen Strand
Barrow
Gibraltar Point
Finisklin
Rathedmond
Br Ht 3.89m
Hosp
Coll
Farranaca
Bellanode
SLIGO
Sligead

36
Rinn
Cartron
Scardan
Barrow
Knappagh More
Sch
Rathquarter
Br Ht 4.03m
Abbey
Fire Stn
Minehead
Garvoge

35
Tully
Lecarrow
Rathonoragh
Ballydoogan
Mound
Stone Row
Standing Stone
Magheraboy
An Machaire Buí
Racecourse

34
Rathcarrick
Drinaghan
Barnasrahy
Tobernaveen
Barrows
Derrydarragh
Caltragh
Cleaveragh De
Megalithic Tomb
Maeve's Cairn
327
Knocknarea
Cnoc na Riabh
Megalithic Tomb
Slieveroe
Carrowmore Megalithic Tomb Cemetery
Grange North

62 63 64 65 66 67 68 69 70 71

1 KILOMETRES 0 1 2 3 4 5 6 7 1 KILOMETRES 8

City Street Maps and Town Plans

In the previous two chapters, we examined Ordnance Survey (OS) maps of 1:50,000 scale. In this chapter, we will examine maps of even larger scales.

- **City street maps** are made in a variety of scales, depending on the size of the area and the level of detail which the map-makers wish to show (see page 152, for example).
- **Town plans** are made to an extremely large scale of 1:1,000. They show very small areas in very great detail (see page 155).

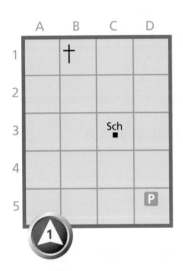

City Street Maps

Locating Places on City Street Maps

A **letter-and-number system** is normally used to give general locations on a street map.

To give a grid reference on a street map, do the following:

1 Find the **letter** across the top of the map.

2 Find the **number** on the side of the map.

3 Put the **letter and number** together to give the location of a **grid square**.

For example, in Figure 1:
- A school is located at **C3**
- A church is at **B1**
- A car park is at **D5**.

Symbols

Street maps use **symbols** to show features. These symbols and their meanings will be found in a **key** or **legend** given with each map.

Figure 2 shows some of the symbols that relate to the street map of **Dublin** shown on page 152.

Activities

Study the street map of Central and East Central Dublin on page 152.

1 Give a grid reference location for each of the following: North Wall; East Wall; St Stephen's Green.

2 Name the principal sports grounds at each of the following grid locations: E1; F3; G3.

Some symbols relating to the street map on page 152

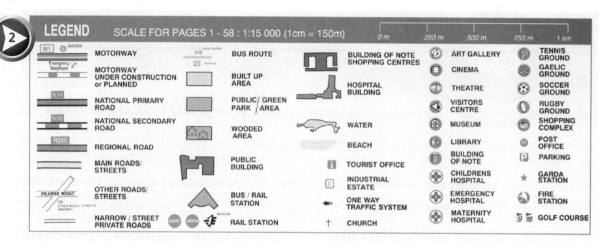

Activities

Identify and give a grid reference for each of the following features on the Dublin street map on page 152: (a) a maternity hospital south of the River Liffey; (b) a DART station north of the River Liffey; (c) a fire station south of the River Liffey.

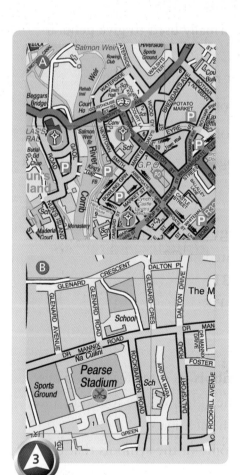

The Shapes of Urban Areas

Street maps can show whether part of an urban area is unplanned or planned.

Unplanned areas are usually **irregular** in form:
- Streets may meet at random angles.
- Individual streets may wind or may vary in width.

Some *old, inner-city areas* are often unplanned and irregular in shape.

Planned areas are laid out in **regular** shapes:
- Streets are normally straight and join other streets at right angles.
- Streets may form a grid pattern, leaving rectangular 'blocks' between them.
- Squares, ornamental parks and 'green areas' provide recreational facilities and a sense of space.

Some inner city areas were planned during the Georgian period. But planned areas are more usually found in *modern suburbs*.

Study the map extracts A and B.
(a) Contrast the shape or form of the areas shown.
(b) Which of the extracts shows the older urban area?

Merrion Square, a planned Georgian square in Dublin

(a) *How do you know that this is a planned area?*

(b) *Describe the Georgian-style buildings at the sides of the square.*

(c) *Identify the street labelled X on the photograph and the function of the buildings at Y and Z.*

Street Maps and Transport

Street maps provide very useful information on transport facilities within a city (see Figure 4).

A Streets are shown and named.

B One-way traffic systems are identified on some maps.

C Bus routes are identified on some maps.

D Parking areas are shown.

E Railway lines and stations are shown.

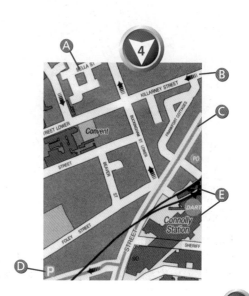

Street Map of Central and East Central Dublin

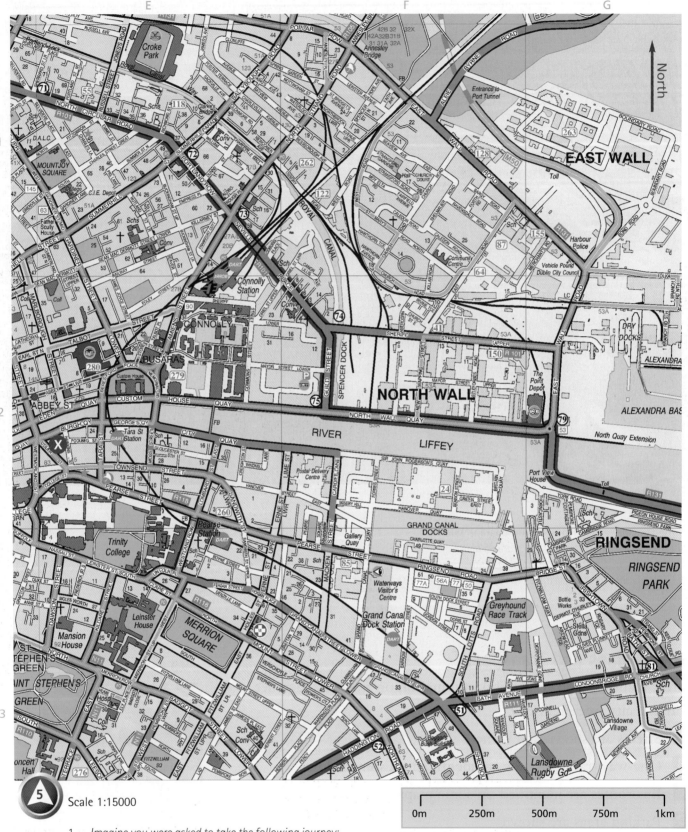

△5 Scale 1:15000

| 0m | 250m | 500m | 750m | 1km |

1. Imagine you were asked to take the following journey:
   Begin at the Custom House (E2) and follow Amiens Street. Then go northwest along Portland Row and North Circular Road.
   Turn north-northeast along Russell Street into Jones's Road.
   Which large building would then be on your right?
2. Name and locate on this map two pieces of evidence that Dublin is a sea port.
3. Name three pieces of information given on this map but not on the photograph on the page opposite.

Central and East Central Dublin

The place labelled X on this photograph is also labelled X on grid E2 of the street map on the previous page. Use the street map to help you answer the following questions:

1. Name the roads labelled A, B and C on the photograph.
2. Name the water area labelled D and the park labelled E.
3. Identify the functions of the areas labelled F and G.
4. The River Liffey is shown on the centre middleground of the photograph. In which direction does this river flow?
5. Suggest a reason for the name given to the street labelled H in the photograph.

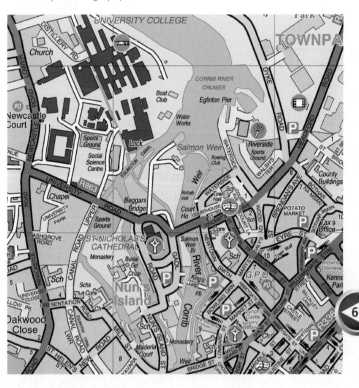

Urban Functions and Services

Street maps provide many clues about the functions or services that a city provides now or provided in the past.

- **Street names** sometimes describe (usually former) functions of an area; for example, *Abbey Street* suggests the presence or former presence of an abbey nearby.
- **Named buildings** or other structures, such as those listed in the box below, provide useful clues.

6 Part of a street map of Galway City
What clues about the functions of Galway are provided by the street names and buildings shown here?

Functions	Some buildings and structures that give clues to functions and services
Defence	*Castle, tower, town wall, town gate* (all refer to former function)
Religious	*Monastery, abbey, priory, presbytery* ('Presby'), *church, convent* (those in gothic print refer to former functions)
Manufacturing	*Factory, plant, works, creamery* (*mill* or *mill race* suggest a former function)
Market	*Market square, market house, fair green* (all former functions), *co-operative mart, creamery* (present functions)
Port	*Quay, dock, wharf, mooring post, warehouse, boat slip, lifeboat station, lighthouse, beacon* (the presence of sand or mud might suggest that the port is not now in use)
Other commercial	Most city centre streets will contain *shops, banks, offices, hotels* or other commercial buildings. These might not be named on the map
Administrative	*City corporation, county council* or *urban council buildings, town hall, municipal building*
Legal	*Courthouse, Garda station*
Medical	*Hospital, infirmary*
Educational	*School, college, academy, library, museum*
Holiday resort	*Beach, pier, hotel, caravan park, youth hostel, golf course, pitch and putt course, antiquities*
Other recreational	*Cinema, ballroom, hall, park, sports ground, library, theatre*

 Activities

Using map evidence only, describe six principal functions of the Central Dublin area shown on page 152.

Town Plans

Town plans are drawn to a very large scale of **1:1,000**. They show **very limited areas in great detail**.

 Activities

Examine the town plan in Figure 7.

1 What details can you find on this plan which could not be found in maps of smaller scales?

2 For what purposes might maps of 1:1000 scale be used?

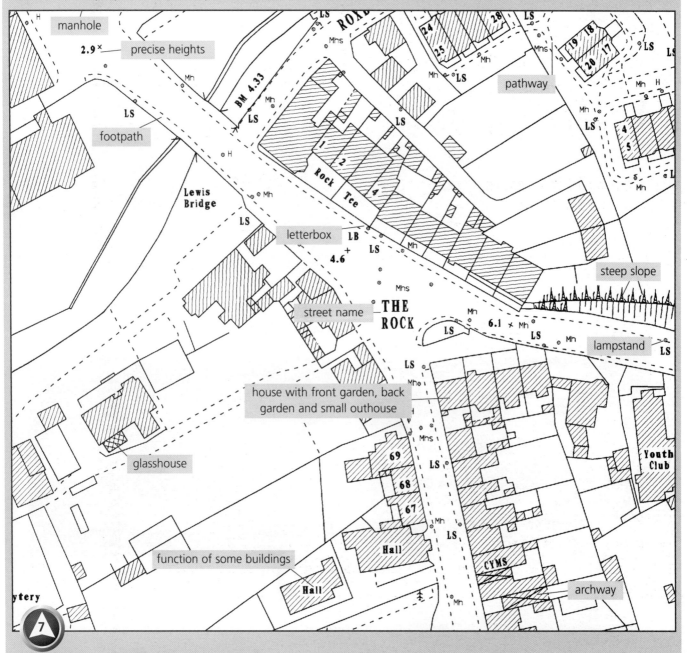

Figure 7

See Chapter 26 of your Workbook

27

Aerial Photographs

Note:
It is best to study Chapters 24 and 25 before beginning this chapter.

Types of Aerial Photograph

Aerial photographs are photographs of the land surface taken from the air. There are two broad types of aerial photographs: *vertical* and *oblique*.

- **Vertical photographs** are taken with the camera pointing *directly down* on the area being photographed (Figure 1).

- **Oblique photographs** are taken with the camera looking *down and across* at the area being photographed (Figure 2).

①

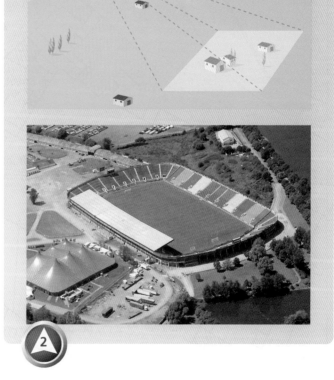

②

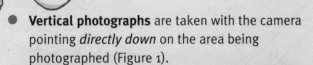

Activities

Are the following photographs vertical or oblique?

(a) Central and East Central Dublin (page 153); (b) Figure 6 (page 158); (c) Figure 8 (page 158).

Locating Places on Photographs

Vertical Photographs

Vertical photographs should be divided into nine equally sized areas, which are named as shown in Figure 3. A feature's location is described by referring to the area that it mainly occupies.

Figure 3 labels: Top Left, Top Centre, Top Right, Middle Left, Middle Centre, Middle Right, Bottom Left, Bottom Centre, Bottom Right.

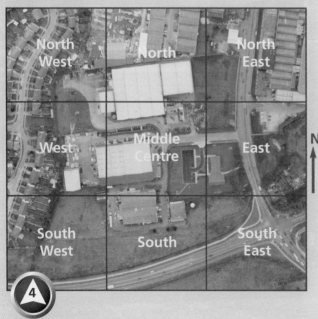

Figure 4 labels: North West, North, North East, West, Middle Centre, East, South West, South, South East.

N

Some vertical photographs will contain an **arrow** indicating north. In such cases, use *compass directions* to describe the locations of places, as shown in Figure 4.

Oblique Photographs

Oblique photographs should be divided into nine areas, as shown in Figure 5. Note that *foreground* areas are nearest to the camera. They cover small areas only, but objects on them will appear to be large. *Background* areas are furthest from the camera. They cover large areas, but objects in them will appear to be small.

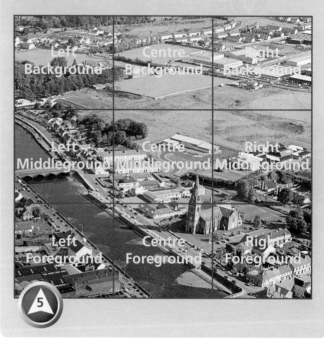

Figure 5 labels: Left Background, Centre Background, Right Background, Left Middleground, Centre Middleground, Right Middleground, Left Foreground, Centre Foreground, Right Foreground.

Activities

1. Indicate the location of each of the following features in Figure 4: road junction; a large building with a white and reddish roof; a car park.

2. Indicate the location of each of the following features in Figure 5: a church; a bridge; a group of factories.

3. Indicate the location of each of the following on the photograph of Cork on page 177: a church labelled 2; a convent labelled 4; houses labelled A.

Recognising Features on Photographs

Use the photographs on this and the
following page to help you recognise a
variety of physical and human features (the
physical features are *in italics*). Then do the
activities on page 159.

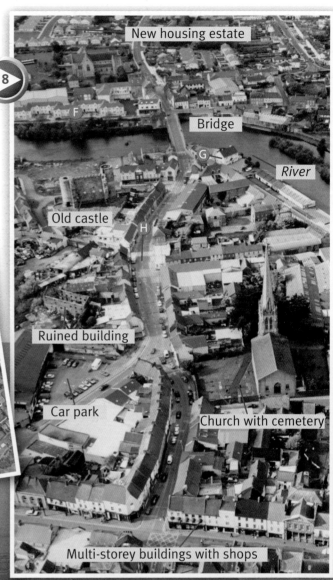

New housing estate

Bridge

River

Old castle

Ruined building

Car park

Church with cemetery

Multi-storey buildings with shops

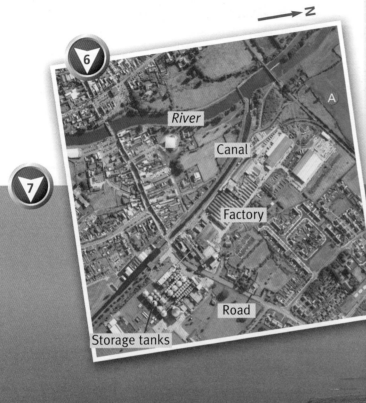

River

Canal

Factory

Road

Storage tanks

Cliffs and headland

Rocky coast

Bungalow

Bay

Pier

Small boats

Sandy beach

Caravan park

Roundabout

Single-storey house

Rough ground

Arable (tilled) field
Farmhouse
Deciduous trees
Pasture
River estuary
By-pass road
Mud/silt
Housing estate
Factory
Main shopping street

9

10

Large factory
Old bridge
Old dock
Dockside apartment building
Motte (old defence feature)

Activities

Examine the photographs Figures 6 to 10.
Match each of the features labelled **A** to **Q** on the photographs with the list of features listed in the box below. Try to make the 'easiest' matches first. Three matches have been made for you.

Feature	
Arable land	
Pasture (grassland)	
Housing estate	
Seaside hotel	
Coastline	O
Roundabout	
Riverside housing scheme or apartments	
Coastal rocks	
Street	
Terraced houses	
Riverside, detached two-storey house	
Church	
Woodland	
Small boat	P
Rough ground suitable for building	
Small river	K
Caravan park	

Colour and Photographs

Colour can help us to identify land uses and other features in aerial photographs. Observe the following from the labels on the photograph in Figures 11 and 12.

1. **Pastureland** is green. Thicker grass or unripe crops are usually of a deeper green.

2. **Trees** are usually (though not always) dark green. Conifers usually appear darker than deciduous trees.

3. **Ripe cereals** or newly cut cereals are yellowish or golden in appearance.

4. Freshly **ploughed land** is brown.

5. **Rivers, lakes** or **sea** may vary in colour from dark blue to silver, depending on how much light is reflected on them.

6. **Roads** are usually light grey.

7. **Factory roofs** are often (though not always) light in colour.

8. **Old castles and other stone buildings** are usually grey.

9. **Areas in shadow** will appear much darker than places in sunshine.

To Identify the Time of Year from Photographs

The following clues can help you to identify the approximate time of year in which a photograph has been taken:

In summertime

- *Deciduous trees and bushes* will be covered in foliage (May to October).
- Ripe *cereals* or cut hay bales may be seen in some fields (July to September).
- *Farm animals* are more likely to be grazing in the fields.

In wintertime

- *Deciduous trees and bushes* will appear to be without foliage (November to April).
- *Freshly ploughed fields* may be common (November to February).
- *Farm animals* will be absent from the fields.
- *Chimney smoke* would indicate cold weather.

Activities

1. Identify five ways in which the use of **colour** helps to identify land uses and landscape features in (a) the photograph in Figure 9, page 159; (b) the OS map on page 133.
2. At what time or **times of year** were the photographs in Figures 11 and 12 above taken? Explain your answers.

Distances and Photographs

To calculate the distance between two places shown on a photograph, we need the help of an **Ordnance Survey map** of the same area.

What to do:

1 Identify the two places on the *map*.

2 Measure the distance between the two places on the map.

Example question

Examine the photograph in Figure 13. Calculate in kilometres the distance between the tip of the pier labelled **A** and the tip of the pier labelled **B** on the photograph.

Solution

- Find the two piers in question on the Ordnance Survey map in Figure 14 (one pier is at V 990 486 and the other pier is at V 969 494).
- Use a straight edge of paper and the linear scale provided with Figure 14 to measure the distance between the two piers on the map.

You should get an answer of 2.15 kilometres

Activities

1 Calculate the distance between the tip of the pier labelled **C** on the photograph and Rabbit Island.

2 Calculate the distance between the pier labelled **C** and the headland labelled **D** on the photograph.

3 Use the map to help you name the features labelled **E** and **F** on the photograph.

Finding Camera Directions (on Vertical Photographs)

- A photograph, whether vertical or oblique, might sometimes contain **an arrow that indicates north**. You can use this as a guide to find all other directions.

- If no arrow is given you can still calculate directions with the help of an **Ordnance Survey map** of the area shown in the photograph. You can calculate the direction between places shown in the photographs simply by studying their positions on the *map*.

Activities

Examine the vertical photograph in **Figure 6** (page 158):

1 What direction is it from the place labelled **A** to the bridge on the top left (south west) of the photograph?

2 What is the direction from the 'storage tanks' label to the 'factory' label?

3 In which direction does the river flow? (Assuming that it flows from left to right.)

Example

Question: Observe the pier labelled **A** on the photograph of Wicklow Port in Figure 15. In which direction would you travel if you walked out towards the end of the pier?

Solution: Identify the pier on the map fragment in Figure 16. (It is at T 318 943.) You will see from the map that the answer to the question is **northeast or east-northeast**.

Now answer the following, with reference to Figures 15 and 16:

(a) In what direction would you travel if you walked out towards the end of the pier labelled **B** on Figure 15?

(b) What direction is it from the tip of the pier labelled **B** to the bridge labelled **C** on Figure 15?

(c) What direction is it from the bridge labelled **C** to the large ship shown by the dockside in Figure 15?

(d) In what direction does the river flow between the two bridges shown in Figure 15?

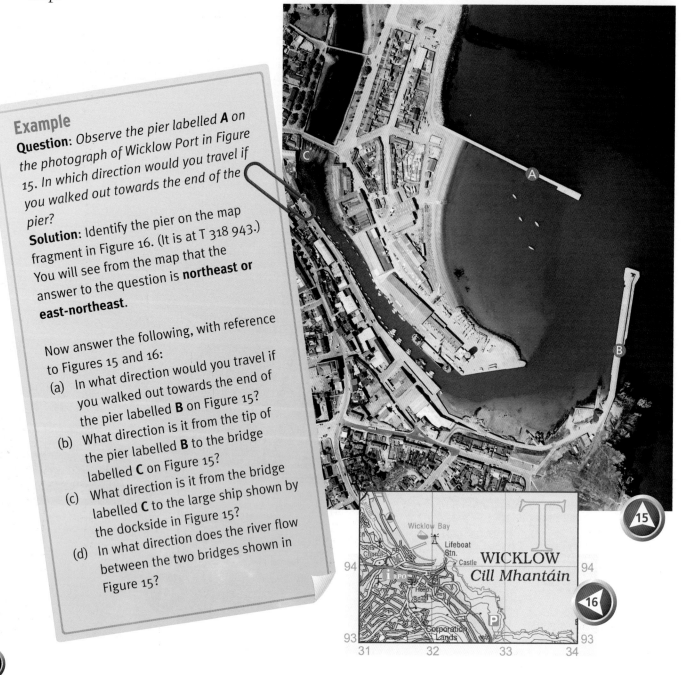

Finding Camera Directions (on Oblique Photographs)

- If a **north arrow** is given on the photograph, you can use it to find the direction in which the camera was pointing when the photograph was taken.

- If no **north arrow** is given, you can find the camera direction with the help of an **Ordnance Survey map** of the area.

    What to do:

    1 Select a prominent feature in or near the centre foreground of the **photograph.** Select another feature in the centre middleground or the centre background. Draw an *arrow line* through these features, with the arrow pointing towards the background.

    2 Find the same two features on the **Ordnance Survey map** and draw a similar *arrow-line* through them.

    3 Read the **direction** of this line from the **map**.

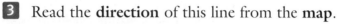

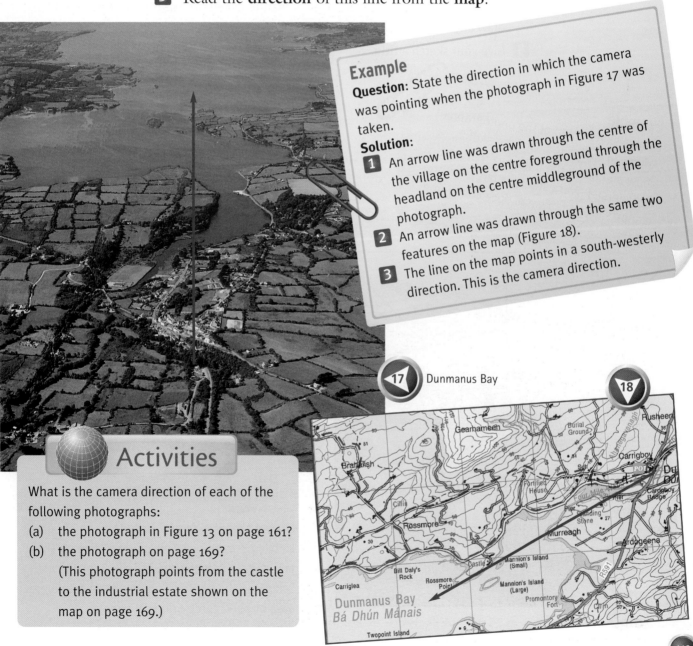

Example

Question: State the direction in which the camera was pointing when the photograph in Figure 17 was taken.

Solution:

1 An arrow line was drawn through the centre of the village on the centre foreground through the headland on the centre middleground of the photograph.

2 An arrow line was drawn through the same two features on the map (Figure 18).

3 The line on the map points in a south-westerly direction. This is the camera direction.

17 Dunmanus Bay

18

Activities

What is the camera direction of each of the following photographs:

(a) the photograph in Figure 13 on page 161?

(b) the photograph on page 169?
    (This photograph points from the castle to the industrial estate shown on the map on page 169.)

Making a Sketch Map of a Photograph

You may be asked to draw a sketch map of a photograph in order to highlight certain landscape features.

To make a sketch map:

1 Using a *pencil*, draw the **rectangular frame** of your sketch. This frame must be the *same shape* (though not necessarily the same size) as the photograph. It is usually suitable to draw a rectangle of half the length and half the breadth (which is one-quarter of the size) of the photograph.

2 Lightly divide the photograph and sketch map into **segments** (see Figures 19a and 19b). Use these segments to guide you when positioning features on your sketch.

3 Insert on your sketch the **coastline, skyline or horizon** if they appear in the photograph.

4 *Draw* the outline or boundary of **each feature asked for**. *Label* each feature. Do not draw any 'extra' features.

5 Give your sketch a **title**.

Example
Draw a sketch map of the photograph of Arklow in Figure 19a. On your sketch, show and name the following features: two piers; a river estuary; a large factory; a sports ground; a small dock containing boats.

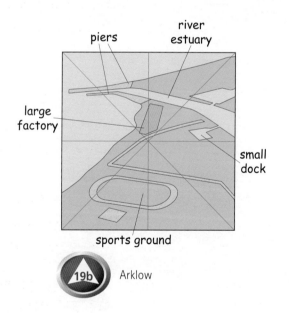
Arklow

19a Arklow

Activities

Draw a sketch map of the photograph of part of Dublin on page 153. On your sketch map, show and name the following: the river; the largest bridge on the photograph; a railway line; a green area or park; three principal streets.

Settlement and Photographs

Former (Historic) Settlement

Photographs may show evidence that people lived in an area in the past. Look out for the following clues:

- **Castles**
- **Ancient churches, monasteries, round towers** or **graveyards**
- **Ring forts** (which were ancient dwellings)
- **Dolmens** (which are stone-age burial places).

What signs of former settlement can you see in this photograph?

20

Rural Settlement

Rural settlement consists of individual houses and villages. You learned on pages 140 and 141 about the density and patterns of rural settlement. *Revise these materials.*

Urban Settlement

Many photographs contain towns or cities and you may be asked questions relating to a town's *location*, *functions*, *traffic problems* or *urban planning*.

The Locations of Towns

Factors affecting the locations of towns were described on page 142 in relation to Ordnance Survey maps. *Revise page 142.*

(a) *Describe how the following factors helped to cause the growth of the settlement shown on this photograph: the land; the roads; the river; the bridge.*

(b) *Attempt to explain why the settlement shown is built, not on the riverbank, but a little way back from the river.*

21

Refer to the photograph when answering the questions above.

Revise page 143

The Central Business District

* Most shops and other retail premises are situated in an urban area called the Central Business District (CBD). This area is usually in the town centre and, in the case of a small town, normally includes the principal street.

Town Functions (Services)

Towns develop because of the functions (services) that they provide or once provided for people. Most towns have several functions. Many of these were described on page 143.

The following is a list of some **urban functions** that might be visible on a photograph:

- **Residential** (houses)
- **Transport** (roads, rail, car parks, etc.)
- **Retail*** (shops, shopping centres, etc.)
- **Religious** (churches, abbeys, convents, etc.)
- **Industrial** (factories, industrial estates)
- **Port** (docks, cargo ships, etc.)
- **Recreational** (playing fields, tennis courts, golf courses, parks, etc.)
- **Tourism** (beaches, golf courses, caravan parks, etc.)
- **Medical** (hospitals)
- **Defence** – a former function (castles, towers, town walls)
- **Educational** (schools, colleges, etc.).

Limerick City

22

Activities

1 Identify the urban function or probable urban function of each of the buildings or areas labelled A–G on figure 22.

2 Give the location on the photograph of the city's CBD. What makes you think that the area you have identified is the CBD?

3 Explain briefly one advantage and one disadvantage of living in the CBD of an Irish city.

Traffic Problems

Traffic congestion is now a big problem in most Irish towns and cities. You can tell from aerial photographs where urban traffic congestion is most likely to happen. The following places usually have most problems:

- main **shopping streets** (the CBD)
- places **where streets become narrow**
- places **where streets meet**, such as near a bridge.

Do you think that the urban area shown here might suffer from traffic congestion? Explain your answer.

23

Traffic Solutions

The following traffic management solutions can be used to reduce traffic congestion in urban areas:

- **traffic lanes** with arrows or other markings
- **traffic lights** at busy street junctions
- **'yellow box' traffic grids**, which regulate the flow of traffic into busy junctions
- **roundabouts**, which reduce traffic delays where busy roads meet
- **parking restrictions** (watch for yellow lines along the sides of streets)
- roadside **parking places** or off-road **car parks**
- **one-way streets**
- **pedestrianised streets**, where no vehicles are allowed
- **by-pass or ring roads**, which divert traffic away from a town.

24

Describe four traffic management measures that are being used to reduce traffic problems in the area shown in this photograph.

Urban Planning

Some urban areas show evidence of being laid out in a planned way. Here are some examples of urban planning:

- There may be evidence of **traffic management** (described on page 167).

- Special **zones** (areas) may be set aside for separate functions, such as housing, industry or shopping.

- **Streets** will meet at right angles. They may sometimes form an orderly 'grid' system between 'blocks' of buildings.

- **Buildings** will be laid out in an orderly manner (as in housing estates).

- There may be parks or other **green areas**. These give a sense of space and provide places for people to relax.

- Town **squares** may serve as central, focal points for urban areas.

- **Trees** planted along the sides of streets offer greenery and shade.

Blanchardstown, Dublin

Activities

Examine the urban areas shown in Figures 25 and 26. Are these areas planned or unplanned? Explain your answer by referring to both pictures.

Kinsale, Co. Cork

Economic Activities and Photographs

By recognising features in a photograph, you can discover many of the **economic activities** that take place in the area shown. This will reveal **what many people in the area do to make their living**.

- **Primary activities** are those in which people obtain natural resources from the land or the sea. They include farming, fishing, mining and quarrying. *(Look for fields, crops, farm buildings, farm animals, fishing boats, piers, small ports, lighthouses, quarries, etc.)*

- **Secondary activities** include all kinds of manufacturing industry. *(Look for factories and industrial estates.)*

- **Tertiary activities** are those which provide useful services, such as transport, education, religion, health, recreation and tourism. *(Look for railway stations, schools, colleges, churches, hospitals, sports grounds, golf links, caravan parks, hotels, etc.)*

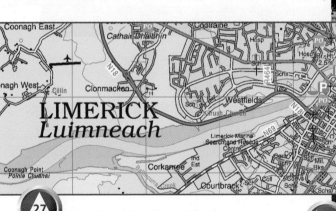

27 Part of Limerick City and its hinterland

28

 Activities

1 Show, with reference to the photograph in Figure 28, that people in the Limerick area make their living from primary, secondary and tertiary activities.

2 List evidence of some economic activities that can be seen on the map in Figure 27, but not on the photograph in Figure 28.

Recreation, Tourism and Photographs

You learned on page 145 how to recognise tourist or recreational attractions and services on Ordnance Survey maps. Similar attractions can be found in aerial photographs.

Examine the recreational and tourist attractions and services to be seen in the photograph in Figure 29.

cliff (*scenic*)

Revise page 145

sea (*swimming, sailing, fishing*)

hotel (*accommodation*)

sandy beach (*sunbathing*)

town (*shops, restaurants, bars*)

car parking facilities

amusement park

ornamental lake (*possible paddle-boat rides*)

29

Locating Large Buildings

Revise pages 146 and 147. Then do these activities.

You may be asked to use a photograph to suggest a suitable location for a large building, such as a factory, a leisure centre or a school. This and other related matters have been covered on pages 146 and 147.

Activities

Referring to the photograph of Ballina on page 173:

(a) Identify a site that you think would be suitable for building a new leisure centre.

(b) Describe two advantages that this leisure centre would bring to Ballina.

(c) Describe two objections that might be raised against the new leisure centre. Refer to the photograph in your answer.

Comparing Maps with Aerial Photographs

Maps and photographs each have special advantages in the ways in which they show landscape. Some of these advantages are shown in Figures 30 and 31 below, which show a map and a photograph of the same area.

Maps

All maps are drawn to a single *scale*, so we can calculate **distance** from them. (Only vertical photographs are to scale.)

Maps use *contours* and *spot heights* to show the precise **heights** of places.

Maps give the **names** of places.

Maps indicate the *grades* (and therefore the importance) of **roads**.

Photographs

Photographs show **features** realistically. (Maps indicate features only by means of symbols.)

Photographs can indicate weather conditions, crop growth, traffic and other **day-to-day information.**

Can you think of any advantages or disadvantages of maps or photographs that are not mentioned on this page?

Activities with Maps and Photographs

The questions in this chapter are modelled on Junior Cert examinations.

Map One – Ballina Area

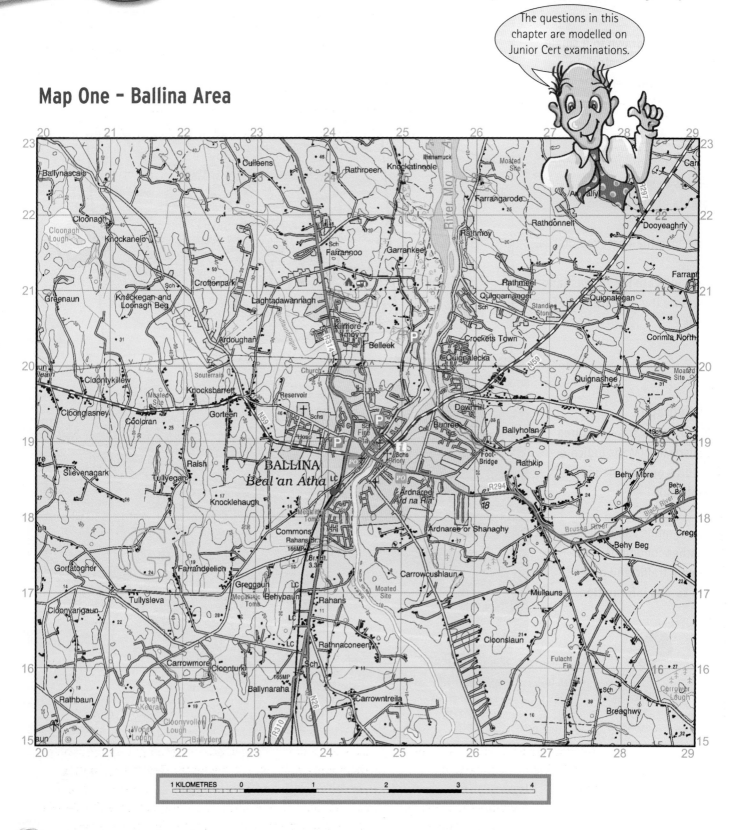

1 KILOMETRES   0   1   2   3   4

Photograph One - Ballina Area

Map One - Questions

1. Measure the distance in kilometres of the N59 roadway.
2. Suggest one reason for the low population density in grid square G 25 15 and one reason for the higher population density in grid square G 27 16.
3. Why did Ballina develop where it did? Give three explanations.
4. The town of Ballina provides a variety of services. With reference to the Ordnance Survey map, describe three of these services.
5. Referring to the map, give three different proofs of former (historic) settlement in the area shown.

Photograph One - Questions

1. Explain two ways in which the use of colour helps you to understand land use on this photograph.
2. With the help of the OS map, state the direction in which the River Moy flows between the two bridges shown on the photograph.
3. Describe three possible ways in which the river might have influenced the development of Ballina.
4. Do you think that the factories on the right background of the photograph are suitably located? Referring to the photograph, give three reasons for your point of view.
5. At what time of year was this photograph taken? Referring to the photograph, give one reason for your answer.

Map Two - West Dublin Area

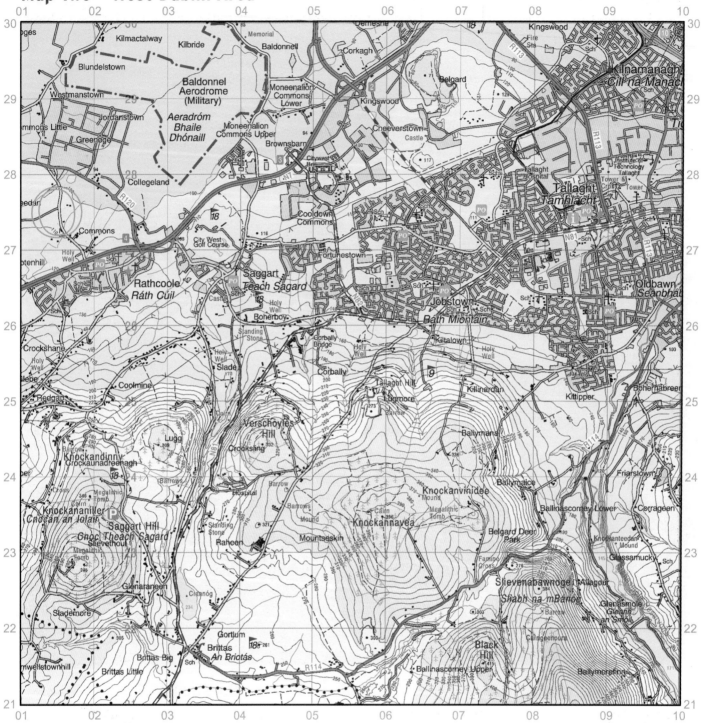

Map Two - Questions

1. What direction is it from Jobstown (O 06 26) to Kilnamanagh (O 09 29)?
2. Calculate the area represented by the map.
3. Calculate the length in kilometres of the R114 roadway between Brittas (O 032 217) and the road junction at O 099 262).
4. Name and state the height of the highest point on the map.
5. Identify the overall settlement pattern at each of the following locations (i) O 02 25; (ii) O 06 28.
6. There is no settlement at O 05 23. Suggest three reasons for this.
7. Do you think that Baldonnel Military Aerodrome (on the north west of the map) is well situated? Give two reasons for your answer.

Photograph Two - West Dublin Area

Photograph Two - Questions

1. Is this an oblique or a vertical aerial photograph?
2. The road junction that is labelled X on the photograph is located at O 090 273 on the **map of the West Dublin area** on the previous page. (a) Name and classify the road labelled **A** on the photograph. (b) What is the function of the building labelled **B** on the photograph?
3. Do you think that the building labelled **B** is well located? Referring to the photograph, give three reasons for your answer.
4. *'The area shown on the photograph is a planned urban area with plenty of services and public amenities.'* Referring to the photograph and to the **West Dublin area map**, show that the above statement is true.
5. Draw a sketch map of the photograph. On your sketch map show and name each of the following:
   (a) The R113 roadway; (b) The N81 roadway; (c) A public park; (d) A housing estate that is south of the N81 roadway; (e) A wooded area in the north east of the photograph.

Map Three - Cork

Map Three - Questions

1. Identify the feature at each of the following places on the map: (i) W 693 721; (ii) W 709 686; (iii) W 677 691.
2. Calculate in square kilometres the area represented by that part of the map which is east of Easting 70 and north of Northing 67.
3. Calculate in kilometres the shortest distance from the car park at W 665 660 to the castle at W 724 720.
4. Identify **four** methods of transport used in the Cork area. Refer in your answer to evidence on the OS map.
5. An industrial estate is located at W 71 72. Describe three advantages that this site has for an industrial estate.
6. Draw a sketch map of the map. On your sketch map show and name each of the following: the national primary roadways; a golf course; a tourist information centre in the city; an airport; a steep, north-facing slope.

Photograph Three – Cork

Photograph Three – Questions

1. With the assistance of the OS map of Cork on page 176, name the river that appears on the photograph above.
2. Describe two ways in which you think the river might have influenced or affected the development of Cork City. You may refer in your answer to the photograph and/or to the OS map on page 176.
3. Link each of the places labelled **A–C** on the photograph with each of the places listed below:
   - A place that has undergone modern redevelopment.
   - A place that was being redeveloped at the time the photograph was taken.
   - An older urban area that might be suitable for future redevelopment.
4. Suggest a function or former function for each of the buildings labelled **1–2** on the photograph.
5. Contrast the buildings labelled **3** and **4** on the photograph.

Map Four – Galway

Map Four – Questions

1. In which general direction does the River Corrib flow in the area shown on the map?
2. (a) Locate by four-figure grid references: (i) a place where settlement is generally dispersed; (ii) a place where settlement is generally ribboned (linear); (iii) a place where there is no settlement.
   (b) Explain briefly why there is no settlement in the place you identified in your answer to (iii) above.
3. *'Galway City is the focus (meeting point) of several different types of transport.'*
   Show that the above statement is true, referring to the map in your answer.
4. What evidence exists on the map to suggest that Galway City is a port?
5. Prove from the map that Galway would be a suitable tourist destination for people with a variety of leisure interests.
6. Imagine that it is proposed to build a large post-primary school at the place located at M 267 235 on the map. Describe three advantages of this site for such a development.

Photograph Four – Galway

Photograph Four – Questions

1. Is this an oblique or a vertical aerial photograph?
2. Draw a sketch map of the photograph. On your sketch map show and name each of the following features:
   (a) a river; (b) a large church in the left middleground; (c) a housing estate in the right background; (d) a green area in the right foreground.
3. Identify two ways in which Galway city uses traffic management to reduce traffic problems. Use evidence from the photograph to support your answer.
4. Outline three reasons for the development of the city of Galway. Use the Ordnance Survey map on the previous page and/or the photograph to support your answer.
5. Describe two contrasts between the urban area in the left foreground and the urban area in the right background of the photograph.
6. Was this photograph taken at a time between May and October or at a time between November and April? Refer to evidence from the photograph in your answer.

Population: A Growing Concern

The world's population has increased greatly over time. But this growth has been uneven and has included periods of decrease as well as increase (see Figure 1).

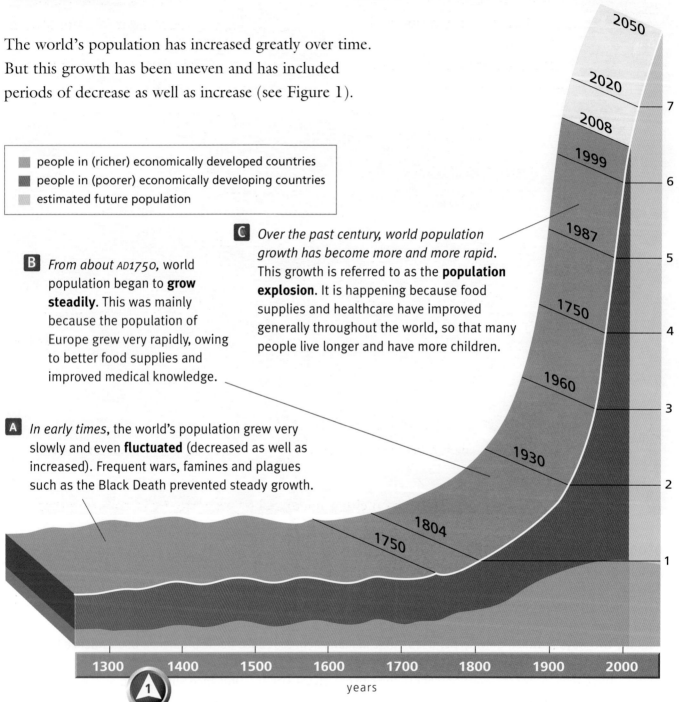

- people in (richer) economically developed countries
- people in (poorer) economically developing countries
- estimated future population

B *From about AD1750,* world population began to **grow steadily**. This was mainly because the population of Europe grew very rapidly, owing to better food supplies and improved medical knowledge.

C *Over the past century, world population growth has become more and more rapid.* This growth is referred to as the **population explosion**. It is happening because food supplies and healthcare have improved generally throughout the world, so that many people live longer and have more children.

A *In early times*, the world's population grew very slowly and even **fluctuated** (decreased as well as increased). Frequent wars, famines and plagues such as the Black Death prevented steady growth.

world population in billions (thousands of millions)

years

1 World population growth

Say whether the following statements are true or false:

(a) *The world's human population is now just over 8 billion.*

(b) *Our planet's population had periods of increase and decrease up to AD1750.*

(c) *The world's population has grown as much in the past 50 years as it did over all time before that.*

(d) *The populations of poor countries are growing much faster than the populations of rich countries.*

Calculating Population Change

Population change – called *natural change* – is calculated by measuring birth rates against death rates.

● **Birth rate** is the number of live births in one year per thousand of the population.

● **Death rate** is the number of deaths in one year per thousand of the population.

When the birth rate is greater than the death rate, a **natural increase** results.

When the death rate is greater than the birth rate, a **natural decrease** results.

For example:

If the birth rate was	22 (per thousand)
And the death rate was	12 (per thousand)
Natural increase would be	10 (per thousand)

For example:

If the birth rate was	17 (per thousand)
And the death rate was	21 (per thousand)
Natural decrease would be	4 (per thousand)

Birth rates and death rates in two countries

Country	Birth rate	Death rate
● Brazil	16.3	6.9
● Germany	8.9	10.7

(a) Calculate the natural change in each of these countries.
(b) Which of these countries is a rich, First World country?

Changes in Population Growth

Population change has been and continues to be very uneven throughout the world.

● In the past, population either fluctuated or **grew slowly** in countries that were *very underdeveloped* economically.

● Population growth is now **very rapid** in many *developing* (Third World) countries.

● Population growth is **very slow** in rich, *developed* countries. Some developed countries show a natural decrease in population.

Trends such as these have led geographers to the following idea:

As the economy of a country develops, its population may first grow very slowly, then very rapidly and finally very slowly or not at all.

This idea is called **demographic transition** or the **population cycle**.

Geographers have drawn up a simplified diagram called a **model** to show how these changes take place. The *Demographic Transition Model* is shown in Figure 3.

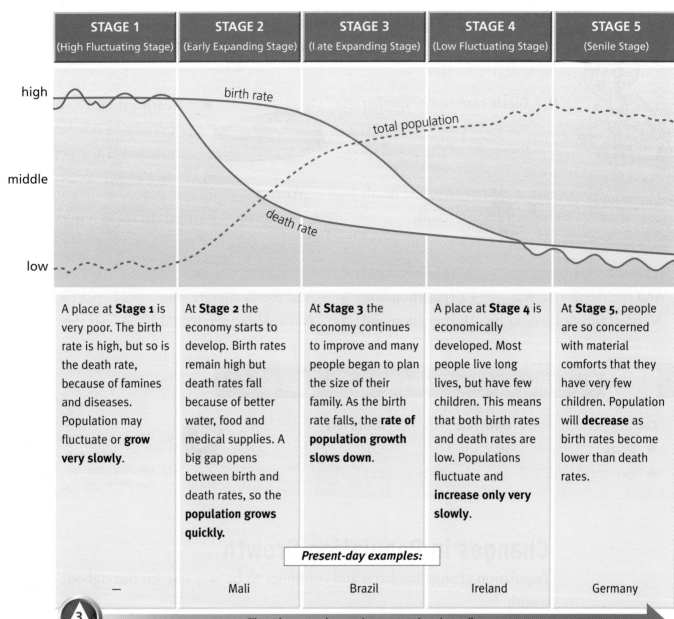

STAGE 1 (High Fluctuating Stage)	STAGE 2 (Early Expanding Stage)	STAGE 3 (Late Expanding Stage)	STAGE 4 (Low Fluctuating Stage)	STAGE 5 (Senile Stage)
A place at **Stage 1** is very poor. The birth rate is high, but so is the death rate, because of famines and diseases. Population may fluctuate or **grow very slowly**.	At **Stage 2** the economy starts to develop. Birth rates remain high but death rates fall because of better water, food and medical supplies. A big gap opens between birth and death rates, so the **population grows quickly.**	At **Stage 3** the economy continues to improve and many people began to plan the size of their family. As the birth rate falls, the **rate of population growth slows down.**	A place at **Stage 4** is economically developed. Most people live long lives, but have few children. This means that both birth rates and death rates are low. Populations fluctuate and **increase only very slowly.**	At **Stage 5**, people are so concerned with material comforts that they have very few children. Population will **decrease** as birth rates become lower than death rates.

Present-day examples:

—	Mali	Brazil	Ireland	Germany

Time (country becoming more developed)

Activities

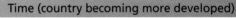

Study the model of demographic transition in Figure 3 and answer the following questions:

1. At which of the five stages is the birth rate **and** the death rate highest?
2. At which stage is the total population smallest?
3. Why do you think Stage 1 is called the 'High Fluctuating Stage'?
4. Why are Stages 2 and 3 called 'expanding' stages?
5. At which stage is the death rate declining most rapidly?
6. At which stage is the total population growing most rapidly? Why?
7. Name two differences between Stage 1 and Stage 4.
8. At which stage was Europe during the Middle Ages, when many wars, famines and plagues affected the people?
9. Into which stage do you expect Ireland to enter in the future?

Factors that Influence the Rate of Population Change

'Developed' countries such as **Ireland** and Germany experienced rapid population growth in the early nineteenth century. But they now have *little or no natural increase*. Some developed countries, such as **Germany**, are now at Stage 5 of demographic transition. They experience a slight *natural decrease* in population.

Most developing countries have rapidly increasing populations. **Brazil** is a developing country at Stage 3 of demographic transition. Its population continues to grow, though not as rapidly as in the recent past.

> **Learn!**
> **Factors that influence population change**
> - Food supplies
> - Health
> - Improved technology (better machines, etc.)
> - War
> - Education
> - The place of women in society

Food Supplies

When a country begins to develop, its food supplies usually improve. People then become healthier, live longer and so have more children. All this results in population growth.

Learn more about **Brazil's** population on page 189.

- The population of **Germany** increased rapidly at the beginning of the nineteenth century, when the 'Agricultural Revolution' resulted in improved food supplies.
- The population of **Ireland** was reduced rapidly by the Great Famine of 1845 to 1849. Food supplies for the poor collapsed when the potato crop failed and other foodstuffs continued to be exported for profit.
- In recent times, food production increased steadily in some better-off developing countries such as **Brazil**. This is partly why Brazil's population has more than trebled in the past fifty years.

When food supplies fail
Famine broke out when drought and desertification caused crops to fail in the African state of **Niger** in 2005. The population of Niger decreased suddenly as many people died. *What is meant by the terms **drought** and **desertification**?*

'If you want to measure the health of a country, count its water taps – not its hospital beds'

(a) *Attempt to explain the above statement.*

(b) *Explain as fully as you can the connection between clean water supplies and population growth.*

Health

Over the past century, **public health** has improved in many parts of the world. This has been due to better food supplies, medicines and – especially – clean water supplies. Deaths from easily curable diseases, such as measles, whooping cough and gastroenteritis (diarrhoea and vomiting) have declined as public health has improved. As death rates declined, populations grew.

- In **Ireland** and **Germany**, medical and sanitary conditions began to improve greatly about a century ago. Population increased at that time.

- Some poor **Brazilians** do not have access to clean water. As a result, many children die of illnesses such as gastroenteritis. But improved public health and health education have reduced such deaths by more than half since 1970. Brazil's population has risen as a result.

Improved Technology

Some **technology** and **machinery** helps people to **live longer** and so causes population growth. *Farm machines* such as tractors help to increase food supplies. Electric *pumps* and water treatment equipment improve water supplies and public health. *Medical equipment* and life-saving drugs also help people to live longer.

- Improved technology has helped to prolong life and to increase population growth in **Ireland** and **Germany** over the past century. **Brazil** is a country with a huge gap between rich and poor. The benefits of improved technology have therefore prolonged the lives of many but by no means all Brazilians.

War

Wars reduce populations. They cause the deaths of soldiers and civilians. They also reduce birth rates by separating husbands from their wives.

- **Germany** lost seven million people during the First and Second World Wars. These losses reduced Germany's population. Thousands of **Irish** soldiers also died during the World Wars.

- The settlement by **Brazilians** of large tracts of the Amazon Basin has resulted in the deaths of many defenceless forest people. Although war was never pursued officially against the forest people, many were murdered by invading armed colonists from other parts of Brazil.

The German city of Dresden at the end of World War Two
Explain how wars such as this can cause population change.

What is meant by the term 'literacy'?

Fact!
Ninety-nine per cent of Irish and German women, but only 87 per cent of Brazilian women, are literate.

Education

Better educational facilities often lead to lower birth rates. People who are literate (can read and write) are more likely to understand and take part in **family planning** schemes aimed at reducing birth rates. Educated women are more likely to work outside the home rather than have large families.

- In **Germany** and **Ireland**, education is compulsory and of a high standard. Many couples plan small families so that both men and women can have careers outside the home.

- Many poorer **Brazilians**, especially poorer women, receive little formal education and seldom have the option of pursuing a career. They tend instead to have large families.

Fact!
In 2008, Brazilian women had an average of 1.9 children each. This was almost as low as Irish women (1.85) and German women (1.4).

The Place of Women in Society

When women enjoy **equality** with men, they are **empowered** to make more decisions relating to their own lives and lifestyles. In general, as the decision-making power of women increases, birth rates tend to decrease.

- In countries such as **Ireland** and **Germany**, improved education and awareness of equality has resulted in general equality between males and females. Women can normally choose to use family planning and to work outside the home. This results in falling birth rates. Forty years ago, Irish mothers had an average of four children each. They now have an average of under two.

- In **Brazil**, 13 per cent of women are illiterate and some are still tied to traditional roles of marrying young and having large families. This contributes to Brazil still having a higher birth rate than either Ireland or Germany. But Brazil's birth rate has fallen rapidly in recent years, as more and more women are choosing to have fewer children.

Population Change: What of the Future?

People who study population hold different opinions on the future growth of world population.

'Pessimistic' and 'optimistic' forecasts of world population growth
What will the population of the world be in the year 2060:
(a) according to the 'pessimistic' forecast;
(b) according to the 'optimistic' forecast?

The 'pessimistic' view
Some people fear that the present world population explosion will continue for a long time. They say the world's population will double within 40 years and that terrible strain will be put on resources such as land, forests and food supplies.

The 'optimistic' view
Many scientists remember the lessons of the Demographic Transition Model (Figure 3). This model suggests that birth rates and population growth will decline as more countries move towards the later stages of economic development. This is already happening in countries such as Brazil.

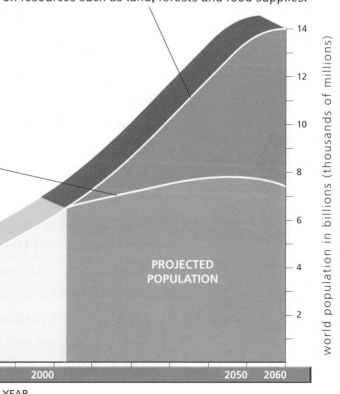

PROJECTED POPULATION

1920　1950　2000　2050　2060
YEAR

Rapid Revision

- World population has **increased unevenly over time**. In the beginning, it grew slowly and even fluctuated. Over the past century growth became ever more rapid, resulting in a population explosion.

- **Natural change** in population is calculated by measuring *birth rates* against *death rates*.

- The **Demographic Transition Model** shows that as a country develops economically, its population changes according to a fixed pattern. When a country begins to develop, death rates decline and birth rates remain high. The result is a population explosion. Following further economic growth, birth rates also decline. Population growth then slows down and finally stops.

- The following **factors** influence population change:

  ➤ As **food supplies** and **public health** improve, more people live long enough to have more children. Population increases as a result.

  ➤ **Technology,** such as farm machinery and medical equipment, has helped to reduce death rates and so to increase population growth.

  ➤ **Wars** kill people and separate husbands from wives. Population decreases as a result.

  ➤ **Education** and **equality** between males and females result in more women having careers outside the home. Birth rates decrease as a result.

- Some people take a **'pessimistic' view** of future population growth. They believe that the population explosion will continue well into the future. The **'optimistic' view** is that, as countries develop economically, their birth rates will fall. Population growth will then modify.

Activities

1 Say whether each of the following statements is *true* or *false*:

(a) The population of the world has increased steadily over time.

(b) Population increases rapidly at Stage 2 of demographic transition.

(c) Most developing countries are at Stage 2 or Stage 3 of demographic transition.

(d) The Demographic Transition Model suggests that world population will eventually stabilise.

2 The pictures show an adult literacy class and a health clinic in the developing world. Explain how such classes and clinics could contribute to population changes in developing countries.

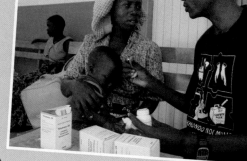

See Chapter 29 of your Workbook

Test Yourself
eTest.ie

Population Make-Up

People who study population may need to know certain things about its **structure** or make-up. They need to know:

- The **age structure** of the population. This is the proportion of people who are in different age groups.

- The **sex structure** of the population. This is the proportion of males to females.

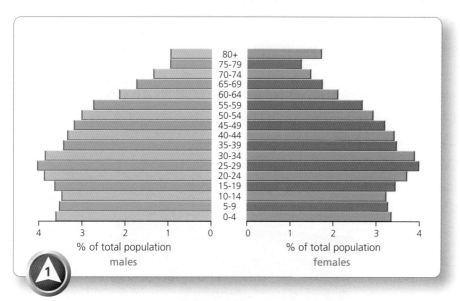

% of total population
males

% of total population
females

The best way to illustrate age and sex structures is to use a diagram called a **population pyramid**. Figure 1 shows a population pyramid for Ireland. Note the following things about it:

- The pyramid is made up of a **series of bars**. The bars are laid flat, one on top of the other.

- The length of each bar shows the percentage of the population (or sometimes the actual number of people) within a certain age group. A **scale** near the base of the pyramid lets you measure these *percentages or numbers*.

- The **youngest** group (usually 0–4 years) is placed at the **base** of the pyramid. The next youngest group (usually 5–9 years) is placed on top of this, and so on, until the **oldest** group is placed at the **top** of the pyramid.

- The bars are divided near the middle by a vertical space or line. This separates **males (on the left)** from **females (on the right)**.

 Activities

Answer the following questions related to Figure 1.

Calculate the percentage of the total population of each of the following:
(a) girls under 5;
(b) all children under 5;
(c) boys aged between 10 and 14;
(d) men over 80.

Case study 1: Contrasting Population Structures of Brazil and Germany

Figure 2 shows contrasting (differing) population pyramids for Brazil and Germany. You will see from it that some population pyramids are not actually pyramid-shaped.

- **Brazil** is a developing Third World country. It has a **growing** population.
- **Germany** is a 'developed' First World country. Its population recently became static (neither grew nor declined) and is now beginning to **decline**.

Study the differences between the population pyramids of Brazil and Germany as shown in Figure 2.

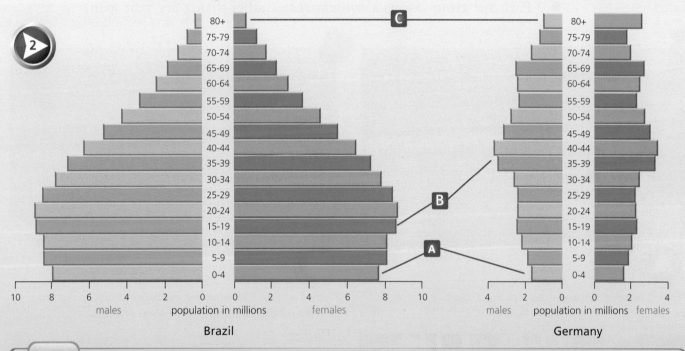

Brazil

Germany

Contrasts between the population structures of Brazil and Germany

BRAZIL

A A **high** if declining **birth rate** means that a large proportion of Brazil's population are children. This causes its population pyramid to have a fairly **broad base**.

B Most of Brazil's population is in the **lower part** of the pyramid. The country has a **young age structure**.

C Brazil has a **high death rate**, so relatively few of its people **survive to old age**. This causes its population pyramid to have a **narrow peak**.

GERMANY

A Family planning has led to a very **low and declining birth rate** in Germany. This means that a small proportion of Germany's population are children, so its population pyramid has a rather **narrow base**.

B More of Germany's population is in the **middle-to-upper part** of the pyramid. Germany has an **older population** structure than Brazil.

C Germany has a **low death rate**, so it has many old people. This causes its population pyramid to have a **broader peak**.

189

Case study 2: Population Structures of Local Areas

Population pyramids can also be drawn to show the population structures of small, local areas. The pyramids in Figures 3 and 4 (page 191) are the results of **local studies**. One shows the population structure of part of a new housing estate in Dublin. The other shows the population structure of part of a remote rural parish in the West of Ireland. Notice that these pyramids differ in two ways from the ones examined already.

- Each bar shows the *actual number* (rather than the percentage or millions) of people in each age group.
- Each age group covers a *ten-year span* (rather than a five-year span).

New housing estate – factfile

Young couples, many of whom have children, occupy most houses. Birth rates and the proportion of young people in the area are high.

There is a small proportion of elderly people in the area.

Figure 3 on page 191 shows the population structure of a small part of a **new housing estate** in Dublin.

Remote rural parish – factfile

Many young adults have left this area to live in towns or cities. Birth rates and the proportion of young people in the area are therefore low.

There is a high proportion of elderly people in the area. Some of them are (male) bachelor farmers.

Figure 4 on page 191 shows the population structure of a small part of a **remote rural parish** in the West of Ireland.

Scene of local study in housing estate

Scene of local study in remote rural parish

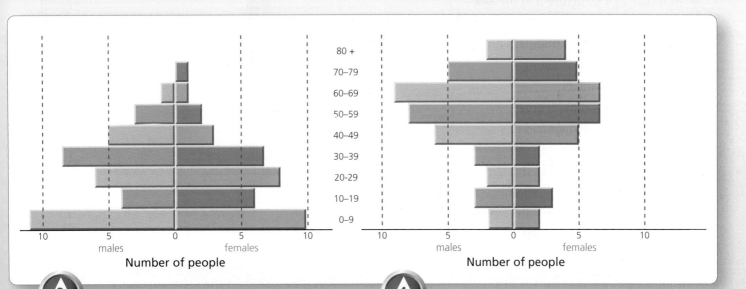

Number of people — males / females (left figure)

Number of people — males / females (right figure)

3

Population pyramid for part of a new housing estate in Dublin

(a) How many children under the age of 10 live in the area represented by Figure 3?

(b) In your opinion, why are there fewer children aged between 10 and 19 than there are aged between 0 and 9?

(c) How many men over the age of 50 live in this area?

4

Population pyramid for part of a remote rural parish in the West of Ireland

(a) What is the sex ratio (sex structure) of people between the ages of 10 and 19?

(b) On average, Irish women tend to live longer than Irish men. To what extent is this shown in Figure 4?

(c) Describe three contrasts between the population structures in Figures 3 and 4.

Uses of population pyramids

Population pyramids provide useful information for **political leaders** and **planners**. For example:

● A pyramid with a **broad base** shows a high birth rate. This means that more money might soon be needed for *education*.

● Workers between the ages of 19 and 60 pay most tax. If a large proportion of the population is between these ages, it will be easier for the government to raise the *taxes* it needs.

● A pyramid with a **broad top** shows a large proportion of older people. More money might be needed for *pensions and health care*.

Ireland's population structure is now 'greying'. Its proportion of older people is getting larger. How might this affect government spending in the future?

Rapid Revision

A **population pyramid** can be used to show the **age structure** and the **sex structure** of an area.

Places with different population structures have contrasting population pyramids.

- **Brazil** has a rapidly growing population. Its pyramid has a broad base and a narrow top.
- **Germany** has an almost static population. Its population pyramid has a much narrower base and wider top than that of Brazil.

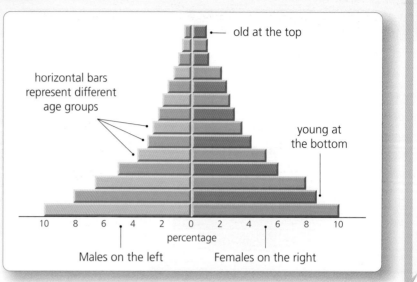

old at the top

horizontal bars represent different age groups

young at the bottom

| 10 | 8 | 6 | 4 | 2 | 0 | 2 | 4 | 6 | 8 | 10 |

percentage

Males on the left   Females on the right

See Chapter 30 of your Workbook

Activities

A

X

Y

(a) Match each of the photographs A and B with the appropriate population pyramid X or Y.

(b) What is the principal difference between the population structures of the two places shown on the photographs?

(c) Try to explain this difference.

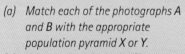

B

31

People on the Move

Throughout history and at the present time, people have **migrated** or moved from one place to another to live. Migration takes place on different scales. Some people migrate small distances within the same country. Other *international migrants* move great distances to foreign lands.

Begin your study of human emigration by learning the terms that appear on the border of this page.

These people, fleeing from persecution or severe hardships in their home country, are seeking permission to live in Ireland

(a) Which of the terms given in the border of this page best describes the people shown?

(b) Has anyone in your family migrated to another country? If so, to where and why?

- **Migrant:** One who moves from one place to live in another place.

- **Internal migrant:** One who migrates from one part to another part of the same country.

- **Immigrant:** One who migrates into a country.

- **Emigrant:** One who migrates out of a country.

- **Refugee:** An immigrant who gets special permission to live in a country because they are being persecuted in their own country.

- **Asylum seeker:** An immigrant who applies for permission to be accepted as a refugee.

- **Individual migrations:** Migrations that are planned and carried out by the migrants themselves. Most migrations are individual migrations.

- **Organised migrations:** Migrations that are planned and carried out by governments or other powerful groups.

Why People Migrate – Push and Pull Factors

A combination of reasons usually causes people to migrate. These reasons are divided broadly into *push factors* and *pull factors*.

- **Push factors**: People may decide to leave a place if they dislike certain things about it. These unattractive things are called push factors or **repellent reasons** for migration.

- **Pull factors**: People may migrate to a place because they think that certain things about it are attractive. These things are called pull factors or **attractive reasons** for migration.

Push factors, pull factors and barriers to migration

1

- Too many people for the farmland
- War and unrest
- Cold, wet climate
- Natural disasters such as floods and earthquakes
- Friends and family left behind
- Severe pollution
- Famine
- Lively social life
- Warm and sunny climate
- Religious or racial persecution
- Fear of the unknown
- Good job opportunities
- A promise of freedom
- Better schools, colleges and other services
- Overcrowding
- Good housing
- High cost of travel
- Government immigration laws
- Unemployment and under-employment
- A shortage of educational facilities

Push factors Repellent reasons for migration	**Barriers to migration**	**Pull factors** Attractive reasons for migration
• _____	• _____	• _____
• _____	• _____	• _____
• _____	• _____	• _____
• _____	• _____	• _____
• _____		• _____
• _____		• _____
• _____		• _____
• _____		
• _____		
• _____		

2

Copy the three boxes in Figure 2 (you may need to enlarge them). In the appropriate spaces, write the push factors for migration, the pull factors for migration and the barriers to migration named in Figure 1.

Case study of Individual Migration:
From the West of Ireland to Dublin and the United States

Many years ago, Oliver Harrington left his home in the West of Ireland to go to live in Dublin. Around the same time, other members of his family migrated to the United States. In this interview, Mr Harrington explains why.

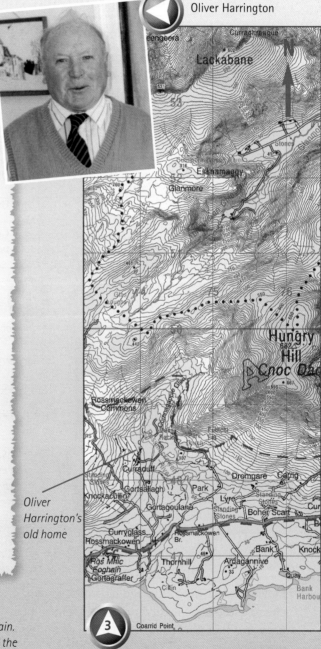

Oliver Harrington

Mr Harrington, were you born and reared in the West of Ireland?
Yes, directly beneath the mountain called Hungry Hill and close to the border between Cork and Kerry.

Why did you leave your old home?
Mainly for the work that I knew I could get in Dublin. The only employment at home in those days was to work for a farmer, but that was paid too poorly to provide a real living. In Dublin there was work available in factories and plenty of buildings being constructed. I was young and strong and I knew I would find work in the building trade there. My sisters also left home. Only my brother Joe stayed to work the family farm.

Where did your sisters go and why?
To Boston and to other cities in the United States. They went partly in search of adventure, but mainly for work. My sister, Eileen, for example, became a nurse in Boston.

Were there any other reasons that your sisters left home?
Another reason was overcrowding. Families were big in those days and there were fifteen of us crowded into our three-bedroom house. Not many families lived in the area around Hungry Hill. But the area was overpopulated, because the land could not provide for those that were there.

Oliver Harrington's old home

Answer the questions below, which relate to the interview above.
(a) Were Oliver and Eileen Harrington internal migrants or emigrants? Explain.
(b) Name two attractive reasons and two repellent reasons that influenced the migrations of Oliver and Eileen.
(c) Oliver mentioned that 'not that many lived in the area around Hungry Hill.' Why do you think that this was so? Use the map in Figure 3 to help you answer.

3

(a) Which direction is it from Oliver Harrington's old home to Hungry Hill?
(b) A shortage of services might be a push factor for migrants from rural areas. Identify one service present in the area shown on the map.

Case study of an Organised Migration:
The Plantation of Ulster

What do you already know about the Plantation of Ulster?

In Irish history, a **plantation** meant removing Irish people from their lands and replacing them with English and Scottish settlers, who were described as 'planters'.

The Plantation of Ulster began in 1609, when almost four million acres in the province of Ulster were confiscated by the king of England. Most of this land was divided into estates, which were rented cheaply to English and Scottish planters (see Figure 4).

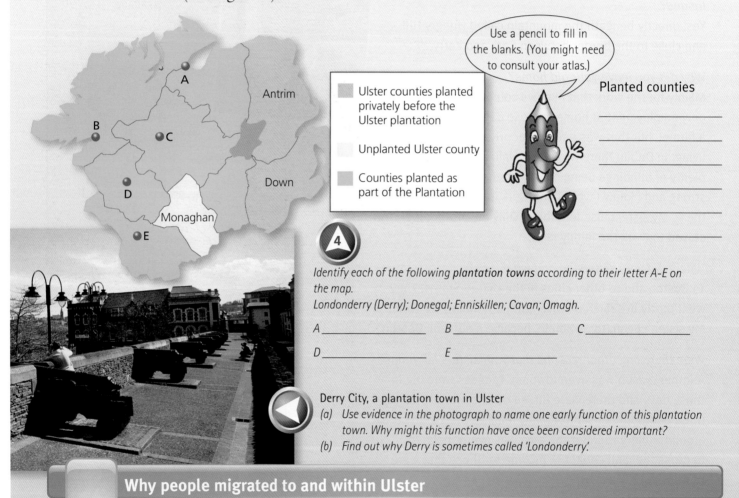

Use a pencil to fill in the blanks. (You might need to consult your atlas.)

Ulster counties planted privately before the Ulster plantation

Unplanted Ulster county

Counties planted as part of the Plantation

Planted counties

_____
_____
_____
_____
_____
_____

4

Identify each of the following *plantation towns* according to their letter A–E on the map.
Londonderry (Derry); Donegal; Enniskillen; Cavan; Omagh.

A_____   B_____   C_____

D_____   E_____

Derry City, a plantation town in Ulster
(a) Use evidence in the photograph to name one early function of this plantation town. Why might this function have once been considered important?
(b) Find out why Derry is sometimes called 'Londonderry'.

Why people migrated to and within Ulster

PULL FACTORS
- Most *planters* were attracted by promises of **cheap estates**. Scottish farmers were enticed by promises that they could rent farms cheaply from the planters.
- Some *planters* were anxious to 'civilise' Ulster by introducing **Protestantism and English culture** to the region.

PUSH FACTORS
- Parts of England and Scotland were becoming **overpopulated**, which made some *planters* willing to migrate to a new land.
- Many *Irish people* were **forced from their land** by the planters. Some were moved to smaller estates. Others hid in the forests, from where they attacked the planters.

Some Long-term Effects of the Ulster Plantation

- **Cultural effects**: The planters brought the English language and the Protestant religion to Ulster. They also introduced English farming methods, with more crop growing and less cattle farming than before.

- **Divisions**: Deep divisions developed between the Protestant settlers and the dispossessed Catholic Irish. These divisions contributed to unrest and violence in Northern Ireland up to recent times.

- **Settlement patterns**: Whereas the Irish had been rural dwellers, the settlers built towns throughout Ulster. These towns provided market centres and places of protection for the planters.

(a) *Contrast the scenes shown in these two photographs.*

(b) *How did the Ulster Plantation contribute to such a contrast?*

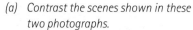

Rapid Revision

- People often **migrate** (move to live) from one area to another.

- **Push factors**, such as overcrowding, might persuade people to leave an area. **Pull factors**, such as economic opportunities, might attract people to another area.

- **Individual migrations** are planned and carried out by the migrants themselves. Many people left the West of Ireland and moved in search of economic opportunities to Dublin, to Britain or to the United States.

- The Ulster Plantation is an example of an **organised migration**. Planters from overpopulated parts of England and Scotland were attracted to Ulster by cheap land offered to them by the English government. Irish people were 'pushed' from their land by the settlers. The Plantation brought cultural changes and bitter divisions to Ulster.

See Chapter 31 of your Workbook

Test Yourself
eTest.ie

Where are the People?

1. **Population density** is the average number of people per square kilometre (km²).

2. **Population distribution** is the spread of people in any given area.

How to calculate population density

Divide $\dfrac{\text{The total population}}{\text{The total area}}$

Example:
The Republic of Ireland's population is 4,240,000. The area of the Republic is 70,283 square km. Calculate the population density of the Republic.

Our human population is distributed very unevenly throughout the world, throughout countries and even over very small areas. This chapter will examine:

● How **resources** and **terrain** (landscape) can affect population densities.

● How **social and historical factors** can affect population densities.

Resources, Terrain and Population Densities

Case Study 1: Some Population Variations within Italy

Figure 1 shows two regions in Italy which have contrasting population densities.

The **North Italian Plain** is densely populated. It has a population density of approximately 230 people per square kilometre.

Southern Italy is less densely populated. It contains an average of about 160 people per square kilometre.

Some Factors that Affect Population Distribution in Italy

North Italian Plain	Factor	Southern Italy
The north of Italy consists of an almost flat **plain**. It is covered largely in rich **alluvial soil**, which has been deposited by the River Po.	**LAND**	The Apennine Mountains dominate much of the south of Italy and some 80 per cent of the region is **mountainous**. Soil cover is thin.
Flat land, rich soil, plentiful rainfall and summer heat give rise to **prosperous agriculture**. Intensive farms provide a high yield per hectare.	**AGRICULTURE**	Mountainous land, poor soil and long, dry summers have created **difficulties for agriculture**. Many farms are small and unproductive.
Flat land has favoured the building of roads, railway lines and canals. This region has a **dense transport network**, which assists trade and encourages settlement.	**TRANSPORT**	Mountainous land has made the building of roads and railway lines **difficult and expensive**. This has discouraged communications, trade and settlement in southern Italy.
The North Italian Plain is the **industrial heart** of Italy. Milan, for example, is Italy's chief industrial and business city.	**MANUFACTURING**	A shortage of capital, communications and industrial tradition **discouraged manufacturing** in southern Italy.

The North

The South

Describe three contrasts between these scenes of northern and southern Italy.

There is more about northern and southern Italy in Chapter 69.

The Dublin region has a rapidly growing population and now contains one-third of all people in the Republic of Ireland. But population densities vary considerably throughout Co. Dublin.

The Dublin Mountains – very low density

The Dublin Mountains are a short distance from Dublin's southern suburbs. They have been preserved as an **amenity** (recreational) **zone**, so urban development on them is not allowed. They are therefore very lightly populated.

West County Dublin – high density and growing rapidly

The western fringe (edge) of Dublin has experienced very rapid population growth.

- It contains many rapidly growing outer **suburbs** such as Bluebell and Greenhills.
- Big **satellite towns** such as Tallaght, Lucan and Clondalkin have grown rapidly outside the western suburbs of the city.
- Some satellite towns serve as **dormitory** or **commuter towns** to Dublin. Many of their inhabitants work in Dublin and commute (travel) to and from the city each day.

North County Dublin – moderate density

- The expansion of city suburbs into North County Dublin has been hindered by the presence of **Dublin Airport**. It is also hindered by the fact that Fingal (North Dublin) County Council wishes to maintain **market gardening** on the fertile land of this area.
- Near to the coast, however, population densities are much higher. **Satellite towns** such as Swords have grown rapidly and are connected by Dublin by rail or by roads such as the M1.

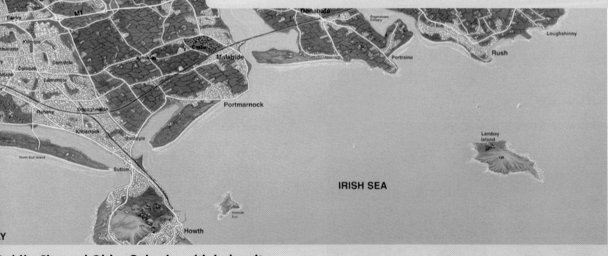

Dublin City and Older Suburbs – high density

- Dublin City is densely populated because there are many **jobs** and **services** available.
- Dublin is Ireland's leading **commercial and industrial city**.
- It is Ireland's chief **port** and is the meeting place of many principal **roads and railway lines**.
- It is our **capital city** – the city where our government meets.
- It is Ireland's biggest **education** centre, with large universities such as University College Dublin and Trinity College.
- Because of the many jobs and services that it offers, many people **migrate** to Dublin from other parts of Ireland.

How Social and Historical Factors Affect Population Densities

Case Study 1: **The West of Ireland**

Population densities in the West of Ireland **varied over time** for *social and historic reasons*. This is shown in Figure 2.

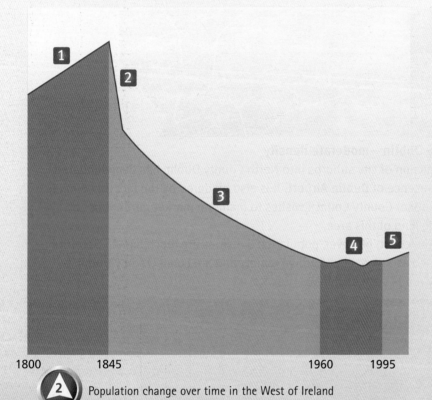

1800   1845   1960   1995

Population change over time in the West of Ireland

1. In the early nineteenth century the *population grew rapidly*. Farmers divided their farms between their sons, so that many people had access to **small plots of land**. They grew **potatoes**, which produced a large amount of food per acre.

2. Between 1845 and 1849, a disease called blight destroyed the potato crop. The **Great Famine** occurred. More than one in four people died or emigrated (left Ireland). The population *fell dramatically*.

3. After the famine, farmers began leaving their farms to their oldest sons only. Fewer people now had access to **land**. Those who had not usually emigrated. The population continued to *fall steadily*.

4. By the 1960s the economy improved and people had **more wealth**. Emigration slowed down and the population began to *stabilise* (remain fairly constant).

5. In the late 1990s Ireland's 'Celtic Tiger' economy resulted in more jobs and **much more wealth**. The population of the West began to *increase*.

Emigrants from Ireland in the 1950s
Name one cause and one effect of emigration such as this.

Population densities in the West of Ireland

You learned on page 202 that the population of the West of Ireland stabilised and began to increase in recent times. In the West, however, population is declining in some rural areas and growing rapidly in some urban centres. Reasons for this are explained below.

In some rural areas:

- The **terrain** (landscape) is hilly, rocky and boggy. Soils are often thin and infertile and **farming** is difficult and unprofitable.

- There are few local industries or services to give **employment. Entertainment** facilities are often limited.

- It is often difficult for people to get **planning permission** to build new homes in picturesque rural areas.

> Some people **migrate** from rural to urban areas:

Resources are more varied and plentiful in **large urban areas** such as Galway, Letterkenny and Tralee.

- Colleges, such as University College Galway, offer excellent **educational services.**
- **Jobs** are plentiful in offices, shops and hospitals. New industrial estates also provide factory jobs.
- Cinemas, clubs, restaurants, etc., provide **entertainment**.

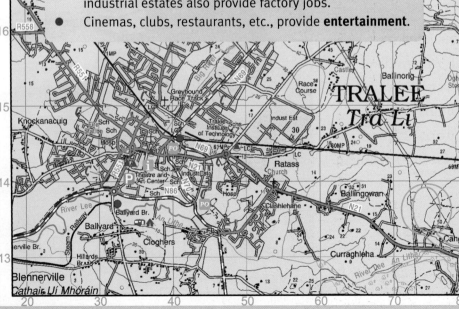

3 Tralee
Identify from this map the resources or services available in Tralee under the following headings: (a) education; (b) manufacturing; (c) recreation.

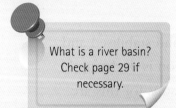
What is a river basin? Check page 29 if necessary.

The map in Figure 4 shows some population densities within Brazil. It shows that:

1 **Coastal areas are the most densely populated.**

2 **The Amazon Basin in the west is very sparsely populated.**

Equator

Amazon Basin

N

Brasilia

Rio de Janeiro

Sao Paulo

Brazil

South America

population densities
- high
- low
- very low

4

Population distribution in Brazil
Describe the population distribution shown.

Most Brazilians live near the coast for these historical reasons:

- In the sixteenth century, the **Portuguese** began to colonise Brazil. They arrived on the East Coast and set up trading towns there.
- Some trading towns eventually grew into huge **industrial cities**, such as Rio de Janeiro and Sao Paulo.
- The Portuguese set up big estates called **plantations** near the coast. They imported millions of kidnapped Africans to work as slaves on the plantations.

Why the Amazon Basin is sparsely populated

The Amazon Basin is home to local 'Amerindian' peoples, but it has not been heavily settled by European colonists. Europeans were not comfortable with the hot, wet **equatorial climate** of the region or with its **dense rainforests**. They called it the 'Green Hell' and made little attempt to settle it until the 1960s. To this day, only seven per cent of Brazil's population live in the Amazon Basin.

In which part of Brazil do you think this picture was taken?

Rapid Revision

Population density is the average number of people per square kilometre. It is calculated by dividing population by area. It varies from place to place and in the same place over time.

Population densities can vary according to the resources or terrain of areas.

- **Case Study 1**

  The **North Italian Plain** is more densely populated than **southern Italy**. The land is flatter and more fertile in the north and agriculture is more productive there. Transport networks are better developed in the north, as is manufacturing industry.

- **Case Study 2**

  Population densities vary considerably throughout **County Dublin**.

  Dublin city – the commercial, educational and administrative centre of Ireland – is very densely populated.

  West Co. Dublin contains large satellite towns such as Tallaght. Its population has grown very rapidly in recent years and its population density is high.

  North Co. Dublin has moderate density. The presence of Dublin Airport and fertile land set aside for market gardening has helped to prevent urban growth there.

  The **Dublin Mountains** keep population very low in the extreme south of Co. Dublin.

Social and historical events also affect population densities.

- **Case Study 1**

  The population of the **West of Ireland** grew rapidly before the Great Famine of 1845. During the famine, it dropped dramatically. For 100 years after that, it continued to decline due to emigration. In the 1960s, it stabilised because of improved job opportunities. In recent years it has grown somewhat.

  Population densities vary **within the West**. Some rural areas have steep terrain, poor soils and few employment opportunities. People migrate from these lightly populated areas to growing urban centres such as Galway City. Such centres provide jobs as well as educational and recreational facilities.

- **Case Study 2**

  The **coast of Brazil** is much more densely populated than the **Amazon Basin**. This is largely because Portuguese colonists settled and brought African slaves to plantations and cities in coastal areas. The Amazon Basin was not heavily settled by Europeans in the past. It contains only seven per cent of Brazil's population.

Activities

1. What is meant by the terms 'population density' and 'population distribution'?
2. (a) With reference to a country that you have studied, name one region with a high population density and one region with a low population density.

   (b) Describe and explain one reason for the high population density and one reason for the low population density. (*J.C. Higher Level*)

   See Chapter 32 of your Workbook

Some Effects of High and Low Population Densities

The population density of an area can greatly affect that area's economy and social conditions.

Some Effects of Very High Population Densities

Very high population densities may result in:

1 Overcrowding

2 Lack of open spaces

3 Shortage of clean water

4 Pollution

These problems are signs that an area is **overpopulated** – it contains more people than its resources can cope with.

Case Study 1: **Kolkata (Calcutta)**

Kolkata is one of India's largest and most densely populated cities. Its rapidly growing population now numbers more than 16 million people. That's about four times the population of the Republic of Ireland!

Much of Kolkata's population is made up of very poor people who *migrate* from rural areas into the city in search of work. These migrants usually crowd into large urban slums called **shanty towns** or **bustees** that grow up in an unplanned way around the edges of the city.

People in the overpopulated city of Kolkata face many problems, some of which are outlined on the following page.

Kolkata is situated on the delta of the River Ganges. It has grown up along a distributary of the Ganges called the River Hooghly. *What is a delta and what is a distributary? (See page 37.)*

1 Overcrowding

Kolkata is one of the world's most densely populated cities. About four million of its people are crammed into overcrowded bustees. One bustee – a place called Barabazar – contains an amazing 100,000 people per square kilometre.

- Most bustee families live in tiny **overcrowded houses**. These houses are sometimes no bigger than an average-sized Irish bathroom.
- Many people live in **temporary shacks** made from pieces of timber, canvas or plastic sheeting.
- More than half a million people have no dwellings at all. These are the **pavement people**, who live on the streets.

Learn more about
Kolkata
in Chapter 48.

Describe this Kolkata family and their dwelling.

2 Lack of Open Space

Kolkata now sprawls for more than 50 kilometres along the banks of the River Hooghly (see Figure 1). It contains very little open space. In the poorer parts of the city especially, buildings are crammed together and people occupy almost every scrap of land.

3 Shortage of Clean Water

Clean water is in short supply. Some drinking water has been poisoned by **lead** from old lead water pipes. Up to 50 people often have to share a single **water tap**. They are the lucky ones! Many pavement people have no clean water at all and are forced to drink **unfiltered water** that was intended only for street cleaning. Drinking this water often leads to serious illnesses such as *dysentery*.

4 Pollution

The poor of Kolkata live with many types of pollution:

- Toilet and kitchen waste flows through **open drains** on some streets. Heavy monsoon rains sometimes flood these drains and flush the waste all over the streets and into people's houses.
- The city cannot afford a proper rubbish collection system, so **garbage** piles up on many streets.
- Kolkata is one of the world's worst cities for **air pollution**. Fumes from motor traffic, industries and cooking fires cause widespread lung conditions such as *asthma*.

How does this Kolkata street differ from those in an Irish city?

Off the south coast of China lies the large and rapidly growing city of Hong Kong. The city occupies the north side of *Hong Kong Island* and spreads across *Kowloon* and parts of the *New Territories* on the Chinese mainland. (See Figure 2.)

Hong Kong is not as crowded as Kolkata and the city's business centre is a place of glittering lights and modern skyscrapers. But more than seven million people live in 1000km² of Hong Kong's territory. This makes it 100 times more **densely populated** than Ireland!

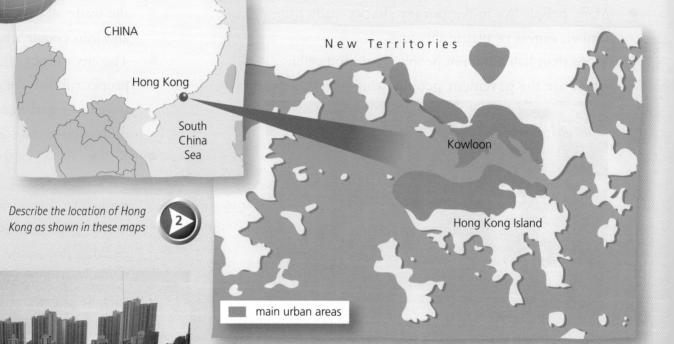

CHINA

Hong Kong

South China Sea

New Territories

Kowloon

Hong Kong Island

Describe the location of Hong Kong as shown in these maps **2**

main urban areas

1 Overcrowding

Hong Kong's population has risen rapidly as large numbers of *migrants* have flocked from rural areas into the city, resulting in severe overcrowding in many parts of the city. Homes are usually very small and most people are packed into big **high-rise apartments**. Some people even live on **houseboats** in the harbour. Many **schools** are so overcrowded that they operate a two-shift day. Some students and teachers attend from 7 a.m. to early afternoon, while others attend from early afternoon until late evening.

Houseboats in Hong Kong Harbour
(a) Why do people live in boats such as these?
(b) Explain how the presence of houseboats might affect the quality of Hong Kong's seawater.

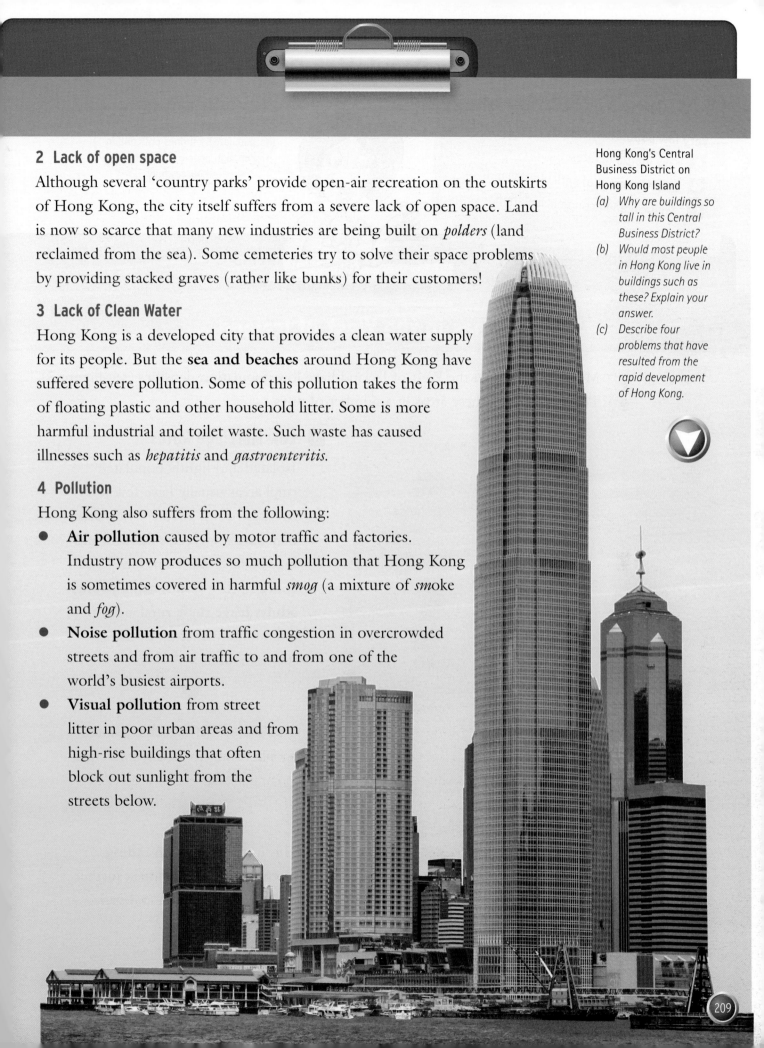

2 Lack of open space

Although several 'country parks' provide open-air recreation on the outskirts of Hong Kong, the city itself suffers from a severe lack of open space. Land is now so scarce that many new industries are being built on *polders* (land reclaimed from the sea). Some cemeteries try to solve their space problems by providing stacked graves (rather like bunks) for their customers!

3 Lack of Clean Water

Hong Kong is a developed city that provides a clean water supply for its people. But the **sea and beaches** around Hong Kong have suffered severe pollution. Some of this pollution takes the form of floating plastic and other household litter. Some is more harmful industrial and toilet waste. Such waste has caused illnesses such as *hepatitis* and *gastroenteritis*.

4 Pollution

Hong Kong also suffers from the following:

- **Air pollution** caused by motor traffic and factories. Industry now produces so much pollution that Hong Kong is sometimes covered in harmful *smog* (a mixture of *smoke* and *fog*).
- **Noise pollution** from traffic congestion in overcrowded streets and from air traffic to and from one of the world's busiest airports.
- **Visual pollution** from street litter in poor urban areas and from high-rise buildings that often block out sunlight from the streets below.

Hong Kong's Central Business District on Hong Kong Island

(a) Why are buildings so tall in this Central Business District?

(b) Would most people in Hong Kong live in buildings such as these? Explain your answer.

(c) Describe four problems that have resulted from the rapid development of Hong Kong.

209

Some Effects of Very Low Population Densities

Very low population densities may result in:

A Low marriage rates.

B Abandonment of agricultural land.

C Political and economic isolation.

These problems are signs that an area is under-populated – it does not contain enough people to develop its resources fully.

Case Study 1: **Rural Areas in the West of Ireland**

Many rural areas in the West of Ireland have low population densities (see Figure 3). This has affected these areas in a number of ways.

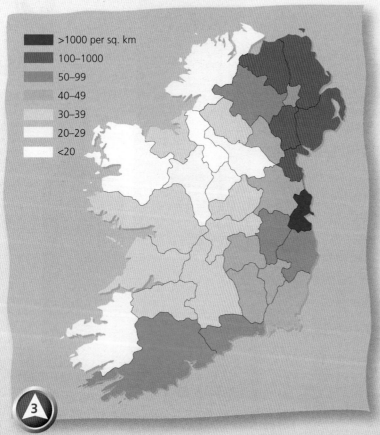

Legend:
- >1000 per sq. km
- 100–1000
- 50–99
- 40–49
- 30–39
- 20–29
- <20

3

The population densities of Irish counties

Are these statements true or false?

(a) The East of Ireland is more densely populated than the West.

(b) Ireland's least densely populated counties are both in Connacht.

(c) Co. Dublin is more than 20 times more densely populated than Co. Mayo.

A Low Marriage Rates

Isolated and lightly populated rural areas usually have **few jobs** to offer young people. They also may have few leisure facilities and may be far away from third-level colleges. As a result, many **young adults leave** these rural areas and migrate permanently to cities such as Dublin.

The loss of marriageable young people results in **fewer marriages** in rural areas.

This in turn results in **falling birth rates** and a gradual, further decline in population and social facilities.

B Abandonment of Agricultural Land

Agricultural land has been either neglected or completely abandoned in some lightly populated areas of the West. Low population densities have contributed to this in the following ways:

- Out-migration and lower marriage rates have caused population densities to fall. As a result, **fewer people** are available to work the land, so land becomes neglected or abandoned.

- It is mainly young adults who migrate from rural areas in the West. Many farms are therefore left in the care of **older people**, who do not always have the energy to work the land fully.

C Political and Economic Isolation

- Lightly populated western areas return far fewer TDs to Dáil Éireann than do densely populated areas such as Dublin (see Figure 4). The West of Ireland is also situated at the edge of the European Union and is far from the political decision-making centres of Dublin and Brussels. These factors reduce the **political influence** of western areas.

- Some remote and lightly populated areas of the West lack the labour force, roads or services needed to attract large-scale commercial or industrial development. Such areas suffer from **economic isolation**, especially since they are situated at the opposite side of Ireland to the economic core-region of Dublin.

Explain as fully as you can why people might abandon farms such as the one shown in this photograph.

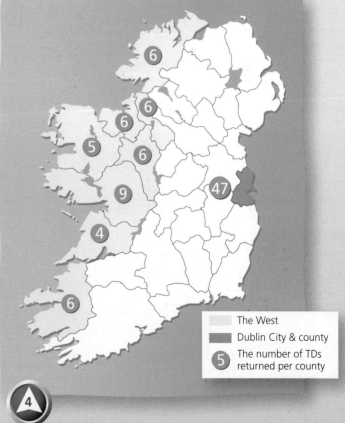

	The West
	Dublin City & county
5	The number of TDs returned per county

(a) 'Dublin has more TDs than the entire West of Ireland.' True or false?

(b) Identify the number of TDs who represent each of the following counties: Co. Kerry, Co. Mayo, Co. Clare.

(c) How might the number of TDs in an area influence its economic development?

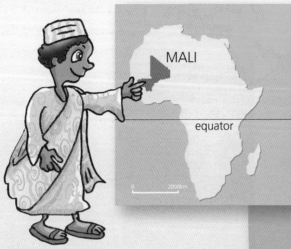

Study **Figure 5** and then decide whether the following statements are true or false.

(a) Mali is a landlocked country, which means that it has no coastline.

(b) Mali is west of Mauritania.

(c) Mali s main city – Bamako – is on the River Senegal.

(d) River water is more plentiful in the south than in the north of Mali.

(e) Northern Mali is part of the Sahel, which is on the southern edge of the Sahara Desert.

The Republic of Mali is 17 times larger than the Republic of Ireland, but it has a population of only 12 million people. This means that Mali has a **very low average population density** of less than ten people per square kilometre. In rural areas, population densities are even lower – sometimes less than one person per square kilometre. Mali's low population density has led to many **problems**, some of which are described on the next page.

(a) Why, in your opinion, is this area so lightly populated?

(b) What effects might low population density have on this area?

A Low Marriage Rates

Many young adults do not want to live in isolated, lightly populated rural areas in Mali. Thousands migrate to cities such as Bamako and Timbuktu in search of work, a better social life and better medical and other services. As is customary in many parts of Africa, it is mainly **young men** who **migrate**. This leaves a surplus of males in the cities and a surplus of females in rural areas, so it **reduces marriage opportunities** in both areas.

B Abandonment of Agricultural Land

* For more on desertification see Chapter 17

- We have seen in the previous paragraph that many **young people migrate** from lightly populated rural areas in search of work, social life and better services.
- Since the 1970s there have been particularly large-scale migrations from the north of Mali, which is part of a region known as the *Sahel*. Droughts and **desertification*** have destroyed animal herds in the Sahel and have forced thousands of hungry people to flee their lands in search of relief aid in the cities.

  Migrations such as these have resulted in severe **rural depopulation**. In many areas, there are no longer enough people left to farm the land or to care for cattle herds. As a result of this, large areas of agricultural land have been completely abandoned.

C Political and Economic Isolation

- In 1850, French armies conquered Mali and made it part of the French empire. Mali's small and scattered population could do little to resist the French, so the country became a remote and **politically isolated** colony of a foreign power.
- Mali became independent of France in 1960. But because the country is poor and very lightly populated, its government cannot afford to build roads across it. There are under 2000 kilometres of paved roads in all of Mali, so most of the country is very **economically isolated**. This prevents economic development. There are parts of Mali, for instance, where rich deposits of gold and iron ore remain untouched, because they are located too far away from roads or from centres of population.

Desertification in Northern Mali
(a) What is desertification?
(b) Name some consequences of desertification.

Rapid Revision

Both Kolkata and Hong Kong suffer from the effects of high population densities.

Problem	Kolkata (India)	Hong Kong (China)
1 Overcrowding	Many bustee-dwellers live in overcrowded houses, temporary huts and even on the streets.	Poor people live in overcrowded apartments and even on houseboats.
2 Lack of open space	There is very little open space in this 50km-long city.	Open space is so limited that buildings are erected on polders.
3 Shortage of clean water	Up to 50 people share a single water tap. Many pavement people have no clean water.	Water supplies are clean, but the sea is polluted by industrial and and household waste.
4 Pollution	Toilet waste and garbage soil the streets. Air pollution causes illnesses such as asthma.	Traffic and factories create air and noise pollution. Litter produces visual pollution.

Both the West of Ireland and Mali suffer from the effects of very low population densities.

Problem	West of Ireland	Mail (Africa)
A Low marriage rates	Many young people of marriageable age migrate from lightly populated areas in the West.	More men than women migrate from rural to urban areas. This reduces marriage rates in both areas.
B Abandonment of agricultural land	As young people leave rural areas there are fewer energetic people left to work the land. Some land is abandoned or neglected.	Many people abandon their land in search of work or social services or to flee from desertification.
C Political and economic isolation	The West of Ireland is removed from the Dublin area, which is the political and economic core of Ireland.	For many years Mali was an isolated colony of France. A lack of roads causes many rural areas to be economically isolated.

 Activities

1 Each of the following multiple-choice questions has appeared on a Junior Certificate examination paper. Tick the correct answer from the alternative answers given in each question.

(i) A place is overcrowded when:

(a) The population is high ☐   (c) The population is growing ☐

(b) There are many big cities ☐   (d) There are not sufficient resources for people ☐

(ii) Bustees or favelas are:

(a) Cattle farms in Mali ☐   (c) Shanty towns ☐

(b) Tropical red soils ☐   (d) Volcanic eruptions in Iceland ☐

(iii) Some of the following problems are associated with over-population:

(a) Overcrowding   (d) High infant mortality rates

(b) Low marriage rates   (e) High living standards

(c) Pollution

Which three of the above answers are correct?

1. (a), (b) and (c) ☐

2. (a), (c) and (d) ☐

3. (a), (b) and (d) ☐

4. (b), (c) and (e) ☐

2 '*The rapid growth of cities in developing countries has led to problems in these cities.*' In relation to a named city in the Third World that you have studied, describe **two** of these problems.
(*J.C. Higher Level*)

3 Describe **two** problems caused by very low population densities in Mali or the West of Ireland.
(*J.C. Higher Level*)

4 Examine the OS map of part of Co. Donegal.

(a) Is there a high or a low population density in the area shown?

(b) Give three reasons for this high or low population density.

(c) Describe three possible effects of this high or low population density.

See Chapter 33 of your Workbook ▶ 6

Test Yourself
eTest.ie

Life and Death in an Unequal World

Rich North - Poor South

One of the biggest problems of today's world is the massive inequality that exists between rich and poor regions of our planet. Figure 1 shows that the world can be divided into two broad regions – the generally rich North and the generally poor South.

The North consists of the wealthy countries of the world, such as those in North America and Europe. It contains only one-fifth of the world's people, but uses 86 per cent of the world's wealth.

THE NORTH

Equator

THE SOUTH

☐ The North
▢ The South

1

The South consists of the poor countries of the world, such as those in Africa and South America. Almost 80 per cent of our human family live in the South, yet the South uses only 14 per cent of the world's wealth. The South is sometimes referred to as the **Third World** or the **Majority World**.

(a) Why are the terms 'North' and 'South' used to describe the two big regions shown on the map?

(b) Name ten countries in the North and ten countries in the South. Consult your atlas if you need to.

	Ireland	Uganda
Area (km²)	70,280	236,040
Child mortality (per 1000 live births)	6	140
Life expectancy (in years)	78	48
Birth rate (per 1000 of population)	14.6	47.4
Percentage of people with AIDS	0.3	4.1

Some contrasts between Ireland and Uganda

(a) Identify three pieces of information in this table which show that Ireland is a rich First World country and that Uganda is a poor Third World country.

(b) Find Uganda on a map of Africa.

Child Mortality - North and South

The term **child mortality rate** refers to the number of young children (usually under five years of age) who die each year, in relation to every 1000 live births in that same year.

Child mortality rates are much higher in the Third World than they are in the First World.

Why More Children Die in Third World Countries

Most people in the Third World live in **poverty**. This is the basic reason why, in Third World countries such as Uganda, one child in seven dies before the age of five.

- Many people in the South do not have supplies of **clean water**. Because of this, many children suffer and die from sicknesses such as gastroenteritis, which causes vomiting and diarrhoea.

- Hundreds of millions of Third World children suffer from **malnutrition**, because they do not enjoy properly balanced diets. Malnutrition weakens resistance against disease. Weak, poorly fed children are more likely to die from diseases such as whooping cough and measles.

- **Preventative medicine**, such as vaccinations against whooping cough and other childhood diseases, would save countless numbers of young lives. But poor people cannot afford such medical treatment and most Third World governments are not well off enough to provide them free to poor people.

A child dies every three seconds in the Third World because of poverty and injustice.

WHEN I GROW UP I WANT TO BE AN ASTRONAUT.

I'LL JUST SETTLE FOR A HALF CHANCE TO GROW UP.

NORTH

SOUTH

BRICK

 What issues are raised in this cartoon?

Child mortality rates in Dublin and Kampala (Uganda) **3**
Describe and give reasons for the difference between the mortality rates shown.

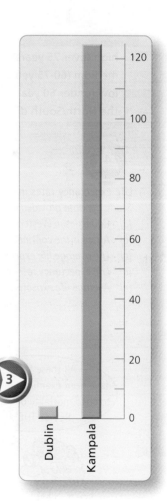

Dublin   Kampala

217

Life expectancy rate is the average number of years which newborn children can be expected to live.

Life Expectancy - North and South

Figure 4 shows that people in the Northern countries generally live longer than people in the Southern countries.

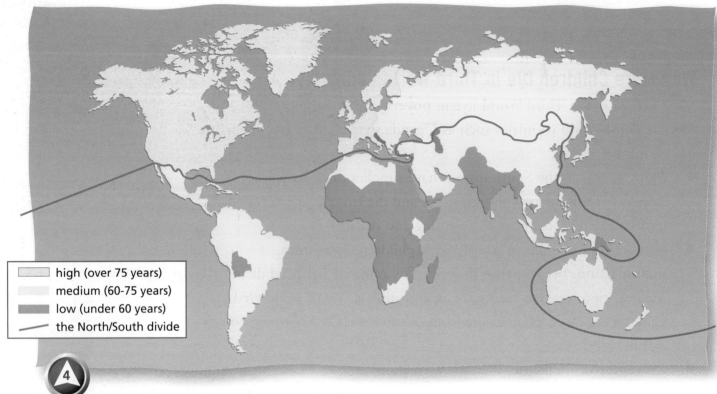

high (over 75 years)
medium (60-75 years)
low (under 60 years)
the North/South divide

4

Life expectancy rates in the North and the South

Study the data provided on this map and state whether each of the following statements is true or false.

(a) Countries in Western Europe and North America all have average life expectancy rates of more than 75 years.

(b) Africa is the continent where life expectancy is lowest.

(c) The average life expectancy rate in South Africa is less than 60 years.

(d) Life expectancy rates are higher in economically developed countries than in poorer, developing countries.

(e) Average life expectancy rates hide big individual life expectancy rates within countries.

All these factors have been examined in relation to child mortality on page 217. REVISE THEM!

Why Life Expectancy is Longer in the North than in the South

- **Child mortality** is much higher in the South than it is in the North. When large numbers of children die in a country in the South, the average life expectancy rate of that country is reduced.

- Other factors affecting life expectancy are the availability of **clean water**, a **balanced diet** and **preventative medicine** — all of which relate to the wealth or poverty of the people.

- **War** is another factor that has lowered life expectancy rates in some countries of the South. It is estimated that in recent times more than one million people a year have died in the South as a result of armed conflict. The US-led invasion of Iraq, for example, resulted in the deaths of up to half a million Iraqis. Some died fighting, while most died as a result of the bombing and chaos that followed the invasion.

- **Aids** has killed millions of young adults and so has reduced life expectancy rates in many African and other Third World countries.

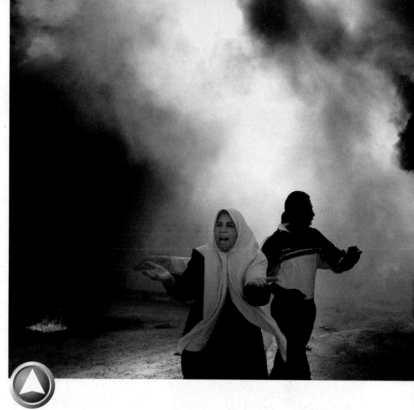

Iraq is bombed at the beginning of the American invasion of 2003. *Describe three ways in which war can reduce life expectancy in Third World countries.*

Rapid Revision

- The world can be divided broadly into the rich, economically developed **North** and the poor, less economically developed **South**. Most people live in the South, but the North controls 85 per cent of the world's wealth.

- **Child mortality** is much higher in the South than in the North. Poverty is the main cause of child deaths in the South. Poverty results from a lack of clean water, from malnutrition and from inadequate preventative medicine. These problems, in turn, result in many avoidable deaths, especially among children.

- **Life expectancy rates** are lower in the Third World than in the North. High levels of child mortality, the effects of poverty, wars and AIDS all reduce life expectancy levels in many parts of the South.

Activities

1. Define the terms 'the North' and 'the South'.
2. Give three reasons why child mortality rates are higher in the South than in the North.
3. Give three reasons why life expectancy rates are higher in the North than in the South.

See Chapter 34 of your Workbook

Norman Settlements in Ireland

Key Idea

The Irish landscape shows evidence of Norman settlements. The locations of such settlements were related to:
- where the settlers came from

and to the availability of:
- water
- food
- communications
- defence

How would you know a Norman town?

Look out for the following clues:
- a *castle*
- a *motte*, which was an early form of timber castle
- old defensive *town walls* or *towers*
- old *abbeys, monasteries* or *friaries*, some of which were built by monks or friars who came to Ireland with the Normans
- Norman *placenames*, such as those including the words 'castle', 'manor' or 'park'.

The Normans built many settlements in Ireland following their invasion of the country in the twelfth century. Most early Norman settlements were at the following locations:

In the east and south

The Normans came to Ireland from England and Wales. They therefore landed in the east and south of Ireland, which were the landing points **closest to where they came from**. Ireland at that time had few roads and much of the country was covered in forests. Most early Normans did not therefore move too far from their landing places. They settled in the east and south.

On fertile land

Land was wealth in Norman times. Good land provided **food**, as well as crops and cattle that could be sold for profit. As the Normans conquered Ireland they usually settled on flat or gently sloping lowlands, where the soil was fertile. The east and south of the country had many such lowlands.

Near rivers

Norman settlements were usually near rivers for the following reasons:
- Rivers provided **water** for drinking and for other domestic purposes.
- Large rivers such as the Suir and the Boyne provided **transport routes** at a time when there were not many roads.
- Rivers sometimes provided **defensive** moats around parts of Norman castles.

What is a *moat*?

Defensive sites

Because the Normans had conquered Irish land, they lived in fear of attack by the native Irish people. Most early Normans therefore lived in or close to easily defended **castles**. Many Normans lived in **towns** that grew up around castles and that were surrounded by strong defensive walls. Some coastal towns, such as Dublin, developed from existing Viking trading ports. Inland towns, such as Trim in County Meath, were founded by the Normans themselves.

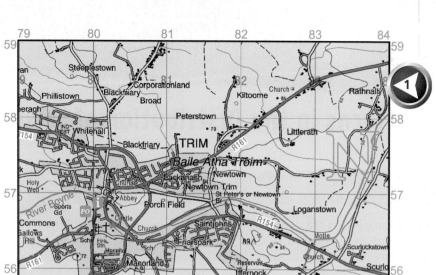

1 OS map of Trim, Co. Meath

(a) To what extent do features and placenames on this map suggest that Normans once settled in the area shown?

(b) Identify one feature on the map that suggests that the area shown was inhabited before the coming of the Normans.

(c) Identify four features of present-day habitation in the town of Trim.

Rapid Revision

Early Normans settled in the following places in Ireland:

- In the **east and south** of Ireland, which was closest to England and Wales, from where they came.

- On **fertile lowlands** that provided plenty of food and wealth.

- Near **rivers** that provided water and sometimes transport routes and defensive moats.

- In defensive sites near **castles** or in **towns**. Some of these towns developed from old Viking trading ports.

See Chapter 35 of your Workbook

Aerial photograph of Trim

(a) Describe evidence in this photograph of Norman settlement.

(b) What role might the river have played in the development of Norman settlement in the area shown?

Patterns in the Distribution of Towns

Key Ideas

Towns or other nucleated settlements are distributed throughout the country in different patterns. There are many reasons for this.

Revise page 141.

The term **settlement pattern** refers to the way in which settlements are distributed or arranged in an area. Individual houses, for example, can be arranged in **dispersed**, **ribboned** (linear) or **nucleated** patterns. You learned about this on page 141.

Most **urban areas** (towns or cities) are themselves nucleated settlements. But these nucleated settlements may be distributed in dispersed, linear or clustered patterns throughout the country. Patterns in the distribution of towns and cities can be related to the following factors:

- **Historical and social factors**, such as the influence of the Vikings or the Normans and the dominant importance of Dublin.
- **Physical factors**, such as altitude, land quality and drainage patterns.

Historic Factors
Viking Towns

The Vikings, who were great sea traders, set up settlements along the east and south coasts of Ireland. Many of these settlements developed into towns, which now form a **linear pattern along or near the coast** (see Figure 1).

- Viking settlement/port
- ☐ Linear pattern of Viking settlements

0   50   100km

1

Ireland's chief Viking settlements
(a) In which general pattern are these settlements arranged?
(b) Why do you think the Vikings established settlements on the south and east coasts rather than on the west coast of Ireland?
(c) With the help of your atlas, identify each of the settlements labelled A to D.

222

Norman Towns

You learned on page 220 that the Normans founded or developed many towns in Ireland. Figure 2 shows some of these towns.

The Primacy of Dublin

Dublin, which is Ireland's **primate city**, dominates the political and economic life of the country.

Dublin's primacy has affected the distribution pattern of Irish towns in two ways:

- Some towns have developed in a **cluster** (nucleated pattern) around Dublin (see Figure 3a).
- Many towns developed along roads leading to Dublin. They are strung along these roads in a **linear pattern** (see Figure 3b).

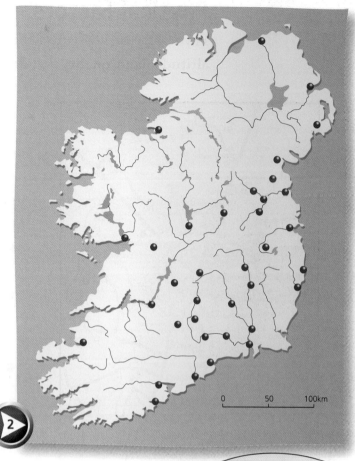

Norman towns in Ireland
Is the general distribution of these gowns dispersed, linear or clustered?

2

A **primate city** is one that has at least twice the population of any other city in the country.

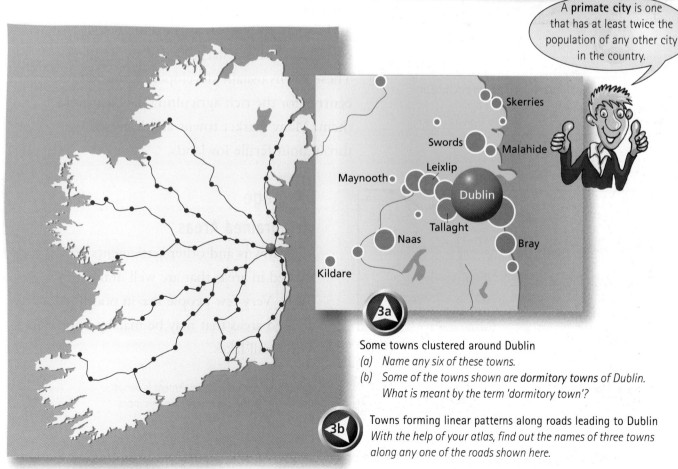

3a

Some towns clustered around Dublin
(a) *Name any six of these towns.*
(b) *Some of the towns shown are dormitory towns of Dublin. What is meant by the term 'dormitory town'?*

3b Towns forming linear patterns along roads leading to Dublin
With the help of your atlas, find out the names of three towns along any one of the roads shown here.

Physical Factors

Physical factors that affect the location and development of towns include **altitude**, **land quality** and **drainage**.

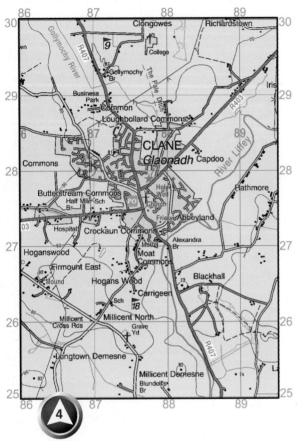

4

Clane, Co. Kildare

*(a) Identify some **services** provided by Clane at present and in the past.*

(b) Why is settlement in the Clane area located some distance from the River Liffey?

Altitude and Relief

Altitude (height above sea level) and relief (shape of the land's surface) influence the location of settlements. Ireland's major towns and cities are generally **scattered throughout lowland areas** for the following reasons:

- Lowlands are generally **flat or gently sloping**. They are therefore easy to build on.
- Lowlands are usually **warmer and less windy** and therefore more pleasant to live in than upland areas.
- Lowlands are usually well serviced by roads, railways or other **transport routes**.

Land Quality

Most large towns are situated in areas of **deep and fertile soils**, such as the alluvial soils that cover many of our flat, lowland river valleys. These towns usually developed as **market centres** for the rich agricultural lands around them. Many market towns are dispersed throughout fertile lowlands.

Drainage
Well-drained Areas

Most towns and other settlements are located in areas that are well drained by rivers. Very few people live in poorly drained areas that may be marshy or littered with small lakes.

5 *Suggest two reasons why settlement is almost non-existent in the area shown on this map.*

How rivers influence the locations of towns

- Many settlements originated in **riverside locations** because rivers provided water for drinking, cooking and other domestic purposes.

- Some large rivers are **navigable.** They may have provided transport routes that helped towns to develop.

- Some towns develop on what are called **dry-point sites**. They are located short distances away from rivers that are likely to flood. These towns are usually found on the flood plains of old or mature rivers.

- Many towns are situated on the **bridging points** of rivers. Roads usually converge (meet) at bridges in order to cross over rivers. Where roads converge, people meet. Where people meet, business develops. Where business develops, towns grow. Many of Ireland's most important towns and cities are located on *the lowest bridging points* of rivers. These bridges are closest to the coast and so control busy coastal routes.

Rivers

Most Irish towns are built near rivers and some towns are distributed in **linear** patterns along the courses of large rivers. Some of the reasons why individual towns are built on rivers are explained in the box.

On which rivers are the following settlements located? Dublin, Cork, Limerick, Galway, Waterford, Kilkenny, Wexford.

Waterford City
Describe three ways in which the river might have contributed to the growth of Waterford

Rapid Revision

- Towns and other urban settlements are dispersed throughout the country in different **patterns**.
- **Historic and social factors: Viking** towns formed *linear* patterns along the south and east coasts. **Norman** towns were *dispersed*, mainly throughout the east and the south. The **primacy of Dublin** caused several towns to be *clustered* around it. Other towns are distributed in *linear* patterns along roads leading to Dublin.
- **Physical factors:** Most towns are *dispersed* throughout **lowland areas** where land is fertile. Towns are also located in **well-drained areas**. Some towns and villages are distributed in *linear* patterns along the courses of important **rivers**.

See Chapter 36 of your Workbook

Test Yourself eTest.ie

New Settlement Patterns in the Dutch Polders

Key Idea

- In recent times, new settlement patterns have been created on the lands reclaimed from the sea.

The Netherlands – the world's most densely populated country – has created extra territory for itself by reclaiming a great deal of land from the sea. **Lands reclaimed from the sea are known as polders**. The polders of the Netherlands are surrounded by walls called *dykes* and are being constantly drained by *drainage ditches* and *canals*.

Did you know that 60 per cent of all Dutch people live in polders that are below sea level?

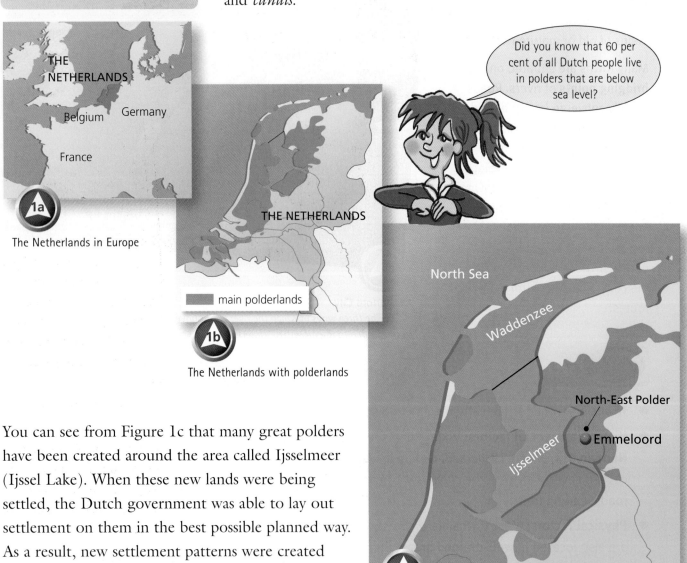

THE NETHERLANDS

Belgium Germany

France

1a

The Netherlands in Europe

THE NETHERLANDS

main polderlands

1b

The Netherlands with polderlands

North Sea

Waddenzee

Ijsselmeer

North-East Polder

Emmeloord

You can see from Figure 1c that many great polders have been created around the area called Ijsselmeer (Ijssel Lake). When these new lands were being settled, the Dutch government was able to lay out settlement on them in the best possible planned way. As a result, new settlement patterns were created which are not to be found in other parts of Europe.

1c

The Ijsselmeer area

Planned Rural Settlement Pattern

Polders that were devoted to agriculture were laid out with rectangular-shaped farms and straight roads. Farmhouses were built along the sides of these roads in **planned linear patterns**. Within the overall linear patterns, small clusters of (usually three or four) farmhouses were sometimes built near each other, so that people could live close to their neighbours.

Identify the settlement pattern shown in this picture.

Planned Urban Pattern – the 'Cartwheel'

The North-East Polder of Ijsselmeer (Figure 1c) is a good example of the way in which towns, villages and roads are arranged in some polderlands (see also Figures 2 and 3).

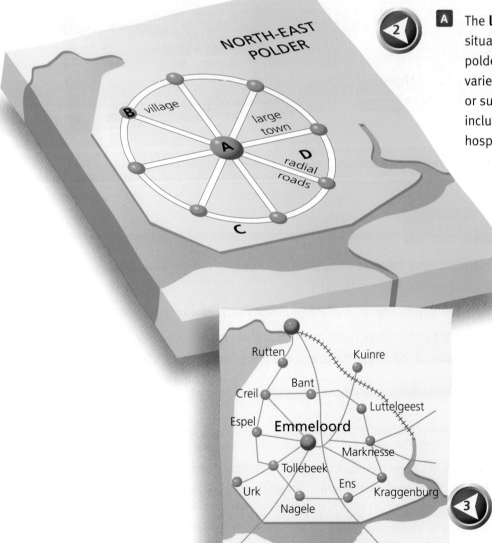

2

A The **largest town**, called **Emmeloord**, is situated in the **centre** or **hub** of the polder, where it can provide a wide variety of services for a large hinterland or surrounding area. These services include specialist stores, theatres, hospital services, etc.

B A ring of **villages** was built along the edge of the polder, forming an approximate circle around Emmeloord. These villages provide small shops and everyday services for the people living close to them.

C A **circular road** connects the villages.

D Emmeloord itself is joined directly to many of the villages by **'radial' roads**, which look like the spokes of a wheel.

3 The North-East Polder
(a) Identify the central town, the surrounding villages, the circular road and radial roads.
(b) Which villages are not joined to Emmeloord by a radial road?

227

How settlement in the North-East Polder is arranged differently from that in Ireland

IN THE POLDER

- Individual **farmhouses** form planned linear patterns along roads.
- **Villages** are arranged in a circle around a large town.
- Ring **roads** join villages arranged in a circle and 'radial' roads connect individual villages with a large central town.

IN IRELAND

- Individual **farmhouses** are scattered throughout the countryside.
- **Villages** often develop at bridging points of rivers.
- **Roads** often follow river valleys or join at **bridging points of rivers**.

(a) One of these photographs was taken in Ireland and the other in the Netherlands. Which photograph was taken in the Netherlands?

(b) Contrast the scenes in the two photographs with regard to (i) relief, (ii) settlement patterns, (iii) land use.

Rapid Revision

- In recent times, new settlement patterns have been created in polders in the Netherlands. **Polders** are lands that have been reclaimed from the sea.
- **Farmhouses** on the polders are usually arranged in *planned linear patterns along straight roadways*.
- Large **towns** may be *centrally placed* within large polders. Small **villages**, connected by **ring roads**, are arranged in *circular patterns* around the large towns and are joined to the towns by radial roads.

Activities

1 In the Netherlands, new settlement has been developed on land reclaimed from the sea. Describe how this settlement is different from settlement in other areas. (*J.C. High Level*)

OR

2 What is a polder? Describe one way in which settlement and land use on polders are different from other areas. (*J.C. Higher Level*)

The Functions of Nucleated Settlements

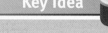
Key Idea

- Nucleated settlements can be classified by their functions.

Functions are the **services and benefits that a settlement provides.** Most towns are **multifunctional**, which means that they have several different functions.

Services in Villages and Towns

A Village

A village is a small settlement that provides only a limited number of services. These services might include a church, a post office, a primary school and a bar or two. There might also be some small shops, which would supply locals with 'everyday' needs, such as bread, milk and newspapers.

Example: Ballingarry, Co. Tipperary
List the services in Ballingarry that are shown on this map.

A Town

A town provides a wider range of services than a village. Together with the basic services offered by a village, a town would have specialised shops (such as jewellers and clothes shops), banks, offices, restaurants, a cinema and perhaps hotels.

Example: Birr, Co. Offaly
Referring to this map and the map in Figure 1:
(a) List the services that are offered both in the town of Birr and the village of Ballingarry.
(b) List some services that are offered in Birr but not in Ballingarry.

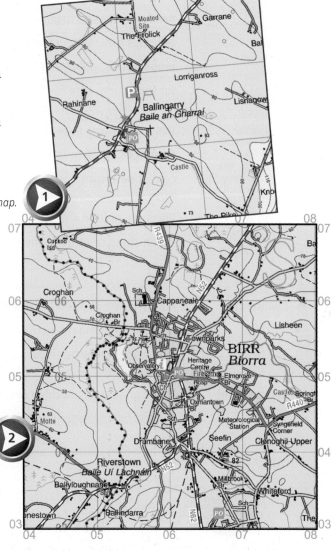

REVISE pages 143 and 166.

Some specific functions of nucleated settlements

Function	Explanation	Examples in the Shannon Basin
● Market	Local country people **shop** in these towns. Many towns had agricultural **fairs** or **co-operative marts** at which local farm produce was bought and sold. Most market towns were surrounded by **fertile farmland**.	*Carrick-on-Shannon, Birr*
● Defence	Medieval (Middle Ages) towns often developed near **castles** that offered protection to local people. Defensive walls surrounded some medieval towns.	*Athlone, Limerick*
● Ecclesiastical	Ecclesiastical settlements provided for people's religious needs. Almost all towns contain **churches** and so provide some religious functions. Some towns developed near old **monasteries, abbeys** or **friaries,** that once provided education for the young, care for the sick and aid for the poor.	*Portumna*
● Resource	Resource towns developed largely as a result of **natural resources** being found nearby. These resources could include coal or peat (turf).	*Shannonbridge*
● Ports	Ports are built in sheltered **harbours** or **estuaries** of rivers on which ships can travel. They usually have docking facilities for ships.	*Limerick*
● Residential	All towns are residential. **Dormitory towns** are especially so, because their main function is to provide housing for people who work in nearby cities.	*Sixmilebridge (near Limerick City)*
● Recreational	These are usually **holiday resorts**, often with facilities such as golfing, fishing, boating and tourist information.	*Killaloe, Portumna*

Activities

(a)   Can you think of one other example (local if possible) of each type of settlement described above?

(b)   Referring to the map in Figure 2 (page 229), describe three functions of **Birr**.

The Shannon River Basin

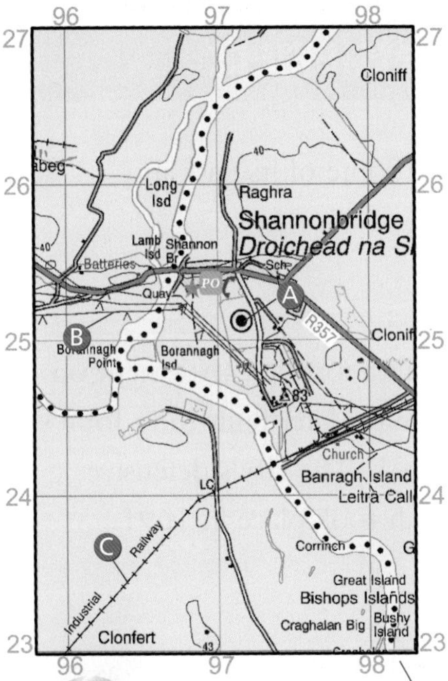

Athlone, Co. Westmeath

(a) Use this photograph to identify three functions of Athlone.

(b) How do you think the river influenced the development of Athlone?

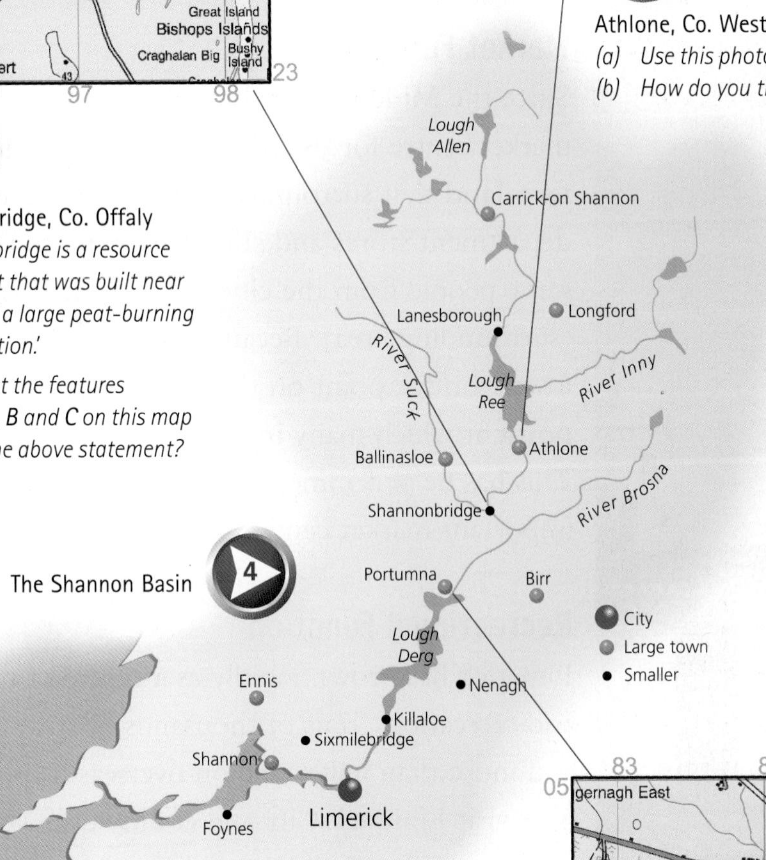

③ Shannonbridge, Co. Offaly

'Shannonbridge is a resource settlement that was built near the site of a large peat-burning power station.'

How might the features labelled A, B and C on this map support the above statement?

④ The Shannon Basin

Area shown in Figure 4

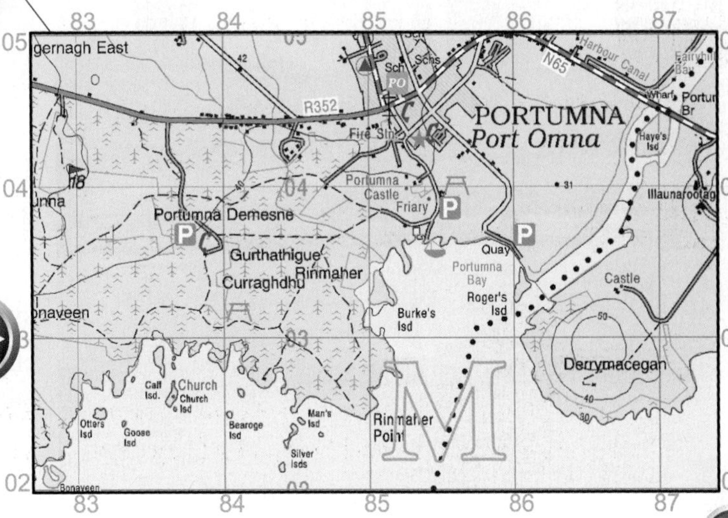

- ● City
- ● Large town
- • Smaller

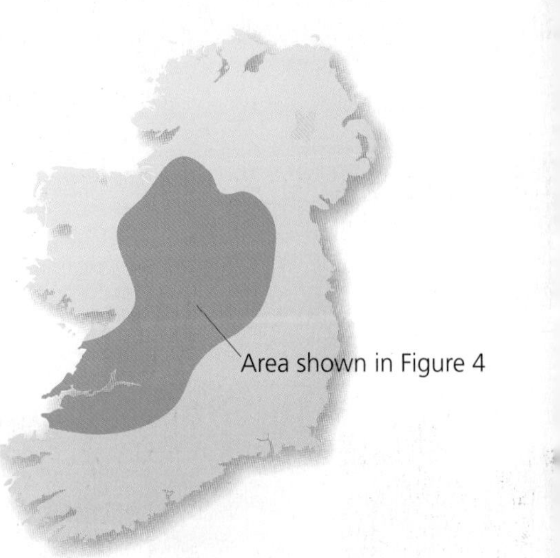

Portumna, Co. Galway

(a) Explain with reference to this map why Portumna developed at the location shown.

(b) Explain how Portumna might make a suitable holiday destination for a group of people with different interests.

Limerick is the largest settlement in the Shannon Basin. Some of its past and present functions are examined below.

Defence Function

Limerick's defence function began when the **Vikings** built a fortified settlement on an island that is now called King John's Island. The **Normans** later built King John's Castle and built walls around the medieval city of Limerick. The city's defensive function lasted up to the famous siege of Limerick, which took place in 1691.

King John's Castle
How has this castle contributed to Limerick's defence and recreational functions?

Market Function

Since the Middle Ages, Limerick has served as a market centre for the produce of the **fertile farmland** that surrounds it. It now has many department stores and **shopping centres** that serve people from the city and its **hinterland** (surrounding area). Because Limerick is at the lowest bridge point on the Shannon, it is a **nodal point** at which many important roads converge. This has helped Limerick to develop into an important market centre.

Recreational Function

Limerick has grown rapidly as a centre of tourism and recreation. Tens of thousands of Irish people and more than half a million overseas tourists now visit Limerick City and county each year.

Limerick's **cultural attractions** include King John's Castle, the Hunt Museum and the Bell Table theatre. Streets such as Cruise's Street contain fashionable shopping malls. Followers of **sport** flock to see hurling, Gaelic football and rugby matches at the Gaelic Grounds and Thomond Park. Limerick City hotels provide 3500 rooms for visitors

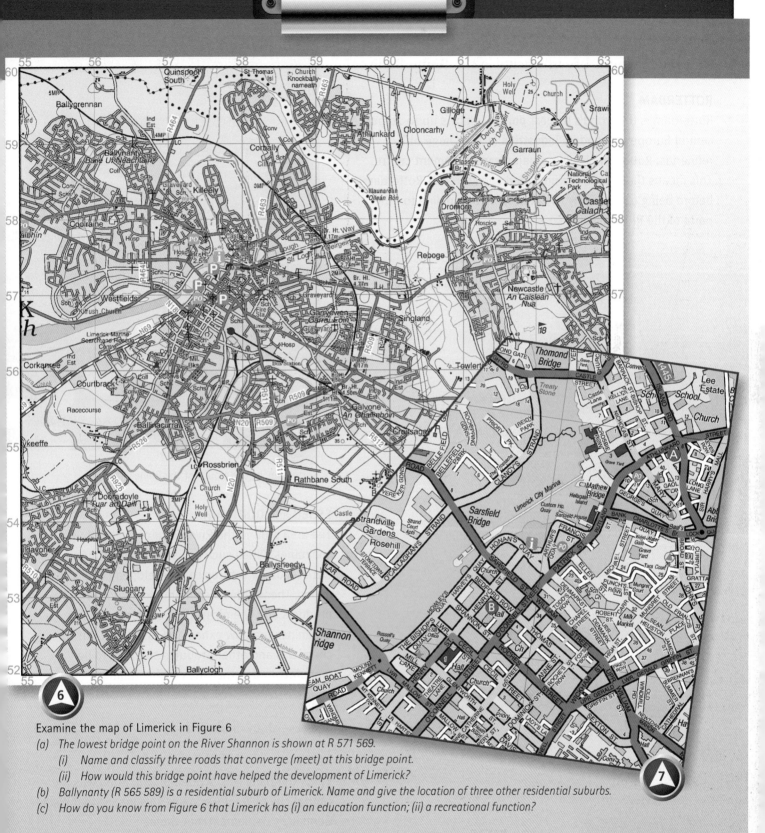

Examine the map of Limerick in Figure 6

(a) The lowest bridge point on the River Shannon is shown at R 571 569.
  (i) Name and classify three roads that converge (meet) at this bridge point.
  (ii) How would this bridge point have helped the development of Limerick?

(b) Ballynanty (R 565 589) is a residential suburb of Limerick. Name and give the location of three other residential suburbs.

(c) How do you know from Figure 6 that Limerick has (i) an education function; (ii) a recreational function?

Examine the street map of part of Central Limerick in Figure 7

(d) Is this map drawn to a larger or smaller scale than the map in Figure 6? Name one advantage and one disadvantage that the map in Figure 7 has over the map in Figure 6.

(e) How does the map in Figure 7 suggest that Limerick: (i) had a defence function; (ii) has or had an ecclesiastical (religious) function; (iii) has or had a port function?

(f) Do you think the area labelled A or the area marked B is the older part of Limerick? Explain your answer.

233

The Rhine River Basin

Figure 8 shows the basin of the Rhine River. It also refers to some functions of settlements in the Rhine Basin.

ROTTERDAM

Rotterdam is the world's busiest **port**. It imports up to 20 per cent of Europe's oil and its **industries** include huge oil refineries. Rotterdam is also a major **trans-shipment centre**. This means that goods are unloaded and stored at Rotterdam before being delivered by river, road, rail or pipeline to other parts of the Rhine Basin.

Rotterdam, at the mouth of the Rhine

Area shown in Figure 8

ESSEN and DORTMUND

The area around the River Ruhr contained huge coalmines. Cities such as Essen and Dortmund were **resource centres** that developed close to the mines. These cities also manufactured steel, iron products and chemicals derived from coal. The coalmines are now exhausted (used up); but cars, chemicals and other products continue to be **manufactured** in the cities of the Ruhr.

KÖLN

See case study on page 235.

BONN

When Germany was divided in two, Bonn was the **capital** city of West Germany. This means that West Germany's parliament met there.

RÜDESHEIM

Rüdesheim is an important **recreation** centre. It is located on the beautiful Rhine Gorge and is a busy destination for river cruises.

BASLE

Basle is a **river port** and **industrial** centre. Its industries include chemicals and medicines.

Case Study : Köln – A Multifunctional Settlement

Market Function

Köln is an important market centre for the surrounding **fertile flood plain** of the River Rhine. It is a big shopping, banking and business city and its international **trade fairs** attract people from all parts of the world.

Important roads and railway routes meet at the bridge points of the Rhine at Köln. The city is therefore a major **nodal point** and this increases its importance as a market centre.

Port Function

Köln is one of Europe's busiest **river ports**. Ocean-going vessels can reach its six different port terminals, which handle ten million tonnes of cargo each year.

Köln is a nodal point of road and rail transport, so trucks and trains can carry goods landed at its port to other destinations. Köln is therefore an important **transhipment centre**.

Some of Köln's **manufacturing** industries, such as its shipbuilding and ship repair yards, are related to its port function.

Recreational Function

Köln is an important tourist destination:

- It is a beautiful city and contains Germany's largest **historic city** centre. Many of its older buildings, such as its great Gothic cathedral, were built in the Middle Ages.
- Köln is an important centre for Rhine **river cruises**.
- Many of Köln's oldest streets have been pedestrianised and are lined with coffee shops, art galleries and other **tourist facilities**.

> **Köln Cathedral** is said to be Europe's finest Gothic church. Its building began in the thirteenth century and it took 600 years to complete. Its two great towers are each as high as a 50-storey building.

Köln
What functions of the city are suggested in this photograph?

Rapid Revision

- The **functions** of a settlement are the services or benefits that it provides.

- **Villages** provide a small number of basic functions. **Towns** provide a larger number of more specialised functions.

- Large settlements in the **Shannon Basin** and some of their past or present functions include: *Limerick City* (defence, market, recreational); *Athlone* (defence, manufacturing); *Portumna* (ecclesiastical, recreational); *Carrick-on-Shannon* (market, residential).

- Cities in the **Rhine Basin** and some of their past or present functions include: *Rotterdam* (port, manufacturing); *Essen* (resource, manufacturing); *Köln* (market, port, recreational); *Basle* (port, manufacturing).

Activities

1 Examine the settlement in this photograph. Using evidence from the photograph, describe three past or present functions of the settlement shown.

2 Name four major settlements in the Shannon River Basin and four major settlements in the Rhine River Basin. Identify *two* functions of each settlement you have named.

3 Examine the aerial **photograph** of part of Limerick City on page 169. Using evidence from the photograph, show that Limerick has or had each of the following functions: (a) defence, (b) ecclesiastical, (c) residential.

4 The **aerial photograph and Ordnance Survey map** in Figure 9, page 237 show the town of Carrick-on-Suir, Co. Tipperary. Answer the questions that appear beneath the photograph and map fragment.

See Chapter 38 of your Workbook

Carrick-on-Suir

(a) Use evidence from the map and/or the photograph above to show the following:
- that Carrick-on-Suir might once have had a defence function;
- that Carrick-on-Suir has a residential function;
- that Carrick-on-Suir has a recreational function;
- that Carrick-on-Suir might be a market town.

(b) Name the river that can be seen on the photograph.

(c) In which general direction does the part of the river that is shown on the photograph flow?

(d) At what time of year do you think the photograph was taken? How do you know?

Change in Urban Functions over Time

Key Idea

The functions of settlements may change over time, for example:
- where mining takes place;
- where large-scale industrial development takes place.

Case Study 1: Navan – A Major Mining Town

Navan in Co. Meath is an important mining town. Its functions have changed over time.

1 A Monastic and Defence Town
Navan probably began its existence as a monastic site. During **Norman** times, it became an important walled town, which functioned as a defence settlement until the sixteenth century.

2 A Market Town
The gently sloping lowlands around Navan contain fertile limestone-based soils that are excellent for **farming**. Navan developed as an important market town for this rich agricultural area.

3 A Resource (Mining) Settlement
On the western fringe of Navan lies **Tara Mines**, the largest zinc mine in Europe. With 650 workers, Tara Mines is easily the largest single employer in Navan. The ore (zinc-rich rock) is *extracted* from the deep mine at Navan and is *processed* into fine powder called concentrate.

   This concentrate is then *transported* to Dublin Port, from where it is *exported* to different parts of Europe to be *smelted* into zinc. This finished product is *used* mainly for rust proofing (galvanising) iron.

4 A Dormitory Town
Navan is now also a dormitory town of Dublin. Most of Navan's workforce **commute** (travel each day) to and from work in Dublin. Many of these are Dublin people who now live in Navan because houses are cheaper there than in the city.

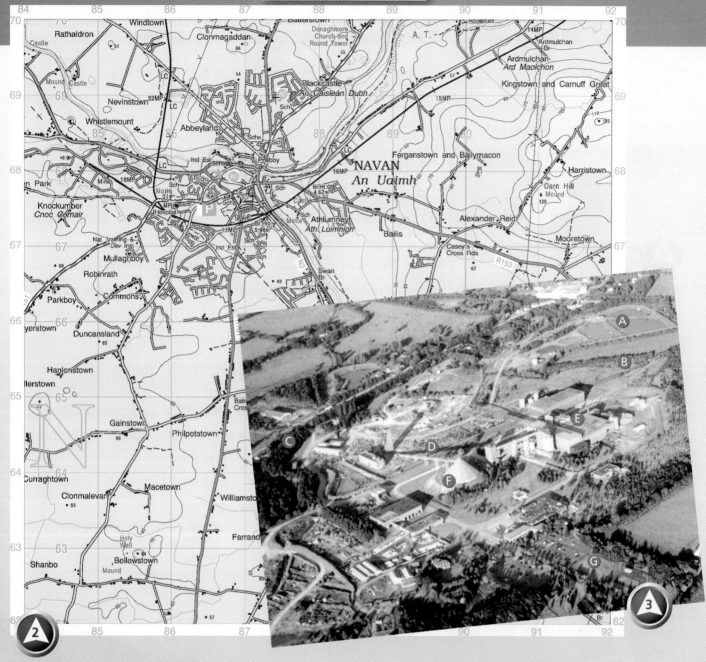

(a) Which placename in Navan town (Figure 2) suggests that the Navan area once had an **ecclesiastical** function?

(b) Referring to the map, identify two different pieces of evidence which suggest that Navan was once a **defence** settlement.

(c) Describe, without using a grid reference, the location in **Figure 2** of Tara Mines at N 851 678.

(d) What means of transport is used to carry zinc concentrate from Navan to Dublin Port? Justify your answer with evidence from **Figure 2**.

(e) Examine the **aerial photograph** of Tara Mines in **Figure 3**. Which of the labels A–G on the photograph represent each of the following features?

1. A conveyor that carries zinc ore from the mine to a cone-shaped storage building.
2. A cone-shaped building that stores ore before it is processed.
3. The main plant, in which ore is processed into concentrate.
4. A road, used to carry zinc concentrate to Dublin Port.
5. Settlement ponds that collect waste from the mine.
6. A car park and tennis courts.
7. Trees used to shield the mine from public view.

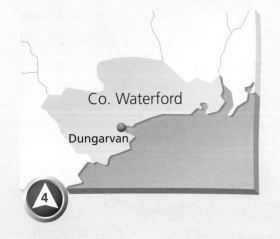

Co. Waterford

Dungarvan

Dungarvan, Co. Waterford, has had several important functions in the course of its long history. Some changes over time in these functions are outlined below.

1 Defence and Ecclesiastical (Church) Functions

- Nearly 800 years ago the Anglo-Normans (English) built a castle to defend Dungarvan from attack. A five-metre high wall was later built around the town.
- Friars of the Order of St Augustine first landed in Dungarvan in 1290 and set up an abbey in the part of the town now called Abbeyside. An Augustinian friary and college still operate in Dungarvan.

2 Port Function

Dungarvan is an ancient port that once traded successfully with England, France and Spain. But a sand spit at the mouth of the harbour was a danger to shipping. The port fell into decline at the end of the nineteenth century.

Dungarvan port in 1900
(a) For what were the buildings on the right used?
(b) Does the condition of these buildings suggest that the port of Dungarvan was prospering in 1900?
(c) What goods for export can you see on the dockside?

Dungarvan today
Contrast this scene with that of 1900. What has changed and what has remained the same?

240

A fair day in Dungarvan's town square in the 1950s

(a) Describe the scene. Mention the people, the animals and traffic in the town.

(b) How did the town square contribute to Dungarvan's market town function?

3 A Market Town

Dungarvan was once an important agricultural market town.

- It has a large hinterland of mainly fertile land.
- Several roads and a railway line (now closed) enabled goods to be transported to and from the town.

Agricultural fairs were held in the town square up to the 1950s and a cattle mart still operates on the outskirts of Dungarvan. The town is also an important shopping venue for people in the surrounding countryside.

4 Manufacturing Industry

By the late 1980s, manufacturing was thriving in Dungarvan. From the late 1990s, however, traditional industry declined and a large creamery and crystal glass factory closed down. But other industries continue to employ several hundred people. The largest of those is *Glaxo SmithKline*, a pharmaceutical company. Other factories include *Microchem* (pharmaceuticals) and *Radley Engineering* (which manufactured 'The Spike' of O'Connell Street, Dublin).

The Glaxo SmithKline factories at Dungarvan

Do you think that these factories are suitably located? Explain your answer.

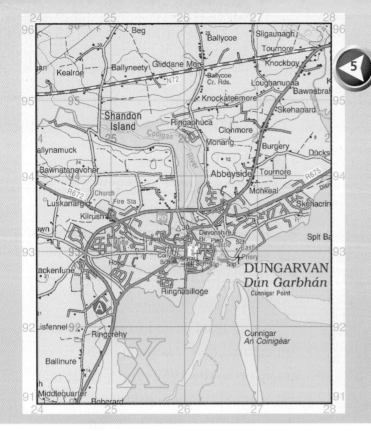

5 Dungarvan, Co. Waterford

(a) What evidence is there on the map that Dungarvan has or once had:
   (i) a defence function
   (ii) a religious function.
(b) What name is given to the sand spit close to the mouth of the harbour that damaged Dungarvan's role as a port?
(c) Identify some of the converging (meeting) roads that helped Dungarvan to become an important market town.
(d) How do you think Abbeyside (on the east side of the Colligan estuary) got its name?
(e) A large Glaxo SmithKline factory is located at the place labelled A on the map. Give three reasons why this is a suitable location for a factory.

Rapid Revision

The functions of settlements may change over time.

Navan, Co. Meath	Dungarvan, Co. Waterford
• Navan was originally a **monastic** settlement and was a walled **defence town** in Norman times.	• Dungarvan originally had **defence** and **religious** functions.
• It then became an important **market town**.	• Its ancient **port** function fell into decline at the end of the nineteenth century.
• Since the opening of Tara Mines in 1977 **mining** has become Navan's most important employer. It also provides employment and profit to local service industries.	• A fertile agricultural hinterland and converging roads helped to make Dungarvan an important **market** town.
• Navan is now also a **dormitory town** to Dublin.	• **Manufacturing** companies, such as *Glaxo SmithKline*, are now major employers in Dungarvan.

See Chapter 39 of your Workbook

Activities

1 *The function of a town may change over time.*
   (a) Name a town that you have studied whose function has changed.
   (b) Describe and explain the change in function that has taken place. *(J.C. Higher Level)*

2 Describe the importance of mining as a present-day function of any Irish town of your choice.

3 With reference to your local town, investigate and describe briefly how its functions have changed over time.

Movement, Communication Links and the Growth of Settlements

Key Idea

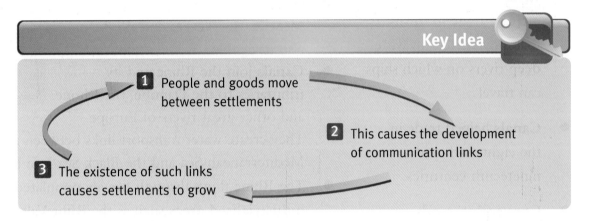

1. People and goods move between settlements
2. This causes the development of communication links
3. The existence of such links causes settlements to grow

Irish Roads

- As **urban settlements** developed throughout Ireland, people and goods moved between them.

- This led to the **development of road networks** between settlements. Roads are now the most commonly used mode (type) of transport in Ireland.

- **Good road links** increase *trade* and so **encourage the further development of settlements**.

  1. Some towns have developed *along main roads*, such as those which link Dublin with Cork, with Limerick or with Galway.

  2. The *convergence of roads*, such as at the bridging points of rivers, has led to the growth of numerous settlements. Dublin, our principal city, is at the meeting point of several important roads.

  3. The growth of *new towns* such as Tallaght in Co. Dublin and Shannon in Co. Clare has been made possible by the excellent road links that exist between these towns and the nearby cities of Dublin and Limerick.

Part of the Dublin–Belfast motorway

(a) Why has a motorway been built between Dublin and Belfast?

(b) How might this motorway affect the growth of towns along its route?

How communication links help to develop settlements

- **Sea transport** has developed port activities in some coastal towns.

- **River transport** might increase trade in towns that are situated on **wide**, **deep** rivers on which ships can travel.

- **Canals** helped trade in the eighteenth and nineteenth centuries.

- **Converging roads** increase trade.

- **Railway stations** assisted the development of market towns and seaside resorts in the past.

- **Airports** help the development of light industry, tourism and other businesses in nearby towns.

Case Study: River Transport on the Rhine

- The Rhine itself is **navigable** from the North Sea to Switzerland.
- Its principal **tributaries**, such as the Moselle, the Neckar and the Main, are also navigable.
- **Canals** join the Rhine and its tributaries to the Danube, the Rhone and other great rivers of Europe. They create water transport links between the North Sea, the Mediterranean Sea and the Black Sea (see Figure 1).
- The Rhine flows through heavily populated and **industrialised areas** such as the Ruhr Valley.

- **Navigable** waters are those on which ships can travel.
- The term **inland waterway** could refer to a navigable river, lake or canal.

Ships and barges carry imported **raw materials** up the Rhine from the North Sea. These raw materials include oil and iron ore for the manufacturing industries of the Rhineland. The **finished products** of those industries are carried down the Rhine for export. They include chemicals and cars. This river traffic is so heavy that the Rhine has been called '*the main road of Germany*'.

The Rhine, its tributaries and canals **link numerous cities** and other settlements in the Netherlands, Germany, France and Switzerland. Many of these settlements have developed into important **industrial cities** and **ports** because of their locations on the Rhine waterway. Others have become **tourist resorts** for people who take river cruises on the Rhine. Some Rhine cities are described on page 245.

Activities

Examine the Ordnance Survey map that shows **Galway City** on **page 178**. Describe how communication links helped the development of Galway. Use evidence from the map to support your answer.

The beautiful Rhine Gorge *What is the function of the boat that is shown in this picture?*

Some important settlements on the Rhine

- **ROTTERDAM** is the world's largest seaport. It was described on page 234.
- **DUISBURG** is located where the River Ruhr meets the Rhine. It is the largest river port in Western Europe. It makes steel and heavy machinery.
- **KÖLN** is a busy port, manufacturing city and tourist centre. It was described on page 235.
- **KOBLENZ** is the German word for *confluence*, which means *the meeting place of rivers*. It is a busy river port because it is located where the rivers Rhine, Moselle and Lahn meet.
- **FRANKFURT** is a major port and bridge point on the River Main. Road and rail routes converge at Frankfurt, which has developed into a large industrial and banking centre.
- **BASLE** is Switzerland's only major river port. Its position on the Rhine has helped it to grow into Switzerland's second largest city.

Map labels:

X

Rotterdam
R.Rhine
①
Duisburg
A Dortmund
R.Rhur
②
Dusseldorf
Köln
B
Koblenz
R. Lahn
Frankfurt
C
Mainz
R.Main
D
Main-Danube Canal
R.Meuse
R.Moselle
R.Neckar
③
F
E
R.Danube
(To the Black Sea)
Basle
④
Rhine-Rhône Canal
R.Rhône (To the Mediterranean Sea)

- City
...... Canal

You may need to refer to page 234 to help you with these questions.

Puzzle it out:
Why is the Rhine in Netherlands known as 'the Lower Rhine' and the Rhine in Switzerland known as 'the Upper Rhine'?

1 The Rhine Waterway
(a) Identify the sea labelled X on the map.
(b) Name the canals that link the Rhine Basin:
   (i) to the Mediterranean Sea; and (ii) to the Black Sea.
(c) Name each of the cities labelled A to F on the map.
(d) Identify the countries at the places labelled 1 to 4.

Telecommunications

Information now travels instantly by electronic equipment such as telephone, fax, email, computer and video link. These types of communications are also called telecommunications or '**telecom**'.

Telecom permits people from all parts of the world to communicate instantly with each other. This allows some businesses to become **footloose**, which means that they can be run equally successfully in a wide variety of places. As a result, some businesses leave large cities and relocate in smaller towns where costs are lower or where the environment is more pleasant. Such towns may then develop economically and grow in size.

Case Study: The Information Age Town of Ennis

A business park or industrial estate near Ennis, Co. Clare

(a) Are the businesses shown here modern or traditional? Explain your answer.

(b) Most of the businesses shown here are *footloose*. What does that mean?

(c) How did developments in *telecom* help the growth of Ennis?

Proximity to Shannon Airport also helped the growth of Ennis. *How?*

1 In 1997 Ennis in Co. Clare was declared an **Information Age Town**. Big Eircom grants were invested in improving telecommunications and IT (information technology) in the town.

2 Ennis soon passed out other towns in the development of business websites and email addresses. A special **Information Age Park** with highly equipped buildings was set up to attract IT companies to the town.

3 **Companies** such as *Magico Software* and *Shannon Showcase* opened in Ennis and employed many people there.

4 As people moved to Ennis in search of work, several housing estates sprang up at the outskirts of the town. **Ennis grew** quickly to become Ireland's sixth largest town, with a population of nearly 25,000 people.

Rapid Revision

● People and goods move between settlements. The development of these **communication links** causes settlements to grow.

● **Road networks** connect Irish settlements. Towns have grown along main roads or where roads meet. New towns have developed in areas connected by major roads to nearby cities.

● **Water transport** on the Rhine and its tributaries link many cities such as Rotterdam in Netherlands, Duisburg in Germany and Basle in Switzerland. Many of these cities have developed as ports and industrial centres. The Rhine waterways are connected by canals to those of the Rhône, the Danube and other rivers.

● **Telecommunications** such as email and video link allow the instant movement of information between people and settlements in all parts of the world. This has encouraged the movement of some businesses from large cities to smaller settlements. Towns such as Ennis have benefited from the spread of information-based businesses.

Activities

1 Write one sentence about each of the following terms to show that you know what it means:
confluence, navigable, inland waterway, telecommunications, footloose industry.

2 *'River transport on the Rhine has linked and developed settlements in different countries.'* Show that the above statement is true.

3 Use evidence from the Ordnance Survey map in Figure 2 to explain how communication links may have contributed over time to the development of Ballinasloe, Co. Galway.

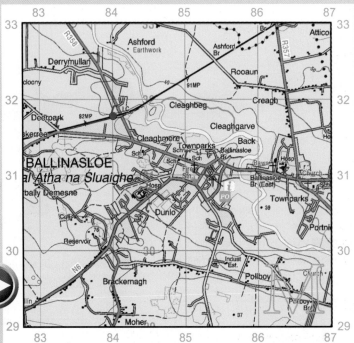

See Chapter 40 of your Workbook

Urban Growth: The Story of Dublin

Throughout history there has been a steady growth in both the number and size of urban areas (towns and cities) throughout the world. This growth is sometimes called **urbanisation**.

Most large urban areas have grown because of the development of the following activities:

- **Economic activities**, such as manufacturing, trading and transport.
- **Administrative activities**, such as those connected with the government and management of a country, a region or an urban area.
- **Social activities**, such as the provision of housing and leisure facilities for people.

> Dublin is the Republic of Ireland's **primate city**. That means it has more than twice the population of any other city in the state.

The Growth of Dublin

The gradual growth of Dublin provides the largest single example of urbanisation in Ireland (see Figure 1).

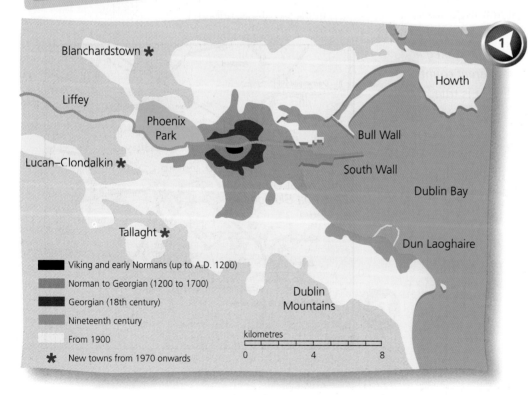

Blanchardstown ✱
Liffey
Phoenix Park
Lucan–Clondalkin ✱
Tallaght ✱

Howth
Bull Wall
South Wall
Dublin Bay
Dun Laoghaire
Dublin Mountains

- ■ Viking and early Normans (up to A.D. 1200)
- ■ Norman to Georgian (1200 to 1700)
- ■ Georgian (18th century)
- ■ Nineteenth century
- □ From 1900
- ✱ New towns from 1970 onwards

kilometres
0   4   8

1 The growth of Dublin over time
Study the map and then say whether each of the following statements is **true** *or* **false**:
(a) Like most cities, Dublin grew outwards from its approximate centre.
(b) The River Liffey was important to the early development of Dublin.
(c) Dublin first developed north of the River Liffey.
(d) The Dun Laoghaire area was developed more than 100 years ago.
(e) Dublin grew more in the twentieth and twenty-first centuries than it had over all time before then.
(f) The Dublin urban area stretches for more than 40km from Howth in the east to Lucan in the west.
(g) Howth was urbanised before Dun Laoghaire.

1 Viking Beginnings

By the tenth century, a group of Vikings had built a small settlement on high ground on the south side of the River Liffey. This settlement was near a dark-coloured pool, which provided shelter for the Vikings' ships. Copying the Irish words for a black pool – *dubh linn* – the Vikings named their settlement *Dyflinn*.

The Vikings were traders and seafarers. So Dublin developed as a **port**.

2 The Normans Take Over

From 1170, the Normans took control of Dublin and began to extend it. By the fourteenth century, Dublin had grown into an important **medieval city**. Its crowded, narrow streets were surrounded by a big stone wall and defended by the Norman-built Dublin Castle.

The Normans had important trading links with English towns, so the **port** of Dublin grew in importance.

Dublin Castle became the centre of English rule in Ireland. As the English gradually extended their control over the country, Dublin became Ireland's main **administrative centre**.

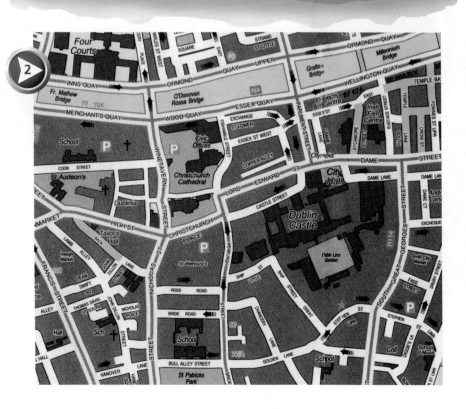

Viking and medieval Dublin
This modern street map shows the approximate location of the old Viking 'Dyflinn' and the medieval city of Dublin.

(a) In what way does the street pattern suggest that the area shown is an old urban area?

(b) The River Liffey and its tributaries once occupied more space than they do today. Which street name suggests that this was so?

(c) Cook Street, Fishamble Street, Winetavern Street and Castle Street all got their names in medieval times. Why do you think each of those streets is so called?

249

3 Georgian Dublin

During the Georgian period of the eighteenth century, Dublin became one of Europe's most splendid cities. The old medieval walls were swept away. Straight, broad streets (such as O'Connell Street) and elegant squares (such as Merrion Square) were built.

A picture and map of Merrion Square can be seen on page 151

- Ireland had its own parliament until 1800, so Dublin was the **administrative** capital of Ireland. Many wealthy landlords built beautiful Georgian townhouses in Dublin and came with their families to live there while parliament was in session. Dublin became one of the largest and most fashionable cities in Europe.

- **Trade** improved with the development of the Grand and Royal Canals and with the building of the North and South Walls to shelter Dublin's port. **Manufacturing** thrived in the old part of the city known as the Liberties, where textiles, coaches and beer (Guinness) were made.

Servants' rooms on top floor

Family bedrooms

Houses usually built of red brick

Upstairs family living rooms, music room, etc.

Main reception rooms on ground floor

Kitchen, laundry and servants' working areas in underground basement

Heavy wood-panelled door

Wrought iron railings

Remember that only a tiny **minority** of Dublin people lived in fine houses such as these. Most people lived in very poor conditions in old parts of the city such as the Liberties.

Georgian townhouses in Dublin
These elegant houses are considered to be among the finest designed buildings in the country.
(a) Find out what is meant by the term 'Georgian'.
(b) Are there any Georgian houses near where you live? If so, describe them.

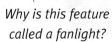

Why is this feature called a fanlight?

By the nineteenth century, many Georgian houses were controlled by slum landlords. Some of these houses then contained more than 100 people – and no indoor toilet or bathroom!

4 The Nineteenth Century

The nineteenth century saw the growth of fashionable new suburbs, but the decay of many older parts of Dublin.

- In 1800, the **Act of Union** abolished the Irish parliament. Dublin declined as a centre of administration and fashion. Many wealthy people abandoned the city and sold their Georgian houses. Some of these houses were bought by 'slum landlords' and rented – room by room – to poor families.

- The coming of the **railway** linked Dublin with new suburbs such as Dun Laoghaire, Dalkey and Killiney. Many wealthy people went to live in these fashionable new suburbs.

- With manufacturing in decline, the **port** area became the centre of Dublin's economic life.

5 From 1900 Onwards

Dublin's **most rapid growth** has taken place since the beginning of the twentieth century (see Figure 1). Some reasons for this are outlined in the box.

Economic reasons	Social reasons	Administrative reasons
• Dublin is the focus of Ireland's road, rail and other **transport** routes. It contains Ireland's chief port and airport. • It is Ireland's biggest **manufacturing** city. • It is our chief **commercial** centre and port and it contains the headquarters of several Irish banks and other commercial firms.	• **Rural to urban migration** greatly enlarged the population of Dublin. • The migration of people from the city centre to the **suburbs** caused Dublin to expand outwards. Most growth today is in **new towns** to the west of the city. Tallaght, for example, contains more people than does Limerick City.	• After independence in 1921, Dublin once again became the **capital*** of Ireland. • Our **civil service** operates mainly out of Dublin.

* The *capital* is the city in which the Government meets.

Blanchardstown, Co. Dublin
In recent times, large new towns such as Blanchardstown developed on the west of Dublin.
(a) How does this picture suggest that Blanchardstown is a new town?
(b) To what extent might the following have contributed to the growth of urban areas such as Blanchardstown?
- The high cost of land in Dublin City.
- Human migration.
(c) Name two new towns, other than Blanchardstown, in Co. Dublin.

Rapid Revision

- Dublin has **grown over time** because of the development of economic, administrative and social activities.
- The **Vikings** set up a small trading settlement, which they called 'Dyflinn'.
- The **Normans** later developed the Viking settlement into a medieval port and defence city.
- By the eighteenth century, Dublin had become an important manufacturing and administrative centre. Beautiful **Georgian** houses and squares made Dublin one of the most elegant cities in Europe.
- The **nineteenth century** saw the decline of Georgian Dublin and the development of rail-linked suburbs such as Dun Laoghaire.
- **From 1900 onwards**, Dublin extended rapidly. It is Ireland's primate city, capital, chief port and leading industrial centre.

Activities

1 The items or activities in the box below all relate to the growth of Dublin over time. Indicate whether each item relates mainly to the *economic life*, the *administrative life* or the *social life* of the city.

> Dublin Port; Georgian townhouses; rural to urban migration; Dublin Castle; the Royal Canal; Dáil Éireann; Merrion Square; the Guinness brewery; medieval city walls; the North Wall; the railway; coach making in the Liberties.

2 Describe the development over time of an Irish city of your choice. Write three paragraphs, one under each of the following headings: *economic activities*, *administrative activities*, *social activities*.

Functional Zones within Cities

Many different activities or **functions** go on in cities. Most cities have areas or **zones** that are used mainly for specific functions. A list of such functional zones is given in the box below.

Some functional zones in a city

- The central area for business and shopping, which is called the **Central Business District** (CBD).
- A number of smaller **shopping areas**.
- Numerous **shopping centres**.
- **Industrial** (factory) areas.
- **Residential** (housing) areas.
- **Open spaces** for recreation (such as parks and playgrounds).

Grafton Street

Phoenix Park

Firhouse

Jervis Street

Which functional zone is illustrated by each of the four images of Dublin given on this page?

Case Study: Functional zones in Paris

Paris dominates the social and economic life of France. It is also the capital (centre of government) of the country.

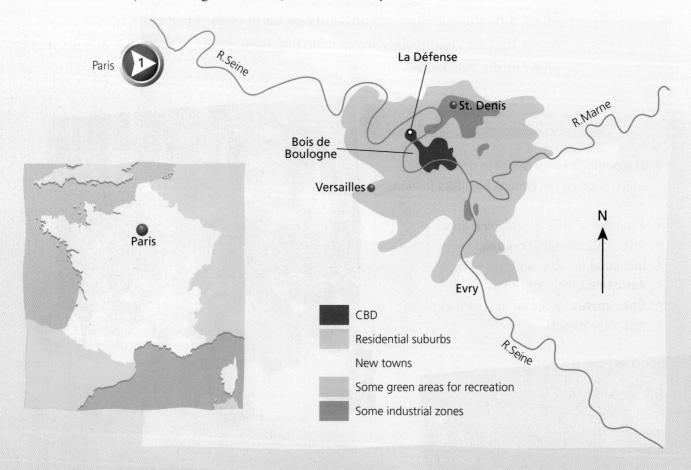

Paris

R.Seine

La Défense

St. Denis

R.Marne

Bois de Boulogne

Versailles

Paris

Evry

R.Seine

N

- CBD
- Residential suburbs
- New towns
- Some green areas for recreation
- Some industrial zones

CBD

The CBD of Paris is located in the heart of the city around **famous streets** such as the *Champs Elysées*. It is the main **commercial area** of the city and its tall buildings contain many large offices, banks, fashionable department stores and high-class specialist shops such as jewellers. The CBD has many world-famous **public buildings**. These include *Notre Dame Cathedral*, the *Eiffel Tower* and *the Louvre*, which is the world's largest art gallery.

The centre of Paris
Identify Notre Dame Cathedral in the picture

Shopping Areas

Paris has several large shopping areas outside its CBD. Some of these were the CBDs of other urban areas, such as *Versailles* and *St Denis*, which have been 'swallowed up' by the growing city of Paris. Others are the commercial centres of new towns, such as *Evry* (see Figure 1).

Most shopping areas contain large **shopping centres**, where people can visit several stores in a single roofed area.

Residential Areas

- Most people live in **residential suburbs**. Some suburbs are more fashionable and wealthy than others. Western suburbs, for example, tend in general to be wealthier than most eastern suburbs.
- Five new **satellite towns** have been developed on the fringes of Paris (see Figure 1). These new towns now house a total of more than a million people.

Industrial Areas

Paris has several industrial areas.

- Most manufacturing takes place in specially planned **industrial estates** on the urban fringes and in satellite towns.
- Paris is an important river port. Chemical and other industries are situated in **dockside locations** along the River Seine.
- Some expensive luxury items, such as jewellery and cosmetics, are still made at **city centre** locations.

Open Spaces for Recreation

Paris contains several open-air recreation areas. Some of these, like the beautiful *Luxembourg Gardens*, were once the gardens of great palaces. Others, like the *Bois de Boulogne*, were once royal hunting forests.

Two sides of Paris
- *The beautifully redeveloped La Défense area (above) reminds us that Paris is one of the world's wealthiest cities.*
- *But some of the city's eleven million people live in extremely poor suburbs such as that shown below.*

See Rapid Revision on page 262

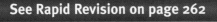

How Land Values Affect Land Use in Cities

1 At the City Centre

Both the value of land and the intensity of land use tend to increase towards the city centre.

The city centre (CBD) is the place where the city's most important streets meet. It is where many people go to work or shop. It is the **busiest part of the city**.

Shops and other businesses like to locate in the busy city centre because this is where they will attract most customers. This results in a **huge demand** for city centre land.

High demand pushes up the value of land in the city centre. **Land values** are higher there than in any other part of the city.

Because businesses pay very high prices for city centre sites, they must put these sites to the best possible use. They do this by using city centre sites very **intensively**.

CBD   INCREASING   LAND   **VALUES**

At the city centre
- Highest land values
- Highest-density buildings

Some high-rise commercial buildings
Examples:
Custom House Quay, Dublin
Connolly Hall, Cork

Near the city centre
- High land values
- High-density buildings

Multi-storey apartment blocks
Examples:
Grand Canal Street, Dublin
South Terrace, Cork

How to use city centre sites intensively

- Build **very tall** buildings. Such buildings allow several 'layers' of use to be obtained from each site.
- Use each building for a **variety of purposes**. Ground floors are usually occupied by department stores or specialist shops. Higher floors are often used as offices.

2 Moving Away from the City Centre

Land values decrease gradually as one moves away from the busy city centre. As land values decrease, **so does the intensity** with which the land is used.

- Land is used less for commercial reasons and more for **residential purposes**.
- Housing **densities** (the number of dwellings per hectare) and the **height** of houses **decrease** gradually as one moves away from the city centre.
- Spacious single-storey schools, factories, shopping centres and houses become more common as one approaches the **outer suburbs**. Land is more plentiful and less expensive here, so buildings can be developed horizontally rather than vertically.

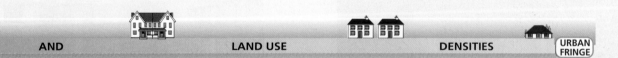

AND   LAND USE   DENSITIES   URBAN FRINGE

In the suburbs
- Lower land values
- Medium-density buildings

Semi-detached houses
Examples:
Dundrum, Dublin
Bishopstown, Cork

In the outer suburbs ('urban fringe')
- Still lower land values
- Low-density buildings

Detached houses
Examples:
Rathfarnham, Dublin
Rochestown Road, Cork

See Rapid Revision on page 262

Variations in City Housing

The information in this chapter shows that the age, type and quality of housing in Irish cities vary greatly.

Age of Housing

Houses tend to be older in inner city areas and newer towards the suburbs.

Most cities grow from their centres outwards, so most of the older houses tend to be situated in or near inner city areas (photograph A). York Street in Dublin and Cove Street in Cork provide examples of this. **But . . .** *many old dwellings have now been replaced by new ones in 'renewed' inner city areas.*

Because most cities grow outwards, the newest houses are usually to be found in the outer suburbs of cities, such as at *Clonsilla* in Dublin and at *Douglas* in Cork (photograph B).

Type of Housing

Homes tend to be smaller in the inner city than they are in the suburbs.

Most **inner city** homes (photograph A) are **high-density**, small terraced homes or apartments. Many do not have front or back gardens. Land is so valuable in the inner city that large houses with gardens would cost too much.

Houses at the **edge of a city** (photograph B) tend to be larger than houses near the city centre. These **low-density** houses are usually semi-detached or detached, with front and back gardens. This is because land is much cheaper here than it is in the city centre.

Quality of Housing

The quality of housing varies greatly within Irish cities.

Wealth is distributed unevenly in Ireland. This is shown by the varied quality of housing in our cities.

- **Public housing estates**, built by city councils or corporations, usually contain dwellings that are modest in size and quality. While such houses may themselves vary, they are typically three-bedroomed terraced or semi-detached houses with small front and back gardens. *Kilbarrack* in Dublin and *Knocknaheeny* in Cork contain large corporation estates.

- Wealthier parts of our cities contain many **privately built houses or housing estates**. Some of these estates contain large, high-quality houses for rich buyers. Top-of-the-range detached houses may contain five or six bedrooms, three bathrooms and large front and back gardens. Suburbs such as *Foxrock* in Dublin and *Rochestown Road* in Cork provide examples of such houses.

Corporation houses in Dublin

Contrast this privately owned house in Dublin with the corporation housing shown in the photograph above.

See Rapid Revision on page 263

On the Move: City Traffic Patterns

There are clear patterns in the daily movement of people within cities.

Each day, most of us travel to and from our homes for different reasons. One of the most common reasons for the daily movement of adults in Irish cities is to commute (travel) to and from work. Many people who work in cities live in suburban or rural areas. This contributes to daily **traffic patterns**, such as those illustrated in Figure 1.

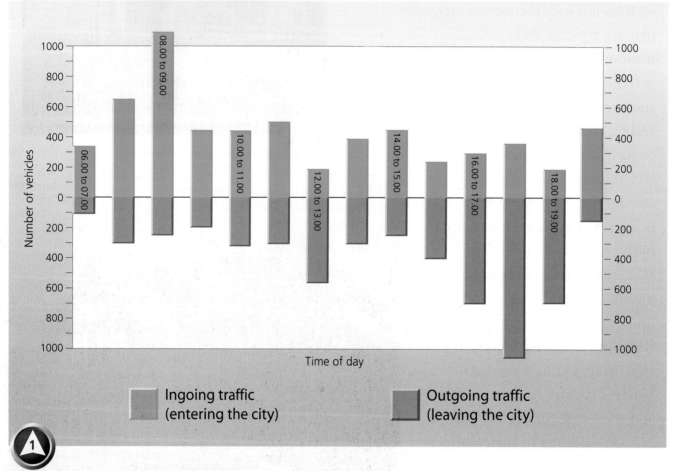

Number of vehicles

Time of day

08.00 to 09.00
06.00 to 07.00
10.00 to 11.00
12.00 to 13.00
14.00 to 15.00
16.00 to 17.00
18.00 to 19.00

■ Ingoing traffic (entering the city)   ■ Outgoing traffic (leaving the city)

1 Weekday traffic on some principal roads in and out of Cork City from 0600 hours to 2000 hours

(a) Which hour shown has most ingoing traffic (traffic entering the city)?
(b) During which hour shown is there least outgoing traffic?
(c) Which two hours of the day can be best described as 'rush hours' with 'peak' traffic?
(d) Why is traffic so heavy during each of these rush-hour periods?
(e) What is the main difference between traffic flows during the morning rush hour and traffic flows during the evening rush hour?
(f) How might traffic patterns on a Sunday differ from those shown on the graph above?
(g) Say whether each of the following statements is true or false:
　(i) There is more traffic shown between 0600 and 0700 than there is between 1800 and 1900.
　(ii) More vehicles enter Cork between 1300 and 1400 hours than between 1500 and 1600 hours.
　(iii) Cork streets are likely to be busy between 1600 and 1900 hours.

Traffic Congestion

The daily movement of working people to and from the same parts of a city at the same time contributes to serious traffic congestion.

Malahide

Howth

Docklands

Citywest

Tallaght

Sandyford

Greystones

—— Dart line
—— Luas line
▨ Dublin urban area

②

Dublin's *DART* and *Luas* railway lines

Some ways of reducing city traffic congestion

- Improve city **bus** services and restrict the use of private cars in inner city areas.
- Use urban and suburban **railways** and **tramways**, such as Dublin's *DART* and *Luas* systems.
- Build **metro** (underground railway) systems.
- Build **ring roads** around cities.
- Build **motorways** through cities.
- Use one-way traffic systems and other **traffic solutions** (see page 167).

Did you know?
- **DART** refers to *Dublin Area Rapid Transport*.
- **Luas** means *speed* in Irish.

Waterford City

(a) How many different modes (types) of transport can you see in this picture?

(b) Why do you think traffic congestion might occur in the urban area shown?

(c) How many traffic management devices can you identify in the photograph?

See Rapid Revision on page 263

Rapid Revision

Chapter 42

Cities such as *Paris* have several **distinct functional zones**.

- The **Central Business District (CBD)** is the main commercial area. Its offices and specialist shops occupy tall buildings in the city centre. It contains busy streets such as the Champs Elysées.
- **Smaller shopping areas** might include the CBDs of older towns, such as Versailles, that have been 'swallowed up' by Paris, or the CBDs of new towns such as Evry.
- **Shopping centres** are large buildings that each contain several shops.
- Most **industry** is located in industrial estates near the fringes of the city. But some old or luxury industries, such as jewellery making, are still located near the centre of Paris.
- Most **residential areas** are in the surburbs or the five large satellite towns that have developed on the fringes of Paris.
- Paris contains many **open spaces** for recreation. These range from small playgrounds to large parks such as the Luxembourg Gardens.

Activities

(a) In urban geography, what is meant by the term 'functional zone'?

(b) In the case of Paris **or** London **or** New York, name *three* different functional zones and give one urban example of each zone that you name.

Rapid Revision

Chapter 43

- Both land values and intensity of land use tend to increase towards a city centre.
- There is a big demand for land near the busy **Central Business District**, so land is very expensive there. Because of this, buildings tend to be very **intensively used**. They are usually tall and multipurpose buildings.
- As one moves **outwards** from a city centre, land tends to become less expensive. Buildings are lower. They do **not** need to be used as **intensively** in order for their owners to profit from them.

Activities

Name a city or large town that you have studied. Suppose you were travelling from the centre of the town or city outwards towards the countryside. Describe the change you would notice in the average height of the buildings. Suggest an explanation for this change. (*J.C. Ordinary Level*)

Rapid Revision

Chapter 44

● The **age, type** and **quality of housing vary** within cities such as Dublin.
● Because cities grow outwards, **houses near city centres are usually older** than houses in the suburbs. (But many inner city houses have now been 'renewed' or replaced.)
● **Smaller, high-density housing is usual near city centres**, where land is very valuable. Houses are usually larger in the suburbs and edges of cities.
● Houses in some **private estates** are much **larger** and more **expensive** than most houses in corporation or city council estates.

Activities

The type, quality and age of houses vary in towns and cities.
Give **two** reasons why this statement is correct. In your answer refer to specific places you have studied.
(J.C. Ordinary Level)

Rapid Revision

Chapter 45

● There are **clear patterns in the daily movement of people** in a city.
● Morning and evening rush hours are caused by **commuters**, who enter a city for work each morning and leave it after work each evening.
● Rush-hour traffic congestion is common. It is reduced by the use of ring roads, one-way traffic systems, the increased use of public transport and other **traffic management devices**.

Activities

(a) Name and explain three ways in which traffic congestion is caused in any town or city you have studied.
(b) Look at Figure 3. What purpose does the M50 roadway have in reducing traffic congestion in Dublin?
(c) Describe three ways, other than that referred to in your answer to question (b) above, of reducing urban traffic congestion.

(J.C. Ordinary Level)

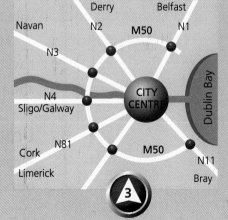

See Chapters 42 to 45 of your Workbook

Rapid change in our cities has resulted in a number of problems for urban dwellers.

Some urban problems

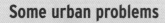

- Zones of **decline** in inner city areas and of **suburban sprawl** at the edge of the cities.

- **Inadequate services** in some areas of decline and sprawl.

- The **disruption of communities** as people move from city centre areas to suburbs.

- **High unemployment** in some areas.

- **Crime**

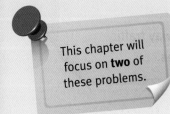

This chapter will focus on **two** of these problems.

Focus One: Areas of Decline and Urban Sprawl

One of the greatest changes that occurred in Irish cities in recent times was the **decline of some inner city areas** and the growth of **urban sprawl at the edges of cities**.

Urban Decline

Between 1960 and 1990, many Irish inner city areas fell into decline.

Poor **housing** and increasing **traffic congestion** made some inner-city areas unattractive to live in. Traditional industry declined rapidly and caused serious **unemployment** in these areas. Inner Dublin, for example, lost 30 per cent of its industry in the ten years after 1966.

As the population of inner city areas declined, so did their **appearance and services**. Old houses fell further into decay, while inner city shops and schools began to close. As the problems of decay increased, more and more people were encouraged to leave for the suburbs.

Many Irish inner-city areas are no longer in decay, because they have been **redeveloped** or **renewed**. This means that their buildings and other amenities have been improved.

Urban Sprawl

Urban sprawl is the **rapid growth of housing from urban areas outwards into the countryside**. This growth was especially rapid during the 'Celtic Tiger' economic boom up to 2008.

The following **problems** are associated with urban sprawl.

- Valuable **farmland** – such as fertile market gardening land in North Dublin – was used for building purposes.

- **Villages**, such as Dundrum in Dublin and Douglas in Cork, were swallowed up by urban growth. They have lost their unique identities and become mere parts of a large, impersonal city.

- Some large **suburbs are boring**, 'soulless' places with few recreational or social amenities. They are almost deserted by day, when most of their inhabitants are at work.

Inner city decay

In the 1980s, the Henrietta Street area of Dublin suffered from serious decay. Many buildings were owned by *speculators*, who left them boarded up for years waiting for property prices to rise before selling them. Most of these inner city areas have now been redeveloped.

What problems have been associated with urban decay in Irish cities?

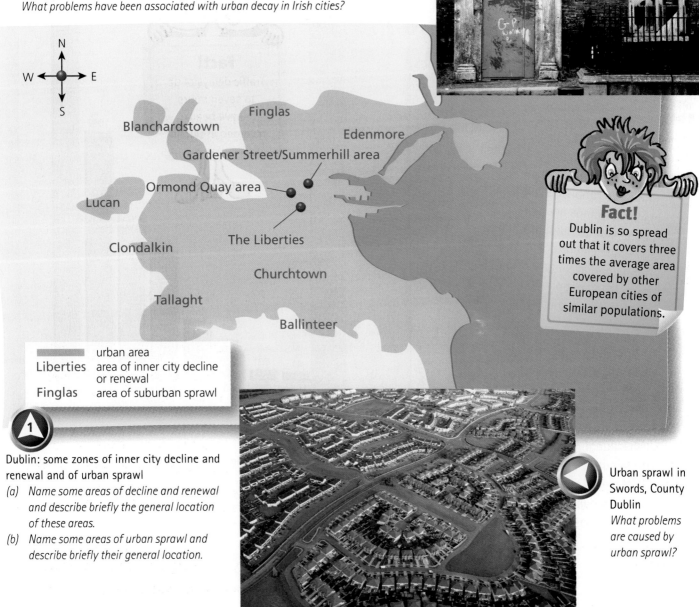

Fact!
Dublin is so spread out that it covers three times the average area covered by other European cities of similar populations.

urban area
Liberties area of inner city decline or renewal
Finglas area of suburban sprawl

1

Dublin: some zones of inner city decline and renewal and of urban sprawl

(a) Name some areas of decline and renewal and describe briefly the general location of these areas.

(b) Name some areas of urban sprawl and describe briefly their general location.

Urban sprawl in Swords, County Dublin
What problems are caused by urban sprawl?

Transport

Our public transport services (buses and trains) do not meet the needs of growing cities such as Dublin. More and more city dwellers therefore rely on private cars for transport. But most of our city streets and roads cannot take ever-increasing car traffic. Huge traffic jams result, causing long delays and frustration to road users.

Water supplies

Water quality has declined in some rapidly growing urban areas. Polluted water supplies made 200 Galway City people ill in 2007. The residents of 90,000 homes in Galway were then forced to use boiled or bottled water for drinking, cooking and even for washing their teeth.

Waste disposal

As urban areas grow, so do their problems of waste disposal. More and more rubbish is buried in 'landfill' dumps and plans have been made to build huge waste-burning incinerators at Poolbeg in Dublin and at Ringaskiddy near Cork. Many people oppose the use of incinerators on health grounds.

Recreation facilities

When private developers build urban suburbs, they often fail to provide adequate recreational facilities. Many suburban areas lack adequate playgrounds, community halls or other facilities that would help young people to develop happily within their communities.

Schools

Some schools in growing urban areas cannot easily cope with their increasing student numbers. This situation has led to overcrowded classrooms and play areas.

Focus Two: Inadequate Services

People need basic **infrastructural services** to live in comfort. Such services relate to *transport, water supplies, waste disposal, recreation* and *schools*. As urban areas grow, some of these services become inadequate. People's quality of life then suffers.

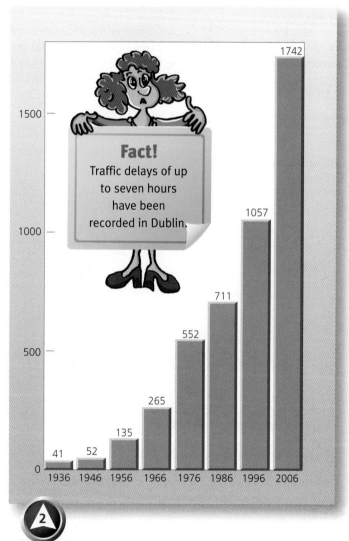

Numbers (given in thousands) of private cars in Ireland between 1936 and 2006.

(a) Over which ten-year period did car numbers increase most?

(b) What was the increase in car numbers over that ten-year period?

(c) By which year shown did Irish car numbers first exceed one million?

(d) How might the trends illustrated in Figure 2 affect infrastructural services that relate to transport?

(e) List three environmental problems associated with increasing car numbers.

Suburban teenagers

(a) Why would the provision of properly equipped recreational facilities be important for these teenagers?

(b) Name other infrastructural services that would be needed in urban suburbs such as this one.

Rapid Revision

- Some Irish urban areas suffer from **problems** such as urban decline, urban sprawl and inadequate services.

- Urban decline and suburban sprawl are serious urban problems. Poor housing, failing industry, declining services and traffic congestion have been associated with **urban decline** in inner-city areas such as Ormond Quay in Dublin. Many of these areas have now been renewed. **Urban sprawl** is the rapid outward spread of suburbs such as Finglas in Dublin. Urban sprawl uses up farmland and 'swallows up' nearby villages. Some suburbs are 'soulless' and poorly serviced.

- **Inadequate services** can create problems relating to traffic congestion, poor water supplies, waste disposal, inadequate recreational facilities and overcrowded schools.

Activities

1 Explain the meaning of the terms 'urban decay' and 'urban sprawl'. Referring to areas that you have studied, describe some of the problems associated with urban decay and urban sprawl.

2 Irish cities have problems that are associated with rapid urban growth. Describe carefully one such problem (do not use urban decay or urban sprawl). (Based on *J.C. Ordinary Level*)

See Chapter 46 of your Workbook

Test Yourself
eTest.ie

Urban Solutions

In Chapter 46 you learned about problems such as inner city decay and urban sprawl. City planners in developed countries try to solve these problems by the following means:

- **Urban redevelopment and renewal** are used to combat *inner city decay*.
- **New towns** are built to reduce uncontrolled *urban sprawl*.

Inner City Development

There are two forms of inner city development.

Urban Redevelopment

Old, run-down houses and other buildings are demolished. Local people are rehoused in the suburbs or in new towns. The valuable inner city sites are then used mainly for offices, shops and other **commercial uses**.

Urban Renewal

Old dwellings are refurbished or replaced by new houses. Community centres and other facilities are provided so that existing inner city **residents** are encouraged to remain in their old localities.

Cork City
(a) Identify an area on this photograph: (i) that has undergone urban redevelopment; (ii) that was undergoing redevelopment when the photograph was taken; (iii) that seems suitable for future redevelopment.
(b) How do you know that this photograph shows urban redevelopment rather than urban renewal?
(c) What urban problem or problems are solved by urban redevelopment?

Case study: The Renewal of Fatima Mansions

Fatima Mansions are situated in the Dolphin's Barn area of inner city Dublin (see Figure 1). They have undergone large-scale renewal.

The old *Fatima*

The old *Fatima Mansions* consisted of nearly 400 corporation flats in 15 large apartment blocks. From the late 1970s, serious problems emerged in the area:

- **Unemployment** rose rapidly as inner-city industries began to close.
- **Drug abuse** and drug-related **crime** increased dramatically.

People gradually left the area, so that most of *Fatima's* apartments lay abandoned and vandalised.

The New Fatima

In 2004, Dublin City Council, with the help of local people, began to renew Fatima Mansions. The old apartment blocks were demolished and replaced by new, high-quality homes. The new Fatima differs from the old in the following ways:

- It has a mixture of **public and privately owned housing**, so that people of different income levels live in the area.
- **Dwellings** include a variety of semi-detached, terraced and duplex houses, as well as flats.
- **Shops and social services**, such as a crèche and a homework club, are included.

Local people are confident that the renewed *Fatima Mansions* will be a happy and safe place to live.

Urban renewal at Fatima Mansions
Compare these dwellings with those of the old Fatima Mansions shown above.

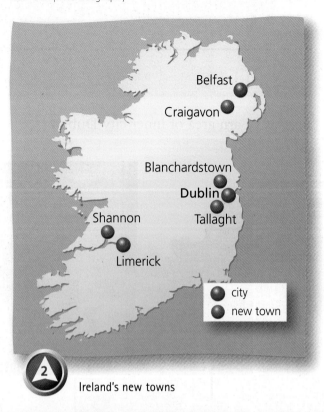

2 Ireland's new towns

New Towns

In order to reduce urban sprawl, new towns are sometimes built near large cities. Some new towns in Ireland are shown in Figure 2.

Characteristics of New Towns

- They do not grow naturally. They are **deliberately built** to house a planned maximum population.
- They are built near cities and are connected to the cities with good transport systems. Their main function is to house the **overspill populations** of nearby cities and so prevent urban sprawl.
- They contain carefully planned **industrial estates**, as well as **services** such as shopping centres.

Case study: Tallaght – A New Town

Examine the photograph and map extract of Tallaght in Figure 3.

1. Refer to the *map only* to answer the following:
   (a) How do you know that Tallaght is a planned urban area?
   (b) Identify four different services in Tallaght.
2. Referring to the *photograph only*, identify four different functions or land uses in Tallaght.
3. The place labelled *X* on the *photograph* is at grid reference O 091 273 on the *map*. With the help of the map, identify the following:
   (a) the type and number of the road labelled *A* on the photograph;
   (b) the functions (uses) of each of the buildings labelled *B* and *C* on the photograph.

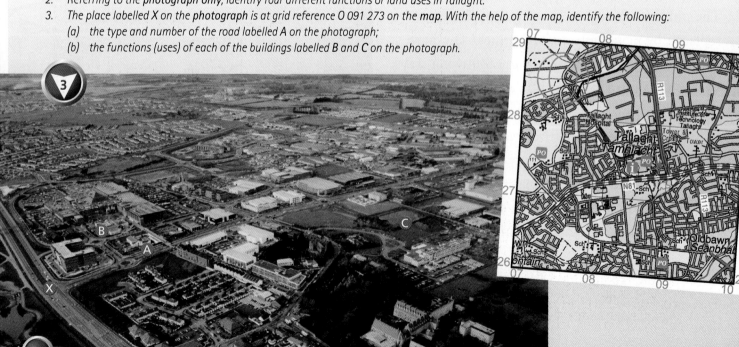

Tallaght was developed to the south-west of Dublin City. It is in many ways **typical of a new town**:

- It is designed to reduce urban sprawl in Dublin by housing some of the city's **overspill** (out-migrating) population.
- Its **population has grown rapidly**. It now contains more than 65,000 people, which is more people than live in Limerick City.
- It is **connected to the city** with excellent roads and with a *Luas* tramway link.
- It has its own **industrial estates** to provide jobs. The Greenhills Industrial Estate is an example.
- It provides a wide range of **services**. They include a hospital, a third-level Regional Technical College, a theatre, cinemas and shopping centres.

Tallaght Town Centre
How is this different from the centres of most Irish towns?

Rapid Revision

- Urban redevelopment and urban renewal are used to fight inner-city decay. **Redevelopment** involves the use of inner city areas, largely for commercial purposes. **Renewal** usually aims to preserve inner-city communities and to upgrade their environments. **Fatima Mansions** in Dublin have undergone urban renewal.

- **New towns** are sometimes built to control the suburban sprawl of nearby cities. **Tallaght** is a new town to the south-west of Dublin. It was purpose-built to take some of the overspill population from the city. It contains several industrial estates, as well as services such as shopping centres and a hospital. It is well connected to Dublin by good roads and by the *Luas* tramway.

Activities

1. *Urban planning can sometimes improve the environment in which people live.* In relation to a named example of an Irish city or town that you have studied, explain two ways in which urban planning has improved the environment.

   (J.C. Higher Level)

2. Describe the principal characteristics of any named Irish new town that you have studied.

See Chapter 47 of your Workbook

Urban Problems in Kolkata

Urbanisation or the growth of cities is going on very rapidly in the Third World. Cities in the South grow at a different pace and in a different manner from Western European cities. They also experience problems that are different from those of cities in the rich North.

> You must study **two** of these problems in detail.

Some problems of Third World cities

- They are growing very rapidly.
- They contain large, unplanned shanty towns.
- There are few clearly planned functional zones.
- There is great inequality between rich and poor.
- There is a lack of infrastructural services, such as schools and hospitals.

> **Revise** what you learned about **Kolkata** on pages 206 and 207.

Case study: **Kolkata and its Problems**

Revise what you learned about Kolkata on pages 206 and 207.

1

(a) In what part of India is Kolkata situated?
(b) Near which bay and country is Kolkata situated?

Kolkata (Calcutta) contains almost 15 million people and is one of India's largest and most rapidly growing cities. Its rapid growth has led to many problems.

Problem 1: The Unplanned Development of Shanty Towns

Kolkata is growing very rapidly as millions of people migrate from the countryside into the city. Most migrants live in hastily built slums called shanty towns or **bustees**, which have grown up around the edges of the city. Kolkata's bustees now contain more than four million people. That is as many people as live in the entire Republic of Ireland!

Because Kolkata grew so rapidly, its bustees developed in an **unplanned** way. Their narrow alleyways wind chaotically around many makeshift houses, many of which are made of wood, straw or even flattened metal boxes or barrels. Homes are packed closely together and are extremely crowded. Some bustees contain over 150,000 people per square kilometre.

Living in a Bustee
(Based on reports by Irish development workers)

The Patel family lives in a *bustee* at the edge of Kolkata. Ten years ago, they migrated from a rural area to the city in search of work.

Their house is built mainly of concrete blocks and old timber, with a corrugated iron roof and a hardened earthen floor. It contains one room and is about the size of an average Irish kitchen.

Mr and Mrs Patel and their three children eat, live and sleep in their single-roomed dwelling. Like most bustee-dwellers, the Patels are **squatters**. This means they do not own the land on which their little house stands. But this situation does not worry them too much. Like the rubbish-strewn streets and open sewers, it is part and parcel of the unplanned nature of Kolkata's overcrowded bustees.

Mrs Patel keeps her little house clean and tidy. This is especially difficult in summer, when heavy monsoon rain sometimes washes sewage from open drains into the bustee dwellings. Mr Patel works hard as a street trader. Their eldest child – a boy of not yet ten years old – has found rather dangerous work in a makeshift factory that mixes gunpowder to make fireworks.

Mrs Patel knows that her house is much better than most bustee dwellings. 'Think of the pavement people,' she says. 'They have to live under bridges or on the streets. And when they die, their bodies are often thrown into the Hooghly (River), in which other pavement people wash and bathe.'

(a) What does this extract tell you about: (i) the house; and (ii) the work of the Patel family?
(b) How does the extract show that bustees are unplanned developments?
(c) Which of the following climate types exist in Kolkata? *Tropical; equatorial; monsoon; boreal. How do you know?*
(d) Who are 'pavement people' and what does the extract tell you about them?

The Patels' home in Kolkata
Describe the scene.

Problem 2: Lack of Services
The provision of **infrastructural services** such as clean water, electricity, schools, hospitals and rubbish-collection facilities costs a lot of money – something which is in short supply in most Third World cities. Poorer areas of Kolkata suffer especially from a shortage of basic services.

Inadequate services

1 While most people can get **clean water**, it is usual for up to 40 families to depend on a single street tap for water supplies. Many homeless 'pavement people' have no clean water. They are forced to rely on unfiltered water supplies intended only for street cleaning or fire fighting.

2 Proper **sanitation facilities**, such as flush toilets, are almost non-existent in the bustees. Human effluent runs through open sewers in the narrow lanes. Heavy monsoon rains often wash sewage into water supplies and people's houses. This endangers health.

3 Most **bustee schools** are poorly built, badly equipped and very short of money. Many classrooms do not even have seats, tables or desks and few children have textbooks of their own. It is very difficult, therefore, for children to make progress at school.

   Many children – especially girls – do not attend school at all. People are so poor that most children need to work from an early age.

4 Despite the fact that parts of Kolkata have an underground rail system, **public transport** is generally very poor. Most buses are old and are so overcrowded that some passengers hang on from the outside. Many people are so poor that they cannot afford to use public transport at all.

See Chapter 48 of your Workbook

Inadequate services in Kolkata
Describe the services shown in these photographs.

See Rapid Revision on page 276.

Economic Activities: An Introduction

Different people make their living by doing different types of jobs. These jobs are called **economic activities** because people earn money from them. There are three main categories of economic activity: **primary activities**, **secondary activities** and **tertiary activities**.

Primary activities are those in which **people obtain natural resources** from the land or the sea. *Farming, fishing, forestry* and *mining* are all examples of primary activities.

Secondary activities are those in which people process or manufacture products. All **manufacturing industries** are secondary activities. Some make things from natural resources, for example when *wheat is processed into flour*. Others take already processed materials and change them further, for example when *flour is processed into bread*.

Tertiary activities include all kinds of useful **services**. People working in tertiary or third-level activities include *teachers*, *truck drivers*, *hairdressers* and *travel agents*.

See Rapid Revision on page 276

Into which category of activities would you place each of the following?
Taxi driver, shipyard worker, TD, potter, farmer, shop assistant, mechanic, forestry worker, chimney sweep, doctor, plumber, fisherman, nun, pop singer.

Rapid Revision

Chapter 48

Majority (Third) World cities such as **Kolkata** have problems that are different from those in Western cities.

- Kolkata is a huge and rapidly growing city. It contains **unplanned bustees**, where narrow lanes separate the makeshift homes of poor people.
- Basic services are **inadequate** in poor areas. *Clean water* is not available to all and most bustee homes do not have proper *toilets*. *Schools* are poorly built and equipped. *Public transport* is poor. Buses are old and are often very overcrowded.

Activities

1. Name five urban problems that you would expect to find in a named Third World city.

2. In the case of any **one** Third World city that you have studied, describe **two** problems resulting from rapid population growth.

Rapid Revision

Chapter 49

- **Primary** activities farm, fish, mine or otherwise obtain natural resources.
- **Secondary** activities manufacture or process resources into useful products.
- **Tertiary** activities, such as nursing or shop-keeping, provide useful services.

Activities

Name and locate evidence of primary, secondary and tertiary activities on the photograph and the OS map shown in Figure 1.

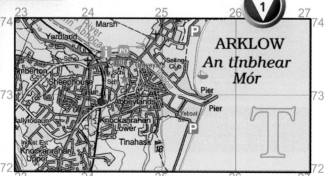

ARKLOW
An tInbhear Mór

See Chapters 48 and 49 of your Workbook

50

Water: A Vital Natural Resource

Which of these are **renewable** natural resources and which are **non-renewable**?

- solar (sun) power
- oil
- iron ore
- peat
- tides
- wind
- electricity
- fish
- coal

Useful things provided by nature are called **natural resources**. Of these, clean air and water are the most important.

A Renewable Resource

Water is a **renewable resource**. This means that it can be used again and again, provided it is properly used and conserved. Nature constantly cleans and renews our planet's water supply. This is done by a process known as the **water cycle** or the **hydrological cycle**. It is shown in Figure 1.

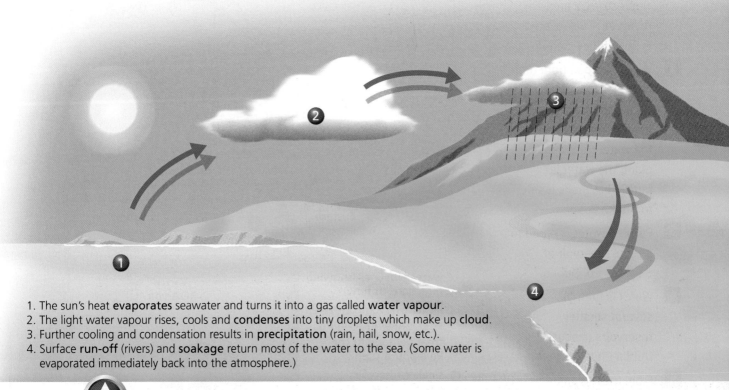

1. The sun's heat **evaporates** seawater and turns it into a gas called **water vapour**.
2. The light water vapour rises, cools and **condenses** into tiny droplets which make up **cloud**.
3. Further cooling and condensation results in **precipitation** (rain, hail, snow, etc.).
4. Surface **run-off** (rivers) and **soakage** return most of the water to the sea. (Some water is evaporated immediately back into the atmosphere.)

The water cycle
(a) How does this diagram show that water is a renewable resource?
(b) How might the presence of permeable or impermeable rock affect the cycle shown here? (Permeable rock allows water to pass through it; impermeable rock does not.)
(c) What effect would the presence of forests have on the cycle? (Hint: find out the meanings of the terms *intervention* and *transpiration*.)

Local Water Supplies in Ireland

County and city councils in Ireland play an important role in supplying fresh water. They collect, store, treat and distribute our water supplies.

The following case study tells the story of South Dublin's main water supply.

Case study: Water for South Dublin

From the Liffey to the Tap

South Dublin gets most of its water supply from the **catchment area** of the River Liffey. (A catchment is the area drained by a river and its tributaries.) Much of this water is drawn from Pollaphuca in Co. Wicklow.

1 Water from the River Liffey and its tributaries is collected in a huge water storage area or **reservoir**. This reservoir is Pollaphuca Lake.

2 Water is **piped** from the reservoir to a water **treatment plant** near Ballymore Eustace. At the water treatment plant, the water is **purified** to make it safe to drink.

3 Purified water is piped to a **large reservoir** at Saggart, Co. Dublin.

4 Water is then piped to **several smaller reservoirs** in south Dublin City.

5 From these small reservoirs, water is piped to the final **consumers** – homes, offices, factories etc.

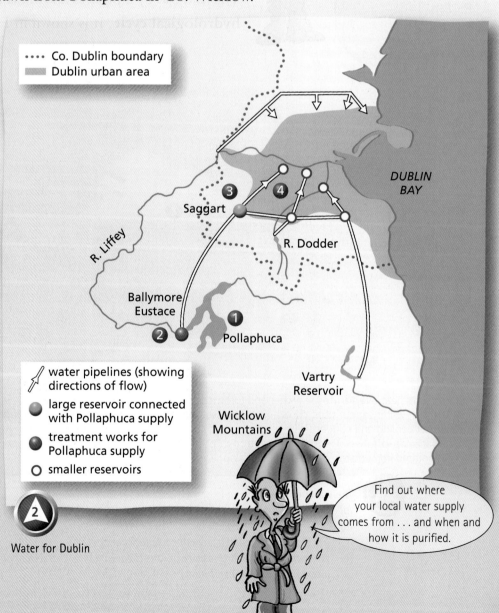

- - - - Co. Dublin boundary

▬▬▬ Dublin urban area

DUBLIN BAY

Saggart

R. Dodder

R. Liffey

Ballymore Eustace

Pollaphuca

Vartry Reservoir

Wicklow Mountains

⚹ water pipelines (showing directions of flow)

🔵 large reservoir connected with Pollaphuca supply

🔴 treatment works for Pollaphuca supply

⚪ smaller reservoirs

2 Water for Dublin

Find out where your local water supply comes from . . . and when and how it is purified.

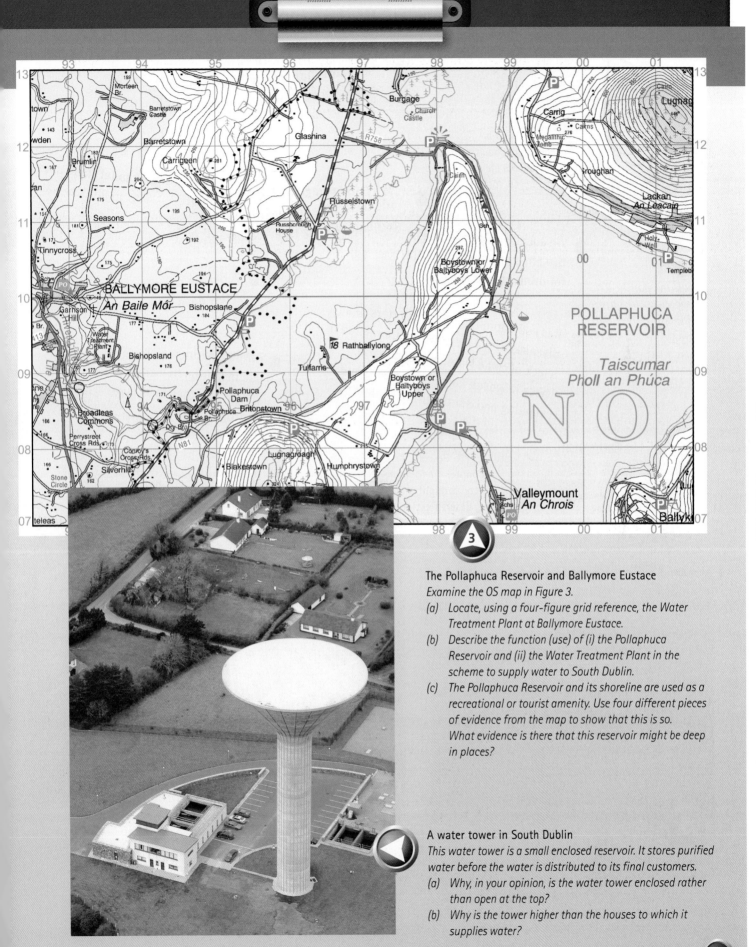

The Pollaphuca Reservoir and Ballymore Eustace
Examine the OS map in Figure 3.
(a) Locate, using a four-figure grid reference, the Water Treatment Plant at Ballymore Eustace.
(b) Describe the function (use) of (i) the Pollaphuca Reservoir and (ii) the Water Treatment Plant in the scheme to supply water to South Dublin.
(c) The Pollaphuca Reservoir and its shoreline are used as a recreational or tourist amenity. Use four different pieces of evidence from the map to show that this is so. What evidence is there that this reservoir might be deep in places?

A water tower in South Dublin
This water tower is a small enclosed reservoir. It stores purified water before the water is distributed to its final customers.
(a) Why, in your opinion, is the water tower enclosed rather than open at the top?
(b) Why is the tower higher than the houses to which it supplies water?

The Importance of Water

Water is needed to maintain human and animal life and to grow food.

Discuss the statement in the speech bubble above. The ideas given here will help you.

❯ We each need an average of five litres of water a day just for **drinking** and **cooking**.

❯ It is estimated that three-quarters of all **diseases** in the Third World are related to a lack of clean water and sanitation. These diseases range from gastroenteritis (vomiting and diarrhoea) to cholera.

❯ The **plants** that provide us with food need water to grow. Farm **animals** need water and plants in order to survive.

❯ In the Sahel region of Africa **drought** and desertification are resulting in terrible suffering (see Photograph A).

❯ A **toilet flush** uses up to 10 litres of water.

❯ A person can **survive** only a **few days** without water.

❯ Farmers in dry regions often use **irrigation** to increase yields from their land (see Photograph B).

Revise **Chapter 17** for more on **drought and desertification**.

Revise **Chapter 18** for more on irrigation

Photograph A
Drought in the Sahel region of Africa. *This rural area of the Sahel region has suffered from severe drought. The growth of the Sahara desert (desertification) has caused great suffering and has resulted in human migration out of the region.*

Photograph B
Irrigation
(a) *What is meant by the term 'irrigation'?*
(b) *Contrast the scene shown here with the scene in Photograph A. Account briefly for the contrast.*

Polluting Our Water Supplies

Water is vital for our survival and comfort. Despite this, people sometimes **pollute** our precious water supplies.

- The overuse of **fertilisers** sometimes results in too many *nitrates* and *phosphates* entering our rivers and lakes. This causes the rapid growth of weed-like *algae*. The algae can use up so much of the water's oxygen supply that fish and other water creatures die. Some rivers and lakes become so polluted that their surfaces become completely covered with green algae.

- Untreated household **sewage** can pollute water and harm human health. In 2007 up to 200 Galway people became ill when human sewage polluted their water supply.

- **Chemical** or **industrial waste** can pollute water and poison fish life. People who eat fish that have been affected by pollution can also be poisoned.

Algae on an Irish waterway
What are the causes and the consequences of such algae?

Rapid Revision

- Water is a **renewable resource,** which can be used again and again.

- The water cycle includes the following:

Condensation of water vapour into cloud ⟶ **Precipitation** (rain etc.)

↑   ↓

Evaporation of water into water vapour ⟵ **Surface run-off and soakage**

- South Co. Dublin gets much of its **water supply** from the River Liffey. The water goes from a reservoir at Pollaphuca to a nearby treatment plant. The purified supplies are then pumped to other reservoirs nearer Dublin before being distributed to consumers.

- Water is needed to maintain **human life.** We need it for drinking, cooking and for good sanitation. Water is also needed for plant growth and for the survival of animals.

- People **pollute** water by the over-use of fertilisers and by allowing raw sewage and harmful chemicals to enter it.

See Chapter 50 of your Workbook

Test Yourself
eTest.ie

51

Energy Sources: Focus on Oil and Gas

Energy Guzzlers

The world today uses up huge amounts of energy. Most of this is being consumed in rich, Western countries, where wasteful consumer societies use more and more of the world's resources. We in the North make up less than 25 per cent of the human family, yet we consume 85 per cent of the world's energy.

Fact!
The world uses 140,000 litres of oil every second.

USA

Ethiopia

Fact!
The average American uses as much energy as 340 Ethiopians.

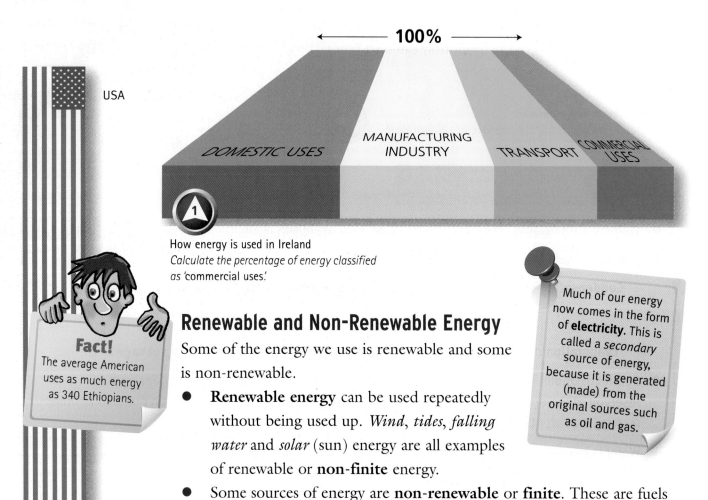

←————— **100%** —————→

DOMESTIC USES

MANUFACTURING INDUSTRY

TRANSPORT

COMMERCIAL USES

1

How energy is used in Ireland
Calculate the percentage of energy classified as 'commercial uses'.

Much of our energy now comes in the form of **electricity**. This is called a *secondary* source of energy, because it is generated (made) from the original sources such as oil and gas.

Renewable and Non-Renewable Energy

Some of the energy we use is renewable and some is non-renewable.

- **Renewable energy** can be used repeatedly without being used up. *Wind, tides, falling water* and *solar* (sun) energy are all examples of renewable or **non-finite** energy.

- Some sources of energy are **non-renewable** or **finite**. These are fuels that must be burned in order to release their energy. Once burned, they cannot be used again. Finite resources include *oil, gas, coal* and *peat*. They will eventually be used up.

Case study: Saudi Arabia – A Leading Oil-Producing State

Saudi Arabia contains one-quarter of the world's crude (unrefined) oil and is the world's leading oil-exporting country. The location of Saudi Arabia is shown in Figure 2.

Saudi Arabia was once a poor country, inhabited mainly by *nomad* farmers who wandered from place to place in search of grazing for their camels and sheep.

Oil wealth has now made Saudi Arabia one of the world's richest countries. Its citizens enjoy a high standard of living, plenty of employment and ultra-modern hospitals, schools and other services. But oil, being a **finite resource**, will eventually be used up. The country must therefore use its vast existing wealth to **diversify** (develop other aspects of) its economy.

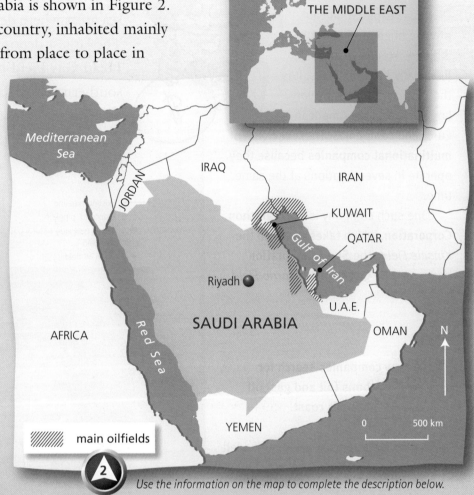

main oilfields

2

Use the information on the map to complete the description below.

Saudi Arabia lies between the _____ Sea in the west and the _____ of _____ in the east. To its north lie the countries of _____ and _____. Most of Saudi Arabia's oil fields are to the east/west of the country. The capital of the country is _____. Saudi Arabia lies in that part of the world called The _____ _____.

Saudi Arabia, though extremely wealthy, is a very traditional country. Its king is an absolute monarch and the rights of women are severely restricted.

Case study: The Search for Hydrocarbons (Oil and Gas) in Irish Waters

Multinational Companies

Oil or gas exploration can provide huge profits, but it is a very expensive and financially risky business. It is therefore carried out by very large and wealthy American or European companies. These are called **multinational companies** because they operate in several nations at the same time.

One such company is the **Marathon Corporation**, which takes gas from the *Kinsale Field*. The **Shell Corporation** hopes to take gas from the *Corrib Field*.

How companies search for hydrocarbons (oil and gas) off Ireland's coast.

Sea areas off the Irish coast are divided into **blocks**. The companies rent some of these blocks from the Irish government.

Companies carry out **rock studies** to see if hydrocarbons exist beneath their rented blocks.

If the rock studies are satisfactory, **test holes** may be drilled to see how much oil or gas exists.

If supplies are sufficient, platforms (rigs) are set up. Oil or gas is then **drilled and brought ashore** through a pipeline.

Large deposits of oil and natural gas may exist under the seabed off the Irish coast. Figure 3 shows sea areas where deposits have already been located. The largest deposits have been found in the **Kinsale Head Gas Field** beneath the *Celtic Sea* off our southern coast. Gas deposits have also been found beneath the Atlantic in the **Corrib Gas Field** off Co. Mayo. Only the Kinsale Head Gas Field has so far been used.

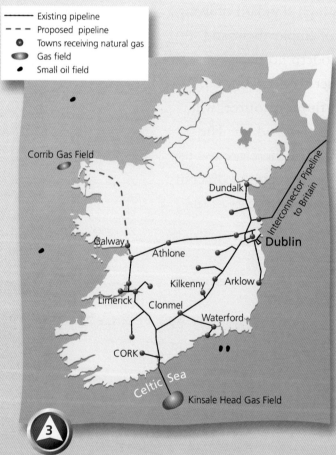

Legend:
- ——— Existing pipeline
- – – – Proposed pipeline
- ● Towns receiving natural gas
- ⬭ Gas field
- ● Small oil field

Corrib Gas Field, Dundalk, Galway, Athlone, Dublin, Kilkenny, Arklow, Limerick, Clonmel, Waterford, CORK, Celtic Sea, Kinsale Head Gas Field, Interconnector Pipeline to Britain

3

Natural gas, oil and Ireland
(a) Name the two gas fields shown on the map.
(b) Which gas field is being exploited?
(c) Name six cities or towns that receive natural gas.
(d) With which country is Ireland connected by pipeline?
(e) Suggest two reasons why gas is supplied to more towns in the east and south-east than in the north-west of Ireland.

A gas rig at the Kinsale Gas Field
(a) Identify the location and ownership of this oil/gas platform.
(b) What evidence is there that oil workers do not travel to and from the platform by ship?
(c) What is the probable function of the ship?

Drilling for oil is an **extractive industry** because the oil is taken from the earth's crust. Name one other example of an extractive industry.

The Benefits of Kinsale Gas

The Marathon Corporation uses a buried, underwater pipeline to carry Kinsale gas to the coast. The gas is then sold to an Irish semi-state company called **An Bord Gais Éireann**, which distributes the gas to various customers. The uses of Kinsale gas include the following:

- It is used to generate **electricity** at Aghada, near where the pipeline reaches the coast.
- It is piped to several **town supplies** throughout the country (see Figure 3).
- It has provided almost 20 per cent of Ireland's energy needs for 25 years.

Some problems with oil and gas

- When they are burned, oil and gas produce carbon dioxide, which contributes to **global warming** (see page 62).
- Oil **spillages** can pollute beaches and harm sea birds and other wildlife.
- Oil and gas are **finite resources**. Kinsale gas is expected to run out by the year 2012.

Describe the effect of an oil spillage like the one shown here.

Case study: The Corrib Gas Land Use Dispute

Shell and other multinational oil companies want to develop the Corrib Gas Field following the plan shown in Figure 4. But many people fear that this plan is dangerous, and some local people set up the **Shell to Sea** group to oppose it. Some arguments for and against the Corrib project are outlined in the speech bubbles below and on page 287.

Gas will be drilled from the offshore Corrib Field

Untreated gas will be pumped ashore through a high-pressure undersea pipe

Belmullet | • Ballina
Co. Mayo
• Castlebar
Westport

Rossport

Belmullet

Ballanaboy

Untreated gas is much more likely to explode than 'cleaned' gas. We want the gas to be cleaned at sea before it is pumped ashore. This is what happens at the Kinsale and other gas fields.

Untreated gas will contain particles of sand, minerals and gases that could erode the pipeline from the inside. This increases the danger of an explosion.

The gas will be 'cleaned' at an inland terminal at Ballanaboy. It will then be piped at lower pressure to other parts of Ireland.

Offshore treatment would be so costly that the entire project might be abandoned!

The pipeline will be quite safe. It is extra thick, and is designed by experts to high international standards.

The Rossport Five
Five local Rossport people – three farmers and two teachers – were so opposed to the Corrib gas project that they went to gaol for obstructing the laying of the pipeline. They spent 94 days in prison and are known as the Rossport Five.

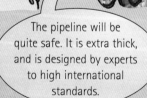

A *Shell to Sea* protest in Castlebar, Co. Mayo.

Class Activity

- Divide the class into five groups. Each group should consider carefully the arguments on both sides and then make a group recommendation on whether or not the Corrib project should go ahead in its proposed form. A spokesperson for each group should report his/her group's decision and the reasons for it. Reasons should be ranked (listed) in order of importance.
- When all the groups have reported their recommendations, hold a general class vote on whether or not the Corrib project should be supported. Each student should vote in secret and according to his/her final, private opinion.

Rapid Revision

- People in rich countries use **enormous amounts** of energy for domestic, industrial, transport and commercial purposes.

- **Renewable** energy sources can be used again and again without being used up. **Non-renewable** sources will eventually be used up.

- **Saudi Arabia** has become very wealthy as the world's leading oil-exporting country.

- The multinational *Marathon* Corporation recovers gas from the **Kinsale Gas Field** off Co. Cork. On being piped ashore, this gas is distributed by *An Bord Gais Éireann*. It is used for town supplies and to generate electricity.

- The *Shell* Corporation wants to exploit gas from the **Corrib Gas Field** off the coast of Co. Mayo. Many people object to the plan to pipe untreated gas under very high pressure close to people's homes.

A French beach polluted by the shipwrecked *Erika*

Activities

1   (a)   Name a place in the **Celtic Sea** where natural gas has been found and drilled commercially.
     (b)   Describe three economic benefits of this gas find.
     (c)   What is meant by the term 'multinational oil company'? Describe briefly how multinational companies search for and recover oil or gas deposits.

2   (a)   Describe three environmental problems associated with a major oil spill that are referred to in the extract in Figure 5.
     (b)   Name one environmental problem associated with oil that is not referred to in the extract.

3   (a)   Name three sources of **renewable energy**.
     (b)   Suggest some advantages and possible problems associated with the widespread use in Ireland of renewable energy.

See Chapter 51 of your Workbook

Oil-spill Disaster in France
More than 200,000 birds on the west coast of France are thought to have died as the result of fuel spilling from the shipwrecked oil tanker *Erika*. 'It is so sad,' said an observer. 'The birds try to pick the oil from their feathers and only end up swallowing it. They die an agonising death.'

Local tourist beaches have been blackened by the thick, treacly crude oil. One beach has suffered a twelve-kilometre long oil slick.

Meanwhile, local fishermen are worried what effect this latest oil spill might have on their livelihoods.

Using Our Peat Bogs

An **extractive industry** is one that removes non-renewable resources from the earth. The harvesting of peat is an extractive industry. Which of the following activities are also extractive industries?
Mining, farming, oil-drilling, fishing, quarrying.

Key Idea

- As technology developed, Ireland's peat bogs were exploited more rapidly.

Thick **raised bogs** with an average peat depth of 8 metres. They are found mainly on flat or gently sloping land in the Midlands.

Thin **blanket bogs** with an average peat depth of only 1.5 metres. They are found mainly on mountain slopes and areas of heavy rainfall, especially in the West of Ireland.

About five per cent of Ireland is covered by peat bogs. Irish people have for centuries extracted peat or 'turf' from these bogs as fuel for cooking and for heating their homes. Up to the middle of the twentieth century, only basic hand tools were used to harvest the peat, so exploitation of the bogs was slow.

Then in 1946 the Irish Government set up **Bord na Móna** to develop the peat industry in a large-scale commercial way. Bord na Móna's use of modern technology greatly speeded up the exploitation of the bogs.

Bord na Móna exploits **raised bogs**, which are mainly situated in the Midlands (see Figure 1). Raised bogs are deep and contain large quantities of turf. They are also relatively easy to exploit because they are usually quite flat.

Exploiting Our Midland Bogs – Past and Present

The diagram below outlines four main steps in the use of Irish peat resources. In each step the role of modern technology has played an important role in increasing the rate of exploitation.

Step One
The bogs are **prepared**. They are drained, levelled and supplied with railway tracks.

Step Two
The peat is **harvested**.

Step Three
The peat is **transported** from the bog.

Step Four
The processed peat is **marketed**.

Step 1 – Preparing the Bogs

The drainage of water from the bogs is the first and often the most difficult part of the preparation. Most bogs have a 95 per cent water content. These bogs are so soft that it is difficult even to stand on them without sinking.

In the Past . . .

Many bogs remained unexploited, because people were unable to drain them.

With Newer Technology . . .

Newer technology made the drainage and preparation of bogs much easier and faster.

- A special drainage machine called a **ditcher** has been developed. This machine does not sink into the soft bog, because it travels on extremely wide tracks that distribute its weight over a large area. The ditchers *dig a network of drains* across the bog. Surplus water is allowed to run through these drains until, after about three years, the bog becomes dry and firm enough for the next stages of preparation.

- **Graders** (which are machines rather like bulldozers) then *level the bog surface*. This makes it easier for big harvesting machines to do their work later on.

- When the surface has been levelled, **heavy tractors** help to *lay down railway tracks* across the bog. Rail transport is later used to carry away the harvested peat.

A ditcher at work
(a) Explain why this heavy drainage machine does not sink into the soft bog.
(b) Describe what the machine is doing.

Step 2 – Harvesting the Peat
With Newer Technology . . .

- Most peat is now harvested as *milled peat*. In this process, a **miller** *scrapes* about half a centimetre of peat from the surface of the bog and tears it up into tiny fragments.

- The milled peat is then left to dry for some days, usually being *turned over* by a **harrow** to speed up the drying process.

- The dry milled peat is then gathered into small ridges by **ridgers** and later into larger ridges by **harvesters**.

Describe the work being done by this harvester.

In the Past . . .

A special type of shovel called a **slean** was used to cut *turf sods* from the bog. These sods were then **footed** or placed in small stacks and left to dry (see picture). This hand-harvesting was very slow.

In the Past . . .

Animal-drawn carts were used to take the peat from the bogs. Transporting the peat in this way was laborious and very slow.

In the Past . . .

In the past, almost all of Ireland's harvested peat was in the form of *sod peat*. This was **used solely as a household fuel** and only in areas *within easy reach of the bogs*. The market for peat was therefore limited and this was another factor that slowed the development of our peat resources.

Step 3 – Transporting the Peat
With Newer Technology . . .

Each large Bord na Móna bog now has its own railway line. Special **turf trains** carry large quantities of peat to electricity power stations and to briquette factories.

Step 4 – Using the Processed Peat
Since the Foundation of Bord na Móna . . .

- Large quantities of **milled peat** are now used to generate electricity at ESB power stations. Milled peat is also compressed to make **peat briquettes**, which are sold throughout the country.

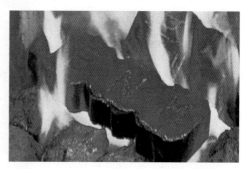

- **Moss peat** – lighter peat found near the top of the bog – is now exported to 27 countries, mainly as a soil conditioner.

- Small quantities of **sod peat** are sold as household fuel in areas near the boglands.

Future Uses of Our Bogs

Ireland's raised bogs are being used up. People are now trying to decide:

- How much of our remaining raised bogs should be used up or preserved?
- What should be done with our cutaway (already used up) bogs?

Should We Use Up or Preserve what Remains of Our Raised Bogs?

Some people think we should **harvest our remaining bogs**. They would provide us with milled peat to generate electricity and to make peat briquettes. This would reduce the amount of fuel that we need to import.

More than 20,000 hectares of raised bog are to be **preserved**. Many people believe this is not enough. Almost all of Europe's bogs have now been used up. This makes Ireland's remaining bogs very important for the survival of endangered plants and birds.

What do you think we should do?

What Can We Do with Our Cutaway Bogs?

1. Some cutaway bogs are used to grow **coniferous trees**. These trees will be harvested to provide raw materials for roof beams and other timber products.

2. Cutaway bogs near the River Shannon are being preserved as swampy **wetlands** that provide valuable habitats for a wide range of plant and animal life.

3. Some cutaway bogs could be suitable sites for **wind farms**.

   - Most boglands are unpopulated. Wind farms located on them would not therefore create *noise* pollution for local people.
   - Most cutaway bogs are flat or low-lying. Wind farms built on them would therefore not have major *visual* impacts on the countryside.
   - Flat land assists *access* to cutaway bogs. This would make it easier to build wind farms on them.

A wind farm on a cutaway bog

(a) *What advantages does this site have for a wind farm?*

(b) *Describe some advantages and/or disadvantages of wind as a source of energy.*

Rapid Revision

- Improved **technology** has resulted in the more rapid development of peat bogs. Bord na Móna has developed the deep and relatively flat **raised bogs** of the Midlands.

- In the past, some bogs were too wet to be drained. Wide-tracked **ditchers** are now used to dig drains, **graders** level the bog-surface and **heavy tractors** lay railway tracks.

- In the past, people used **sleans** to harvest sod peat. **Millers** are now used to scrape milled peat from the bogs. **Harrows** turn the milled peat over to dry. **Ridgers** and **harvesters** then gather it into heaps.

- In the past, **animal-drawn carts** carried peat from the bogs. **Turf trains** are now used to transport milled peat.

- In the past, turf was used only as a household fuel and only in the vicinity of bogs. Now milled peat is used to generate **electricity** and to make **peat briquettes**. Moss peat is widely used as a **soil conditioner**.

- There is disagreement over how much of our remaining bogs should be **harvested** or **preserved**. Some *cutaway bogs* can be used to grow coniferous *trees*, as *wetlands* or as sites for *wind farms*.

Activities

1 (a) Explain why most of the bogs exploited by Bord na Móna have been the raised bogs of the Midlands.

(b) Describe two ways in which technology has helped in peat production. (*J.C. Higher Level*)

2 Examine the ***Ordnance Survey extract*** in Figure 2:

(a) Suggest a reason for the absence of settlement at N 42 35.

(b) What proof is there that the area shown on the map includes bogland?

(c) Identify the feature at N 431 359. Suggest a precise use for this feature.

(d) Boglands have uses other than those relating to the harvesting of peat. With reference to the map extract, identify two such uses.

(e) Identify the feature at N 435 346.

See Chapter 52 of your Workbook

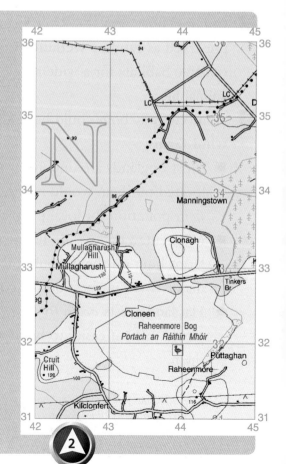

53

Over-Fishing

Examine Figure 2, which shows cod stocks in the Irish Sea between 1982 and 2004. *Indicate whether each of the following statements is true or false.*
(a) *Cod stocks declined steadily over time.*
(b) *Stocks have been depleted over time.*
(c) *Stocks were highest in 1982 and lowest in 2005.*
(d) *Stocks in 2005 were less than one quarter of those in 1982.*
(e) *Stocks have been critically low since 1994.*
(f) *Over-fishing has probably taken place in the Irish Sea.*

Key Idea

● The over-use of a resource may lead to its depletion.

Fish are a **renewable resource** because they can renew their numbers through breeding. If used carefully, therefore, the world's fish stocks need never be depleted (used up).

But some renewable resources, including fish, can be seriously depleted if they are **over-exploited** (over-used). In many parts of the world, over-fishing is so great that fish cannot recover their numbers through breeding. When this happens, fish stocks decrease quickly and become **depleted**.

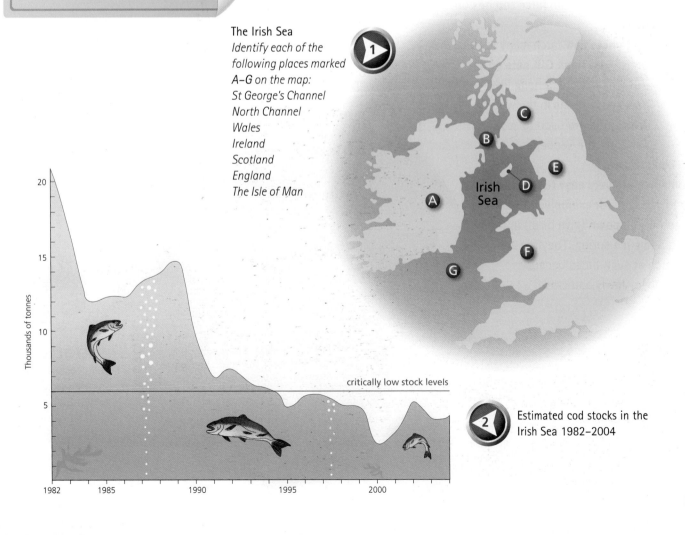

The Irish Sea
Identify each of the following places marked A–G on the map:
St George's Channel
North Channel
Wales
Ireland
Scotland
England
The Isle of Man

1

2 Estimated cod stocks in the Irish Sea 1982–2004

Why over-fishing takes place

● Big ships

Some of today's trawlers (boats) are as tall as seven-storey buildings and as long as Croke Park. These '**super-trawlers**' often travel together in **fleets**, which usually include **factory ships** that process fish at sea. This system allows trawlers to fish without pause for months on end. They kill vast quantities of fish, which can be stored for long periods in massive, refrigerated **holds** (rooms) in the trawlers.

● Modern equipment

Modern boats are so well equipped that it is very difficult for fish to escape them:

- **Echo sounders** and **sonar equipment** are used to locate fish, while **radar** reveals the location of nearby rocks or ships.
- Powerful **motorised cranes and winches** can haul huge catches on board.
- Huge **nets** can catch many tonnes of fish at a time. **Gill nets** of up to 21 kilometres long hang like massive curtains in the water. **Trawl nets** are used to scoop up fish from the seabed.

● Easy targets

Some fish are very easy to catch. Big shoals of cod, for example, gather together to **spawn** (give birth) in the Irish Sea each spring. They are easy to catch at such times because they move slowly and close together.

Hi-tech equipment in a modern trawler
How might such equipment contribute to over-fishing?

What is happening in this photograph?

Stock depletion

Over-fishing has led to serious stock depletion. In northern European waters, for example, a fish is now 20 times less likely to survive to adulthood than was the case 60 years ago. Some fish species are now in danger of extinction.

Fact!

If over-fishing continues at its present rate, all world fish stocks will collapse within 50 years.

What is being done to save our fish stocks?

Only **sustainable fishing** can save our fish stocks for the future. The following efforts are therefore being made to control fishing so as to prevent stock depletion:

- **Fishing fleets** have been reduced in size to lessen the pressure on fish stocks. Ireland's fishing fleet is to be reduced by one third.
- The European Union has set **quotas** or limits on the quantities of fish that each of its member states can catch each year. These quotas are reduced when fish stocks become dangerously low.
- Fishing for endangered fish species may be **forbidden**. Parts of the Irish Sea, for example, have been closed to cod fishing.
- **Fishery exclusion zones** have been set up to reduce the amount of fishing that takes place in rich coastal fishing grounds. For example, only Irish boats may normally fish within ten kilometres of the Irish coast.
- Irish Navy **fishery protection vessels** patrol our coast to prevent poaching (illegal fishing) by foreign trawlers.

The Atlantic Dawn – a 'super trawler'
This vessel is 145 metres long and cost a staggering €63 million to build for an Irish owner. It can employ 100 people and hold enough fish to provide meals for 14 million people.

'The Atlantic Dawn' fishes off the west coast of Africa, where it can catch more than a tonne of fish every five minutes.

An Irish fishery protection vessel on the look-out for poachers
Poaching by foreign trawlers is a major cause of fish depletion in Irish waters. Convicted poachers may face heavy fines and may have their boats and nets confiscated. But Ireland has a long coastline and it is difficult for Ireland's eight fishery protection vessels to patrol our coast effectively.

Rapid Revision

● Fish are a **renewable resource**, but **over-fishing** can lead to the **depletion** of fish stocks.

● Several factors have contributed to **over-fishing**:
 (a) *Super-trawlers* take vast catches.
 (b) *Modern equipment* has made fishing very efficient.
 (c) Some fish, such as cod in spawn, are *easy to catch*.

● Over-fishing has led to the **depletion** of fish stocks such as cod in the Irish Sea.

● The following means have been used to **preserve fish stocks**:
 (a) Fishing *fleets* have been reduced in size.
 (b) *Quotas* (limits) have been set on fish catches.
 (c) The catching of endangered fish species has been *banned*.
 (d) Fishery *exclusion zones* have been set up.
 (e) Fishery *protection vessels* prevent poaching.

Activities

1 Which of these statements best describes the fishing industry in Europe?
 (a) Fish are a non-renewable resource, so there has to be a limit on the amount caught.
 (b) Fish are a non-renewable resource, so there is no need to limit the amount caught.
 (c) Fish are a renewable resource, so fishermen can catch as many as they want.
 (d) Fish are a renewable resource, but new technology has led to over-fishing. (*J.C. Higher Level*)

2 Describe the trend shown by the figures in the table. (*J.C. Higher Level*).

Fish Type	1997	1998	1999	2000
Cod	5,706	5,294	3,860	2,928
Herring	57,155	58,248	45,334	42,114

3 Explain two reasons why over-fishing has occurred in Irish waters. (*J.C. Higher Level*)

4 Describe two steps that are being taken to limit the over-exploitation of fish. (*J.C. Higher Level*)

See Chapter 53 of your Workbook

54

Farming: An Example of a System

Key Idea

- Many primary activities are systems, with *inputs*, *processes* and *outputs*.

What is a System?

A system is something that takes inputs and processes and changes them into useful products or outputs.

Inputs are the things that *enter the system*. Some of these things are changed by the system's processes. Others are used to help the processes to work.

Processes are the activities that *change* some of the inputs into outputs.

Outputs are the things that *leave the system* as a result of the processes.

Is your school a system? Discuss.

Farming as a System

A farm is a good example of a system. This chapter will examine **mixed farming** as a system. A mixed farm is one that grows crops and raises animals.

Which of the following relate to primary activities *and* are examples of systems?

- a computer factory
- a restaurant
- a farm
- a rock
- a hospital
- a mine.

(a) Is the farm shown in this picture a mixed farm? How do you know?

(b) How might relief (slope, etc.) of the land favour farming in the area shown?

(c) At what time of year do you think the picture was taken? Explain your answer.

Case Study: Garryvoe Farm: A Mixed Farm in Co. Cork

The account in Figure 1 below was given by the owner of a mixed farm near Garryvoe in Co. Cork. Use information in the account to fill in the blank spaces in Figure 2 on page 301.

Are the things shown in these pictures farm inputs or farm outputs?

Our family farm contains just over 60 hectares of low-lying, well-drained land. We are fortunate in that its rich brown soils, southerly aspect and moist, temperate climate favour crop growing and livestock raising alike.

There are several farm buildings near to our dwelling house. There are large cattle sheds and a milking parlour for our 20 milking cows, 36 calves and 30 beef cattle. We have two large machinery sheds. These house a tractor, several trailers, a sower, a manure spreader and a mower for cutting grass. There is also a silage harvester, a sprayer and a combine harvester.

These machines cost a great deal of money, so capital is quite important to us. Much of our capital is generated from farm profits, although EU and government grants also help us greatly.

Most of the labour is done by my brother and me, though we also hire extra help during the harvesting season. We are nearly always busy. All through the year we must milk cows, feed livestock and maintain machinery. Spring is a busy time of sowing and fertilising the land. During summer we harvest and bale silage, which we use to feed our cattle. In autumn we harvest our tillage crops, the most important of which are barley and wheat. In winter – the least busy season – we clear fences and plough the land.

Milk is a major output of our farm. It is sent to a nearby Dairygold creamery. The Dairygold co-operative also buys our wheat and feeding barley. We send fattened cattle to a cattle factory in Waterford, while our best-quality malting barley is sold to Guinness to make beer. But some of our outputs stay on the farm and become inputs into our farm system. For example, we rear and fatten some of our own calves, use our silage and grass to feed our livestock and spread our animal manure on the land as fertiliser.

Description of a mixed farm near Garryvoe, Co. Cork

The Farm System

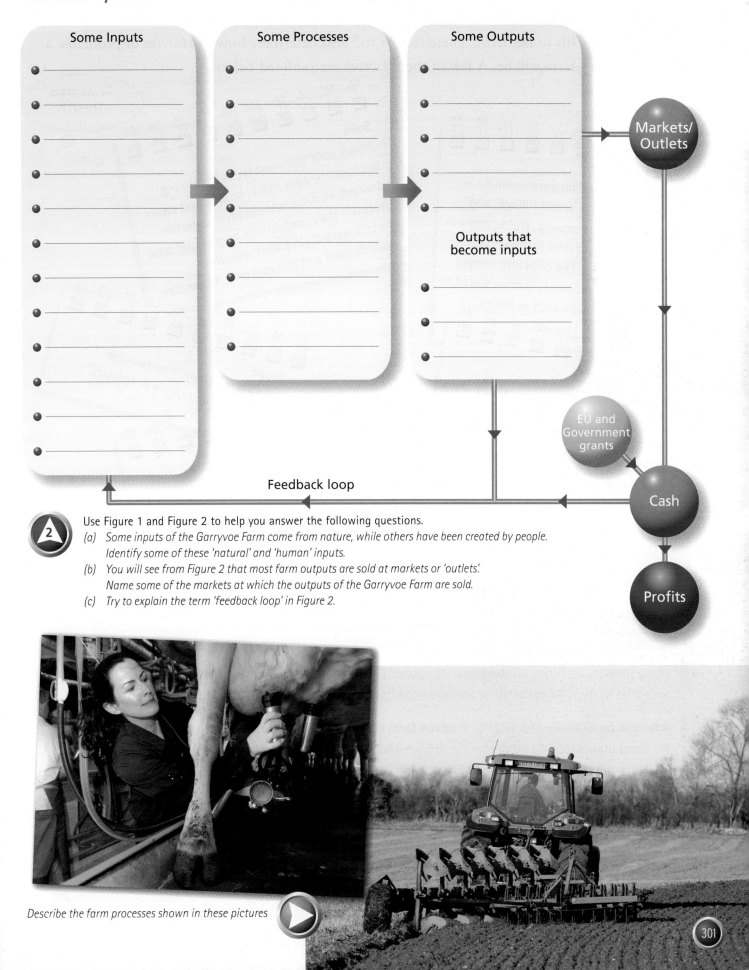

Some Inputs

- _____
- _____
- _____
- _____
- _____
- _____
- _____
- _____
- _____
- _____
- _____

Some Processes

- _____
- _____
- _____
- _____
- _____
- _____
- _____
- _____

Some Outputs

- _____
- _____
- _____

Outputs that become inputs

- _____
- _____

Markets/ Outlets

EU and Government grants

Cash

Profits

Feedback loop

2 Use Figure 1 and Figure 2 to help you answer the following questions.

(a) Some inputs of the Garryvoe Farm come from nature, while others have been created by people. Identify some of these 'natural' and 'human' inputs.

(b) You will see from Figure 2 that most farm outputs are sold at markets or 'outlets'. Name some of the markets at which the outputs of the Garryvoe Farm are sold.

(c) Try to explain the term 'feedback loop' in Figure 2.

Describe the farm processes shown in these pictures

Things that Influence Production on a Farm

Many factors act together to influence what crops or animals a farmer will have on his or her farm. These factors will also determine how *productive* or profitable a farm will be. A few of these factors are outlined below.

Climate

Ireland's moist and moderate climate is well suited to both arable (tillage) and pastoral (grazing) farming. Wetter areas in the West of Ireland tend to favour grass and cattle rearing. The drier and sunnier south-east of the country is more suited to growing cereal crops such as barley.

Revise pages 116–117.

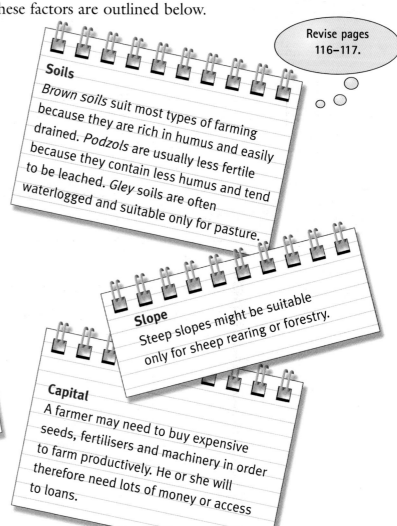

Soils

Brown soils suit most types of farming because they are rich in humus and easily drained. Podzols are usually less fertile because they contain less humus and tend to be leached. Gley soils are often waterlogged and suitable only for pasture.

Markets

Farmers like to grow products for which there is a reliable demand and good prices. Some farmers in Leinster, for example, grow barley to supply the Guinness brewery in Dublin.

Slope

Steep slopes might be suitable only for sheep rearing or forestry.

Capital

A farmer may need to buy expensive seeds, fertilisers and machinery in order to farm productively. He or she will therefore need lots of money or access to loans.

Rapid Revision

Many primary activities are **systems**. All systems contain **inputs**, **processes** and **outputs**. The inputs enter the system. Some of these are processed or changed into products called outputs.

A farm is an example of a system. A **mixed farm** concerns itself with cattle as well as with crop growing.
- **Farm inputs** include land, climate, labour and farm machinery.
- **Farm processes** include ploughing, sowing, harvesting and milking.
- **Farm outputs** include barley, wheat, fat cattle, milk and wool.

Many factors influence production on a farm. They include climate, soils, markets and capital.

See Chapter 54 of your Workbook

Secondary Activities as Systems

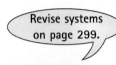
Revise systems on page 299.

In Chapter 49 you learned that the phrase **secondary economic activities refers to manufacturing industries**. In these industries, raw materials are processed (changed) or processed materials are changed further. These processes usually take place in factories.

A factory works like a system with **inputs**, **processes** and **outputs**.

- The industry gathers together the raw materials and anything else it needs to make the manufactured product. These things are called the **inputs** of the system.
- The system then **processes** (changes) some of the inputs into outputs.
- The **outputs** of a factory include manufactured products, by-products and any wastes that are produced by the manufacturing process.

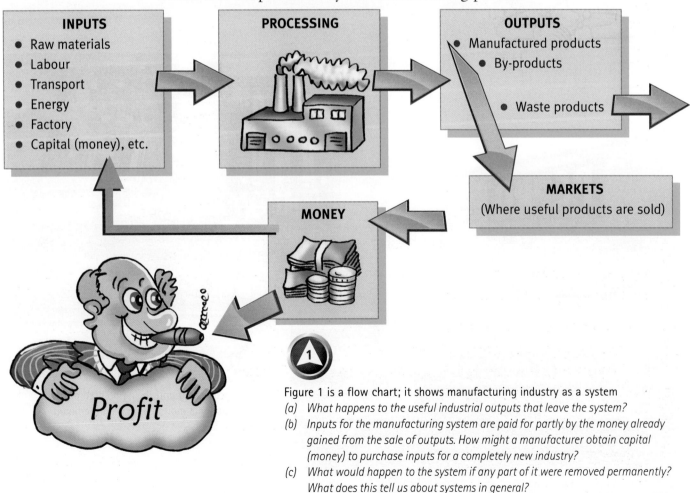

Figure 1 is a flow chart; it shows manufacturing industry as a system

(a) What happens to the useful industrial outputs that leave the system?

(b) Inputs for the manufacturing system are paid for partly by the money already gained from the sale of outputs. How might a manufacturer obtain capital (money) to purchase inputs for a completely new industry?

(c) What would happen to the system if any part of it were removed permanently? What does this tell us about systems in general?

(d) Why is this diagram called a 'flow chart'?

The inputs

Inputs include a modern **factory building**, in which **20 employees** assemble personal computers from **imported components** (parts). Each computer contains the following components:

- A **case** that surrounds the computer.
- A **motherboard,** which is the base on which some of the computer's parts are fitted.
- A **central processing unit** that performs all the computer's calculations. This matchbox-sized component is the 'brain' of the computer.
- A **hard disk** that *stores information* in the computer.
- A **video card** that *converts information* from electronic to visual form.
- A **monitor** that *shows* visual *information* on its screen.
- A **keyboard**.
- A **mouse**.

PC Pro is an Irish-owned *computer assembly plant* located in the Southside Industrial Estate in Togher, Cork City. Like all factories, it works as a *system*.

A central processing unit (being pointed out) and other components mounted on a motherboard

The PC Pro Plant at Southside Industrial Estate, Togher, Cork

The processes

1. When components arrive at the factory, they are **tagged and shelved** in the factory warehouse.
2. When a customer orders a computer, specific components are **selected** and brought to the production area.
3. The computer is assembled (put together) in the production area.
4. **Quality control** workers then ensure that the computer has been assembled properly.
5. The computer undergoes **burn-in**. This means it is test-run for a period of 12 hours to ensure that it *works properly*.
6. The new computer is **packaged and delivered** to customers.

An assembled PC Pro computer
Identify the components labelled A–D.

The outputs

Assembled computers are the principal output, although PC Pro also sells *software packages and individual computer parts*.

Rapid Revision

Secondary economic activities are those in which raw materials are processed, or in which processed materials are processed further.

- All manufacturing industries are **systems**. PC Pro – a computer assembly plant in Togher, Cork – is an example.
- **Inputs** include the factory itself, the workforce and the resource materials. For *PC Pro*, these materials include components such as hard disks, monitors and keyboards.
- The **processes** or activities of *PC Pro* include tagging, shelving, assembling and quality controlling components.
- The **outputs** of *PC Pro* include assembled computers, monitors and software packages.

56

Industry in Ireland

Heavy and Light Industry

HEAVY INDUSTRIES use large amounts of bulky raw materials and usually produce big or heavy products in *large factories*. Cement making and steel making are examples of heavy industry. Name some other examples.

The Irish Cement factory near Drogheda, Co. Louth

(a) How would you know from this picture that the industry shown is an example of heavy industry?

(b) Identify a quarry, a railway line and a road on the picture. How would each of these features assist cement manufacturing?

Irish Cement's Platin Factory – An Example of Heavy Industry

Irish Cement Ltd operates a large cement-making factory at Platin near Drogheda, Co. Louth. The company is now part of a large multinational building materials group named *CRH*. A **multinational company** is one that owns factories in several different countries.

LIGHT INDUSTRIES use less bulky raw materials and usually make smaller products than do heavy industries. Some light industries are located in specially built industrial estates at the edges of towns or cities. Making computers and textiles are examples of light industry. Name some other examples.

PC Pro - An Example of Light Industry

PC Pro is a small but growing computer assembly company. Its factory is situated in the Southside Industrial Estate in Togher, on the outskirts of Cork City. The inputs, processes and outputs of this plant were described on pages 304 and 305.

Industrial estates

Many modern light industries are located in **industrial estates,** which are areas set aside especially for industry. Industrial estates provide factories with top-quality **infrastructure** (services), such as electricity, water supplies and waste disposal.

- Industrial estates are usually located near **major roads,** which makes transporting factory inputs and outputs more efficient.

- Some estates are situated near **airports,** which might be used by managerial staff or to transport light, valuable goods.

- Estates are usually located at the edges of large **urban areas** – close enough to be convenient for workers but far away enough from city or town centres to avoid severe traffic jams.

- Estates are divided into industrial plots on which **advance factories** are sometimes built. These factory buildings are available for manufacturers to buy or to rent.

The location of PC Pro
Identify the letter label that shows each of the following in the picture: an industrial estate; a major road; Cork Airport; part of a housing estate; land being redeveloped.

The Location of Industry

Industrialists take great care in deciding where to set up a new factory. They examine several **locational factors** before deciding the best overall location for their plant. Figure 1 identifies some of these factors.

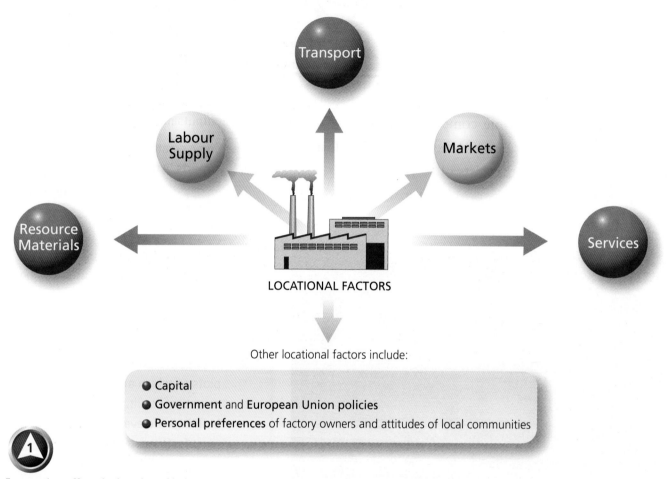

Other locational factors include:

- Capital
- **Government** and **European Union policies**
- **Personal preferences** of factory owners and attitudes of local communities

Factors that affect the location of industry

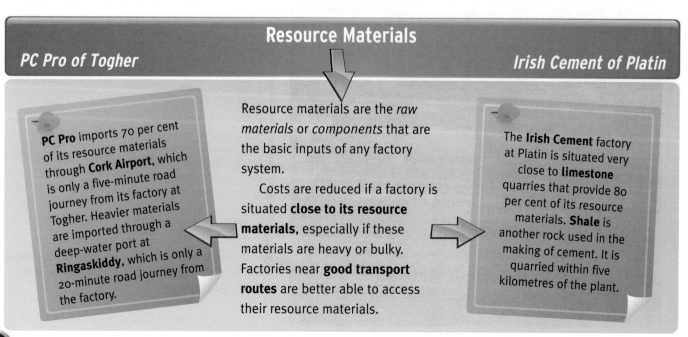

Resource Materials

PC Pro of Togher

PC Pro imports 70 per cent of its resource materials through **Cork Airport**, which is only a five-minute road journey from its factory at Togher. Heavier materials are imported through a deep-water port at **Ringaskiddy**, which is only a 20-minute road journey from the factory.

Resource materials are the *raw materials* or *components* that are the basic inputs of any factory system.

Costs are reduced if a factory is situated **close to its resource materials**, especially if these materials are heavy or bulky. Factories near **good transport routes** are better able to access their resource materials.

Irish Cement of Platin

The **Irish Cement** factory at Platin is situated very close to **limestone** quarries that provide 80 per cent of its resource materials. **Shale** is another rock used in the making of cement. It is quarried within five kilometres of the plant.

Labour Supply

PC Pro of Togher

Irish Cement of Platin

Most factories are located near cities or **large towns** that can supply large numbers of workers. Some industries, such as those involved in computer manufacturing, may be located **near universities or colleges** that provide highly trained and skilled employees.

All workers at the **PC Pro** plant are from **Cork**. Local **colleges**, such as University College Cork and the Cork Institute of Technology, provide some workers with useful *skills* ranging from computer science to accountancy.

Irish Cement employs a large workforce of 200 people. Most workers live in the nearby town of **Drogheda**. An excellent **road network** makes it easy for workers to commute to and from the factory.

Transport Materials

PC Pro of Togher

Irish Cement of Platin

Reliable transport is needed to carry resource materials, finished products and workers to and from factories. Most factories are therefore built near good **road** or **rail** networks or within easy access of **seaports** or **airports**.

The **PC Pro** plant is easily accessible because it is situated just off Cork's important **South Link** roadway. The factory is only five minutes by road from **Cork Airport** and 20 minutes from the deepwater port at **Ringaskiddy**.

The **Irish Cement** plant is located within one kilometre of the **M1 motorway** that links Dublin with Northern Ireland. This is important because 90 per cent of the factory's products are transported by road. A **railway line** runs through the plant and trains are used to carry some cement to Dublin. A coal-like fuel called petroleum coke is imported for the factory through the nearby **Port of Dublin.**

The M1 motorway near Drogheda
Why is it important for the Irish Cement factory at Platin to be located near good roadways such as the M1?

Market

PC Pro of Togher

Irish Cement of Platin

Cork City provides a market for 40 per cent of PC Pro's products. Because the factory is on the outskirts of the city, such products can be delivered to their customers within a few hours of orders being ready.

The **market** is the place or places in which the finished products of an industry are sold. It is important for a factory to be near or within easy access of its markets. This is especially so if its **finished products** are **heavy** (as in the case of cement) or **fragile** (as in the case of computers).

The **Irish Cement** plant is connected to its markets by a network of good roads. It is connected to its main **Dublin** market by the *M1 motorway*, which runs within a kilometre of the factory. It is also connected to Dublin by a *railway* line that runs through the plant.

Services

PC Pro of Togher

Irish Cement of Platin

Superior fibre-optic telephone lines provide PC Pro with instant **internet and e-mail** communications. The Southside Industrial Estate is also well serviced by **roads, drainage** and **electricity**.

Local **printing** and **packaging** firms make brochures and packages for PC Pro, while a firm called *Interlink* provides local **courier** services.

- Factories need **on-site services** such as electricity, water supplies and good e-mail and Internet communications. While these services are available in most parts of the country, they are always at hand in or near large *urban areas*.
- Many factories enjoy **linkages** with other nearby firms. These firms might provide a plant with services ranging from electrical maintenance to couriers.

The processes of the Irish Cement plant require a great deal of power and water. An **ESB sub-station** has been built on the factory site to service the plant alone. Water is supplied from reservoirs on the nearby **River Boyne**.

Local **electrical firms** carry out maintenance work on the factory. **Gypsum Industries** of Kingscourt, Co. Cavan, provides the factory with a mineral called gypsum that is used in making cement.

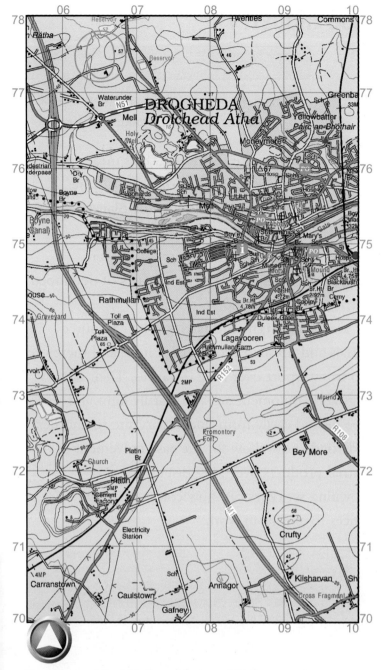

The location of the Irish Cement factory at Platin

(a) Use a four-figure grid reference to locate the cement factory at Platin.

(b) Identify (i) the transport route at O 070 734; (ii) the transport route at O 060 710 and (iii) the river at O 065 754.

(c) Explain briefly how each of the three features mentioned in question (b) above has influenced the location of the cement factory at Platin.

(d) What is the shortest distance in kilometres between the cement factory at Platin and the centre of Drogheda at O 090 750?

(e) What advantage is the nearby town of Drogheda to the cement factory at Platin?

Other Locational Factors
Capital

Capital is the money needed to set up and run a factory. Most capital is now provided by banks and by people who purchase shares in manufacturing companies. Capital *is no longer a major influence* on the location of Irish industry, because it is equally available to potentially profitable factories in all parts of Ireland.

Government and European Union (EU) policies

- The **Irish government** set up the **Industrial Development Authority (IDA)** to give grants to new industries. It also encouraged industry by charging a *tax rate* of only 12.5 per cent on industrial profits.

- The **EU** has provided **Structural Funds** to build roads and other vital services throughout the country.

These policies have encouraged industry throughout Ireland as a whole, but they have little influence on the precise location of any particular factory. They are therefore *of minor importance* as a locational factor for industry.

Personal Preferences and Local Attitudes

- Some factory owners have **personal preferences** about the location of their factory, but this usually applies to small family businesses rather than to large-scale plants.

- **Local communities** can also influence the locations of factories. They may oppose the setting up of plants that they fear will pollute their environment. They may welcome plants that will provide jobs for local people.

In the *nineteenth century*, most factories were very limited in their choice of location.

- Many factories needed to be near their **resource materials** or **sources of power**. Steel plants, for example, were usually built near coalmines. *Coal* was used as their source of power and it was too bulky to be transported from place to place.

- Many industries had to be located in the heart of a city. This was to be near their **workers**, who had to walk to and from work each day.

This old steelworks in the German city of Duisburg was typical of heavy nineteenth-century industry. It had to be located on the Ruhr coalfield because it used coal as its source of power.

A modern industrial estate
The factories in this industrial estate are typical of light, footloose industry.
Why are these industries more footloose than the steelworks shown on this page?

Footloose Industry

Key Idea

- Modern industry, unlike industry in earlier centuries, tends to be **'footloose'**.

Most modern industries are **footloose**. This means that **they are not tied to any one location, but can be situated successfully in a wide variety of places**. Modern industries are footloose because:

- They use **electricity** as their source of power. Electricity is equally available in all parts of developed countries such as Ireland.

- They are usually **light industries**. Their resource materials and finished products are light and therefore cheap to transport over long distances. Their factory fittings and equipment are also usually light and so can be moved easily from one factory site to another.

- **Good roads** now allow for the easy movement of industrial products over long distances.

- Car-owning **workers** can now commute long distances to and from work.

Rapid Revision

- **Heavy industries** use bulky resource materials to make heavy products. *Irish Cement* of Platin is an example.
- **Light industries** use less bulky resource materials to make relatively small products. *PC Pro* of Togher is an example.

Several locational factors determine the locations of industries.
- Factories need easy access to **resource materials**.
  - PC Pro imports materials through nearby *Cork Airport* and *Ringaskiddy seaport*.
  - Irish Cement is situated close to limestone and shale *quarries*.
- Factories usually locate close to a suitably skilled **workforce**.
  - Many workers at PC Pro were trained at local *Cork colleges*.
  - *Irish Cement* gets most of its workforce from nearby *Drogheda*.
- Reliable **transport** networks are needed to carry resource materials, finished products and workers to and from factories.
  - PC Pro is ideally situated just off the *South Link roadway* and close to *Cork Airport* and *Ringaskiddy seaport*.
  - Irish Cement is situated close to the *M1 motorway* and has a *railway line* running through its plant.
- **Markets** are the places where factories sell their products.
  - *PC* Pro sells 40 per cent of its computers locally in *Cork City*.
  - Irish Cement is well connected by road and rail with its main *Dublin* market.
- Factories need on-site **services** such as Internet access, roads, drainage and electricity. They may also have linkages with other nearby industries.
  - PC Pro uses the services of local *printing*, *packaging* and *courier* firms.
  - Irish Cement gets electricity from an on-site *ESB sub-station* and gets water from *reservoirs* on the nearby River Boyne.
- **Other locational factors** include:
  - *Capital* or the money needed to set up and run a factory.
  - Government and EU *policies*.
  - The *personal preferences* of factory owners and the attitudes of local people.

- **In earlier times,** factories were limited in their choice of location. They had to be built close to bulky resource materials or sources of power such as coal. They usually had to be located within walking distance of their workers.
- Modern industries are **footloose**. They can be situated successfully in a wide variety of locations. Their source of power is electricity, which is available everywhere in Ireland. Modern roads allow for the easy transportation of workers, light resource materials and finished products.

See Chapter 56 of your Workbook

57

Change over Time in the Location of Industry

Chapter 56 explained the factors that affect the location of industry.

Changes occur over time in the relative importance of each of these factors. Because of this, some manufacturing areas suffer from **industrial decline**, while other areas may experience **industrialisation** or the growth of industry.

The **British iron and steel** industry provides a good example of change over time in industrial location.

The British Iron and Steel Industry

1 Before the Industrial Revolution – By Forests and Rivers

Britain's early ironworks were situated in places such as the *Forest of Dean* near Bristol and *the Weald* in south-east England (see Figure 2). These places provided the following resources needed by this *resource-based industry*:

- Local rocks, which were rich in **iron ore.**
- Forests, which provided the wood from which **charcoal** could be made. Charcoal was used as a source of energy to smelt the iron ore.
- **Rivers**, which provided water power as well as river transport.

Main raw material:
Iron Ore

Sources of power:
Coal, Oil, Gas, etc.

Processes:
- Iron ore is *smelted* (melted) into liquid steel.
- Liquid steel is *moulded* into bars and sheets of steel.

Outputs:
Bars and sheets of steel are sold to engineering firms to make cutlery, parts of cars and other steel products.

How the steel industry works

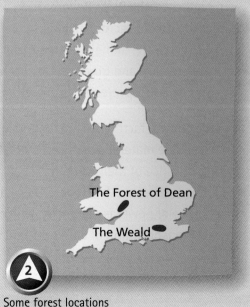

The Forest of Dean

The Weald

Some forest locations

Has any manufacturing industry in your locality changed its location?

If so, try to describe this change and explain why it took place.

2 The Industrial Revolution – By Coalfields

By 1800, most of the great *forests had been cut down* and a new, better source of power had been discovered. This source of power was **coal**. As old ironworks declined, new works were built near Britain's great **coalmines** in places such as *South Wales* and *Yorkshire* (Figure 3).

An old coal-based iron and steel plant at Margam in Wales.

3 From 1950 Onwards – On the Coasts

During the second half of the twentieth century, the great coalfield sites began to suffer industrial decline and Britain's iron and steel industry moved to coastal sites such as *Port Talbot* and *Teeside* (see Figure 4). There were several reasons for this.

- Britain's **coal** and **iron ore** mines were almost **exhausted** (used up).
- **Oil** had become more efficient than coal as a source of power.
- Coal, iron ore and oil were by then all being **imported by sea** into Britain.

3

Some coalfield locations

4

Some mainly coastal locations

From coalfield to coast
A modern coastal steel mill at Port Talbot in Wales (left) and the ruins of an old coal-based steel plant at Merthyr, Tydfil, Wales (below).

Why did Britain's steel industry relocate from coalfield to coastal sites?

Industrial Inertia

Sheffield in England is an old inland steel-making location. But Sheffield's steel industry survived for the following reasons:

- Sheffield steel is used to make specialised **high-quality products** such as surgical instruments and cutlery. There continues to be a big demand for such products.

- Sheffield has such a **famous reputation** for making fine steel that business would decline if it were to move elsewhere.

- Sheffield's **workers** are very skilled. It would take much time and money to train a similar workforce elsewhere.

- A great deal of money has been invested in **modernising** Sheffield's steel plants. It would be costly to abandon these factories and to build others elsewhere.

- The British government gave **subsidies** (financial aid) to Sheffield steel in order to fight rising unemployment in the English Midlands.

It sometimes happens that an industry does not move to a new location, even when changing locational factors seem to suggest that it should do so. This is called **industrial inertia**.

Steel-making in Sheffield (see Figure 4 on page 315) is a good example of industrial inertia.

Rapid Revision

Changes in the importance of various locational factors have caused **changes over time in the location of the British iron and steel industry.**

- Before 1800, steel plants were located near **forests** that provided charcoal and near **rivers** that provided water power and transport routes.
- During the Industrial Revolution, steel plants relocated at **coalfield sites**. Coal was a better source of power than charcoal.
- From 1950 onwards, steel-making was carried out at **coastal locations**. Imported iron ore and oil could be brought more easily to these sites. In any case, British coal supplies were becoming exhausted and inland steelworks were out of date.

Some industries do not move to new locations, even when locational factors change in importance. This is called **industrial inertia**. Steel-making has remained in Sheffield for the following reasons: the area is famous for fine steel; the local workforce is skilled; new plants would be costly; the British government has subsidised Sheffield steel plants.

Activities

1. Industrial inertia means: (tick the correct box)
   - [ ] that an industry fails to change location when it would seem profitable for it to do so
   - [ ] that a factory may locate in many different places
   - [ ] that government policy reduces the efficiency of an industry
   - [ ] that new sources of resource materials are not exploited *(J.C. Higher Level)*

2. In the boxes provided, match each letter in column **X** with the number of its pair in column **Y**.

	Column X		Column Y		
A	Yorkshire	1	Deepwater, steel-making location	A	
B	Sheffield	2	Old coal-fuelled, steel-making location	B	
C	The Weald	3	Location associated with industrial inertia	C	
D	Port Talbot	4	Ancient steel-making location	D	

3. The general location of Britain's iron and steel industry has changed over time.
   Explain why this happened. You may use the diagram below to assist you. *(J.C. Higher Level)*

 Ancient forest sites → Industrial Revolution coalfield sites → Modern coastal sites

See Chapter 57 of your Workbook

Women in Industry

The roles of women in industry have changed over time. This chapter will examine some of these changes in Ireland and in China.

Case Study 1: Ireland

In recent years there have been many changes in the roles of women in Irish manufacturing industry. But Irish women still do not enjoy equality of employment with men.

Changes Have Taken Place . . .

1 **More women** are now in paid employment. Most women choose to work outside the home. Some are forced to do so by high living costs.

2 Within industry, more women are doing **skilled** and semi-skilled work.

3 Women's industrial **wages have increased** steadily. There is equal pay for equal work and sexual discrimination within the workforce is illegal.

But . . .

- Nearly a third of all female employees are **part-time** workers and most of those women are in low-paid jobs.
- Most women continue to work in what is seen as **traditional employment** – office work, catering and other service industries. Ninety-two per cent of nurses but less than 20 per cent of manufacturing workers are women.
- A much smaller proportion of women than men are in **management** positions. Only 18 per cent of Irish industrial managers are female.
- Women's average industrial **wages** are still only 76 per cent of those of men.

Why do you think this is so?

Fact!
Women make up 61 per cent of post-primary school teachers. But only 35 per cent of school principals are female.

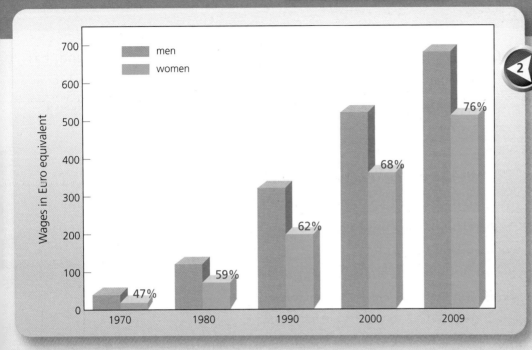

2 Average weekly earnings in the Irish manufacturing industry between 1970 and 2009. The percentages refer to female earnings as a percentage of male earnings.
1. Indicate whether each of the following statements is true or false:
   (a) Male and female wages rose steadily between 1970 and 2009.
   (b) In 2009, the average female wage was more than three-quarters that of the average male wage.
   (c) The average male wage in 1990 was higher than the average female wage in 2009.
2. Make three statements about the trends (changes) in female earnings between 1970 and 2009.

Things that Prevent Change

The following factors have hindered change in the roles of women in Irish industry.

- **Prejudice**

  Many Irish men – and women – still have set ideas about what they see as 'suitable' working roles for women. An EU survey showed that only 50 per cent of Irish people believe that women are just as capable as men of working as bus drivers, surgeons or TDs.

- **Education**

  Young men and women still tend to receive different types of educational training. More girls than boys study subjects such as home economics. More boys than girls learn industrial subjects such as metalwork, car maintenance and woodwork.

- **Domestic duties and childcare facilities**

  Women perform most childminding and household duties. This, together with a shortage of affordable childcare facilities, prevents many women from entering full-time employment outside the home.

What could be done to encourage equality between men and women in industry?

"AH, MRS BROWN, WE WERE WONDERING IF THERE'S ANY PARTICULAR REASON YOU'RE NOT APPLYING FOR THE NEW MANAGERIAL POSITION...?"

3 Study the cartoons shown here and in Figure 1 on the previous page.
(a) Describe the message of each cartoon.
(b) Do you think that each cartoon presents a fair and accurate view of Irish life? Explain your point of view.

Case study 2: China

China is a huge country in Asia. It is 117 times the size of Ireland, has a population of more than 1 billion (1000 million) people and is now one of the world's leading industrial countries. The roles of women in Chinese industry have changed greatly over time.

4

China

In the Early Years of Communism

China became a Communist country in 1949. The Communist government brought in many reforms that **encouraged women** to work outside the home:

- *Discrimination* against women was *forbidden* in the workplace.
- *Manufacturing was developed*, so that more jobs were made available for women.
- Pressure was put on each Chinese family to have only one child. This '*one child policy*' was very controversial. But it gave more women the opportunity to work outside the home.

As a result of these policies, millions of Chinese women began to work in industry. Most found permanent employment in **state-owned factories**, where China's labour laws usually protected their rights.

New Policies

In 1979, the Chinese government decided to open its economy to Western investors and to trade freely with the rest of the world. This decision brought big changes to Chinese industry, some of which are described on the next page. The changes that occurred helped to turn China into one of the world's leading manufacturing countries, but they also brought terrible **hardship** to many female workers.

5

Percentages of men and women in Chinese industry between 1947 and 2007
Describe the trends shown here. Quote percentages as you do so.

	Women	Men
1947	7	93
1977	32	68
1997	44	56
2007	48	52

Sweatshop Abuse

The Chinese government set up **Export Processing Zones** or **EPZs**, which are special areas where thousands of factories make goods for export. Factories in the EPZs are quite different from state-owned factories. They are *privately owned* and many of them make goods for *American and European companies*. They often ignore China's labour laws and force employees to work in *'sweatshop'* conditions.

Many **Western companies** have closed their own factories in Europe and America and now have their products made cheaply in China instead.

- Most workers in the EPZs are **young, single women** who have migrated from poor rural areas in search of work.
- Many **work** 14 hours a day for 360 days a year. Sometimes they are forced to work almost round the clock. They are **paid** the equivalent of as little as €40 a month and they normally receive no extra pay for overtime.
- The work is often **dangerous** as well as tiring. Some women drop dead from exhaustion. Many lose limbs in machine accidents. Those who lose limbs are usually sacked.
- China's labour laws are not usually enforced in the EPZs. Many women who work there are therefore at the mercy of **exploiters** who place profit before people.

EPZ goods are very cheap because they are made by **very cheap labour**. Young women make up most of the labour force.

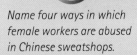

Name four ways in which female workers are abused in Chinese sweatshops.

China's Toy Story
Women in Southern China produce almost 70 per cent of the world's toys. Many work in Export Processing Zones.

See Rapid Revision on page 327

Test Yourself
eTest.ie

Classifying Global Regions According to Industry

Key Idea

- Regions may be identified on a global scale as being 'industrialised', 'newly industrialised' or 'industrially emergent'.

Industrialised Regions

Industrialised regions include the rich First World countries of the North. These countries have skilled labour, plenty of capital and **long traditions of industry**. They still produce most of the world's high-value industrial goods.

- *Germany, the **United Kingdom** and the **United States of America** are examples of industrialised countries.*

Newly Industrialised Regions

These regions contain Third World countries where **new industries are growing** very rapidly. Industrial growth in some East Asian countries is so great that these countries are said to have 'tiger economies'. Cheap but skilled labour attracts many multinational companies to newly industrialised regions.

- ***China**, **India** and **Brazil** are newly industrialised countries.*

Industrially Emergent Regions

These regions include the Least Developed Countries (LCDs) of the Third World. LCDs have **very little large-scale industry**. They were all once colonies of First World empires. As colonies, they had no chance to develop industries. They were used instead to produce cheap raw materials for their ruling imperial powers.

- ***Peru**, **Ethiopia** and **Uganda** are industrially emergent countries.*

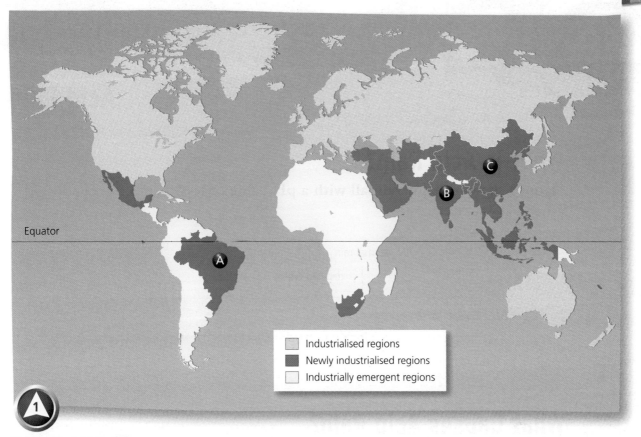

Global Industrial Regions

(a) Say whether each of the following statements is true or false:
> Most industrially emergent countries are in Africa and South America.
> All industrialised countries are north of the Equator.
> Most newly industrialised countries are in Asia.

(b) Name each of the newly industrialised countries labelled A to C.

(c) Find out why Ireland has been called 'The Celtic Tiger.'

Changes in export earnings in three leading industrial countries
Use the information given in Figure 2 to help identify the correct alternatives in the passage below:

Of the three countries shown, *US / China / UK* shows the greatest increase in export earnings between 1993 and 2008. The increase in China's earnings over that period was to the value of more than *400 / 500* billion US dollars. In 2008, China's exports were *more / less* than six times their 1993 value. China is considered to be an *industrially emergent / newly industrialised* country.

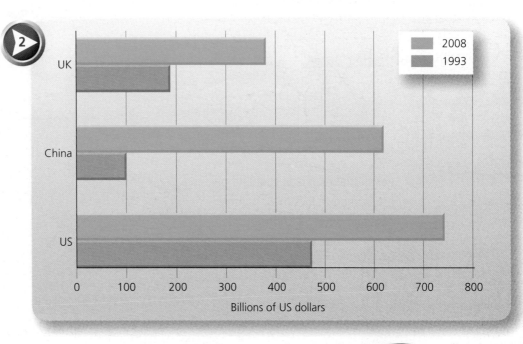

Acid Rain

What is Acid Rain?

Figure 1 shows that any **rainfall with a pH value of less than 5.6** is considered to be acid rain.

What Causes Acid Rain?

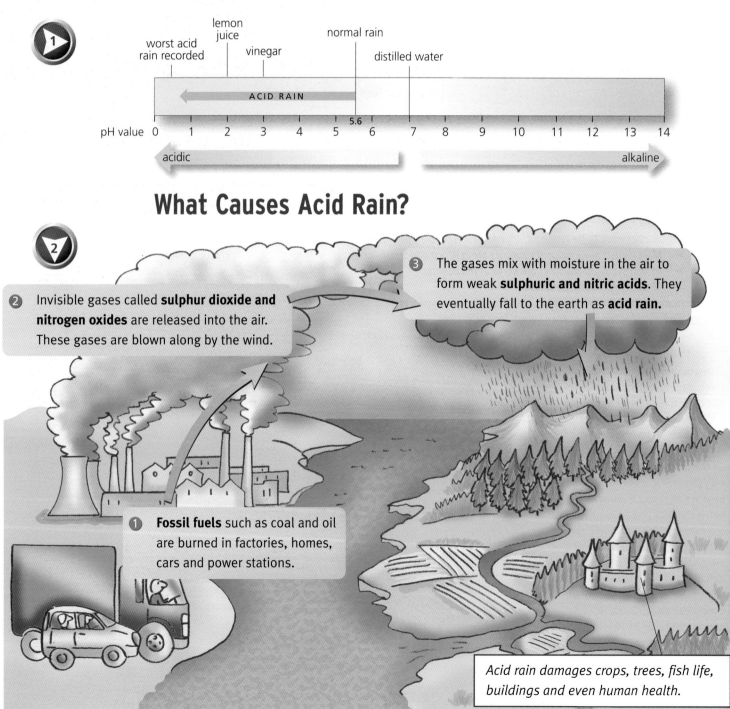

3 The gases mix with moisture in the air to form weak **sulphuric and nitric acids**. They eventually fall to the earth as **acid rain.**

2 Invisible gases called **sulphur dioxide and nitrogen oxides** are released into the air. These gases are blown along by the wind.

1 **Fossil fuels** such as coal and oil are burned in factories, homes, cars and power stations.

Acid rain damages crops, trees, fish life, buildings and even human health.

Some Consequences (Effects) of Acid Rain

Damage to Agriculture

Acid rain creates **acidic soils** that are less able to support healthy crops. It also causes severe **leaching**, which results in valuable crop nutrients being washed out of topsoils. Soils in some parts of Norway are now ten times more acidic than they were 50 years ago.

Damage to Forests

Heavy **leaching** caused by acid rain deprives tree roots of the nutrients they need. Trees then become 'malnourished' and are more likely to become diseased and die. More than half of Germany's trees have now been damaged by acid rain.

Damage to Tourism

- Acid rain can destroy food chains in rivers and lakes. **Fish** can die because they are part of these food chains. Acid rain has thus destroyed fish life in thousands of angling lakes in Norway and Sweden.
- The surfaces of old **buildings** flake away as they suffer severe chemical weathering by acid rain. Famous 'tourist trap' buildings such as the Coliseum in Rome have suffered as much acid rain damage in the past 20 years as they did in the previous 2000.

Damage to Human Health

- The acidification of **water supplies** in Sweden has been linked to foul-tasting water and outbreaks of diarrhoea. It has even caused people's hair to turn green after washing!
- Acid fog can cause an increase in illnesses such as **asthma**.

See Rapid Revision on page 326

Describe and explain how acid rain has affected trees in the Black Forest region of Germany (above) and the stone statue in London (below).

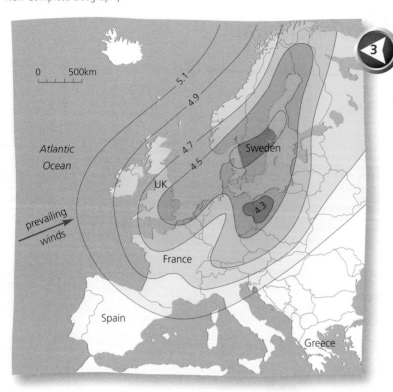

Acid rain levels in Europe

③

(a) *Rank* the following countries according to their acid rain levels. (Begin your list with the country that has the highest levels of acid rain.)
France, Greece, Spain, Sweden.

(b) Does Ireland or the UK suffer more from acid rain? Try to explain why this is so.

(c) Sweden is not as heavily populated or as industrialised as some other parts of Europe, yet it has high levels of acid rain. Try to explain why this is so.

(d) 'Acid rain is an international problem.' Explain this statement with reference to Figure 3.

Rapid Revision

Acid rain is caused when **fossil fuels** are burned and **sulphur dioxide** and **nitrogen oxides** enter the air. These invisible gasses **combine with moisture** to form **acid rain**.

Acid rain causes great **damage** to our wellbeing and to our environment.

- It damages **agriculture** by making soils acidic and by causing severe leaching.
- It damages **forestry** by causing severe leaching.
- It damages **tourism** by killing fish and by weathering beautiful buildings.
- It damages people's **health** by causing diarrhoea and asthma.

 ## Activities

1 Explain briefly the message of the cartoon in Figure 4.

2 Explain how human activity causes acid rain.
Draw a diagram as part of your answer and label it carefully.
(J.C. Ordinary Level)

3 Describe the consequences of acid rain on our environment.
(J.C. Higher Level)

See Chapter 60 of your workbook

Chapter 58

The roles of women in industry have changed over time.

In **Ireland**:

● More women are in paid, **skilled** employment and female **wages** have increased steadily.

● But women's average **pay** is still lower than that of men. Many women work in poorly paid **part-time** jobs. Relatively few work in well-paid **management** positions.

● **Prejudice, domestic duties** and a lack of affordable **childcare** facilities make it difficult for women to achieve equality with men.

In **China**:

● **Labour laws**, a **one child policy** and the **development of industry** have all increased the roles of women in industry.

● But women workers are exploited in **Export Processing Zones**, where privately owned factories ignore China's labour laws and produce goods under 'sweatshop' conditions.

 ## Activities

1 Describe briefly three ways in which the role of women has changed in Irish manufacturing industry in recent years.

2 The picture in Figure 5 shows a female worker in an EPZ in China.
  (a) What is meant by the term 'EPZ'?
  (b) Describe how the setting up of EPZs has affected the role of women in manufacturing industry in China.

See Chapter 58 of your Workbook

 5

Chapter 59

● **Industrialised regions** include Europe and the USA. They have many well-established industries.

● **Newly industrialised regions** include East Asian countries such as China. They have many new, rapidly growing industries.

● **Industrially emergent regions** include least developed countries such as Ethiopia. They have very few large-scale industries.

See chapter 59 of your Workbook

Disagreements about Industry

Disagreements sometimes arise between industrialists and others. This chapter will examine a serious controversy that has arisen in the Cork Harbour area.

Case study: The Ringaskiddy Incinerators – Cork Harbour's Burning Debate

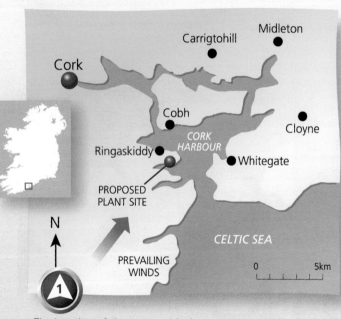

The location of the proposed incinerators

A Belgian-based multinational company named *Indaver* wants to build a large **waste management plant** at Ringaskiddy, in the Cork Harbour area (see Figure 1). The plant would include a large waste storage area. It would also include two big **incinerators** or furnaces. These would burn toxic (poisonous) waste brought from all over Ireland, as well as household and other waste from the Cork area. The incinerated waste would be converted mainly into ash. There would also be some air emissions.

The Indaver proposal has caused serious debate within and outside the Cork Harbour area. Some arguments for and against the building of the incinerators are shown here and on the following page.

A toxic waste plant will harm the environment and the **tourist trade** in this beautiful harbour area.

The waste management plant will provide steady, well-paid work for 50 people.

Prevailing winds could blow air pollution from the incinerators over nearby settlements such as Cobh, Midleton and Carrigtohill.

Incineration is already an out-of-date idea of waste disposal. Waste should be **reduced** and **recycled**, not burned!

These incinerators will not create health hazards because they will be managed properly. In any case, **An Bord Pleanála** (the Irish Planning Board) has approved them.

Even the Indaver Company admits that the incinerator's chimney stacks will emit 'safe levels' of **dioxins** into the air. Dioxins are deadly chemical pollutants that cause cancers, breathing difficulties and other human illnesses. These poisons are so dangerous that their only safe level is zero level!

Air pollutants such as dioxins could penetrate the land around this area and so enter the human food chain. This would endanger human health. It might also ruin local agriculture and damage Ireland's agricultural exports.

Heat from the incinerators can be converted into enough **electricity** to power up to 20,000 homes annually. This would be a useful by-product at a time of rising energy costs.

If Ringaskiddy becomes the 'waste capital' of Ireland, up to 20 trucks an hour will approach and leave the plant. This will greatly increase already heavy traffic in the area. These incoming trucks will carry toxic waste from all parts of Ireland. Surely this would be dangerous.

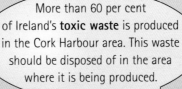

These incinerators might attract **more industries** into the area. This would provide more jobs and increase prosperity.

Only a minority of people have actually objected to the incinerators. These objectors do not know what they are talking about. Ignore them!

More than 60 per cent of Ireland's **toxic waste** is produced in the Cork Harbour area. This waste should be disposed of in the area where it is being produced.

Do the activities given on the next page.

Examine the arguments given on pages 328 and 329 for and against the Cork Harbour incinerators. Then do these activities.

For homework:

● Identify one argument that you think is valueless because it is based solely on prejudice.

● Consider the remaining arguments carefully. Then write a one-page report or prepare a one-minute speech outlining why you are in favour or against the proposed incinerators.

With your class:

● Listen to some of the reports or speeches against the incinerators.

● Discuss the various views expressed.

● Take a class vote on whether or not the Indaver company should or should not be allowed to build the incinerators.

Rapid Revision

A company named *Indaver* wants to build two huge **waste incinerators** at Ringaskiddy on the shores of Cork Harbour.

Indaver argues that the plants:

● Would conveniently burn Ireland's toxic waste, 60 per cent of which is *produced locally*.

● Would be managed safely and would provide 50 permanent *jobs*.

● Would generate a small amount of *electricity*.

Critics of Indaver's proposal say that:

● The plants would pollute nearby settlements with deadly *dioxins*.

● Poisons from the plant might also damage local *agricultural produce* and the *tourist trade*.

● Waste should be *reduced and recycled*, not burned.

Activities

Suppose that the local authorities wished to develop a new manufacturing industry in the area where you live.

(a) Name a possible industry.

(b) Give some reasons why local people might welcome it.

(c) Explain also some reasons why some local people might not welcome the new industry.

(Based on *J.C. Ordinary Level*)

See Chapter 61 of your Workbook

Tertiary Activities

You learned in Chapter 49 (page 275) that there are three types of economic activity: *primary activities*, *secondary activities* and *tertiary activities*.

Tertiary activities are those that **provide services and facilities for people.** There are many different tertiary activities in economically developed countries such as Ireland. Most jobs in developed countries are provided by tertiary activities.

All but four of the occupations listed in the box relate to tertiary activities

(a) Use a pencil to underline the four activities that are not tertiary.

(b) Tourism is a very important tertiary activity. Circle three activities in the box that are directly related to tourism.

> Tour guide, secretary, teacher, nurse, farmer, street cleaner, bar attendant, air pilot, shopkeeper, telesales person, TD, professional footballer, nun, miner, hotel worker, forester, pop star, garda, mechanic, soldier, truck driver, factory worker, judge, bishop, tourist agency worker, accountant.

Figure 1 shows the proportions of people employed in primary, secondary and tertiary activities in an economically developed (First World) country and in an economically developing (Third world) country

(a) Which of the countries, A or B, is the First World country? How do you know?

(b) Contrast the proportions of people working in primary and tertiary activities in the two countries. Give percentages for both countries.

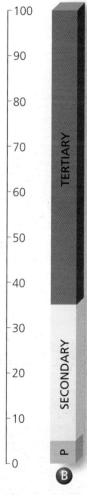

Percentages of workers engaged in primary, secondary and tertiary activities in six countries

Country	Primary	Secondary	Tertiary
A	80	12	8
B	4	18	78
C	6	–	79
D	68	20	–

The table of figures in Figure 2 shows the percentages of workers engaged in primary, secondary and tertiary activities in four countries labelled A–D. Two of these countries are economically developed and two are economically developing.

(a) Two percentages have been left blank. Calculate and pencil in each of these percentages.

(b) Which two countries labelled are economically developed? How do you know?

The *Custom House Quay* area is near the centre of Dublin. In 1987, sixteen hectares of this area was redeveloped into the **International Financial Services Centre (IFSC)** – a modern hub of banking and other services.

The IFSC now contains more than 400 banks, insurance companies and other businesses. It is a hive of tertiary activities within the heart of Dublin.

3

Dublin's IFSC (shaded in brown)
(a) Use this map to describe the location of the IFSC.
(b) Do you think the IFSC is in an attractive location? Explain.

BEFORE

AFTER

The Custom House Quay area before and after the development of the IFSC
(a) The building of the IFSC is an example of urban redevelopment. What is **urban redevelopment**? (Consult page 268 if necessary.)
(b) Use these photographs to contrast the Custom House Quay area before and after the development of the IFSC.

See Rapid Revision on page 339

Tourism and Tourist Attractions

Tourism is the world's biggest and fastest-growing tertiary activity. Figure 1 illustrates the **growth of tourism** over time.

The growth of international tourism 1965–2005
Examine the graph and say whether each of the following statements is true or false:

(a) International tourism grew steadily between 1965 and 2005.
(b) The number of tourists doubled between 1965 and 1970.
(c) Tourist numbers grew most rapidly between 1975 and 1980.
(d) There were 440 million international tourists in 2000.
(e) An international tourist is someone who leaves one country to holiday in another.

Why tourism has grown

- Many people in First World countries have become **wealthier**. They have disposable income (spare cash) to spend on holidays.
- Most people work a five-day week and enjoy at least two paid work-free weeks each summer. This gives people the **free time** they need to go on weekend breaks or on longer holidays.
- **Improved transport** allows tourists to travel long distances quickly, relatively cheaply and in comfort. Air travel, for example, allows Irish people to travel to Spain in approximately two hours.

Tourist Services and Facilities

In Ireland, tourist services and facilities tend to be located in particular regions that offer some of the following attractions:

Name *one other* example of each of the attractions mentioned here.

1. **Areas of natural beauty,** such as the Burren in Co. Clare.
2. **Beaches and coastlines,** such as Brittas Bay in Co. Wicklow.
3. **Recreational and sporting facilities,** such as the Curragh racecourse.
4. **Cities** such as Dublin.

Figure 2 shows that Ireland contains eight different **tourist regions**. Most of these regions possess a combination of some or all of the tourist attractions listed above.

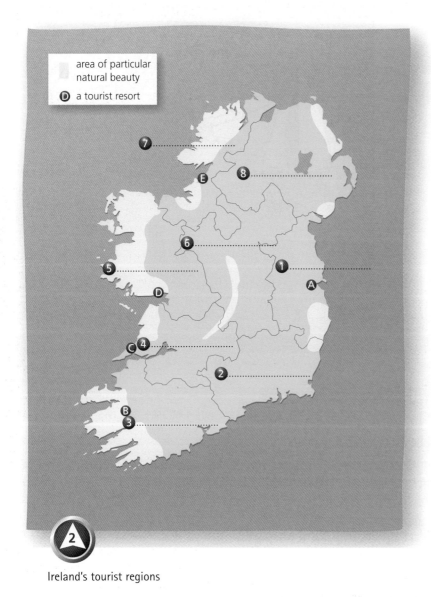

Ireland's tourist regions

(a) Using a pencil, write the names of the tourist regions labelled *1* to *8* on the map in Figure 1. These eight regions are listed below. Four clues have been provided to help you identify the regions on the map.

IRELAND'S TOURIST REGIONS
- *East and Dublin*
- *Invernia (Counties Cork and Kerry)*
- *Ireland West (Counties Galway and Mayo)*
- *Lakeland (in the Midlands)*
- *Northern Ireland*
- *North-West*
- *Shannonside (Counties Limerick and Clare and part of Co. Tipperary)*
- *South-East.*

(b) Identify and name some areas of natural beauty in *any one* of the regions shown.

(c) Examine the tourist resorts labelled *A–E* on the map. Using pencil, write the letters *A–E* opposite the matching resorts named in the grid below. You may need an atlas to help you.

Letter	Resort
	Galway
	Killarney
	Kilkee
	Bundoran
	Dublin

1 Areas of Natural Beauty

Areas of great natural beauty attract tourists to many parts of Ireland. These attractions include the following:

- **Mountain areas** with deep glacial valleys and pretty ribbon lakes provide spectacular scenery for tourists. Such areas include the Wicklow Mountains, and Macgillycuddy's Reeks in Co. Kerry.

- **Lakes** attract tourists to places such as the Midlands ('Lakelands' Region) and Killarney in Co. Kerry. Boat cruises on the Shannon lakes provide people with relaxed holidays in beautiful surroundings.

- **Unusual rock formations** provide spectacular scenery in several parts of Ireland. These include the karst scenery of the Burren in Co. Clare and the famous six-sided basalt pillars of the Giant's Causeway in Co. Antrim.

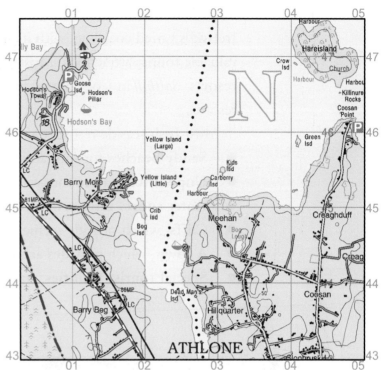

Lough Ree on the River Shannon
(a) What evidence is there that tourists visit the area shown on the map?
(b) Describe three tourist attractions in the area shown.

Glenveagh, Co. Donegal
(a) Why would the area shown here attract tourists?
(b) Can you explain how the valley shown here was formed? (Consult page 44 if necessary.)
(c) The area shown is part of Glenveagh National Park. What is a National Park? (Consult page 22 if necessary.)

(a) What famous tourist attraction is shown here?
(b) How were the columns shown here formed? (Consult page 11 if necessary.)

335

2 Beaches and Coastlines

Ireland's varied coastline, with its many attractive and unspoilt beaches, provides valuable tourist attractions. Most of our tourist regions include busy **seaside resorts**. *Salthill* in Co. Galway and *Bundoran* in Co. Donegal are examples of such resorts.

Most Irish seaside resorts contain a combination of the following attractions:

- **Sandy beaches** for sunbathing and for children to play on.
- **Unpolluted waters** for swimming, sailing, windsurfing and fishing.
- **Water sports infrastructure**, such as piers and yachting marinas.
- **Cliffs**, which provide scenic beauty and pleasant cliff walks.
- **A town**, which provides accommodation, shops, bars and restaurants.
- **Special tourist facilities**, such as caravan parks, campsites and golf courses.

Hi Michelle,

Greetings from Kilkee, Co. Clare. We arrived here this morning. Deirdre and I booked into the hostel. Danny and Michael are staying with Michael's people in the caravan park. Our hostel is right next to a lovely sandy beach, which Deirdre and I hope to make use of for sunbathing purposes. The lads (especially Danny!) are a lot more interested in the golf course. Deirdre says she'll just die if there isn't a good disco here. She keeps saying we should have gone to Spain for the sun, but I think this place will be good craic. We're off now to check out the town for restaurants and bars and to post our cards. I'll have all the news for you next week.

Bye
Kate

Michelle McSwiney

76 Cherrywood Lawn

Ardbeg

Co. Waterford

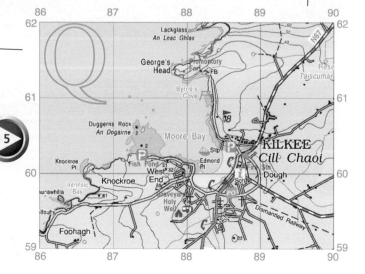

Examine the holiday postcard (Figure 4) and the map fragment (Figure 5)

(a) *Name four tourist attractions or facilities that are mentioned in the postcard and that are also shown on the map. Locate each of those features on the map by means of a six-figure grid reference.*

(b) *List three tourist attractions or services that are shown on the map, but that are not mentioned in the postcard.*

3 Recreation and Sporting Activities

Most regions offer a variety of recreational and sporting activities that attract tourists.

- **Golfing** attracts tourists to many resorts. Many famous golf courses, such as that at Portmarnock (Co. Dublin), are in coastal locations where sand dunes make excellent golf bunkers.

- Mountains, such as the Macgillycuddy's Reeks, entice **hill walkers**. Hill walking routes, such as the Kerry Way, are shown on our 1:50,000 OS maps.

- Bogs and coastal mud flats provide excellent **nature reserves** that attract birdwatchers and other wildlife enthusiasts.

- **Sailing and other boating activities** entice tourists to coastal resorts such as Kinsale in Co. Cork.

- **International sporting fixtures**, such as soccer and rugby matches, attract overseas visitors to Dublin.

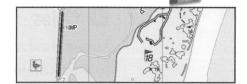

Identify the following outdoor activity attractions on the map fragments above:
- a hill-walking route
- a nature reserve
- a golf course on sand dunes
- boating activities.

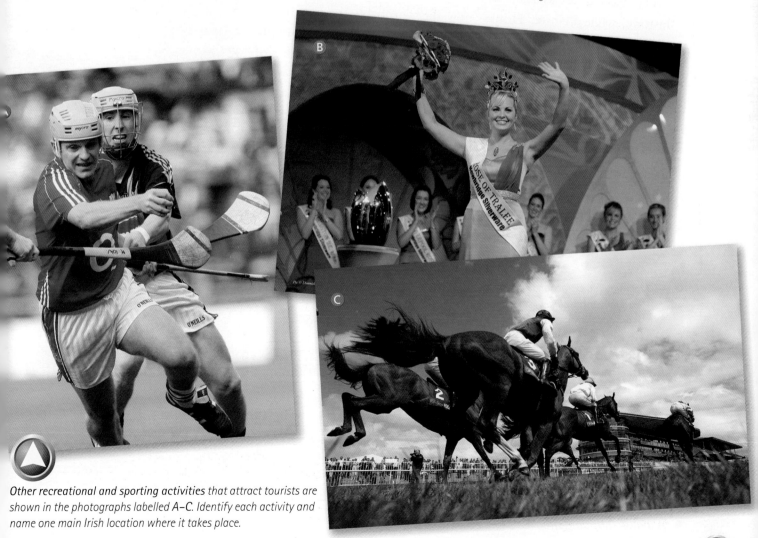

Other recreational and sporting activities that attract tourists are shown in the photographs labelled A–C. Identify each activity and name one main Irish location where it takes place.

4 Cities

Unlike rural areas, cities depend almost entirely on human-made cultural features to attract tourists. Each city has its own unique attractions. Below is a travel-book extract about the attractions of Dublin. Read the extract and answer the questions that follow it.

In recent years, Dublin has become one of Europe's more important tourist city destinations.

The redeveloped Temple Bar area boasts numerous pubs and restaurants. It is lively, colourful, rather noisy and quite expensive.

Dublin is also a city of great culture. It boasts some very beautiful buildings and its Georgian architecture is among the best in the world. Christchurch and Trinity College are as beautiful as they are historic, while Leinster House (now the seat of Ireland's Parliament) is itself a most elegantly designed palatial building. Nearby museums of note include the National Museum and the Museum of Natural History.

The Phoenix Park is credited with being one of the largest urban parks in Europe. St Stephen's Green – though tiny by comparison – does offer the advantage of a beautifully maintained green area in the very heart of the city.

For those who love theatre, a visit to the famous *Abbey* or *Gate* theatres is advised; while more modern centres such as *The Point* host large audiences for performers ranging from Russian ballet dancers to pop stars.

Dublin, like all European capitals, has a host of shopping delights to offer. For visitors with limited time, the elegant and colourful Grafton Street is probably the best bet for a spree. Beware, though! Dublin is one of Europe's more expensive cities. It is no place for the holiday bargain hunter!

Which building, mentioned in the extract, is shown here?

7 Study the extract above. In the spaces provided, name examples in Dublin of the places listed in the box below. Use the other spaces provided to name similar examples in one other Irish city of your choice.

URBAN ATTRACTIONS	Examples in Dublin	Examples in . . . (Name another city)
• An area of pubs and restaurants		
• Historic buildings		
• A public park		
• Theatres		
• A major shopping area		

Rapid Revision

Chapter 62

- Tertiary activities provide **services** for people. Most workers in economically developed countries are employed in tertiary activities.
- Dublin's **International Financial Services Centre** contains more than 400 companies that are involved in banking, insurance and other service activities.

Chapter 63

Tourism is a major tertiary activity. Tourist services are often located in the following areas:

- **Areas of natural beauty**, such as mountains (Macgillycuddy's Reeks), lakes (Killarney) and places of unusual rock formation (the Giant's Causeway).
- **Coastlines** that provide sandy beaches, unpolluted seas, cliffs, etc. Salthill and Bundoran are examples of coastal resorts.
- **Places with recreational and sporting facilities** for golf, hill-walking, sailing, etc.
- **Cities** such as Dublin that offer a busy nightlife (Temple Bar), historic buildings (Christchurch), parks (St Stephen's Green), theatres (the Abbey), etc.

Activities

Test Yourself **eTest.ie**

1. Many regions are important for tourism.
   (a) Name one such region.
   (b) Give three explanations why tourism is important in the region you have named. (*J.C. Ordinary Level*)

2. Tourists are attracted to locations other than beaches for holidays. These locations include:
   - areas of natural beauty
   - cities
   - sporting and recreational facilities.

   With reference to specific examples you have studied, discuss two of the above attractions. (*J.C. Higher Level*)

3. Use evidence from the map in Figure 8 to describe the attractions and facilities that the Strandhill area offers tourists. Refer in your answer to:
   (a) natural beauty
   (b) coastal attractions
   (c) recreation facilities
   (d) access to the area.

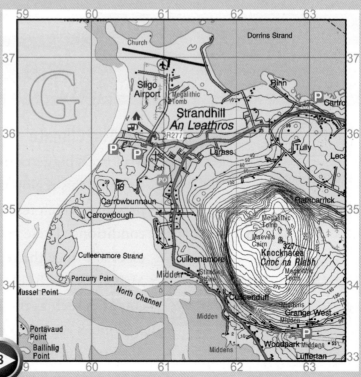
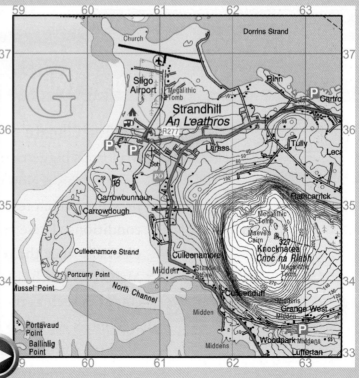

Strandhill, Co. Sligo **8**

64

Fun in the Sun - Mediterranean Tourism

Western Europe is one of the world's most developed tourist areas. **Coastal areas**, especially around the Mediterranean Sea, are particularly attractive to tourists.

Principal coastal tourist areas

France

Riviera

Costa Brava

Spain

Costa Blanca

Costa del Sol

Italy

Mediterranean Sea

Mallorca (Majorca)

Santa Ponça ● Palma

1 Europe's main coastal tourist areas

(a) *Name three countries and three coastal areas that benefit from Mediterranean coastal tourism.*

(b) *Why do you think the Mediterranean attracts more coastal tourism than any other sea in Europe?*

Case Study: Why Mallorca (Majorca) Attracts Tourists

Key Idea

- Climate is an important factor in making some regions attractive to tourists.

Revise pages 106 and 107

1 The Climate

Mallorca's biggest attraction is its **Mediterranean climate**. During the summer, this region is usually under the influence of **high atmospheric pressure**, which results in long periods of **hot**, **dry**, **sunny** and **calm conditions**. These conditions are perfectly suited to **beach holidays**, especially since the region contains many sandy beaches. Each year, Mallorca's beach resorts attract millions of tourists from damp, cool countries such as the United Kingdom, Germany and Ireland.

Winters are damp but mild in Mallorca. At this time, many retired northern Europeans live on the island to avoid the hard, cold winters of their home countries.

A summer beach scene in Mallorca
(a) Describe the scene in as much detail as possible.
(b) In what ways does this beach scene differ from
a beach scene in Ireland?

2 Mallorca's Other Attractions

- The area has a multitude of well-developed **facilities**, such as hotels, apartments and swimming pools.
- There is a **lively nightlife** in resorts such as Palma and Santa Ponça*, with numerous bars, restaurants, discos and leisure centres.
- **Costs** are generally lower than in many European countries such as Ireland.

* Pronounced *Santa Ponza*.

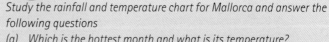

Study the rainfall and temperature chart for Mallorca and answer the following questions
(a) Which is the hottest month and what is its temperature?
(b) Which month is the coolest and what is its temperature?
*(c) Calculate the **annual temperature** range.*
(d) Name the wettest month and estimate its rainfall.
(e) Which are the driest months?
*(f) Calculate the **mean rainfall** for the four driest months of the year.*

Evening in Mallorca
(a) How does the scene shown here differ from
a corresponding holiday scene in Ireland?
(b) Name some other ways in which a
Mediterranean holiday might be different
from a holiday in Ireland.

Some Positive and Negative Effects of Tourism

Tourism brings **unwelcome impacts as well as benefits** to popular tourist areas. Some impacts that relate to *Mediterranean tourism* are outlined below.

> This was once an area of high unemployment. Most local people have now found **jobs** in hotels, restaurants and souvenir shops.

> Tourism is largely a **seasonal business**, with a very busy peak during the summer period. At other times of the year, many seasonal workers are without work.

> The tourist boom has provided lots of work in the **building trade**.

> The **high-rise hotels** that have been built are extremely **ugly**. Many of them are poorly finished, and building work seems to be going on all the time! The long unplanned lines of these hotels dominate the skyline and spoil our beautiful scenery.

> This place used to be far **too dull**! Now there's plenty of entertainment available.

> This used to be a lovely, peaceful place. Now it is **noisy**, **brash** and **littered** and has lost its own distinctive character.

> Roads, electricity, water and sewerage **services** have all been greatly improved.

> These **services are overused** during the peak tourist season. Roads are overcrowded. Swimming pools use so much water that water for local farms is in short supply. The Mediterranean Sea is polluted annually with the sewage of up to 90 million tourists.

> Tourism has brought lots of foreign money to the area. Peoples' **standards of living** have risen as a result.

> The **cost of living** has risen too, especially the cost of food, housing and entertainment. This is particularly hard for those local people who do not make their money from tourism.

> I used to be a small farmer and was quite poor. I made a lot of money **selling my land** at a very high price to the property developers.

> **Land values** have risen so rapidly here that only rich property developers and other wealthy outsiders can afford to buy land. Because of this, local people are gradually losing ownership of their own locality. High land values also mean that fewer public parks or other community amenities are being developed for local people.

- Tourism may lead to the development of transport and communication links.

Tourism and the Development of Transport and Communications

- **Transport** refers to the movement of people and goods between places.
- **Communications** refers to the exchange of ideas and information, *as well as* the movement of people and goods (see Figure 3).

3

- road ⎤
- rail ⎥ transport
- sea ⎥
- air ⎦
- TV and radio
- telephone and fax
- e-mail and other computer links
- printed matter

communications

How Tourism Leads to the Development of Transport and Communications

- Tourism creates a **demand** for better transport and communication links.
- Profits from tourism help to provide the **money** to develop such links.
- Even the **prospect of tourism** encourages governments to develop transport and communication links in potential tourist areas.

Tourism has led to the development of the following:

- Busy **airports** in tourist areas such as Dublin and Palma (Mallorca).
- **Car ferry services** such as those that link the Aran Islands with the Irish mainland and Mallorca with France, Italy and the Spanish mainland.
- **Improved roads** such as those between Killarney and Cork and between Palma and Santa Ponça (Mallorca).
- Improved **telephone**, **fax** and **Internet** services in all tourist areas.

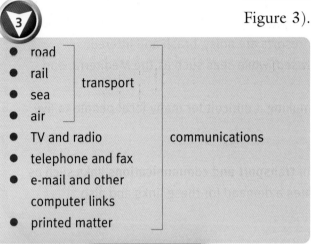

Discuss how the photographs labelled A, B and C illustrate the effects of tourism on transport facilities

Rapid Revision

The **Mediterranean climate** is an important factor in making *Mallorca* attractive to tourists. Hot, dry sunny summers make the region especially suited to beach holidays. **Other attractions** of Mallorca are its well-developed facilities, lively nightlife and relatively low costs.

Tourism brings **unwelcome impacts** as well as benefits to tourist regions.
- *Employment* tends to be largely *seasonal*, leaving people without work in the off-season periods.
- Many high-rise buildings are *ugly* and some tourist resorts are noisy, brash and littered.
- *Services* such as roads and water supplies are *overused*, while seas such as the Mediterranean can be polluted by sewage.
- Land values and other *costs can rise* dramatically, making it difficult for many local people to live in tourist areas.

Tourism may lead to the development in tourist areas of **transport and communications** links such as airports, car ferries, roads and cable cars. Tourism creates a demand for these links and also provides the money needed to pay for them.

Activities

1. *Climate is important in making some places attractive for tourism.*
   Explain this statement with reference to a European example that you have studied.
   (J.C. Higher Level)

2. Using an example that you have studied, name one region in Europe where people go to enjoy a different kind of holiday than they could enjoy in Ireland. Describe and explain the differences between tourism in this region and tourism in Ireland.
   (J.C. Ordinary Level)

3. Using the information in *Figure 4*, give two reasons why some tourists prefer Spain's *Costa del Sol* area to Ireland as a holiday destination.

See Chapter 64 of your Workbook

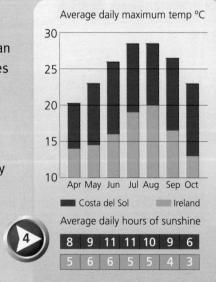

65

Rich World - Poor World

Revise
Chapter 34

You learned in Chapter 34 that the world's wealth is very unequally divided between the generally wealthy **North** and the generally poor **South**.

Measuring Development

There are many ways of measuring development. We can, for example, measure the following:

- The average yearly income per person. This is sometimes called the **GNP (Gross National Product) per capita.**
- The average **life expectancy** of people.
- The **adult literacy rate**, which is the percentage of adults who can read and write.
- The average **years of schooling** that people receive.

Country	GNP per capita ($US equivalent)	Life expectancy at birth (years)	Adult literacy rate (%)	Years of schooling (average)
Brazil	4,470	71.5	83	4.8
China	2,100	73.1	89	5.8
Guinea	328	43.9	28	1.1
India	910	60.6	54	3.9
Ireland	44,578	78.0	99	11.8
Mali	435	44.5	27	1.2
Norway	61,012	80.0	99	12.3
Uganda	323	48.0	34	2.3
USA	45,247	77.5	99	12.3

1

Measurements of development for nine countries

(a) Which three countries would you classify as being 'developed'?

(b) Which country do you think is the **most** developed and why?

(c) Very poor countries are sometimes said to be 'slowly developing' countries. Which three countries would you place in this category?

(d) Which country do you think is the **least** developed and why?

Key Idea

- In economic terms, the world is divided into developed, quickly developing and slowly developing countries.

Developed . . .

- . . . countries are the rich countries of the North.
- They contain only 25 per cent of the world's population but use 80 per cent of its resources.
- They have high GNPs and most (but not all) of their people enjoy fairly high living standards.
- Public services, such as schools and hospitals, are well developed in most developed countries.
- Some countries (such as the USA) are much wealthier than others (such as Poland).

Quickly Developing . . .

- . . . countries are Third World countries whose economies are growing rapidly.
- Some Asian countries, such as South Korea, have developed so rapidly that they are said to have 'tiger economies'.
- Industry is the key to growth in these countries. Many people work in manufacturing, though wages and working conditions are often poor.
- China and India are examples of quickly developing countries.

Slowly Developing . . .

- . . . countries are the poorest in the South.
- These Third World countries have very low (and often declining) GNP levels.
- Most people work in primary activities such as farming.
- Manufacturing and services are very poorly developed.
- Many people suffer from malnutrition and the diseases that accompany it.
- Many African countries, such as Sudan and Uganda, are 'slowly developing'.

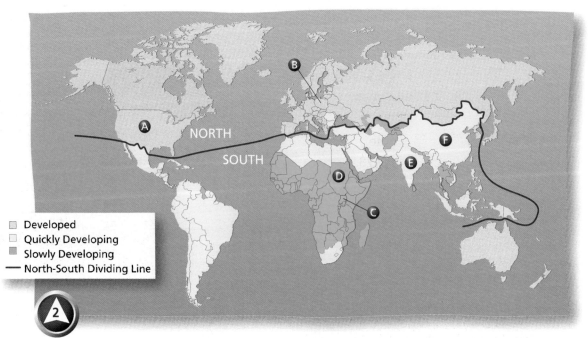

Developed
Quickly Developing
Slowly Developing
— North-South Dividing Line

(a) Name each of the countries labelled A–F on the map. Indicate whether each country you name is developed, rapidly developing or slowly developing.
(b) Which continent has the greatest concentration of slowly developing countries?
(c) Explain briefly the meanings of the terms North and South as used on the map.

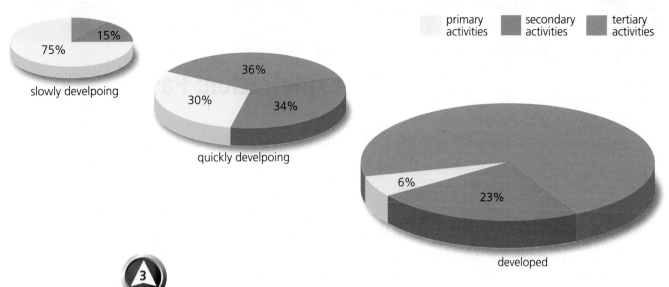

primary activities   secondary activities   tertiary activities

15% 75%
slowly develpoing

36% 30% 34%
quickly develpoing

6% 23%
developed

These three pie charts show the percentages of people working in primary, secondary and tertiary activities in a slowly developing, a quickly developing and a developed country. The size of each pie chart represents the size of that country's economy.

(a) Which of the three countries is the wealthiest? How do you know?

(b) In which country do primary activities dominate the economy?

(c) Which country has the greatest proportion of its workers in manufacturing industry?

(d) Calculate the percentage of people who work in tertiary activities: (i) in the slowly developing country; and (ii) in the developed country.

(e) Suggest why larger proportions of people work in tertiary activities in developed countries than in slowly developing countries.

Rapid Revision

In economic terms, the **world is divided into three categories of country.**

● **Developed countries** are the rich countries of the North, such as the USA and Ireland. These countries have high GNP levels and most people in them enjoy high standards of living and good public services. Most people work in tertiary activities.

● **Quickly developing countries** are Third World countries whose economies are growing rapidly. China and India are examples. Many of their people work in manufacturing industry.

● **Slowly developing countries** are the poorest in the South. They have very low and often falling GNPs. Manufacturing industries and public services are poorly developed. Most people work in agriculture. Such countries include Sudan and Uganda.

See Chapter 65 of your Workbook

66

Exploitation: Past and Present

In Chapter 65 we learned that the world's economic wealth is very unevenly distributed. One reason for this is past **colonialism** – a system by which powerful 'developed' states often exploited (abused) 'less developed' states.

How Colonialism Worked

From the fifteenth century, powerful European countries began to 'discover' other parts of the world. These European countries became *colonial powers* as they began to conquer and *colonise* large parts of Africa, South America and Asia.

The Europeans **exploited** (abused) people in their new colonies:

- They *took gold, silver and spices* from their new colonies, often without paying for them.
- They *stole land* from the colonised peoples.
- They *set up an unfair trading system* that is described in Figure 1. This exploitation made the **colonial powers rich** but kept the **colonies poor.**

> COLONIAL POWERS made big profits by processing the cheap raw materials into expensive manufactured products. Some of these products were then exported back to the colonies or to other colonial powers.

- **Colonialism** is a system in which one country controls other countries.
- A **colony** is a country controlled by another country.
- A **colonial power** is a country that controls colonies.
- An **empire** is the colonial power, together with its colonies.

> COLONIES were used to provide cotton, coffee and other cheap raw materials for the colonial powers.

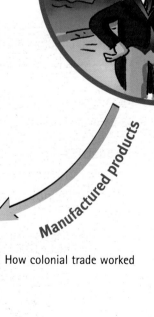

Raw materials

Manufactured products

1 How colonial trade worked

Case study 1: Ireland in the Past

In the past, Ireland was a **colony of Britain**. Like colonies everywhere, Ireland was exploited by its colonial power.

- **Trade** was organised in such a way that Ireland exported farm produce cheaply to Britain, while Britain exported expensive manufactured products to Ireland.
- The British organised **plantations** in which Irish lands were confiscated and given to British colonists. One such plantation – *The Plantation of Ulster* – was referred to on pages 196 and 197.
- As a result of the plantations, almost all of the land of Ireland came to be owned by rich **landlords**. Most native Irish people lived as labourers or as tenants of small farms that they rented from the landlords.

Some effects of exploitation on Ireland

- Irish **crops and cattle were exported** to England, even while Irish people starved during the Great Famine of 1845–49.
- There was **very little manufacturing** industry in most of Ireland. This added to the country's poverty.
- Any wealth that did exist in Ireland was very **unevenly distributed**. A small minority of rich landlords lived in luxury, while most Irish people lived in poverty.

Rich and poor in an exploited land.
The 'great houses' of rich landlords contrasted with the tiny cabins of most Irish peasants in nineteenth-century Ireland.

Unfair Trade Today

Trade or the exchange of goods should help to make people richer. But world trade now sometimes does the opposite. It is organised in such a way that **rich states and companies dominate world markets, making it difficult for many poor countries to develop economically.**

Case study 2: The Coffee Trade

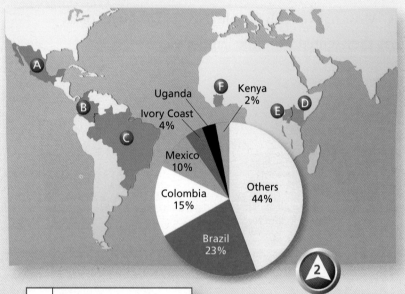

Next to crude oil, coffee is the world's most valuable **commodity**. The coffee we buy comes from coffee beans, which are grown in Third World countries such as Brazil, Kenya and Uganda (see Figure 2). Some coffee is grown in large specialised farms called **plantations**. Many small farmers also grow coffee as a **cash crop**. More than 20 million poor people work in the coffee fields of the Third World.

Some major coffee-exporting countries. The pie chart gives the percentage of world coffee exports per country.

(a) Use the pie chart to calculate the percentage of world coffee exports produced by Uganda.

(b) In the spaces provided, write the names of the countries labelled A to F on the map. Use an atlas to help you.

A	
B	
C	
D	
E	
F	

Meanings of terms:

- **Commodity**: something that is sold in its raw state.
- **Cash crop**: a farm crop that is sold for money.
- **Plantation**: a large farm that specialises in one cash crop.
- **Multinational company**: a large company with branches in many countries.
- **To export**: to send something abroad for sale.

Third World coffee growers sell their coffee beans cheaply to local agents, who in turn sell them to powerful **multinational companies** such as *Nestlé*. These First World companies control the coffee trade. They **export** coffee beans to the First World, where the beans are processed (roasted and ground), packaged and sold.

Rich countries and multinational companies control almost all world trade. They organise trade in such a way as to put their interests before those of poor countries. This has led to the following problems with the coffee trade.

Problems with the Coffee Trade

1 Unfair Terms of Trade

The **terms of trade** (the way that prices are set) are unfair. Third World farmers are forced to accept low prices for raw coffee beans. But First World companies charge high prices for the processed coffee that is sold in shops. Only a tiny part of the profits from coffee goes to Third World producers. More than 80 per cent of the profits end up in rich First World countries.

Where the money for an average jar of coffee goes

3

(a) Of the four categories given in the picture, Third World growers put most work into the production of a jar of coffee. What percentage of the profits goes to the growers?

(b) What percentage of coffee profits goes to the First World?

(c) Half a dozen multinational companies control almost two-thirds of the world's coffee business. Name two such companies.

Third World

Growers 8%

Exporters 10%

First World

Shipping and roasters 57%

Sellers 25%

Child workers in a Central American coffee plantation
How might the coffee trade affect the lives of these children?

351

2 Falling and Fluctuating Prices

Over the past 30 years the price of processed coffee has grown steadily. But over the same period the price of coffee beans has actually **decreased** on the world market. The price of coffee beans has also been allowed to **fluctuate** (rise and fall) wildly. This makes it impossible for coffee-producing countries to plan their economies properly (see Figure 4).

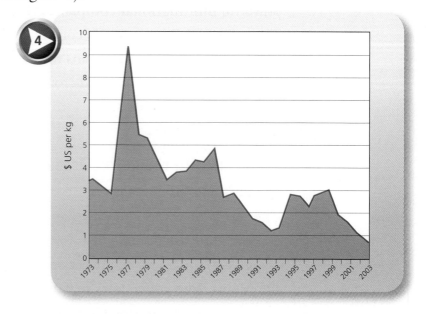

Changes in unprocessed coffee prices 1973–2003
(a) What was the price of coffee in 1977 and in 2003?
(b) How might the price changes shown here affect small farmers who grow coffee as a cash crop?

3 Protectionism

Powerful First World countries pretend that they are always in favour of free trade and 'competition'. But they often **protect** their own economies from Third World competition. The governments of rich countries know that much of the profit from coffee comes from processing coffee beans. They discourage Third World countries processing their own beans by putting higher tariffs (taxes) on any processed beans that enter the First World.

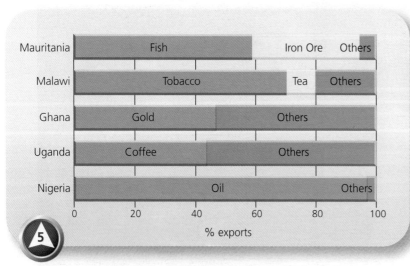

Some African countries' dependence on the export of primary products
(a) What do you think is meant by the term 'primary products'?
(b) Which of the countries shown is most dependent on a single primary product?
(c) Describe Malawi's dependence on primary products. Mention percentages in your answer.

4 Dependency

Some poor countries are **too dependent** on coffee for their export earnings. Uganda, for example, gets **43** per cent of its foreign earnings from coffee. Over-dependency on coffee earnings can create serious problems for a producing country. If the coffee crop fails or if the price of coffee beans collapses, the economy of that country could be ruined.

How Unfair Trade Prevents Development

The domination of world trade by rich countries has made it difficult for many Third World countries and people to develop economically.

- Poor countries get **low and fluctuating prices** for their raw materials. But they have to pay very high prices for products manufactured in rich countries.

- Many **multinational companies** set up factories in Third World countries. But some companies make use of 'sweatshop' conditions to make luxury goods very cheaply with virtual slave labour.

The governments and people of poor countries receive **very little income**. Because of this . . .

1 . . . they lack the **capital** to improve agriculture or to develop industry of their own.

2 . . . they cannot improve education, public health or other **social services**.

3 . . . they may be forced to ask for international aid or to borrow money abroad and so fall into **international debt**. This makes them even more dependent on First World countries and banks.

All this makes it **difficult** for poorer countries to **develop economically**.

Global trade in action

This cartoon offers a viewpoint on trading relationships between rich and poor countries.

(a) How are developed and developing countries represented in the cartoon?

(b) Why are they represented in this way?

(c) What is the overall message of the cartoon?

(d) Do you think that this message is a fair one? Explain your point of view.

Rapid Revision

- In the past, developed states often exploited less developed states. This was done through **colonialism**. Colonies had land and other riches taken from them. They were also used to produce cheap raw materials and had to import expensive manufactured goods from colonial powers.
- **Ireland** was once exploited as a colony of Britain.
  - Irish *land* was confiscated during plantations and passed on to rich landlords.
  - There was *little industry* in the country.
  - Ireland exported *farm produce* and imported manufactured goods.
- **Unfair trade** sometimes contributes to Third World poverty today. The **coffee trade** is an example:
  - The *price* of coffee beans is *low*; while processed coffee is expensive.
  - The price of coffee beans is allowed to *fall* and to *fluctuate*.
  - Rich countries sometimes put *tariffs* on coffee that is processed in Third World countries.
  - The economies of some Third World countries are *too dependent* on coffee exports.
- Unfair world trade **prevents development**. It often does not provide Third World countries with the incomes that they need to develop industry or social services or to pay international debts.

Activities

1 Many poorer countries find it difficult to develop because of unfair trading.
Account for this difficulty in relation to one commodity in world trade.

(J.C. Higher Level)

2 Examine the cartoon in *Figure 7*.
(a) Which of the two people shown represents the North and which represents the South?
(b) What does the cartoon suggest about world trade?

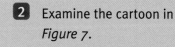

See Chapter 66 of your Workbook

67

Aid to the South

Key Idea

- Aid is given by rich countries to poor countries. Disagreement exists about the effectiveness of aid programmes.

Examine Figure 1, which shows how **international aid** operates.

Givers of Aid

Individuals → (tax) → Governments in richer countries

Sources of Aid

Non-Governmental Aid
This is provided by voluntary groups called *Non-Governmental Organisations (NGOs)*. Examples in Ireland include Trocaire, Concern, Goal, Christian Aid and Oxfam.

Bilateral Aid
This aid is given by one government to another. An example is Irish government aid to the government of Zambia in Africa.

Multilateral Aid
Governments contribute money to international bodies such as the United Nations. These bodies then distribute the aid to Third World countries.

TOTAL AID

Types of Aid

Contrast the types of aid shown in these photographs.

Emergency Aid
This is given in times of crisis, such as after earthquakes or floods or during famines. Its immediate purpose is to prevent people dying.

Examples:
food, shelter, medicine.

Development Aid
This 'long-term' aid is aimed at improving water supplies, health, agriculture, industry, roads and schools in Third World countries.

Examples:
specialists (teachers, nurses, etc.), machinery, money.

Ireland's Non-governmental Organisations

Many Irish NGOs do outstanding work on behalf of people in the Majority World.

Most NGO aid helps to meet people's **basic human needs**.

NGOs projects are effective and **sustainable** because they are small-scale, are run by local Third World people and are aimed at helping people to help themselves.

NGOs such as Trocaire **inform Irish people** of the causes of and possible solutions to Third World poverty.

Many NGOs are respected in the South because they support the dignity and **human rights** of poor people.

Ireland's Bilateral Aid

Only governments have enough resources to greatly reduce poverty in the South. Irish government aid is managed by a body called *Irish Aid*, and is far greater than all the combined aid given by our NGOs.

About 60 per cent of Irish government aid is given directly to Third World governments as **bilateral aid**. Most of this assistance goes to the African and Asian countries shown in Figure 2.

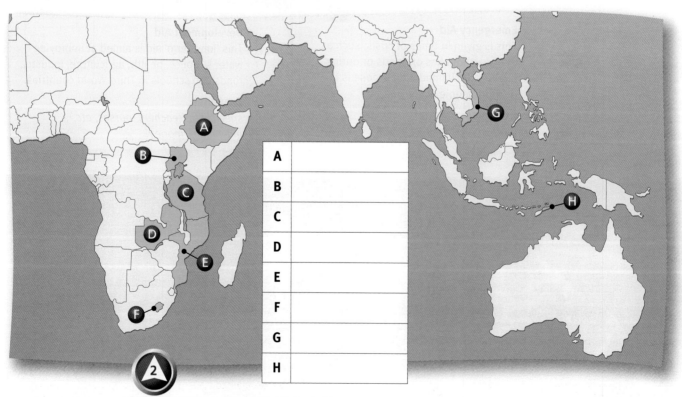

A	
B	
C	
D	
E	
F	
G	
H	

2

Some countries receiving Irish bilateral aid

The following countries are labelled A-H on the map: Lesotho, Zambia, Tanzania, Uganda, Ethiopia, Mozambique, Vietnam and East Timor. With the help of an atlas, use a pencil to write the names of each of these countries in the correct spaces on the grid provided.

Is Irish Government Aid Appropriate Aid?

'Appropriate aid' is aid that helps to meet the *real needs* of poor people. It also helps poor people to *help themselves*.

Does this fact file suggest that Irish bilateral aid is appropriate aid? Explain your point of view.

Fact File:

Aspects of Ireland's bilateral aid programme

- Most Irish bilateral aid goes to the world's poorest or **least developed countries**, such as Tanzania and Ethiopia.

- Many projects are designed to meet **basic human needs**. Irish aid in Lesotho, for example, is used to dig wells that will provide clean water.

- Some projects have helped the government of Lesotho to lay down gravel roads using local labour. These projects aim at the **long-term development** of communities.

- Irish aid helps to make Third World people **self-sufficient**. For example, it helps to improve farm livestock in Tanzania, so that people there can provide better food supplies for themselves in the future.

- Irish adult education projects in Ethiopia help to **empower** people so that they can help themselves better in the future.

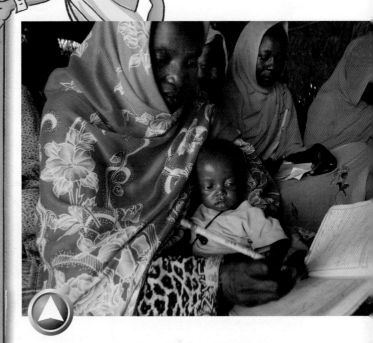

An adult literacy class funded by international aid

(a) Is this an example of emergency aid or of development aid?
(b) Is the aid shown here an example of 'appropriate aid'? Explain your answer.

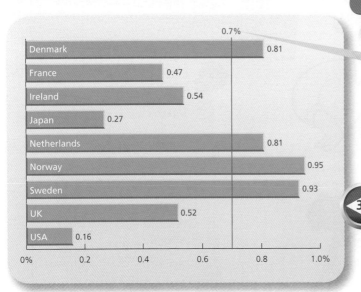

Denmark	0.81
France	0.47
Ireland	0.54
Japan	0.27
Netherlands	0.81
Norway	0.95
Sweden	0.93
UK	0.52
USA	0.16

0.7%

The United Nations (UN) asks First World countries to give 0.7% of their GNP (what they produce) in aid to the Third World. That is 70 cents for every €100 that First World countries produce.

3 Percentages of GNP of a selection of countries given in international aid

(a) Which countries shown have reached or exceeded the UN target on aid?
(b) What percentage of its GNP does Ireland give in aid?
(c) Where does Ireland rank among the countries shown?

How Effective is International Aid?

People disagree on the effectiveness of aid programmes. Debate the topic *How Useful is International Aid*? Use the evidence presented here and on the next page to help you.

In 2005, the world's richest countries promised to double their Third World aid by 2010. This might save the lives of up to 10 million people.

"SEE, PANCHO, BETWEEN US WE *CAN* WIN THE WAR AGAINST POVERTY!"

Arguments for aid

- Emergency aid **saves lives** in times of famine, earthquakes, etc.
- Development aid **helps communities** by improving water supplies, sanitation, roads, housing and education.
- Aid that is targeted at **specific groups** (e.g. literacy courses for women) can have good long-term effects.
- Aid creates friendly links between countries and acts as a limited means of **spreading the world's wealth** a little more evenly.

Aid can be turned on and off like a tap. This gives donor countries great **control** over receiving countries.

Arguments against aid

- Bilateral aid is sometimes **tied**. This means it is given with conditions attached that favour the interests of donor countries.
- **Fair trade** is much more important than aid in overcoming Third World poverty. First World aid may be used to draw attention away from the exploitation of poor people by unfair trading practices.
- Because aid flows from the North to the South, some **people in the North** may feel that they are somehow superior to Third World people.

Uganda was given aid from the **World Bank** on condition that it sold state-owned mines, industries and even banks to private investors. Many of these national assets were sold cheaply to wealthy foreigners.

Ireland's bilateral aid programmes are effective because they are examples of **appropriate aid** (see page 357).

But some international aid does more harm than good. This includes '**military aid**' from powerful countries that may be used to keep corrupt 'puppet' governments in power in the Third World.

CERTAINLY I'M HERE TO DISCUSS HUMANITARIAN AID, BUT FIRST....

5 What is the message of this cartoon?

 Rapid Revision

Aid is given by rich countries to poor countries.

- **Non-governmental aid** is provided by voluntary groups such as Trocaire, Concern and Oxfam.
- **Bilateral aid** is given by one government to another.
- **Multilateral aid** is channelled through international bodies such as the United Nations.

Aid is usually one of **two broad types**:

- **Emergency aid** is given in times of crisis, such as during a famine.
- **Development aid** is aimed at long-term improvements to agriculture, industry, etc.

Most Irish **NGO** and **bilateral aid** tries to meet long-term, basic human needs in least developed countries.

Disagreements exist about the effectiveness of international aid programmes.

Arguments for aid	Arguments against aid
• Emergency aid saves lives. • Development aid helps communities. • Aid redistributes the world's wealth a little.	• Some aid is 'tied' or is in the form of 'military aid'. • Fair trade is much more important.

Activities

1 Describe briefly but clearly the meaning of each of the following terms: *bilateral aid*; *multilateral aid*; *emergency aid*; *development aid*; *tied aid*; *non-governmental aid organisations*.

2 The five statements below refer to the message or messages given by the cartoon. Indicate which of the statements are correct by ticking (✓) the correct box.

1. Rich countries are generous to poor countries.
2. Rich countries are not really concerned about the problems of poor countries.
3. First World aid to the Third World is inadequate.
4. Rich countries do what they can to help poor countries.
5. Third World countries need aid from First World countries.

The correct statements are:

    1, 2, 4 ☐   1, 3, 5 ☐   2, 3, 5 ☐   2, 4, 5 ☐

3 Aid is given by richer states to poorer states.
Describe Ireland's aid programme to developing countries.   (*J.C. Higher Level*)

OR

4 Ireland gives aid to the developing world. Describe one example of
the type of assistance that Ireland gives to developing countries.   (*J.C. Ordinary Level*)

See Chapter 67 of your Workbook

68

Sudan - Things that Hinder Development

Examine the map of Sudan in Figure 1 below.

1

The Sahel

1. In which continent is Sudan located?
2. List the countries that border Sudan.
3. Which sea borders Sudan?
4. What major river runs through Sudan?
5. What is the capital of Sudan?
6. Part of the Sahel is shown on the map. What is the Sahel? (Refer to page 98 if necessary.)
7. Are the following statements true or false?
   (a) Sudan stretches approximately 2,000 km from north to south and more than 1,000 km from east to west.
   (b) The province of Darfur is in the west of Sudan.
   (c) Egypt lies to the south of Sudan.

Sudan is a slowly developing Third World country. In Chapters 66 and 67 we examined the effects of **international trade** and **aid** on the economic development of Third World countries such as Sudan. This chapter will focus on the key idea shown here.

Key Idea

● **Climatic change, population growth, arms expenditure** and **war** all hinder (slow down) the economic development of Sudan.

Climatic Change

North Sudan has a hot dry climate, while Southern Sudan enjoys more moist tropical conditions. But Sudan's climate appears to be changing. Since the 1970s the country has suffered from periods of severe **drought** that have seriously hindered development.

Global warming may be partly responsible for drought in Sudan. You studied global warming on pages 62 and 63

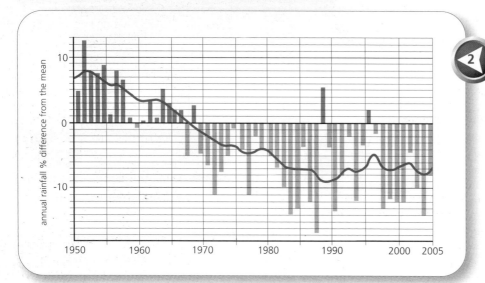

The effects of drought on Sudan

- The Sahara Desert has been spreading southwards into the Sahel region. (This is called **desertification** – you studied desertification in Chapter 17.)
- Grasslands and forestry have been destroyed. Millions of people have been short of **water** and **food**.
- Thousands of country people have had to abandon their land and flee to already **overcrowded cities** such as Khartoum.
- Cattle herders from Northern Sudan have been forced to **migrate southwards** in search of grazing land. Competition for land and water has contributed to **conflict** between northern herders and southern farmers in places such as Darfur (see page 364).

Drought in Sudan
List some effects of drought on development in Sudan.

annual rainfall % difference from the mean

2 Rainfall levels in part of the Sahel between 1950 and 2005
(Values above 0 indicate above-average rainfall. Values below 0 show below-average rainfall.)
(a) *Name the wettest year and the driest year shown.*
(b) *What was the wettest decade shown?*
(c) *How have rainfall levels since 1965 differed in general from rainfall levels before 1965?*

Population Growth

Sudan is not a densely populated country. It has fewer than 16 people per square kilometre. But Sudan is at the 'early expanding stage' of the population cycle (see page 182). It has a very high birth rate and its **population is increasing** at a rapid rate of 2.1 per cent per year. Rapid population growth has already caused some areas to become **overpopulated**. That means they have too many people for their limited resources.

How rapid population growth can hinder development

- A growing population needs more water, food and houses. This puts great strain on Sudan's limited **resources** and slows down development.
- Trees are cut down for firewood and land is cleared for agriculture. The cleared land is often overgrazed or overcultivated. This, combined with drought, causes **soil erosion** and **desertification**. Crops fail, food supplies decrease and people go hungry.
- Hungry people **migrate** into overcrowded cities such as Khartoum. Poverty increases in these cities and hinders urban development.

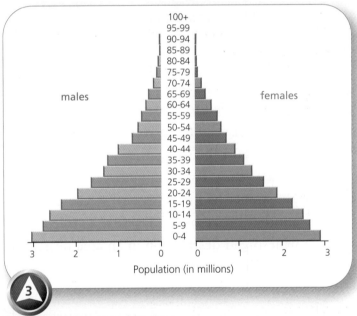

3

The population structure of Sudan

(a) What name is given to this type of diagram?
(b) How does the diagram suggest that Sudan has a high birth rate?
(c) In what other ways is the population structure of Sudan typical of an LDC (Least Developed Country)?

Sudanese children
Try to explain how each of the following factors might contribute to high birth rates in countries such as Sudan:
- high infant death rates
- levels of formal education
- the place of women in society.
(Chapter 29 might help you to answer.)

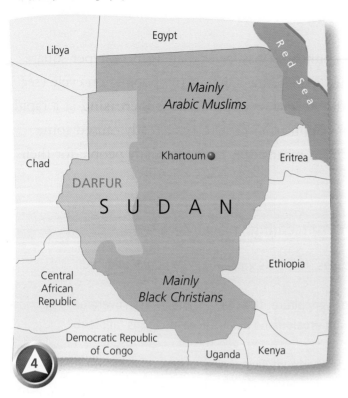

4

People in a Darfur refugee camp in 2008
How has war and arms expenditure affected the development of the people shown here?

Arms Expenditure and War

Civil wars have hindered development in Sudan for more than 25 years.

Causes of the Civil Wars

- Sudan has a majority of **Muslim Arabic** people, most of whom live in the north of the country. It also has many **black Christians** who live mainly in the south and in the western region of Darfur (see Figure 4). For many years there have been tensions between those two groups.
- Severe **drought** forced Arabic herders to migrate southwards in search of grazing for their cattle. Competition for land and water caused conflict between these herders and southern farmers.
- Some Christians were angry when the Sudanese Government passed strict **Islamic laws** in 1983.

These tensions led to **two civil wars**.

- A war between the **government and Southern rebels** began in 1983 and raged for 20 years. Two million people died.
- No sooner had the first civil war ended than another broke out in **Darfur**. This led to widespread destruction in an area nearly six times the size of Ireland.

Effects of the civil wars

- Two and a quarter million people have been **killed**. Millions more have been **injured** or **driven from their homes**.
- Massive **damage** has been done to buildings, crops and livestock. Hundreds of villages have been destroyed in the Darfur region alone.
- Sudan spends 17 per cent of its income on its large **army**. This reduces the amount of money that it can spend on development.

Rapid Revision

The following factors have hindered development in Sudan:

- **Climatic change** – repeated droughts have resulted in desertification and in water and food shortages. They have also caused human migrations to the south and into crowded cities.
- **Population growth** – rapid population growth and overpopulation are putting strains on Sudan's limited resources. This is causing soil erosion, desertification, hunger and rural-to-urban migrations.
- **Wars** – Sudan has endured two civil wars that have resulted in death, injury, the destruction of property and the displacement of people. Wars have also caused money to be spent on military rather than on development projects.

 Activities

1. Explain briefly the meaning of each of the following terms that have been used in this chapter:
   (a) drought
   (b) overpopulation
   (c) desertification
   (d) rural to urban migration.

2. Many factors are responsible for preventing economic development.
   These include the following:
   - climatic change
   - population growth
   - arms expenditure and war
   - colonisation.

   Explain how *any three* of the above factors prevented economic development in a country that you have studied.
   (*J.C. Higher Level*)

3. Which *one* of the following messages does the cartoon in Figure 5 give?
   (a) All people in Sudan dream of food.
   (b) Poor people in Sudan prefer to spend money on arms than on food.
   (c) Arms expenditure is hindering human development in Sudan.
   (d) Sudan is a rapidly developing country.

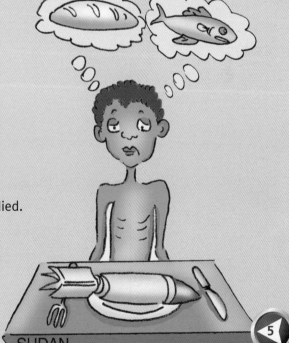

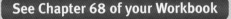
See Chapter 68 of your Workbook

Rich and Poor Regions within European States

Key Idea

● There are differences between rich and poor regions within states.

Case study 1: Regional Differences in Ireland

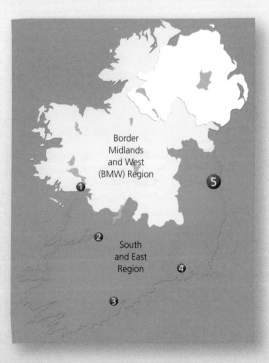

Border Midlands and West (BMW) Region

South and East Region

The Border, Midland and West (BMW) Region and the South and East Region

(a) Identify each of the cities labelled 1–5 on the map.

(b) In which region is each of the following counties? Co. Dublin, Co. Mayo, Co. Wexford, Co. Cork, Co. Donegal, Co. Sligo.

The Republic of Ireland can be divided into two general regions; the *South and East Region* and the *Border, Midland and West (BMW) Region* (see Figure 1). **The South and East Region is more prosperous than the BMW region.**

The South and East Region

● **Agriculture**

Farms are generally larger and more profitable here than they are in the BMW Region. Counties such as Meath and Wexford contain fertile lowlands with well-drained soils.

● **Services**

Tertiary activities are well developed. This is especially so in Dublin, which is Ireland's capital city, chief port and main commercial centre.

● **Population**

The population density of this region is nearly three times that of the BMW region. Three-quarters of the people live in urban areas. Dublin alone contains 1.3 million people.

● **Standard of living**

Average pay levels are 10 per cent higher here than they are in the BMW region. There are many well-paid jobs in industry and services, especially in the Dublin area.

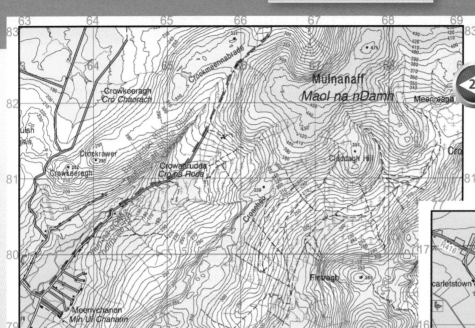

Contrast the Co. Donegal area (BMW Region) in Figure 2 with the Co. Kildare area (South and East Region) in Figure 3. Use the following headings:
- Suitability for farming
- Transport facilities
- Employment opportunities outside farming.

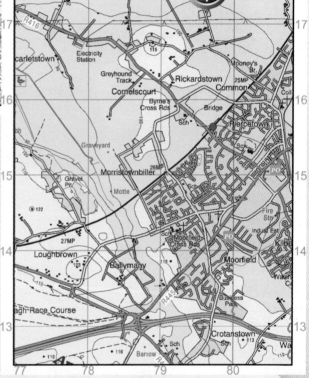

The Border, Midland and West Region

● Agriculture

Farms are generally small and farm incomes are only half of those in the South and East Region. Some land is hilly and boggy and some soils are peaty and waterlogged.

● Services

Tertiary or service activities are generally less well developed here than they are in the South and East. Galway City provides the region's widest range of high-quality services.

● Population

Only 27 per cent of the country's population live in this region and nearly two-thirds of these people live in rural areas. There are few very large towns. Galway is the region's only city.

● Standard of living

This region provides lower farm incomes and fewer well-paid service jobs than those in the South and East. Living standards are therefore somewhat lower in the BMW region.

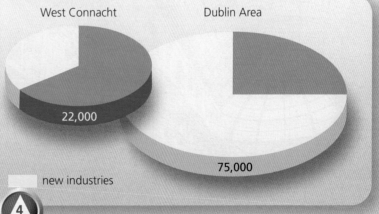

West Connacht · Dublin Area

22,000

75,000

☐ new industries

Manufacturing industries in West Connacht (BMW Region) and in the Dublin area (South and East Region)

Contrast the two areas shown in relation to: (a) total number of manufacturing industries; and (b) proportions of new industries.

367

The **north of Italy** is one of the **richest regions** of the European Union.
The **south of Italy** (also called the *Mezzogiorno*) is one of the EU's **poorest**
regions (see Figure 5).

THE NORTH

Turin Milan

THE SOUTH

SARDINIA

SICILY

5

The north and south of Italy

The rich north

● **Agriculture**

Much of Northern Italy consists of the flood plain of
the River Po. This almost flat north Italian plain is
covered in rich alluvial soils. Summers are hot and
there is plenty of rainfall for pasture and for a wide
variety of crops. Farms are mechanised and profitable.
Crops include maize and rice, while well-known dairy
products include *Parmesan* and *Gorgonzola* cheeses.

● **Manufacturing industry**

Because Northern Italy is a highly populated and
wealthy region, it provides the capital, markets and
good transport networks needed to stimulate industry.
The north Italian plain is the country's industrial
heartland. Milan, for example, is Italy's leading
manufacturing city, while Turin is the headquarters of
the famous *Fiat* motor company.

● **Standard of living**

Northern Italy provides a high standard of living for
most of its people. GNP per person is high,
unemployment levels are low, road and rail networks
are well developed and most urban areas are modern
and attractive. High standards of living have caused
many people from southern Italy to migrate to the
north.

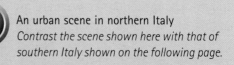

An urban scene in northern Italy
Contrast the scene shown here with that of
southern Italy shown on the following page.

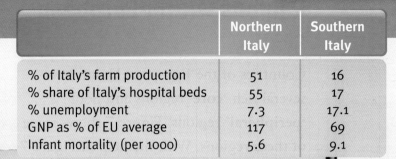

	Northern Italy	Southern Italy
% of Italy's farm production	51	16
% share of Italy's hospital beds	55	17
% unemployment	7.3	17.1
GNP as % of EU average	117	69
Infant mortality (per 1000)	5.6	9.1

The Poor South

● **Agriculture**

Much of Southern Italy is dominated by the steep-sided Apennine Mountains. Soils are poor and thin in most mountainous areas. Summer drought is common in the Mediterranean climate and this limits the crops that can be grown without the help of irrigation. Many farms are small, poorly mechanised and unproductive.

● **Manufacturing industry**

Large-scale industry did not traditionally thrive in Southern Italy. This was largely owing to a shortage of capital, local wealthy markets, good communications and industrial traditions. Some state-owned factories have been built in the South to reduce unemployment there. But industry continues to be less prosperous here than it is in Northern Italy.

● **Standard of living**

Standards of living in the *Mezzogiorno* are much lower than in Northern Italy. GNP per person is only 60 per cent of that in the north, while unemployment is more than twice the northern level. Poor living standards act as a 'push factor' for many southern Italians to migrate northwards in search of work.

What is meant by each of the following terms used in this case study? *Flood plain*; *alluvial soil*; *drought*; *irrigation*; *capital*; *GNP*; *push factor*.

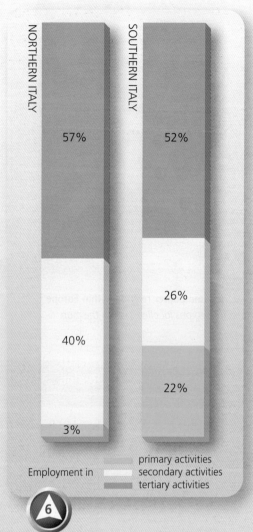

NORTHERN ITALY
57%
40%
3%

SOUTHERN ITALY
52%
26%
22%

Employment in

primary activities
secondary activities
tertiary activities

6

Some economic contrasts between northern and southern Italy
How do the statistics and bar charts provided above indicate differences in prosperity between northern and southern Italy?

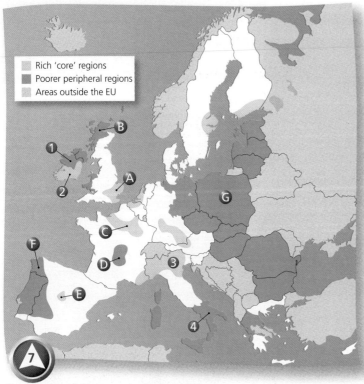

Rich 'core' regions
Poorer peripheral regions
Areas outside the EU

7

Some rich and poorer regions within Europe
Name the regions labelled 1–4 on the map.

Other Rich and Poor Regions within European States

Countries of the European Union have several rich '**core**' regions and poor '**peripheral**' regions. Figure 7 shows some of these regions. With the help of Figure 7 indicate whether each of the regions listed in Figure 8 is a rich core region or a poorer peripheral region. Then memorise the names and locations of three rich and three poorer regions.

Tick the correct boxes

Label on map	Region	Rich or poorer region	
		Rich	*Poorer*
A	London Region (UK)		
B	Scottish Highlands (UK)		
C	Paris Region (France)		
D	Massif Central (France)		
E	Madrid Region (Spain)		
F	Northwest Spain		
G	Poland		

8

Some Ways of Reducing Differences between Rich and Poor Regions in Europe

- **Industrialists** who set up new factories in peripheral areas rather than in core areas could be given special state or EU grants.
- Many peripheral regions are unspoilt scenic areas. Such areas would benefit from the increased development of **tourism**.
- **EU Structural Funds** already provide grants to help develop transport and other infrastructure in peripheral regions.

Rapid Revision

There are differences between rich and poor regions within European countries.

In Ireland

The South and East Region is rich
- Moderate rainfall, higher summer temperatures and fertile lowlands help to make *farming* profitable.
- *Services* are well developed, especially around Dublin.
- *Population density* is higher than in the BMW Region.
- *Pay levels* are higher than in the BMW Region.

The BMW Region is relatively poor
- Small hilly *farms* provide low incomes, especially where soils are peaty and waterlogged.
- *Services* are less well developed.
- *Population density* is small and there are few very large towns.
- *Incomes* are generally lower than in the South and East Region.

In Italy

Northern Italy is rich
- *Farming* is mechanised and profitable on the fertile flood plain of the Po.
- Local capital and wealthy markets helped the widespread development of *industry*, especially around Milan.
- *Standards of living* are high, with high GNP per person and low unemployment. This attracts in-migration.

Southern Italy is relatively poor
- *Agriculture* is hindered by rocky, mountainous land and by summer drought.
- A lack of capital and remoteness from rich markets hinder *industry*. State-controlled factories increase employment.
- *Standards of living* are low, with GNP only 60 per cent and unemployment more than twice that of the north. Out-migration is common.

Economic differences between regions **could be reduced** as follows:
- Offer incentives to industrialists to set up *factories* in poorer regions.
- Develop *tourism* in poor but beautiful regions.
- Use EU Structural Funds to improve *infrastructure* in poor regions.

Activities

1 In Ireland, some parts of the country are less developed than other parts. Describe one example of this which you have studied. (*J.C. Ordinary Level*)

2 (a) Name two regions in the poorest and two regions in the wealthiest areas of continental Europe.
   (b) Explain two reasons for the difference in wealth between the richest and the poorest areas. (*J.C. Higher Level*)

See Chapter 69 of your Workbook

Reducing Economic Inequality – Different Viewpoints

Key Idea

- There are disagreements about the best ways to reduce inequality between the First World and the Third World.

Some people in the **First World** use these arguments.

- Natural disasters such as earthquakes and drought are a major cause of Third World poverty. These disasters are accidents of nature. All that can be done to reduce their effects is to send **aid** to affected regions. Rich countries help to reduce inequality by giving emergency and development aid to the South.

- Corrupt Third World governments and officials often waste the aid we give them. We should insist that Third World countries be ruled properly. Maybe we should use armed intervention to overthrow Third World dictators and to bring Western **democracy** to the South.

- Overpopulation is a major cause of Third World poverty. People in the South would be better off if, like us, they had **fewer children**!

- World **trade** is the best solution to poverty in the South. Third World countries could sell more tea, coffee and other commodities to us, while we could sell more manufactured products to them.

Earthquake
In May 2008 tens of thousands of people died and five million were left homeless following a terrible earthquake in China.

Fact!
The population of the world doubled between 1960 and 2000. This was mainly because of population growth in the South.

The invasion of Iraq
In 2003 the United States and Britain invaded Iraq to overthrow its dictator (whom they had previously armed) and to 'bring democracy' to the country. The invasion led to the deaths of up to half a million Iraqis and to almost five million people being forced from their homes.

Some people in the **Third World** use these arguments.

- Powerful First World countries are a major cause of Third World poverty. In the past, imperial powers invaded our countries and stole our natural resources. Such powers still invade countries such as Iraq and pretend they do so to bring us 'democracy'. Powerful countries should **stop trying to dominate us**.

- Some First World people criticise us for having large families. But we need children to support us when we grow old. First World people should try to **understand** our situation.

- At present, world trade increases economic inequality between North and South. Third World producers are paid little for their commodities, while First World countries charge high prices for their manufactured products. Only **fair trade** can reduce global inequality.

- Most First World countries are quite mean with aid to the South. Almost all give less than 0.7 per cent of their GNPs in aid. In any case, if the North traded fairly with us we would not *need* their aid. We need **justice**, not charity!

The *Fairtrade* logo
An organisation called Fairtrade guarantees fair prices to Third World producers. This logo is to be found on all Fairtrade products.

WHAT DO *YOU* THINK?
Mark both the 'First World' and the 'Third World' set of arguments out of 40. (Award each bullet-pointed argument between 1 and 10 marks.)
(a) Which set of arguments got the more marks?
(b) Which two arguments did you agree with most?
(c) Which two arguments did you agree with least?

New Complete Geography

There are disagreements about the best ways to reduce inequality between the First World and the Third World.

- *Some people in the North* think that:
  - Existing international **aid** and **trade** are the best ways to reduce inequality.
  - Third World countries should have more Western-style **democracy** and **fewer children.**
- *Some Third World people* believe that:
  - Powerful **western countries** should stop invading and exploiting Third World countries.
  - Western people should try to **understand** better the situations of Third World people.
  - **Fair trade** rather than international aid is the best solution to global inequality.

 Activities

1 Do you think that aid is the best way to tackle inequality in the world?   (*J.C. Higher Level*)

2 Choose **two** of the items below and explain how each might reduce differences between developed and developing countries. In your answer refer to one example or country that you have studied.
  (a) Reducing military spending.
  (b) Increasing aid.
  (c) Reforming international trade.   (*J.C. Higher Level*)

3 Explain *briefly* why you **agree** or **disagree** with each of the following statements:
  (a) Some wealthy countries do more harm than good in the struggle to reduce Third World poverty.
  (b) World trade is the best solution to inequality in the world.
  (c) Nature is more to blame than people for Third World poverty.

4 Examine the cartoon in Figure 2. Which one of the following statements represents the message of the cartoon?
  (a) First World people like to buy presents for Third World people.
  (b) The First World is generous to the Third World.
  (c) First world people do not really care about inequalities in the world.
  (d) Third World people enjoy seeking aid from First World people.

See Chapter 70 of your Workbook

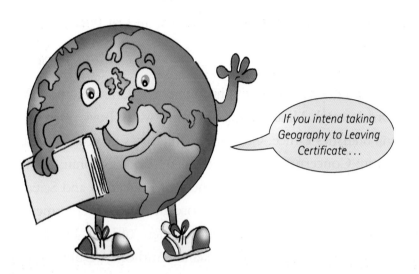

Acknowledgments

The author is deeply appreciative of the many Geography teachers whose shared experiences, advice and encouragement have played a vital part in the creation of this textbook and workbook.

Special thanks to all who played pivotal roles in the preparation, design and production of this work; especially to Anthony Murray, Aoileann O'Donnell, Mairead O'Keeffe, Helen Thompson, Neil Ryan and Hubert Mahony of *Gill & Macmillan*. Thanks also to Dara O'Doherty of Design Image, to illustrators Kate Shannon and Karen Allsopp, copyeditor Jane Rogers, and to Una Nation for her help and advice.

The assistance of the following is greatly appreciated:

Aer Rianta; Archaeology Department, UCD; Peter Barrow (photographer); Colm Bannon; Maria Barry; Joanne Bissett; An Bord Gais; Bord Iascaigh Mhara; Bord na Mona; Mark Boyle; Barry Brunt; Brick; Bus Éireann; Karen Cahill; Central Statistics Office; Chernobyl Children's Project International; Christian Aid; James Clune; Niamh Coggin; Concern; Margaret Conellan; Alex Corcoran; Joan Corcoran; Jane Cregan; Eamonn Cullen; Aileen Cummins; Department of Education and Science; Department of Enterprise, Trade and Employment; Department of Foreign Affairs; Department of the Marine; Department of Transport, Energy and Communications; Department of Irish, UCC; Sheila Dillon; Diageo Ireland; Dochas; Dublin City Council; Dublin Docklands Authority; Dublinia; Ute Duane; Dungarvan Town Council; Kevin Dwyer (photographer); Ennis Chamber of Commerce; Ennis Town Council; Failte Ireland; Fairtrade; Anna Farrell; Fatima Mansions Project; Fatima Regeneration Board; Aiden Ffrench; Brenda Field; Billy and Marion Fitzpatrick; Mike Fitzpatrick; John J. Forde; Mary Forde; Miriam Forde; William Fraher; Mary Furlong; Seán Ganley; Gerry Gannon; Garda Headquarters; Glaxo Smithkline; Goal; Greenpeace; Michelle Guiney; Maura Harrington; Oliver Harrington; Mark Harney; Tim Hayes; Aoife Horgan; Mark Hynes; Iarnród Éireann; IDA; Information Age Park Ennis; Irish Cement; Irish Fisherman Liaison Ltd; Irish Fishermen's Organisation; Irish Landscape Institute; Irish Nurses' Organisation; The Irish Times; George Jacob; Jean Kelly; John Kelly; Anne Kinsella; Frank Larkin; Ian Lawlor; Ann Leahy; Limerick City Council; Lisney and Co.; Brendan Lynch; Joe Maddock; Hugh Mangan; Gerry MacNally; Rita McInerney; Shaun McLaughlan; Eoin McVey; Chris Meehan; Microchem; George Munday (photographer); John Mulcahy; William Murrow; NAPD; Navan Chamber of Commerce; Navan Town Council; Guy Bernard Nimpa; Eoin O'Carroll; Finbarr O'Connell (photographer); Pat O'Connell; Colm O'Connor; Conor O'Donovan; Rosman O'Dwyer; Frankie O'Gorman; Rosaleen O'Leary; Conor O'Loughlan; Aiden O'Sullivan; The Ordnance Survey Office; Oxfam; PC Pro; Pfizer; Eugene Pratt; John Quilinan; Patricia Quilligan; Eibhlin Roche; Anne Marie Rossiter; Self Help Development International; Shannon Development; Elaine Sheridan; Catherine Shiels; Shell Exploration and Production; Shell to Sea Campaign; Ben Siddle; Mary Sleeman; John Smith; John Spillane; Tara Mines; Dick Tobin; Martyn Turner; Trocaire; Alan Whelan; Gillian Whelan; Susan Whelan; Brian White; John White; West Waterford Chamber of Commerce; Youghal Tourism.

Charles Hayes, MEd, MA, HDE
Department of Education, UCC

For permission to reproduce photographs the author and publisher gratefully acknowledge the following:

AEROFILMS: 141T, 165TR; ALAMY: 3BL, 6, 8, 11CR, 12L, 12BR, 13BL, 15, 20T, 20B, 25, 31, 45, 53, 57, 59B, 64BL, 64BC, 64BR, 69CL, 69CR, 73, 86, 91, 92, 97TC, 97TR, 107T, 110, 114TR, 117TR, 118, 140, 190BL, 191, 192CL, 197T, 197C, 204, 207C, 207BR, 208, 209, 212, 213, 244, 250, 253BL, 253CR, 253BR, 255BR, 257BR, 259B, 265T, 274T, 274B, 275T, 275C, 280BR, 281, 285B, 290T, 292CR, 293, 296T, 296B, 300TL, 300BL, 301BL, 301BR, 312L, 316TL, 316TR, 322TL, 341BR, 343TL, 343BL; AN POST: 336; BORD NA MONA: 290B, 291B, 292TR, 292BR; BRICK: 217, 319, 326, 345, 353, 354, 359; THE BRIDGEMAN ART LIBRARY 349B © National Trust Photographic Library/Matthew Antrobus; CAMERA PRESS: 364, 372, 373T; CORBIS: 292TL © Sean Sexton Collection, 50 © Tom Bean, 19 © Yann Arthus-Bertrand; DEFENCE FORCES: 297B; DEPARTMENT OF THE ENVIRONMENT: 46; DEREK SPEIRS: 269T; DOMINICK WALSH: 337CR; DUBLIN CITY COUNCIL: 269B; DUBLIN DOCKLANDS AUTHORITY: 332CR, 332BL; KEVIN DWYER: 34, 55TR, 59T, 136, 141C, 156, 158B, 159BL, 160L, 160R, 161, 163, 165BR, 169, 170, 171, 268, 276, 307, 237; EC/ECHO/FRANÇOIS GOEMANS: 355BL, 355BR; ECOSCENE: 55BR © Sally Morgan; ESB: 40; ESLER CRAWFORD: 141B; EUROPEAN SPACE AGENCY: 37BR; FAIRTRADE: 373B; FINBARR O'CONNELL: 159TL, 177, 236, 225, 241BR; FIRTREE MAPS: 200; FLPA: 32 © Bill Broadhurst, 35 © Chris Demetriou, © 120T Nigel Cattlin, 14T © Steve McCutcheon; GERRY O'LEARY: 271; GETTY: 4, 5TR, 39C, 85, 97TL, 99, 183, 185T, 185B, 227, 228CL, 234, 251, 254, 283, 321, 327, 341TL, 343CL, 363; GREENPEACE: 63BR, 63CR; HARALD M VALDERHAUG: 297T; IMAGEFILE: 3BR, 11BR, 12TR, 14C, 16BL, 16BR, 17, 21, 30BR, 33, 37BL, 38, 44, 47, 72, 107B, 112, 114TL, 117TL, 119, 120B, 139, 190BR, 196, 199BL, 199BR, 203, 211, 228CR, 232, 235, 255TR, 256BL, 256BR, 257BL, 258CR, 259T, 292BL, 296C, 299, 325TR, 325BR, 335BR, 338, 349CR, 368, 369; INPHO PHOTOGRAPHY: 337BL, 337BR; IRISH CEMENT: 306; IRISH EXAMINER: 202; IRISH TIMES: 28 © Irish Times, 286 © Brenda Fitzsimons; JOHN CLEARE: 3TL; MARTYN TURNER: 318, 360; MICHAEL DIGGIN: 335BL; ORDNANCE SURVEY IRELAND: 23, 150, 156, 157TL, 157BL, 158TL, 162, 168B, 175; PA PHOTOS: 5B, 27, 288; PANOS PICTURES: 322BL © Chris Sattlberger, © 280BL Dieter Telemans, 273 © G.M.B. Akash, 184, 187T, 187B © Giacomo Pirozzi, 192BR, 274C © Jacob Silberberg, 357 © Jenny Matthews, 219 © Moises Saman, 362 © Paul Lowe, 24 © Jan Banning; PC PRO: 304BL, 304CR, 305TR, 305CL; PETER BARROW: 151, 153, 157TR, 158TR, 164, 166, 167BL, 167TR, 168T, 173, 179, 221, 231, 243, 246, 252, 261, 265B, 270, 279, 309, 312R; PETER WILCOCK: 287; PHOTOCALL: 62, 258CL; RAY RYAN: 291T; REPORTDIGITAL.CO.UK: 193 © Jess Hurd, 267, 275B © Paul Box; REUTERS: 39CR © Carlos Barria, 322CR © Crack Palinggi; REX ROBERTS: 49; SCIENCE PHOTO LIBRARY: 13BR © British Antarctic Survey, 48 © Dirk Wiersma, 30BL © Dr Morley Read, 77 © European Space Agency, 115 © Kenneth W. Fink, 79CL © Pekka Parviainen, 42, 79BR © Simon Fraser, 79BL © GIPhotostock, 30BC © Michael Marten,

377